PHOTOGRAPHY BY TAM WEST

SUPERGOOD
CHELSEA WINTER

RANDOM HOUSE
NEW ZEALAND

RANDOM HOUSE

UK | USA | Canada | Ireland | Australia
India | New Zealand | South Africa | China

Random House is an imprint of the Penguin Random House group of companies, whose addresses can be found at global.penguinrandomhouse.com.

First published by Penguin Random House New Zealand, 2020

5 7 9 10 8 6

Text © Chelsea Winter, 2020
Photography © Tam West, 2020

The moral right of the author has been asserted.

All rights reserved. Without limiting the rights under copyright reserved above, no part of this publication may be reproduced, stored in or introduced into a retrieval system, or transmitted, in any form or by any means (electronic, mechanical, photocopying, recording or otherwise), without the prior written permission of both the copyright owner and the above publisher of this book.

Design by Helen Gilligan-Reid. Typesetting by Cat Taylor © Penguin Random House New Zealand
Styling by Victoria Bell. Special thanks to: Miss Tash ceramics, Fiona Mackay ceramics
and Monmouth Glass Studio
Prepress by Image Centre Group
Printed and bound in China by RR Donnelley

A catalogue record for this book is available from the National Library of New Zealand.

ISBN 978-0-14-377505-8

penguin.co.nz

KIA ORA

Hello, my dear friends and welcome to book number six! Thank you for waiting so patiently; there was the small matter to attend to of producing a real human being instead of another book baby!

Let's get straight to the point because I've heard cries of 'WTF, SHE'S DONE A PLANT-BASED COOKBOOK!? What about cheese and butter and cream and chicken?! How can the recipes be any good without that?!'

Yep, every single recipe in *Supergood* is free from meat, dairy and eggs (and nearly every recipe has a twist to make it gluten-free). And you know what? This is so not a big deal. For *years* people have begged me to produce more recipes without eggs, dairy and gluten, and especially of late — plant-based recipes.

I figured why not just go the whole hog? After five books along the same vibe, it feels good to offer something different.

Some of you will be thrilled.

Some of you will be curious.

Some of you will be sceptical, and understandably so.

Many of you will be excited, and that's perfect because this is totally exciting! It doesn't really matter who you are or what you normally eat, I can promise this book is still for you. Even if you don't have intolerances and you're not a vegetarian or vegan, the meals in this book are designed for everyday people of all ages and stages, and especially those for whom 'it's not a real meal without meat'.

Ever been tempted to serve up a meat-free dinner but hesitated in anticipation of the outrage that would ensue?

That's why I created *Supergood*, because I want to prove cooking vegetarian and plant-based food can be just as tasty and satisfying as the other recipes you've come to trust me for. These recipes are supremely delicious, with many of them being on a constant rotation at our place (and that should be all you need to hear, because I am *very* picky about flavour).

Also, I think it's safe to say we're all beginning to realise that cooking more plant-based meals is a very good idea on many levels. Whether you do it for your physical health or your family's, the health of the planet, a healthier wallet or a healthy conscience (or all of the above), the value and importance of this way of eating is now too big to ignore. From my own personal experience, eating more plants has been one of the best things I've done. My diet isn't perfect and I'm not obsessively strict; I'm just enjoying the journey. The way I see it, it's not a fad — it's the future.

As always, I'm here to help you create delicious food, to inspire you in the kitchen. With this book I'm opening another door to deliciousness, offering new and exciting recipes that'll make you feel proud to have cooked them. After all, isn't that what we've always been about?

Whether you dip in here once a day, once a week or once a month, it's all good. Supergood, even. I've never been more proud of a book than I am of this one, and I can't wait to hear what you think. Find me on Insta or Facebook and let me know once you've had a crack at the recipes.

Sending so much love, deliciousness and good vibrations to you all.

Chelsea

PS — Before you get started, take a wee look at the 'Say Hello To Your New Friends' section beginning on page 222, where I introduce a few exciting new ingredients into the mix.

CONTENTS

12 —— MEALS, BIG & SMALL

122 —— SWEETS

180 —— BREAKFASTS, BITS & PIECES

222 —— SAY HELLO TO YOUR NEW FRIENDS

232 —— GRATITUDE

234 —— INDEX

MEALS, BIG & SMALL

Welcome to a great whopping selection of every savoury dish you might conceivably have occasion for! Robust and hearty family fare, quick and easy weeknight meals, lunches and brunches, lighter plates for warmer weather, robust and substantial salads, soups and sides, party food and some awesome fun stuff, too (think onion rings in a burger and a carrot in a hot dog). May your journey into the chapter of deliciousness be filled with culinary triumphs and many a licked-clean plate.

CREAMY DAHL & CRUNCHY ROAST POTATOES

PREP 15 minutes   **COOK** 1 hour   **SERVES** 4–6

CRUNCHY POTATOES
1.5kg floury potatoes (e.g. Agria), scrubbed or peeled
⅓ cup grapeseed or sunflower oil

CREAMY DAHL
¼ cup melted coconut or grapeseed oil
2 large onions, thinly sliced
4 cloves garlic, crushed
1 tbsp finely grated ginger
2 tsp ground cumin
2 tsp ground turmeric
1 tsp ground coriander
1 tsp curry powder
1 tsp paprika
½ tsp finely ground black pepper
1¼ cups dried brown lentils, rinsed
3 cups vegetable stock (or use water and stock powder)
1 tsp salt
1 tsp sugar
½ cup coconut cream (I used the UHT one in a tetrapack)
1 tbsp lemon juice

TO SERVE
chopped fresh coriander (optional)
lemon wedges (optional)

IT'S GLUTEN-FREE
(Check your stock, though.)

TIP
+ If you're one of those people who doesn't like coriander because you think it tastes like stink bugs, you can use finely chopped parsley instead.

Please promise me you'll make this dish — embrace the lentil, you simply must. We eat this meal about once a week, and never get tired of it. It's SO good, so much better than an image can show (even this insanely beautiful photo). Creamy, richly flavoured lentil curry softly spooned on top of the most golden, crispy potatoes — pure comfort food that's also good for you. If there's any left over, it's even better for lunch the next day. You can make the dahl in advance; you may just need to thin it down a bit with more stock when you reheat it. If you like some heat, add some chilli powder.

Preheat the oven to 230°C regular bake.

Halve the potatoes (or quarter if very large) and place them in a large saucepan of salted water. Bring to a fast simmer, cooking until the potatoes are about three-quarters cooked through — about 8–10 minutes. Drain well, then return to the pan and place back over the heat for a minute or so to steam off any excess liquid. Add the oil to the pot, put the lid on and shake really vigorously. You want the potatoes to break up a bit, and it's okay to have mushy stuff at the bottom — this will all turn crunchy. Tip everything onto a large oven tray and spread it out as best you can. If some pieces are too large, smoosh them a bit with a wooden spoon. Season generously with salt and set aside.

To make the dahl, add the oil to a large, deep frying pan or flameproof casserole dish over a medium-low heat. Add the onion and a pinch of salt and cook, stirring occasionally, for about 15 minutes until the onion is golden and mushy. Add the garlic and ginger and cook, stirring, for another few minutes. Add the spices and cook for another minute.

Put the potatoes in the oven for 35 minutes, turning once halfway through if you need to.

Add lentils, stock, salt and sugar to the pan with the onion, garlic and ginger. Stir to combine, then cover and simmer on a very low heat for about 30 minutes, or until the lentils are tender. Add the coconut cream and lemon juice, stir through and continue to simmer, uncovered, for as long as it takes for the dahl to thicken up nicely — 15 minutes maybe; it depends how thick your coconut cream is. Season with salt and pepper to taste.

Place the dahl and potatoes in separate dishes on the table. To serve, pile some dahl on top of the crispy potatoes, and sprinkle with coriander and maybe a little extra squeeze of lemon, if you like.

Lovely with some steamed greens on the side.

MACHO NACHOS

PREP 15 minutes **COOK** 30 minutes **SERVES** 4

- extra virgin olive oil or grapeseed oil, for frying
- 1 large onion, finely chopped
- 3 cloves garlic, crushed
- 1 tbsp smoked paprika
- 1 tsp ground cumin
- 1 tsp ground coriander
- ½ tsp chilli powder
- ⅓ cup red wine (optional)
- 1 x 400g can brown or Puy lentils, drained and rinsed
- 1 x 400g can black beans, drained and rinsed
- 2 x 400g cans chopped tomatoes in juice
- ½ cup water
- 1½ tbsp soft brown sugar
- 2 tsp chicken-style or vegetable stock powder
- ½ tsp salt

TO SERVE
- good-quality natural corn chips
- plant-based aïoli (see page 182) or cashew cream (see tips)
- smashed seasoned avocado
- chopped fresh coriander

TO MAKE IT GLUTEN-FREE
Make sure that your stock, corn chips and tortillas are GF.

I can give full credit to Douglas for this recipe; it's his creation, and it's one of my favourites in the whole world! Not just because it's delicious and super-speedy to make using pantry staples, but also because it's such a versatile mixture. Instead of corn chips, we often just serve the bean sauce with cooked rice and fry up a couple of tortillas if we have them. Or you could try rolling it up into a juicy burrito, or piling it into taco shells. Leftovers are always in hot demand for lunch the next day, 'cause the sauce is even better reheated. If you're cooking for a big hungry family I'd double the recipe (you'll need a big ol' pot).

Preheat the oven to 180°C regular bake.

Add about 3 tablespoons oil to a large frying pan over a medium heat. Add the onion and cook, stirring, for about 10 minutes until soft. Add the garlic and cook for another minute or so.

Add the spices and cook for another minute, stirring so that it doesn't stick.

Add the red wine, if using, turn up the heat and let it bubble for 10 seconds.

Add the drained lentils, beans, tomatoes, water, sugar, stock and salt. Stir, then bring to a simmer for about 15 minutes until slightly reduced. Add more salt to taste if need be. Set aside.

Place the corn chips in a roasting tray along with a splash of oil and some salt. Toss to combine and bake for 7–10 minutes, or until crispy.

To serve, spoon the bean sauce over the crunchy chips and top with lots of aïoli and avo and coriander. A squeeze of lime or lemon and some chilli flakes or Tabasco would go down a treat, too.

TIPS
+ To make cashew cream, soak 1 cup of cashews in just-boiled water for 15 minutes, drain, then whizz until smooth in a high-speed blender with ⅓ cup water, 2 tsp lemon juice, salt and pepper.
+ If you have some dairy-free cheese, you can sprinkle some over the corn chips before you bake them if you like.

MARGHERITA PIZZA

PREP 30 minutes, plus 1+ hours rising time **COOK** 10 minutes per pizza
MAKES 4 pizzas — enough for 6 people

Margherita is my all-time favourite pizza flavour — you just can't beat the simplicity. Here, instead of buffalo mozzarella I've made a quick and easy cashew cheese. It may look a little runny when it goes on, but it firms up when you cook it. As with most Italian food, the quality of the ingredients is paramount because you're not using a million different flavours. So the tomatoes on the top need to be rich, red and ripe; if the big tomatoes at your local look hard and floury, go with ripe cherry tomatoes instead. If you can't be bothered making the dough, this still tastes awesome on store-bought bases — I like the Turkish ones.

Place the cashews in a heatproof bowl, cover with boiling water and leave to soak for 20 minutes or until needed.

To make the dough, place the warm water in a small bowl and whisk in the sugar. Whisk in the yeast and leave to sit for 5–10 minutes until the yeast foams up.

Place the flours, semolina, cold water and salt in a large mixing bowl and add the frothy yeast mixture. Stir until it comes together to form a craggy dough, then tip it out on to a lightly floured benchtop and knead for around 10 minutes, or until it's very stretchy and it springs back when you press a finger into it. You can add a little more flour if it seems sticky, but not too much.

Oil inside a large clean bowl and add the dough to it. Cover with a clean cloth and leave in a warm, draught-free place until it's doubled in size — this might take an hour or two.

While the dough is rising, prepare the cheese and tomato sauce. Drain the cashews, then whizz in a high-speed or bullet blender along with the milk or water, nutritional yeast and salt. Season to taste with salt and pepper.

To make the sauce, combine all the ingredients in a small bowl and add salt to taste.

Slice the tomatoes and sit them on paper towels to absorb some of the excess moisture.

Once the dough has doubled in size, break it into 4 even pieces, roll them into balls and place on a well-floured baking tray or benchtop. Leave for another 15 minutes until looking a bit puffy.

Recipe continued on next page

CREAMY CASHEW CHEESE
2 cups cashews
⅔ cup plant-based milk or water
¼ cup nutritional yeast
1 tsp salt

DOUGH
½ cup warm water
2 tsp sugar
2 tsp instant yeast granules
1½ cups high-grade flour
1½ cups plain flour
1 cup fine semolina, plus extra for under the base
1 cup cold water
1 tsp salt

TOMATO SAUCE
⅔ cup tomato paste
½ cup warm water
¼ cup extra virgin olive oil
4 cloves garlic, crushed
1 tbsp brown sugar
2 tsp dried oregano
2 tsp balsamic vinegar

TOPPINGS
500g fresh, very ripe red tomatoes
flaky salt and cracked pepper
chilli flakes
1 cup grated dairy-free cheese (optional)
fresh basil leaves

TO MAKE IT GLUTEN-FREE
Use a pre-made GF base and no semolina.

MARGHERITA PIZZA continued

Meanwhile, preheat the oven to 240°C fan-bake (or basically the hottest your oven will go). Set the rack near the bottom of the oven. If you have a pizza stone, preheat it in the oven now, or preheat a nice thick oven tray instead. If you want to bake more than one pizza at a time, preheat a second pizza stone or oven tray as well.

Sprinkle a large board, or a baking tray without sides, with a layer of semolina so that you can easily shimmy your assembled pizzas onto the hot stone or oven tray.

Squash out each dough ball between your hands, then sort of shimmy it around, holding the edge so that it stretches out a bit using gravity. Place it on top of the semolina and finish pulling it into a rough circle using your fingers and palms. It doesn't matter if it's a bit uneven-looking — just make sure there are no holes. You want the edges to be a bit thicker than the middle bit. You can use a rolling pin, but I don't reckon it works as well.

Spread some tomato sauce out on each base using the back of a dessert spoon. Spread with some of the cashew cheese and arrange tomato slices on top. Season with salt, pepper and chilli flakes. Sprinkle with the cheese, if using.

Open the oven and carefully slide each pizza on to the preheated stone or tray. Bake for 8–10 minutes, until the crust is golden. Slice, top with basil leaves and serve.

TIPS

+ The semolina in the dough helps the base go nice and chewy (which I love), and it also acts as little ball bearings when you're trying to slide the pizza from the board to the stone or tray.
+ If you don't need four big pizzas all at once, you can freeze the balls of dough, well wrapped. Defrost for a few hours in the fridge until workable. The tomato sauce freezes well, too.
+ You can sprinkle some Plant Parmesan over the top before baking if you like — see page 196.

OOZY QUESADILLAS

2 x 400g cans pinto beans, kidney beans or black beans (or a mixture)
neutral oil, for frying
1 large onion, finely sliced
2 cloves garlic, crushed
1 x 35g packet taco seasoning mix
2 marinated roasted red capsicums, finely sliced (optional)
1 tbsp tomato paste
2 tsp sugar
1 tsp salt
1 cup water
2 cups grated dairy-free cheese
flour tortillas (about 12 small or 6 large; see tips)

TO SERVE
smashed avocado
plant-based aïoli (see page 182)
chopped fresh coriander
Tabasco or chipotle sauce

TO MAKE IT GLUTEN-FREE
Use GF tortillas (see tip) and GF taco seasoning mix.

PREP 25 minutes **COOK** 20 minutes **SERVES** 4–5

Oh heck yes, these are so freakin' yum! It's amazing what a couple of humble cans of beans can be whipped into with a little TLC . . . crispy golden tortillas encasing a super-tasty Mex filling and, of course, loaded with the good creamy and hot stuff on top to make it a total flavour sensation. I've cheated a bit by using taco seasoning mix, but you can get some really good ones now and they're handy to have on hand. Choose one without any nasty additives or fillers — you only want spices and the good stuff.

Drain and rinse the beans and set aside.

Heat 3 tablespoons oil in a frying pan over a medium heat. Add the onion and cook, stirring, for about 10 minutes until nice and soft. Add the garlic and cook for another couple of minutes. Add the spice mix and stir for another minute.

Add the drained beans, capsicum (if using), tomato paste, sugar, salt and water. Cook, stirring, for about 15 minutes or until it's thickened right down.

Mash the mixture with a masher to break the beans up. It won't look all that appealing at this point — but worry not! Just make sure it's not too liquidy, or it will all spill out when you fry the quesadillas later. When nice and thick, remove from the heat.

To prepare the quesadillas, arrange a generous amount of grated cheese over a tortilla (this helps hold it together). Spoon over some of the bean mixture and smooth out with the back of a spoon almost to the edges. Top with some more cheese and another tortilla. Repeat until all the tortillas and mixture are used up.

Heat a splash of oil in a clean frying pan over a medium-high heat. When nice and hot, add a quesadilla and fry for a few minutes until golden brown and crispy on one side. Carefully flip and fry the other side. Set aside and repeat with the remaining quesadillas, or serve them as you go.

To serve, cut the quesadillas into halves, quarters or wedges and top with all the delicious goodies piled on top — the more the better, I always reckon.

TIPS

+ Don't over-stuff the quesadillas or the filling will spew out and they'll fall apart.
+ If you can't find a pack of good taco seasoning at your local, use 1 tbsp paprika, 1 tsp smoked paprika, 1 tsp ground cumin, 1 tsp ground coriander, ½ tsp dried oregano and a pinch of chilli.
+ Flour tortillas work best for quesadillas as they are pliable. Gluten-free tortillas tend to break more easily, so you might want to dampen and flash-fry them first to soften them.

MAC & CHEESE

250g egg-free pasta elbows (or similar shaped pasta)
¼ cup neutral oil (I used grapeseed)
3 cloves garlic, crushed
3 tbsp plain flour
3 cups creamy soy or rice milk
6 tbsp nutritional yeast
1½ tbsp cashew butter (optional)
2 tsp lemon juice
1 tsp mustard powder
1½ tsp salt
½ tsp finely ground black or white pepper
¾ cup grated dairy-free cheddar cheese (optional)

SMOKY CRUNCH TOPPING

3–4 small slices good-quality grunty bread
2½ tbsp grapeseed or olive oil
1½ tsp smoked paprika
½ tsp salt

TO MAKE IT GLUTEN-FREE

Use GF pasta, flour and bread.

TIP

+ If you can't find cashew butter it's no biggie — but you can get it at most supermarkets, and it's amazing for making dishes like this instantly creamier and more luxurious without the pain of puréeing cashews!

PREP 15 minutes   **COOK** 10–20 minutes   **SERVES** 4–5

When it comes to contenders for the most luxurious comfort food, I reckon that Mac & Cheese would be standing proudly on top of the podium. It's one of my most beloved meals — not a hell of a lot of nutritional value there, but does that really matter when it's a treat? In any case, you won't feel as heavy and gluggy after eating this unctuous plant-based version (especially if you use gluten-free pasta). It's still creamy and cheesy, and the smoky crumb on the top covers off the crunchy bacon that would normally be there. Feel free to add half a cup of peas before baking, if you like. You can double the recipe if serving a crowd.

Preheat the oven to 200°C fan-bake (210°C regular bake).

Cook the pasta according to the packet directions until *al dente*, then rinse with cold water and set aside in a colander.

To make the smoky crunch topping, pulse all the ingredients in a food processor until you have a nice chunky crumb — some bigger bits are fine. Set aside.

Heat the oil for the Mac & Cheese in a medium-sized saucepan or flameproof casserole dish over a medium-low heat. Add the garlic and cook, stirring frequently, for a couple of minutes until the garlic is fragrant (but not browned).

Add the flour and cook, stirring with a whisk, for about a minute. Remove from the heat and slowly pour in the milk, whisking all the time. Return to the heat and cook, stirring, for a few minutes until thickened.

Add the nutritional yeast, cashew butter (if using), lemon juice, mustard powder, salt and pepper, and stir with a whisk until silky smooth. Add the grated cheese (if using) and stir until melted (it may take a few minutes).

At this point, if you think it's too thick for a macaroni sauce then feel free to add more milk, keeping in mind that the pasta will take up a little of the sauce later.

Tip the pasta back into its cooking pot, add the sauce and stir through, then transfer the mixture to a medium-sized baking dish.

Sprinkle the crumb over the top and bake until the crumb is crispy — maybe 10 minutes or so. If you like, you can grill the crumb at the end to brown it nicely. If you have let your macaroni cool down completely before baking, it may need a little more time.

Serve immediately with a nice crisp salad or some steamed veg.

FUSS-FREE TOMATO PASTA

extra virgin olive oil
4 courgettes, chopped into 2cm pieces
1 large onion, finely chopped
4 cloves garlic, crushed or finely chopped
2 tsp finely chopped fresh rosemary (optional)
1 tsp dried oregano
2 x 400g cans chopped tomatoes in juice
1 tbsp soft brown sugar
2 tsp vegetable or chicken-style stock powder
2 tbsp tomato paste
1 tsp balsamic vinegar
½ tsp salt
¼ tsp finely ground black pepper
500g dried egg-free pasta of choice

TO SERVE
Plant Parmesan (see page 196)
fresh basil leaves or pesto (see page 184; optional)

PREP 10 minutes   **COOK** 15 minutes   **SERVES** 3–4

This is one of the most-cooked dinners in our household. Especially when Sky was a newborn, it was just so easy to throw together with pantry staples, plus whatever veges we had on hand — if we could be bothered. The fried courgette is a must, though, as it adds such a pleasingly juicy little bite to each mouthful. We use pasta made from lentils, which makes it more nutritionally complete as well being more filling and gluten-free. You can get other types of pasta, made from chickpeas, quinoa, etc., but for some reason red lentils seem to work the best. I love red lentil rigatoni for this.

Place 2 tablespoons olive oil in a frying pan over a medium-high heat. When hot, add the courgette pieces in a single layer and leave to sizzle until golden. While they are sizzling, season the tops with salt and pepper. Stir them around and sizzle again until only just tender — don't let them go mushy or turn golden all over. Transfer to a bowl and set aside.

Turn the heat down to medium. Add ¼ cup oil to the pan along with the onion and cook, stirring, for about 7 minutes until soft. Add the garlic, rosemary (if using) and oregano and cook, stirring frequently, for a few minutes until the garlic is fragrant (not browned or too golden).

Add the tomatoes, sugar, stock powder, tomato paste, vinegar, salt and pepper. Stir, then increase the heat a little until the mixture is bubbling gently. Simmer for about 10 minutes, or just until it has reduced to a thick sauce. Season with more salt and pepper to taste.

Cook the pasta according to the packet directions in a large saucepan of generously salted water. Drain and add back to the pan. Carefully tip the tomato sauce in with the pasta, and toss to combine.

Serve immediately with a good helping of Plant Parmesan and fresh basil leaves or a dollop of pesto if you like.

Goes well with a fresh green salad and garlic pitas.

TIPS

+ Sometimes I'll sauté some chopped mushrooms with the onions if we have some. Stirring some chopped spinach through at the end until just wilted is also nice.
+ If you love olives, add a handful to the simmering sauce — Kalamata or Sicilian are delish. Same goes for capers . . . a couple of teaspoons.

CREAMY ALFREDO

1 cup raw cashews

1½ cups unsweetened rice or creamy soy milk

2 tbsp lemon juice, plus extra to taste

3 tbsp grapeseed oil

3 tbsp nutritional yeast

1 large clove garlic

2 tsp chicken-style or vegetable stock powder

½ tsp salt

¼ tsp ground white or black pepper

500g dried egg-free pasta (fettuccine, penne or spaghetti)

⅓ cup finely chopped fresh herbs (parsley, basil, chives), plus extra to serve

Plant Parmesan (see page 196), to serve (optional)

TO MAKE IT GLUTEN-FREE

Use GF pasta and stock powder.

PREP 15 minutes, plus 30 minutes soaking time   **SERVES** 4–5

Pretty much everyone goes crazy for creamy pasta (well, Kiwis do anyway — Italians don't really use cream in their pasta, but that's another story). Up until now, people who can't or don't want to eat dairy may well have been feeling decidedly forlorn at missing out. Never fear! Ol' mate Chelsea is here with a dish that's as creamy, 'cheesy' and comforting as ever — and it's actually far easier to make than most pasta dishes. Literally whizz the sauce up and stir it through hot pasta. *Bada-bing!* Perfect for when you just can't deal with a complicated recipe. As it's quite a simple dish, we sometimes add sautéed chopped mushrooms and wilted spinach or cooked peas to make it more substantial (that all gets stirred through at the end).

Place the cashews in a heatproof bowl and cover with just-boiled water. Leave to sit for at least 30 minutes, then drain.

Tip the cashews into a high-speed blender or bullet blender along with the milk, lemon juice, oil, nutritional yeast, garlic, stock, salt and pepper. Blend until the sauce is silky smooth. Set aside.

In a large saucepan, cook the pasta according to the packet directions. Drain, then return to the pan and add the creamy sauce. Replace over a medium heat for a minute or so, stirring, to thicken it up just a little. Add the herbs and stir through.

Taste, and season with more salt, pepper and lemon juice if you think it needs it. Spoon into bowls and serve with extra fresh herbs and a little Plant Parmesan, if you like.

TIPS

+ If you don't want to use a whole 500g of pasta, just use less and still make the same amount of sauce — extra-saucy pasta is good!
+ You can make the sauce in a food processor, but you'll probably have to whizz it for a good 10 minutes or so.
+ If you have a really high-powered bullet, you don't even need to soak the cashews.
+ If you're reheating the pasta, or it has been sitting a while, you might want to thin it down with more plant-based milk.

PESTO & SPINACH PASTA

⅓ cup raw cashews
⅓ cup raw walnuts
3 tbsp nutritional yeast
2 tbsp lemon juice (or to taste)
2 cloves garlic, peeled
1 tsp fine pink salt
½ tsp finely ground black pepper
1½ packed cups washed basil leaves
2 cups chopped spinach leaves (or use baby spinach)
½ cup extra virgin olive oil
500g dried egg-free pasta of your choice

TO MAKE IT GLUTEN-FREE
Use GF pasta.

PREP 15 minutes   **COOK** 10 minutes   **SERVES** 4

Here, I've put a twist on regular pesto by adding good ol' spinach to make it more cost-effective and to pack in extra green goodness. I'm also featuring walnuts for flavour and cashews for creaminess. And don't forget nooch (nutritional yeast) — all cheesy and amazing. This is one of those quick dinners or lunches that sings with flavour, even though all you have to do is whizz some stuff in a food processor and cook some pasta. Some days, that's all you can be bothered doing. (Actually, some days all I can be bothered doing is making toast, but I can hardly put a recipe for that in the book!)

Place the cashews, walnuts, yeast, lemon juice, garlic, salt and pepper in a food processor and process until you have a coarse crumb.

Add the basil and spinach and whizz again until the leaves are all incorporated into a nice mush. With the motor going, pour in the olive oil in a medium-fast stream until all used up.

Now taste the sauce — you can add more yeast for cheesiness, more salt or pepper, more lemon, even more basil and spinach if you like. Bear in mind that it's going to go through bland pasta, so it's meant to pack a bit of a punch at this point.

Cook the pasta according to the packet directions. Drain, then return to the saucepan. Scrape in the pesto and toss to combine.

Serve immediately. It's lovely with a tomato salad or a green salad on the side; perhaps some fresh bread or garlic bread, too.

TIPS

+ To make this more nutritionally complete, I use pasta made out of red lentils (you can get it at the supermarket). Then you get protein. A nice salad on the side, and you're on your way!
+ If you have some pine nuts lying around, you could toast them to sprinkle on top.
+ Replace the cashews or walnuts with sunflower seeds, if you like.

VEGE BOLOGNESE

PREP 25 minutes **COOK** 1 hour **SERVES** 6

- 3 cups vegetable stock
- ½ cup dried brown lentils, rinsed
- ½ cup dried green (Puy) lentils, rinsed
- 2 medium-sized carrots, roughly chopped
- 2 stalks celery, roughly chopped
- 250g Portobello or shiitake mushrooms, roughly chopped
- ⅓ cup extra virgin olive oil
- 2 onions, finely chopped
- 4–5 fat cloves garlic, crushed
- 1 tbsp finely chopped fresh rosemary
- 2 tsp dried oregano
- ⅓ cup tomato paste
- ½ cup red wine or ¼ cup port (or use ½ cup extra stock)
- 1 x 400g can chopped tomatoes
- 2 tsp sugar
- 1½ tsp balsamic vinegar
- 1 tsp vegetable stock powder
- ½ tsp smoked paprika
- ½ tsp Vegemite or Marmite dissolved in a little boiled water (optional)
- ½ tsp finely ground black pepper

TO SERVE

- 500g dried egg-free spaghetti (or pasta of choice)
- chopped fresh parsley or basil
- Plant Parmesan (see page 196)

TO MAKE IT GLUTEN-FREE

Use GF pasta and stock.

Some of you, like me, are already fans of a tradish spag bol so this cleverly disguised planty version will be a no-brainer. Others of you may have been scarred for life by greasy, grey, tasteless spag bols of your past, so I'm here to help you heal that trauma. This is a diabolically good twist on the classic. It offers a deep, rich sauce, sweet and tangy with tomato, rosemary, red wine and balsamic (with the bonus of lots of hidden veges!). It's good and filling, doesn't cost the earth to make and is pretty easy to do (no frying mince, which is a welcome change). And best of all, it won't leave you feeling heavy and gross. This recipe makes a big batch, so hopefully you'll have leftovers.

Place the stock and lentils in a medium-sized saucepan. Bring just to a boil, then cover and simmer gently for about 20 minutes, or until the lentils are almost tender.

Place the carrot, celery and mushrooms in a food processor and pulse to a coarse crumb. Don't let it turn to mush — you still want a little texture.

Heat the olive oil in a large, deep frying pan or flameproof casserole dish over a medium heat. Add the onion and cook for 5 minutes, stirring, until soft. Add the garlic, rosemary and oregano, and cook for another minute.

Add the vege mixture to the pan. Cook, stirring every now and then, for 5–10 minutes until the mixture is soft and mushy. Add the tomato paste, turn up the heat and stir for a minute or so to sort of caramelise the tomato paste a bit.

Add the wine or port (or extra stock) and let it bubble for 30 seconds or so.

Add the lentils and their cooking liquid to the pan along with the tomatoes, sugar, balsamic, stock powder, smoked paprika, Vegemite/Marmite and pepper. Simmer gently over a low heat until reduced into a nice thick sauce — around 30 minutes, maybe more. You can add a little more liquid if you have time and you want to cook it longer; long and slow is good.

Just before serving, season to taste with salt if it needs it.

Cook the pasta according to the packet directions. Serve the sauce over the pasta with a sprinkling of fresh herbs and a good smattering of Plant Parmesan.

TIPS

+ If you like a little zing, feel free to add some chilli or cayenne powder.
+ You can use all brown or all green lentils if you need to.
+ The wine or port adds a sweet, luscious depth — you could be naughty and add *both* wine and port if you wanted; just make sure you bubble it up well to evaporate the alcohol off.

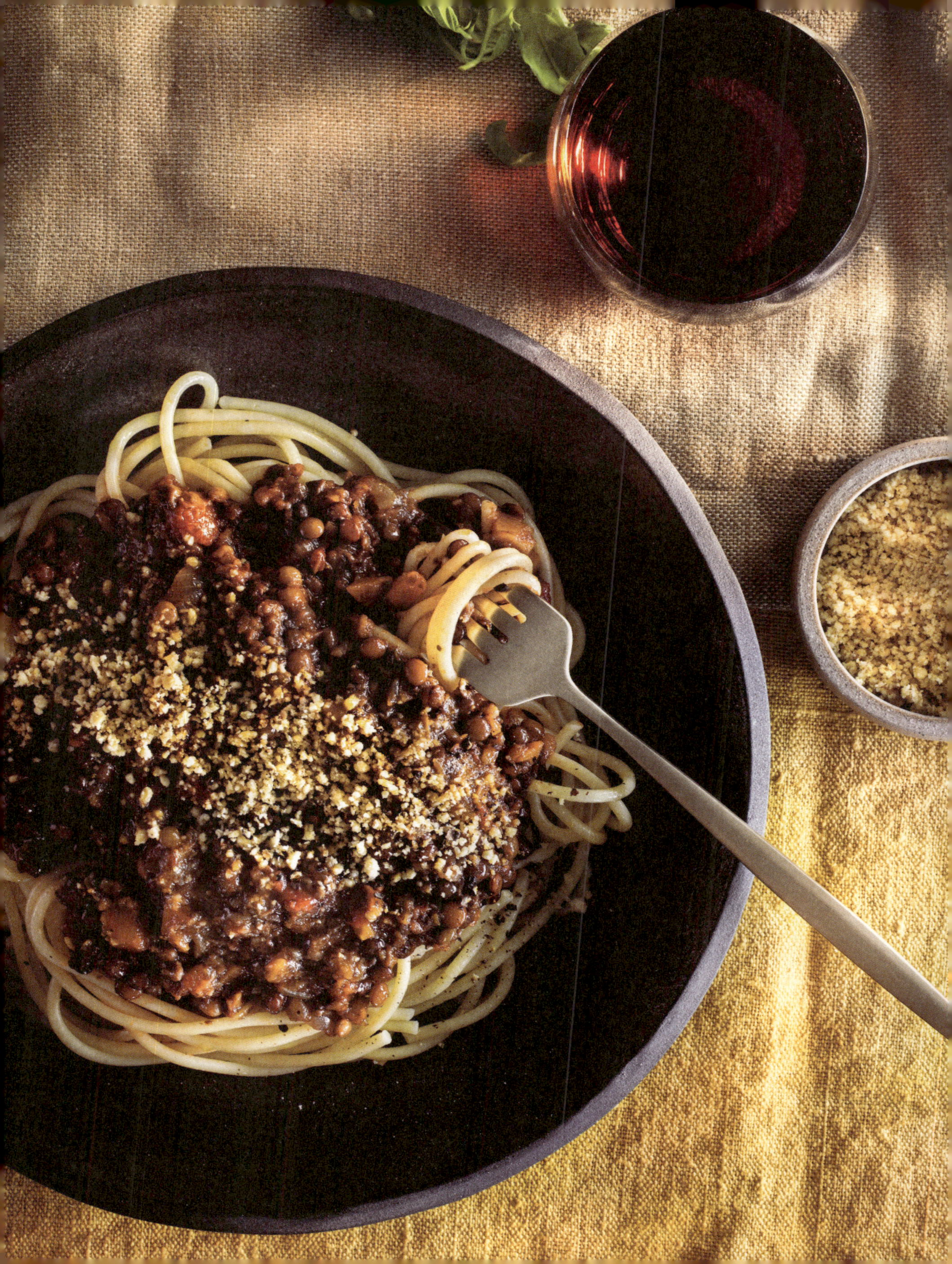

THE BEAST MODE LASAGNE

PREP 1 hour 15 minutes **COOK** 1 hour, plus resting time **SERVES** 10

TASTY-AS SAUCE

400g Portobello or fresh shiitake mushrooms (or a mixture)
⅓ cup extra virgin olive oil
1 onion, finely chopped
1 leek, inner part finely chopped (or use another onion)
2 stalks celery, very finely chopped
1 medium-sized carrot, very finely chopped
8 cloves garlic, crushed or chopped
2 x 400g cans chopped tomatoes in juice
5 cups vegetable stock
¾ cup red wine (optional, or use extra stock)
1 cup dried brown lentils, rinsed
½ cup tomato paste
2 tbsp brown sugar
1 tbsp soy sauce
1 tbsp balsamic vinegar
2 tsp dried oregano
¾ tsp ground black pepper

CREAMY WHITE SAUCE

1 cup raw cashews
½ cauliflower (about 250g), chopped
¼ cup grapeseed oil
¼ cup plain flour
3¾ cups creamy soy, oat or rice milk
1 tbsp Dijon mustard
⅓ cup nutritional yeast
2 tsp lemon juice
2 tsp salt
¾ tsp ground white pepper

TO ASSEMBLE

4 cups roughly chopped spinach leaves (400g bag, stalks removed)
500g (approx.) egg-free lasagne sheets
fresh thyme leaves (optional)
1 cup dairy-free cheese, grated (optional)

Remember The Boss Lasagne from *Everyday Delicious*? Allow me to introduce its plant-based brother, The Beast Mode. Seriously impressive, and seriously hard to tell that there's no meat or dairy there — this one has caused more than a few people to scratch their heads after I've served it up. And I haven't met anyone yet who doesn't love it! Not only does it taste delectable and have a great personality, but it's a bit of a looker as well. A serious contender for best recipe in the book, and definitely one for the plant-based sceptics in the house.

Before you get started, roughly chop the cashews for the white sauce, place in a heatproof bowl and cover with just-boiled water. Leave to sit for 15 minutes or just until you're ready.

To make the tasty-as sauce, chop about two-thirds of the mushrooms into 1cm chunks, and then cut the last ones into larger chunks for texture — maybe 4cm. Set aside.

Heat the extra virgin olive oil in a large lidded flameproof casserole dish or large soup pot over a medium heat. Add the onion, leek, celery and carrot with a big pinch of salt and cook, stirring every now and then, for about 15 minutes until reduced right down and very soft. Add the mushrooms and garlic and cook for another couple of minutes.

Add the remaining sauce ingredients and stir to combine. Cover and simmer over a low heat, stirring every now and then, for about 1 hour, or until the lentils are tender and it's reduced into a thick sauce (if it's taking too long, you may need to turn up the heat). You don't want the sauce too watery or it will make the pasta soggy; but not too dry either, or you'll end up with a dry lasagne. Kind of like a saucy Bolognese is about right. Season to taste with salt.

To make the creamy white sauce (while the tasty-as sauce is cooking), bring a large saucepan of water to the boil, add the cauliflower and simmer until tender. Drain and transfer to a high-speed blender or bullet blender along with the drained cashews and 1 cup of the milk. Whizz until silky smooth.

Place the oil and flour in a medium-sized saucepan over a medium-low heat and cook, stirring with a whisk for about 5 minutes — don't let it brown. Remove from the heat and add the remaining milk in a thin stream, whisking all the time. Replace over a medium heat and stir continuously with the whisk for about 5 minutes, until thickened. Stir in the mustard, nutritional yeast, lemon juice, salt and pepper.

Recipe continued on next page

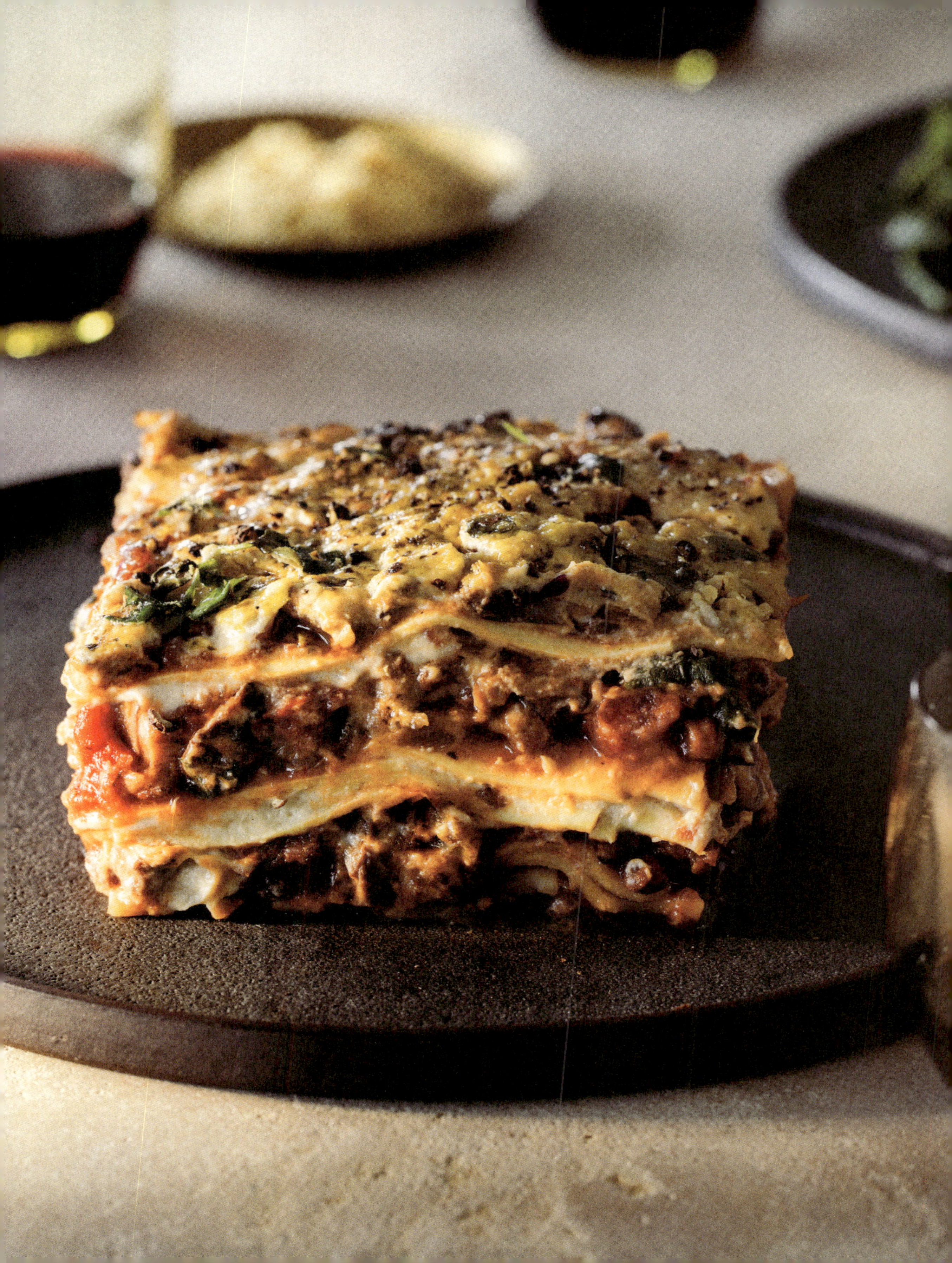

THE BEAST MODE LASAGNE continued

TO MAKE IT GLUTEN-FREE
Use GF flour for the white sauce and GF lasagne sheets. Make sure the stock and soy sauce you use are GF, too.

Add the cauliflower mixture and stir to combine. Taste, and adjust the salt and pepper if you like. If you think it's too thick, you can add a little milk until you're happy with the consistency.

Steam the spinach in a frying pan with a little water until just wilted. Drain, season with salt and pepper and set aside.

Preheat the oven to 180°C regular bake.

To assemble, grease the base and sides of a large baking dish with olive oil. Cover the base in a spoonful of tasty-as sauce, then a layer of lasagne sheets, snapping bits to make it fit if you need to. Cover with a layer of creamy white sauce.

Continue to layer the tomato sauce, lasagne sheets and white sauce until used up, adding a layer of spinach somewhere in there and ending on a layer of lasagne topped with white sauce. Sprinkle with thyme leaves and a little extra oregano if you like. Season again with salt and pepper.

Scatter with the cheese (if using). Cover with foil, poke a couple of steam holes and bake for about 50 minutes. Remove the foil and cook for another 10–15 minutes until the top is golden and bubbling — you can grill it at the end if you like.

Let it sit for 15 minutes out of the oven before you slice up and serve. This will help avoid it being too sloppy when you slice it up.

TIPS

+ 'Beast mode' refers to a state of performing something with extreme power, skill or determination. In this case, it's a lasagne performing at maximum epicness even though it's plant-based.
+ If you're not a fan of mushrooms, you could either bulk it up with extra lentils, and/or add two finely chopped red capsicums or eggplants.

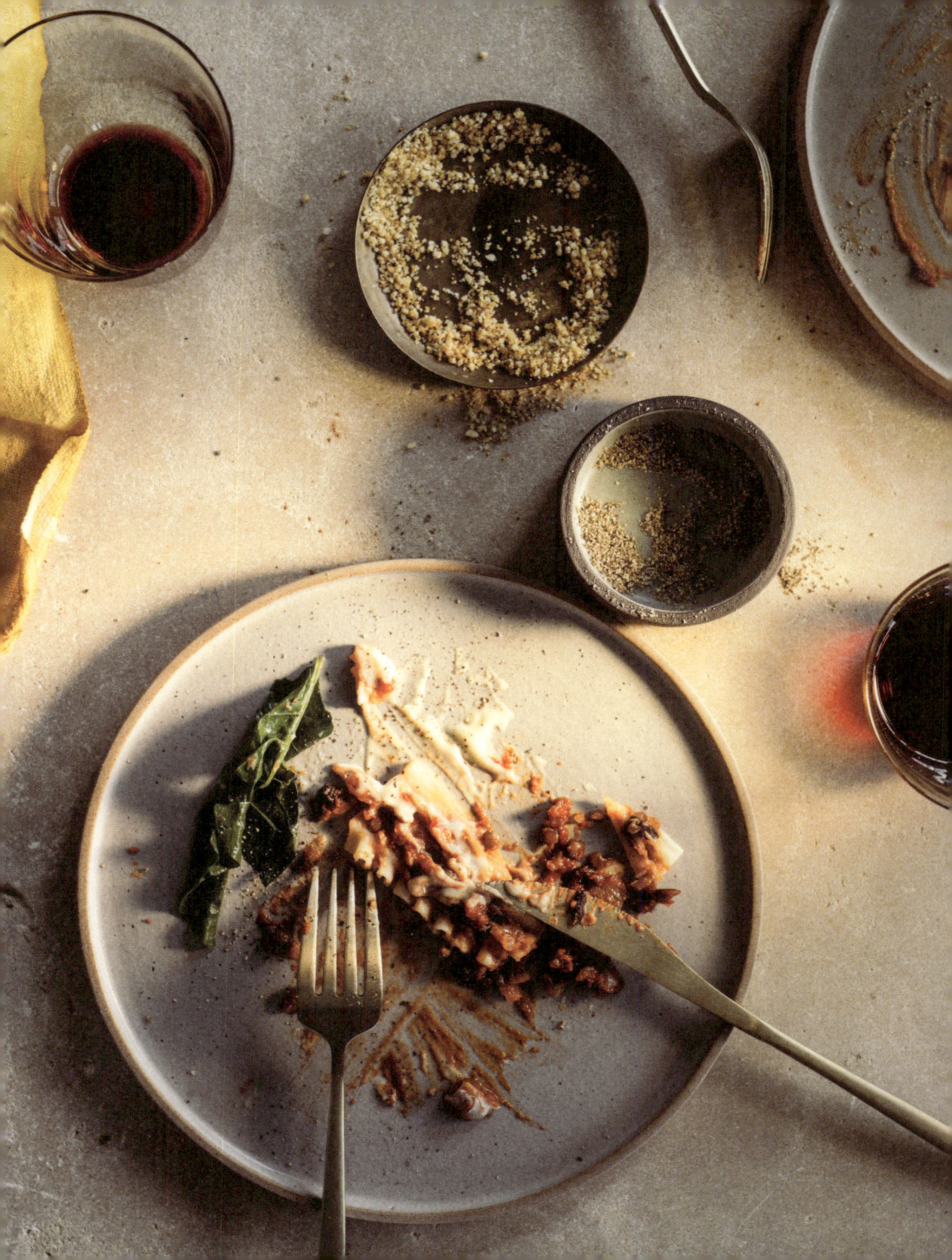

VEG-OUT LASAGNE

PREP 45 minutes   **COOK** 1 hour, plus resting time   **SERVES** 6

RICH TOMATO SAUCE

¼ cup extra virgin olive oil
4 cloves garlic, crushed
5 sundried tomatoes, minced
1 stalk rosemary, leaves finely chopped
2 x 400g cans chopped tomatoes in juice
1½ tbsp soft brown sugar
1 tsp dried oregano
1 tsp vegetable stock powder
½ tsp salt
½ tsp finely ground black pepper

CREAMY WHITE SAUCE

3 tbsp grapeseed or other neutral oil (or use a plant-based butter)
¼ cup plain flour
4 cups creamy soy, oat or rice milk
¼ cup nutritional yeast
¼ cup cashew butter (optional)
2 tsp mustard powder (or 1 tbsp Dijon mustard)
1 tsp salt
½ tsp finely ground pepper

VEGE LAYERS

4 courgettes, sliced lengthways very thinly
1 large eggplant, sliced lengthways very thinly
200g Portobello mushrooms, sliced very thinly
3 marinated red capsicums, sliced

TO ASSEMBLE AND SERVE

200g dried egg-free lasagne sheets
grated dairy-free cheese, for topping (optional)
olive oil, for drizzling
basil leaves (optional)

TO MAKE IT GLUTEN-FREE

Use GF flour, lasagne sheets and stock. Mustard powder is usually GF, but check the label.

This dish is deliciously rich and tasty — even grumbly meat-eaters will be showing up for seconds. The thin layers of golden fried courgette, mushroom and eggplant kind of melt together so you don't get big chunks of anything offensive — perfect for people who aren't vegetable fans. This recipe doesn't make the standard enormous vat of lasagne big enough to feed an army, but you can make roughly 1½ times the recipe if you need to feed a crowd. You can add a layer of mashed roasted pumpkin to the lasagne if you like, to bulk it up or in place of something else. I like to wilt some spinach leaves or chopped silverbeet and add a layer of them when I have some on hand.

To make the tomato sauce, heat the olive oil in a medium-sized frying pan, heavy-based saucepan or flameproof casserole dish over a medium-low heat. Add the garlic, sundried tomatoes and rosemary and cook, stirring, for 5 minutes or so until fragrant but not browned. Add the tomatoes, sugar, oregano, stock powder, salt and pepper. Stir to combine and simmer gently for about 15 minutes until reduced slightly.

To make the creamy white sauce, place the oil and flour in a medium-sized saucepan over a medium-low heat and cook, stirring constantly, for a couple of minutes until puffy (but not browned). Remove from the heat and add the milk in a slow stream, stirring constantly with a whisk, until incorporated. Add the remaining ingredients, return to a medium heat and cook, stirring constantly with the whisk, for a few minutes until thickened up. Season with extra salt if it needs it. Cover and set aside.

Add a good splash of olive oil to a large frying pan over a medium-high heat. When the pan is nice and hot, add the courgette slices and leave to sizzle until golden on the bottom. Turn over and cook until just tender but not mushy. Season with salt and pepper and set aside. Repeat with the eggplant slices and then the mushrooms. The capsicum doesn't need frying.

Preheat the oven to 180°C regular bake. Grease a medium-sized baking dish with olive oil.

To assemble, spread a small amount of the tomato sauce over the base of the dish. Cover with a layer of lasagne, a layer of veges, a layer of tomato sauce and some white sauce. Keep layering until it's all used up — there are no hard and fast rules. It's good to end on a layer of pasta, then a bit of tomato sauce and/or creamy sauce to top it off. Sprinkle with the dairy-free cheese, if using, and a drizzle of olive oil.

Season with salt and pepper, cover with foil and bake for 45 minutes. Remove the foil, turn the oven up to 200°C and cook for another 15 minutes until golden.

Remove from the oven and leave to sit for 10 minutes before serving. Scatter with torn basil leaves if you like.

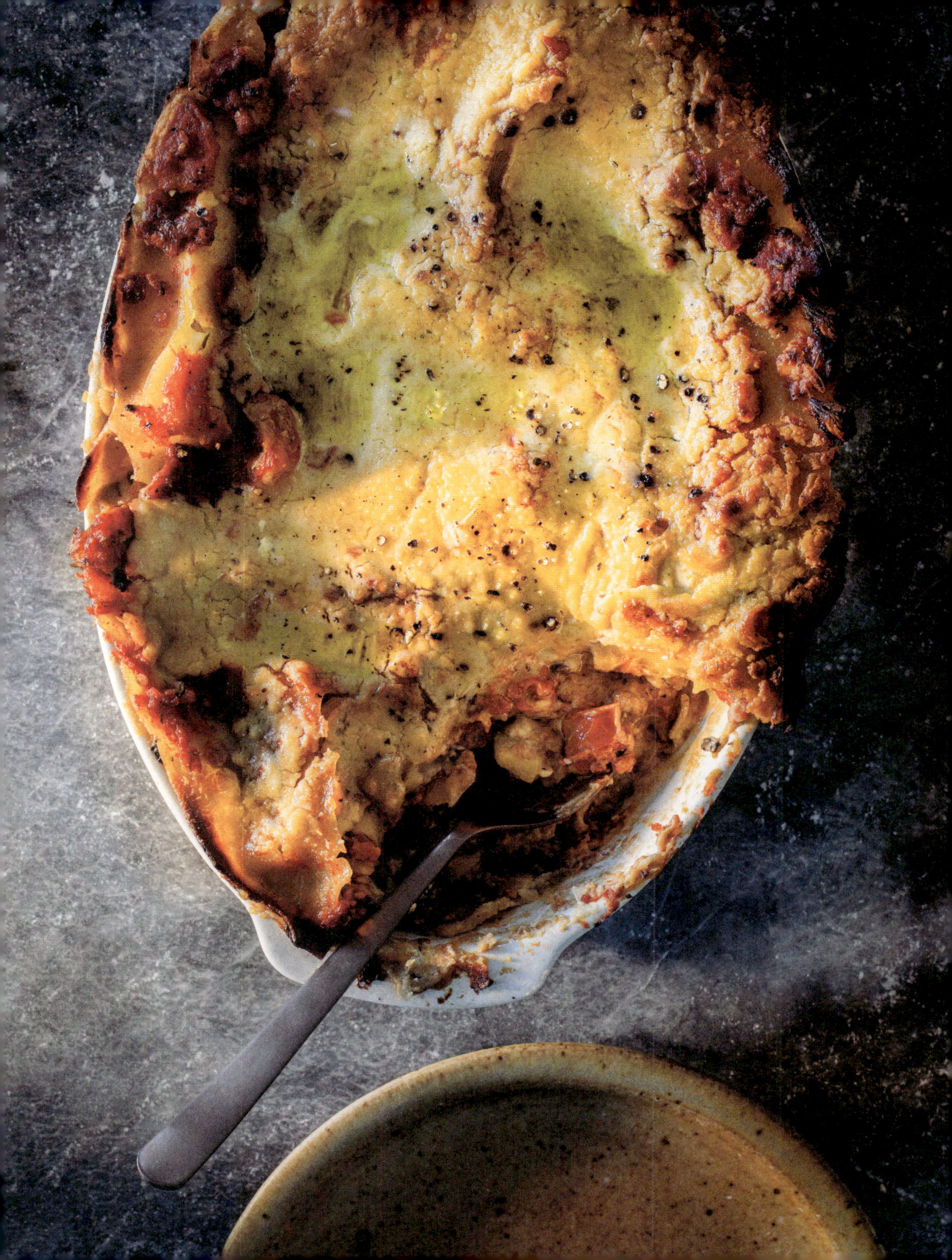

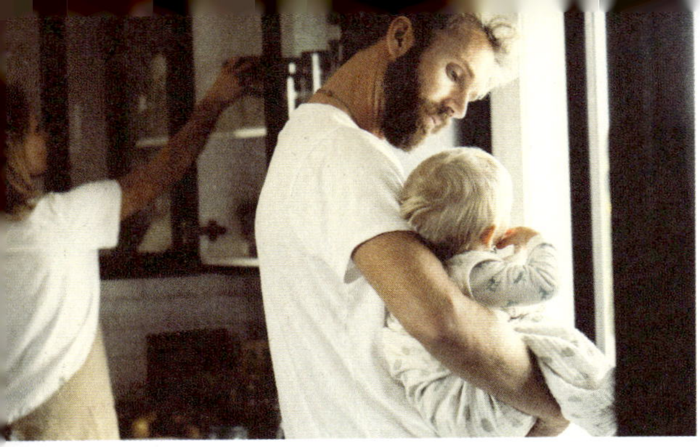
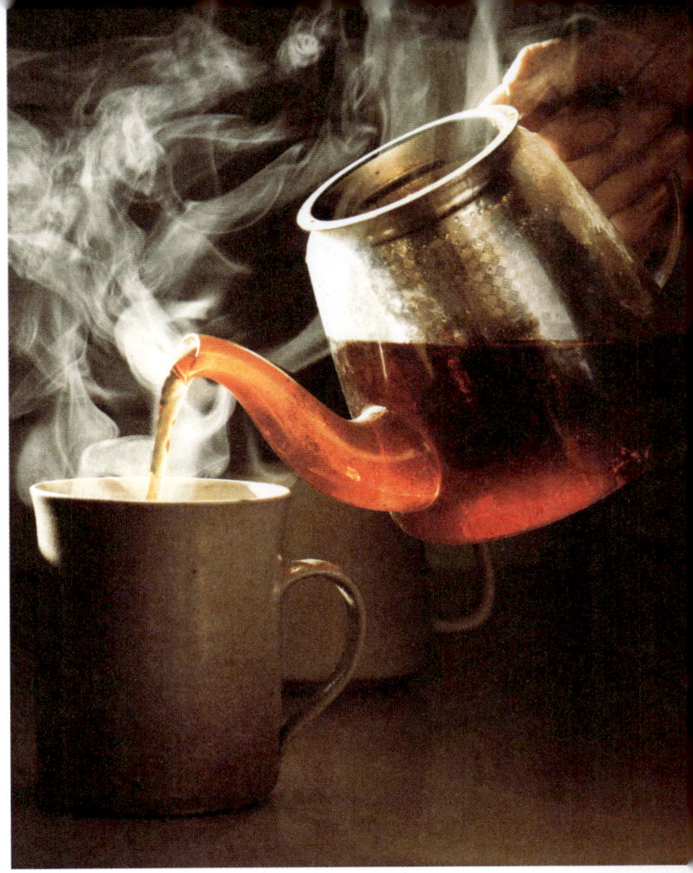
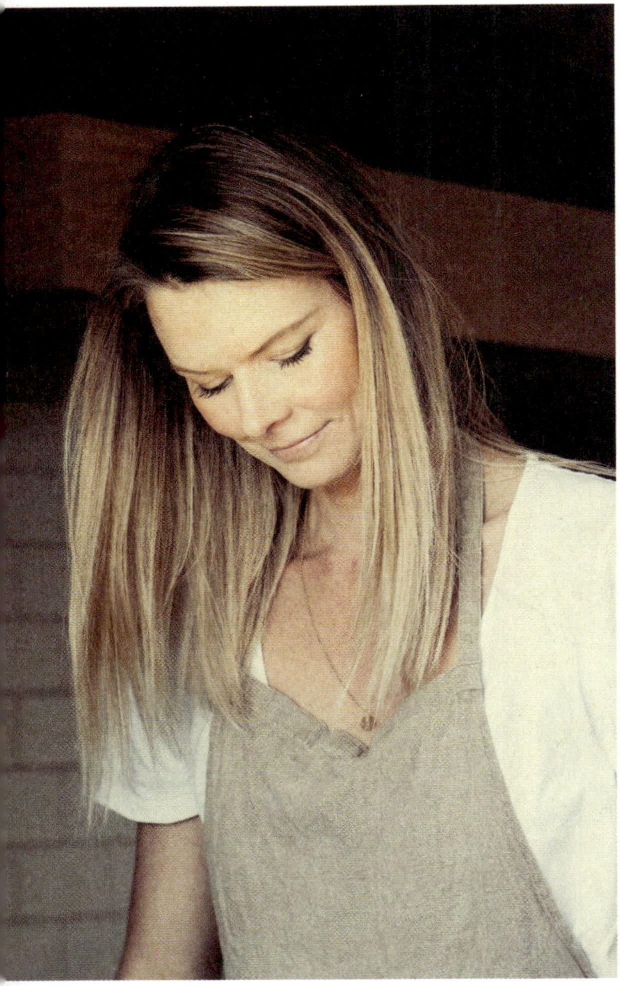
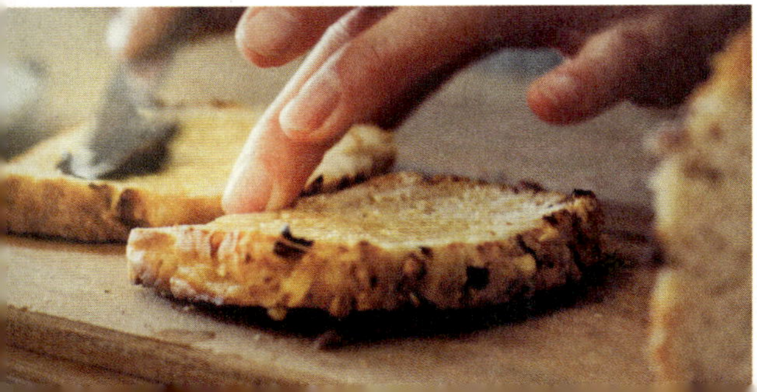
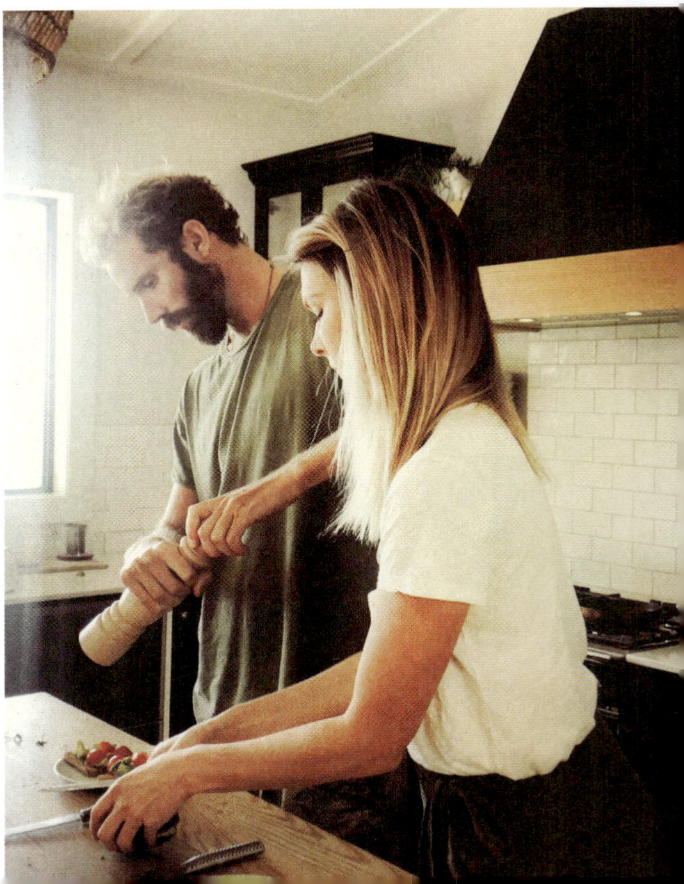

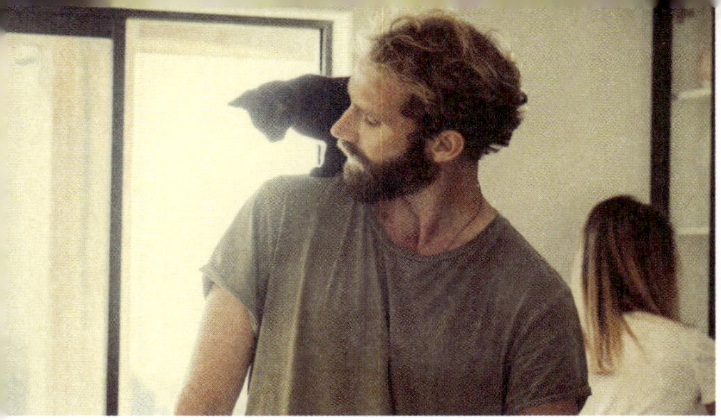
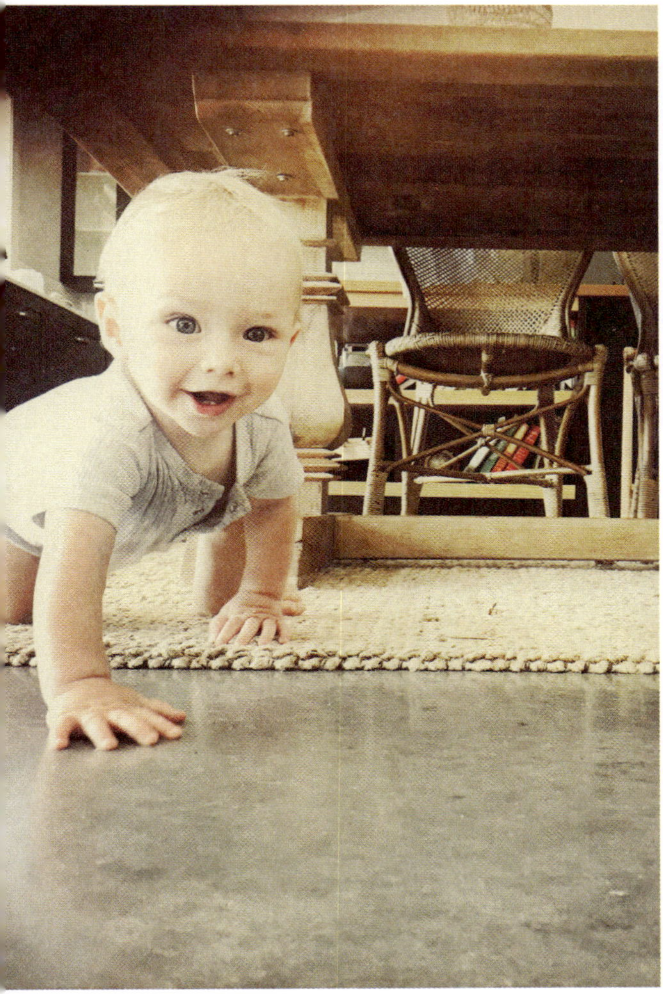
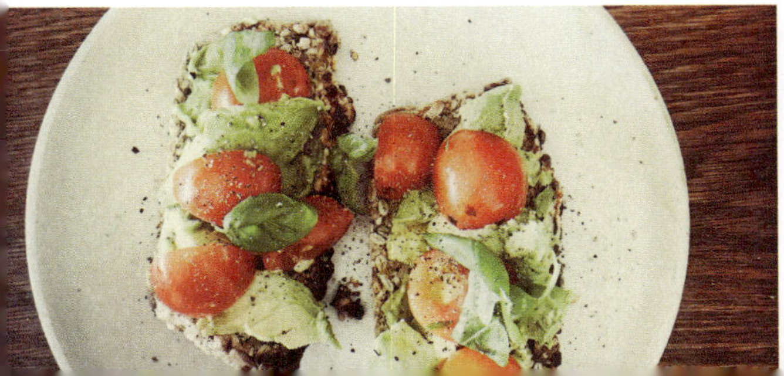
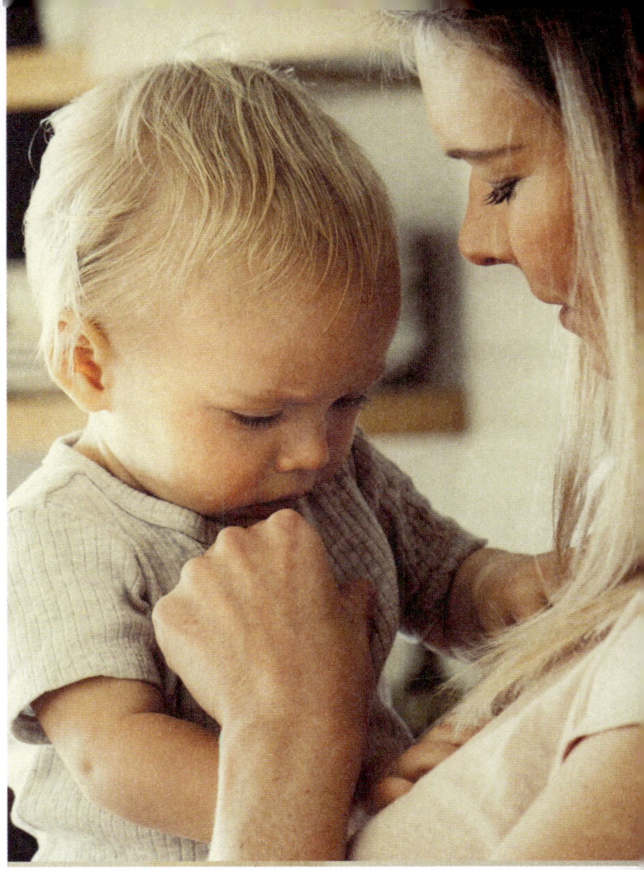
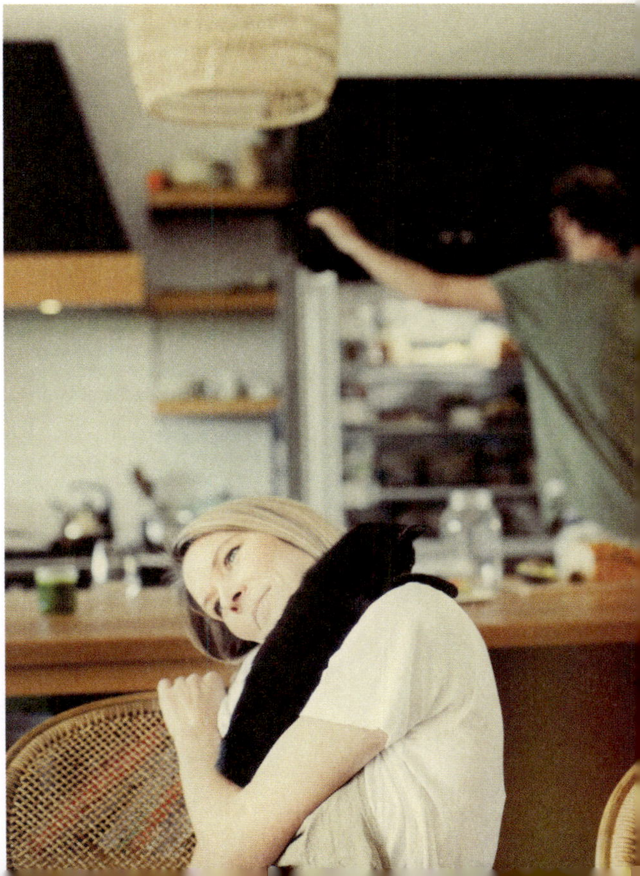

FRENCH TOMATO TART

PREP 20 minutes   **COOK** 35 minutes   **SERVES** 4–6

I created my first version of this tart when I was living in France with Douglas for a couple of months, relishing the crispy pastry, creamy cheese, juicy flavourful tomatoes, fresh herbs and spicy cracked pepper. Back then I used a lovely soft salty white French cheese riddled with herbs and garlic. Naturally, I've created a new version of this, and it's still amazingly good. Only use big tomatoes if they're in season — red and ripe and full of flavour. Otherwise, use a heap of ripe cherry tomatoes. This magnificent dish can be served hot, warm or cold, for breakfast, brunch, lunch or dinner. It's perfect for a shared table, a picnic or a light meal served *al fresco* with a fresh salad and a glass of chilled rosé. *Oh là là*, take me there!

Place the cashews for the cheese spread in a heatproof bowl or jug and cover with just-boiled water. Leave to soak for 20 minutes or so, then rinse.

Slice the tomatoes for the tart about 5mm thick and lay on a couple of layers of paper towel. Sprinkle with salt and press another couple of paper towels on top (or you can use a clean tea towel for this if it's nice and absorbent). Leave for 10 minutes or so.

Place the oil in a medium-sized saucepan over a medium-low heat. Add the shallots along with the salt and sugar and cook, stirring every now and then, for 15–20 minutes until golden and starting to caramelise. Remove from the heat.

Place the drained cashews in a food processor or high-speed blender along with the other cheese spread ingredients except the fresh herbs, and process until smooth. It may take a while, so be patient and keep scraping down the sides. You could also do this with a stick blender. Stir the herbs through at the end.

Preheat the oven to 190°C fan-bake (or 200°C regular bake, but fan-bake is better for pastry) and set a rack in the lower half of the oven.

If your pastry is pre-rolled, lay it on baking paper on a baking tray. Otherwise, roll it out to 3–4mm thick. Prick all over with a fork. Lightly moisten the edges with water and fold the edges over by 1–2cm, pressing down hard to crimp all along with your index finger.

Spread the base of the pastry with the cheese. Top with the shallots and tomato slices. Season with cracked pepper, extra fresh herbs and a little more salt.

Brush the edges of the pastry generously with the aquafaba. Bake for 35–40 minutes, or until the pastry is golden brown and everything is looking lovely and caramelised. Leave it in longer if not — the pastry should be nice and crispy, even underneath.

Keeps well for a day or so at room temperature or in the fridge.

HERBY CHEESE SPREAD

- 1 cup raw cashews (or use tofu; see tips)
- ¼ cup water
- 2 tbsp coconut oil, melted
- 3 tbsp nutritional yeast
- 1 tbsp lemon juice
- 2 cloves garlic, crushed
- 2 tsp Dijon mustard
- 1 tsp dried dill (or 1 tbsp chopped fresh)
- ½ tsp salt
- ¼ tsp finely ground black or white pepper
- 3 tbsp finely chopped fresh parsley and chives
- 1 tbsp finely chopped fresh sage and thyme (or ½ tsp each dried; optional), plus extra to serve

TART

- 1kg ripe juicy tomatoes
- ¼ cup extra virgin olive oil
- 250g shallots, peeled and halved
- big pinch salt
- big pinch sugar
- 350g dairy-free puff pastry
- ¼ cup canned chickpea liquid (aquafaba), for brushing

TO MAKE IT GLUTEN-FREE

Use a GF pastry and mustard.

TIPS

+ If you prefer, you can use 300g tofu for the cheese instead of the cashews. It's easier to make in a food processor, but it won't be quite as creamy.

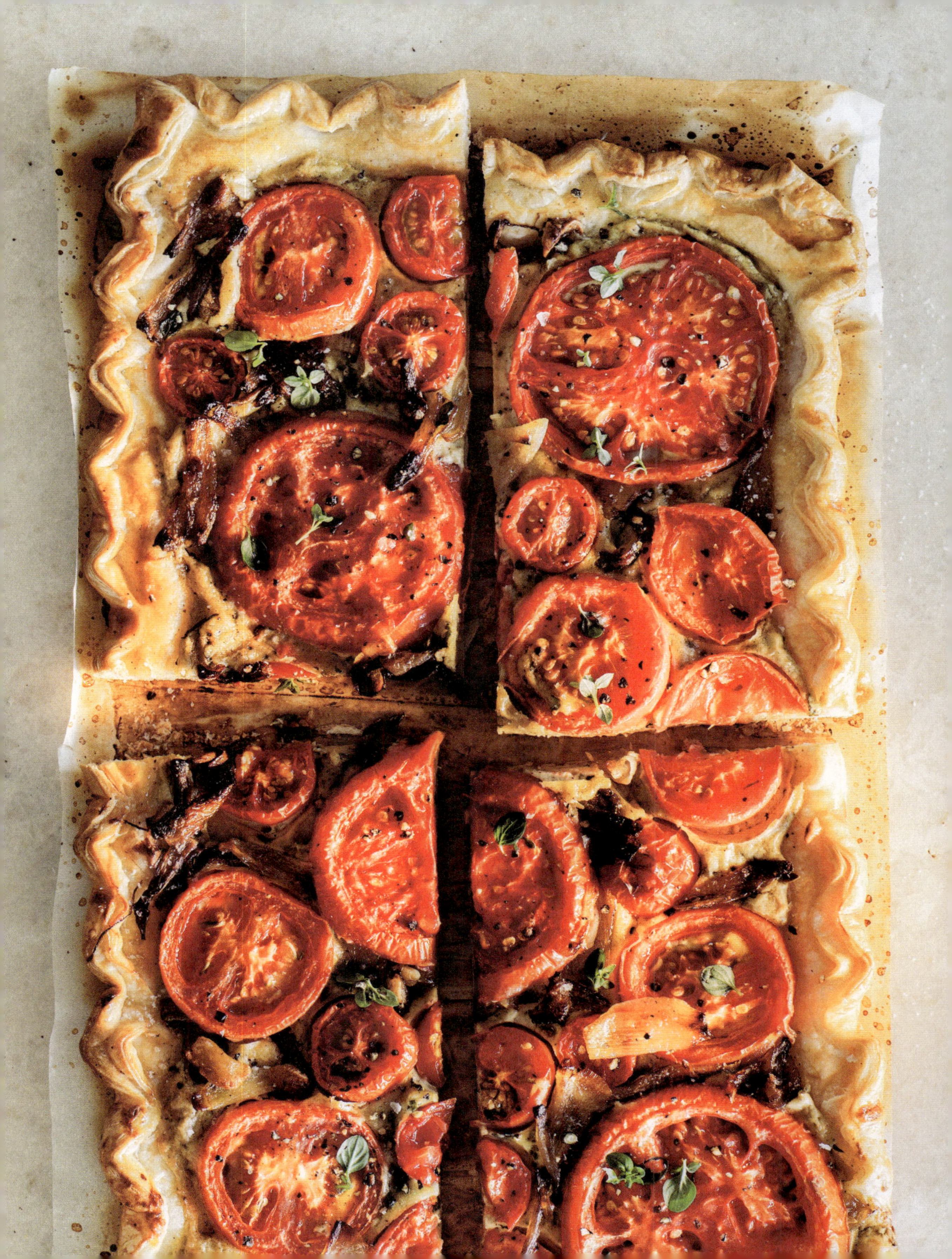

GOLDEN TORTILLA BAKE

extra virgin olive oil, for frying
2 x 500g cans young green jackfruit
1 x 400g can kidney beans, pinto beans or lentils
1 x 400g can black beans
2 onions, thinly sliced
5 cloves garlic, crushed
35g packet taco seasoning mix (see tips)
2 x 400g cans chopped tomatoes
2 cubes vege stock dissolved in 1 cup boiling water
6 medium-sized or 12 small tortillas
150–200g bag natural corn chips, crushed
1½ cups (200–300g) grated dairy-free cheese

TO SERVE

smashed avocado (½ an avo per person at least)
plant-based aïoli or mayo (see page 182)
chopped fresh coriander
chipotle or hot sauce
lime or lemon wedges
chopped pickled jalapeños (optional)

TO MAKE IT GLUTEN-FREE

Use GF tortillas and make sure that your taco mix and stock are GF.

TIP

+ Find a spice mix that only contains spices and natural ingredients (no three-digit numbers or fillers like maize flour, if possible). There are a couple of good brands at the supermarket. If you don't have any, use 2 tbsp paprika, 1 tbsp mild smoked paprika and 2 tsp each coriander and cumin.

PREP 30 minutes   **COOK** 45 minutes   **SERVES** 8

This recipe was actually going to be enchiladas, but the fancy corn tortillas I was using cracked when I started rolling them up, so I just grabbed a baking dish and kinda layered it a bit like a lasagne. The result was so incredibly delicious that my grumpiness at my recipe not going to plan didn't last long. The key is to have as many of the condiment things on your plate as possible, because they are an integral part of the dish and make it texturally balanced and delicious. The kidney and pinto beans make it a filling, sustaining meal, perfect for a family. As much as I love jalapeños, though, I keep them as a garnish so that picky eaters can avoid them.

Preheat the oven to 180°C regular bake and grease a medium-sized baking dish with olive oil.

Rinse the jackfruit pieces in a colander. Squeeze the excess liquid out of the pieces with your hands and shred into meaty chunks, smooshing the hard core pieces with the back of a knife on a board to soften them. Set aside in a bowl.

Drain and rinse the beans. Mash roughly with a masher or a fork, and set aside with the jackfruit.

Add 3 tablespoons oil to a frying pan or flameproof casserole dish over a medium heat. Add the onion and cook, stirring, for about 10 minutes until soft and starting to caramelise. Add the garlic and cook for another minute. Add the taco seasoning and stir for another minute (add a splash more oil if it seems dry).

Add the jackfruit and beans to the pan along with the tomatoes and stock. Simmer over a medium heat for about 20 minutes, or until thickened. Season to taste with plenty of salt and pepper.

Arrange one-third of the tortillas in a layer on the base of the baking dish, tearing them so that they fit evenly. Sprinkle with a handful of crushed corn chips and a smattering of cheese. Top with half the bean mixture, then another layer of tortillas, some more chips and cheese (keeping some for a final layer), then the remaining bean mixture, then a final layer of tortillas.

Sprinkle the top with the remaining cheese and top with a couple of handfuls of crushed corn chips. Season with salt and pepper (I added a smattering of paprika, too) and drizzle with oil.

Cover with foil and bake for 40 minutes. Remove the foil, turn the heat up to 220°C and cook for another 5–10 minutes until golden.

Divide among plates and serve with all the delicious condiments.

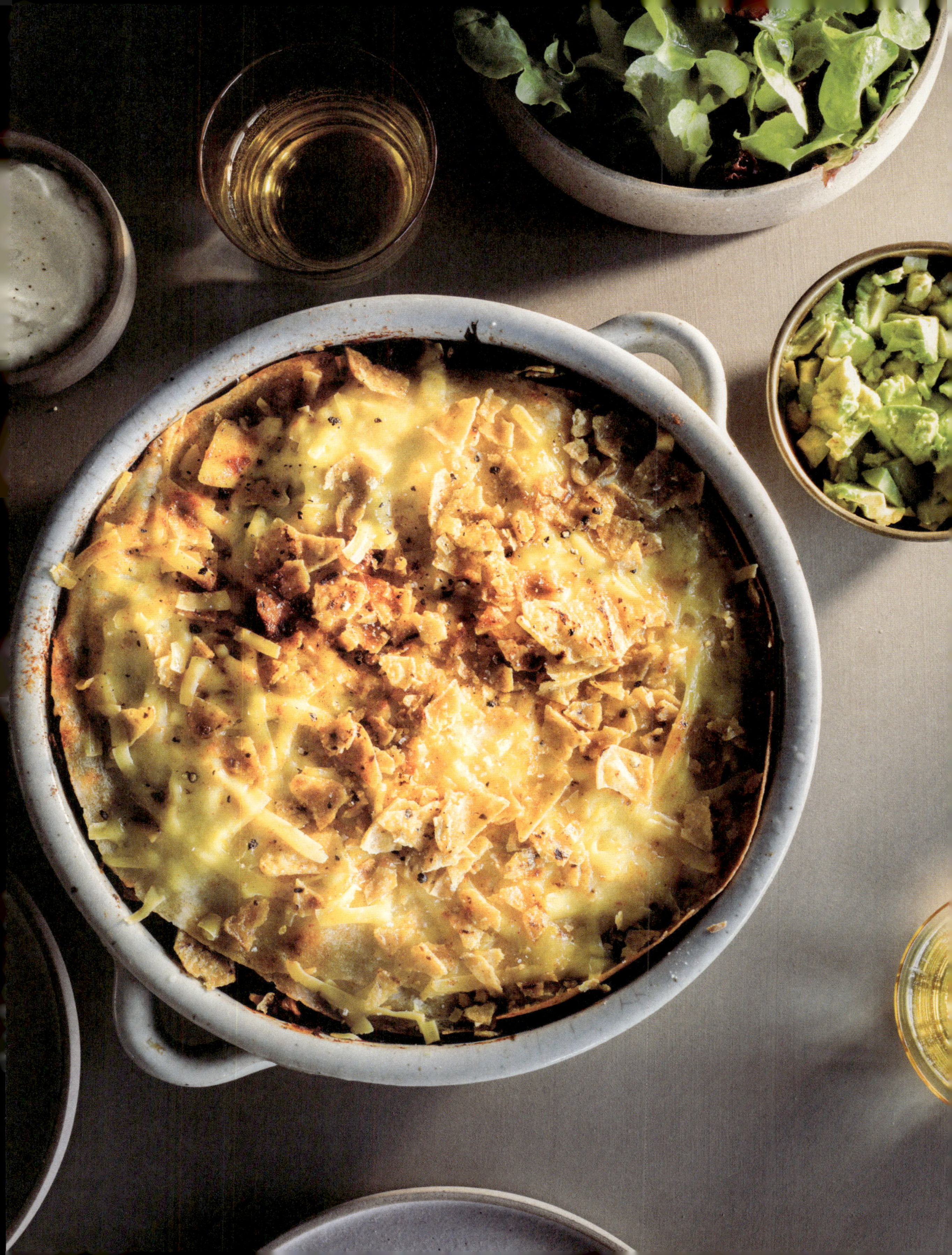

RICE PAPER ROLLS WITH PEANUT SATAY SAUCE

PREP 30 minutes **SERVES** 4–5

Rice paper rolls have always been one of my favourite things to eat. So fresh, so crunchy — like eating a rainbow of deliciousness. To be honest, the dipping sauce is what makes these good as much as anything, so naturally I recommend you make two. The rich, creamy peanut dressing here is to die for and makes it more of a meal, especially with the tofu, but I also use the sauce from the Crispy Tofu Burgers on page 74 for something tangy and fresh. Don't worry about making up enough rolls for the family dinner — everyone can assemble their own at the table. I've put my favourite fillings in here, but you can be creative and use whatever you like (soaked vermicelli noodles are a nice addition).

Slice the tofu into sticks 1–2cm thick and lay on paper towels for a few minutes to draw out the moisture. Season generously with salt and pepper.

To make the dipping sauce, place all the ingredients except the peanut butter in a small saucepan and stir to combine evenly. Bring to a gentle simmer for a few minutes. Add the peanut butter and stir it through. If you think it's too thick when you go to serve it, you can thin it down with a little water. When ready to serve, warm the sauce slightly and pour it into a couple of dipping bowls for the table.

Now prep the veges. If your cucumber has tough skin, peel it first. Halve the cucumber lengthways and scrape the seeds out with a teaspoon. Slice the flesh into thin sticks.

Peel the carrots and slice them into thin sticks (or use a julienne tool; they are amazing).

Arrange all the veges on a platter, cover with a clean, damp tea towel and pop it in the fridge while you fry the tofu.

Heat a little oil in a frying pan over a high heat, add the tofu sticks and fry for a couple of minutes until golden and crispy. Drizzle all over with the tamari or soy sauce, cook a minute or so more on each side, then transfer to a serving plate.

Place the platter of veges on the table along with the sauce, tofu, rice paper sheets, peanuts, herbs and sesame seeds (if using) in separate bowls, so everyone can make their own rolls.

Have a large, shallow bowl of hot water (or use a medium-sized frying pan) on the table for people to dip their rice paper in for 10–15 seconds to soften them. Then just stack up tofu, veges and peanuts in a neat line in the middle of the bottom half of the circle, tuck in the sides as you roll it up, dip in the sauce and away you go. It's up to you whether you allow double-dipping or not!

TASTY TOFU STRIPS
2 x 300g blocks medium-firm tofu (organic is best)
neutral oil for frying
2 tbsp tamari or soy sauce

PEANUT DIPPING SAUCE
1 x 400g can full-fat coconut milk or cream
¼ cup soft brown sugar
2 tbsp mild Thai red curry paste
2 tbsp lemon juice
2 tsp soy sauce
1 tsp salt
¾ cup peanut butter (smooth or crunchy)

VEGES
1 large cucumber
2 large carrots
¼ red cabbage, very finely chopped
2 ripe avocados, finely sliced
1 red capsicum, finely sliced
lettuce leaves, torn

TO SERVE
250g packet rice paper sheets
¾ cup chopped roasted peanuts or cashews (or both)
½ cup chopped fresh soft herbs — coriander, mint, basil
2 tbsp toasted sesame seeds, for sprinkling (optional)

THEY'RE GLUTEN-FREE
If you use a GF curry paste and soy sauce (tamari is GF).

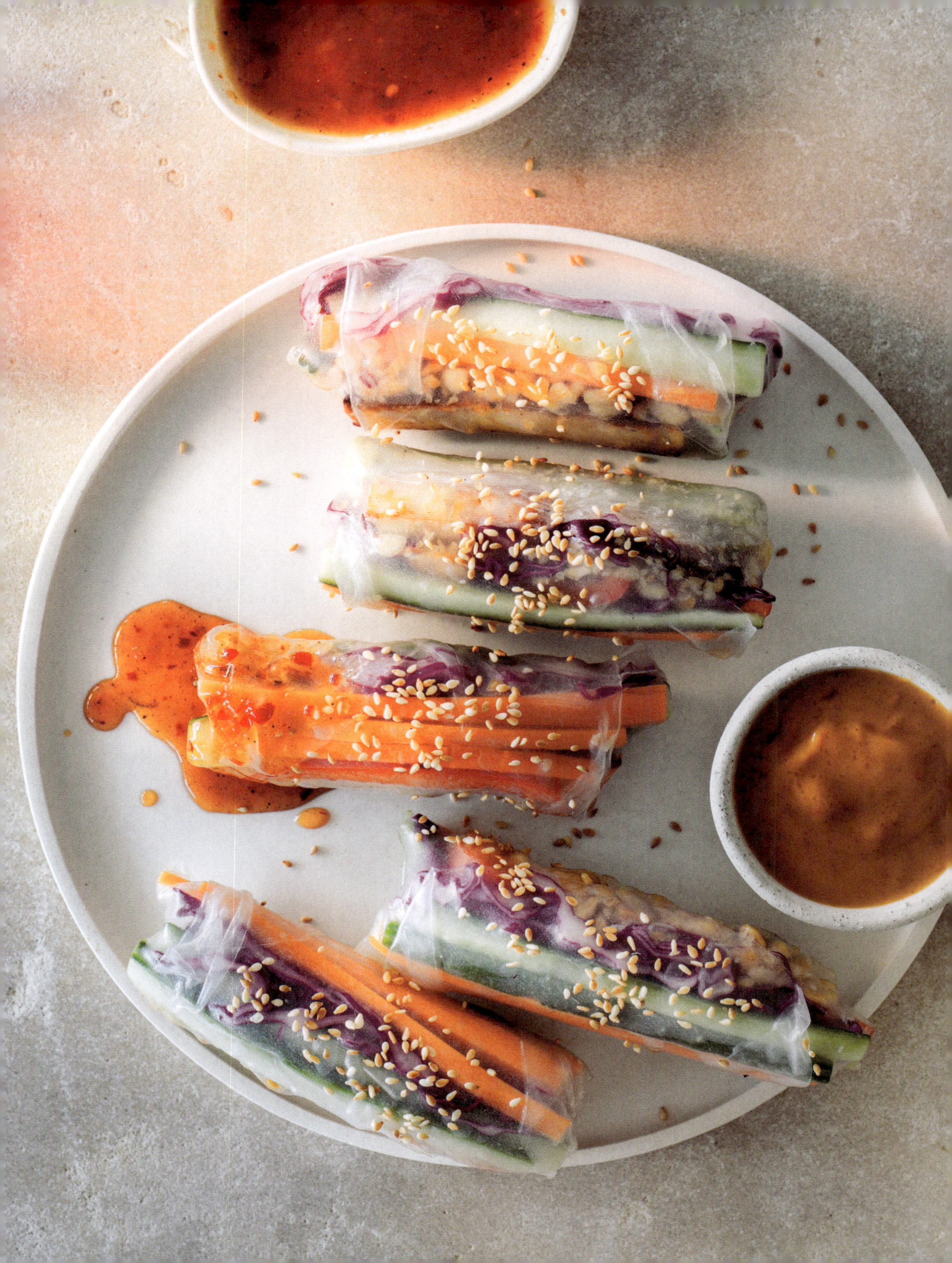

PAD THAI

PREP 30 minutes **COOK** 20 minutes **SERVES** 4

2 x 300g blocks medium-firm tofu (organic is best)

300g dried rice stick noodles (or any rice/wheat noodles)

peanut or grapeseed oil

1 large onion (or 2 small), roughly chopped

4–5 cloves garlic, finely chopped

1 tbsp finely chopped ginger

3 red chillies, deseeded and finely chopped

100g fresh shiitake or button mushrooms, minced (optional)

250g green beans, chopped into 3cm pieces

100g snow peas or sugar snap peas (optional)

½ cup chopped roasted peanuts

2 spring onions, chopped

1 cup mung bean sprouts

⅓ cup chopped fresh coriander (leaves and stalks)

lime wedges, to serve

SAUCE

2 tbsp brown sugar

2 tbsp fresh lime or lemon juice

2 tbsp tamari or soy sauce

¼ cup hot water

3 tsp vegetable or chicken-style stock powder

¾ tsp ground black pepper

TO MAKE IT GLUTEN-FREE

Ensure that your soy sauce, noodles and stock are GF.

Ah, the much revered Pad Thai is always a crowd favourite — you just can't lose with tasty stir-fried noodles. Here's my new plant-based concoction, which stands up pretty well to the original even without fish sauce! I've used grated tofu here in place of the meat or egg — get it nice and crispy when you fry it and it's amazing how perfectly it works, adding a great texture and soaking up the flavour of the sauce. Who knows . . . it might just become your Friday night fave!

Grate the tofu, then spread it out on a few layers of paper towel with a paper towel on top, so that all the excess moisture is sucked out.

Follow the instructions on whatever noodles you have, but cut the soaking time a minute short so that the noodles don't all break up when you stir them at the end.

Mix all the sauce ingredients in a small jug or bowl ready to go, and have the veges chopped and ready, too.

Heat 3 tablespoons oil in a large wok or frying pan over a high heat. When shimmering, season the grated tofu with salt and pepper and add it to the pan. Cook, stirring occasionally, until most of it is crispy and golden brown — a good 8–10 minutes. Set aside.

Add another 2 tablespoons oil to the same pan and add the onion. Stir-fry for a couple of minutes until golden. Add the garlic, ginger, chilli and mushrooms (if using), and stir-fry for another few minutes until everything is golden and fragrant.

Add the fried tofu back to the pan along with the noodles, green beans, snow peas/sugar snap peas (if using) and sauce mixture, and stir-fry for another couple of minutes until the greens are tender.

Just before serving, toss through the peanuts, spring onion, bean sprouts and coriander.

Squeeze over a little more lime juice and season with salt and pepper and extra chilli if you like.

TIPS

+ Some julienned carrot is nice added in, as is red capsicum.
+ You can add a little finely chopped cabbage or spinach, as well as or instead of the beans, to bulk up the veg if you like.

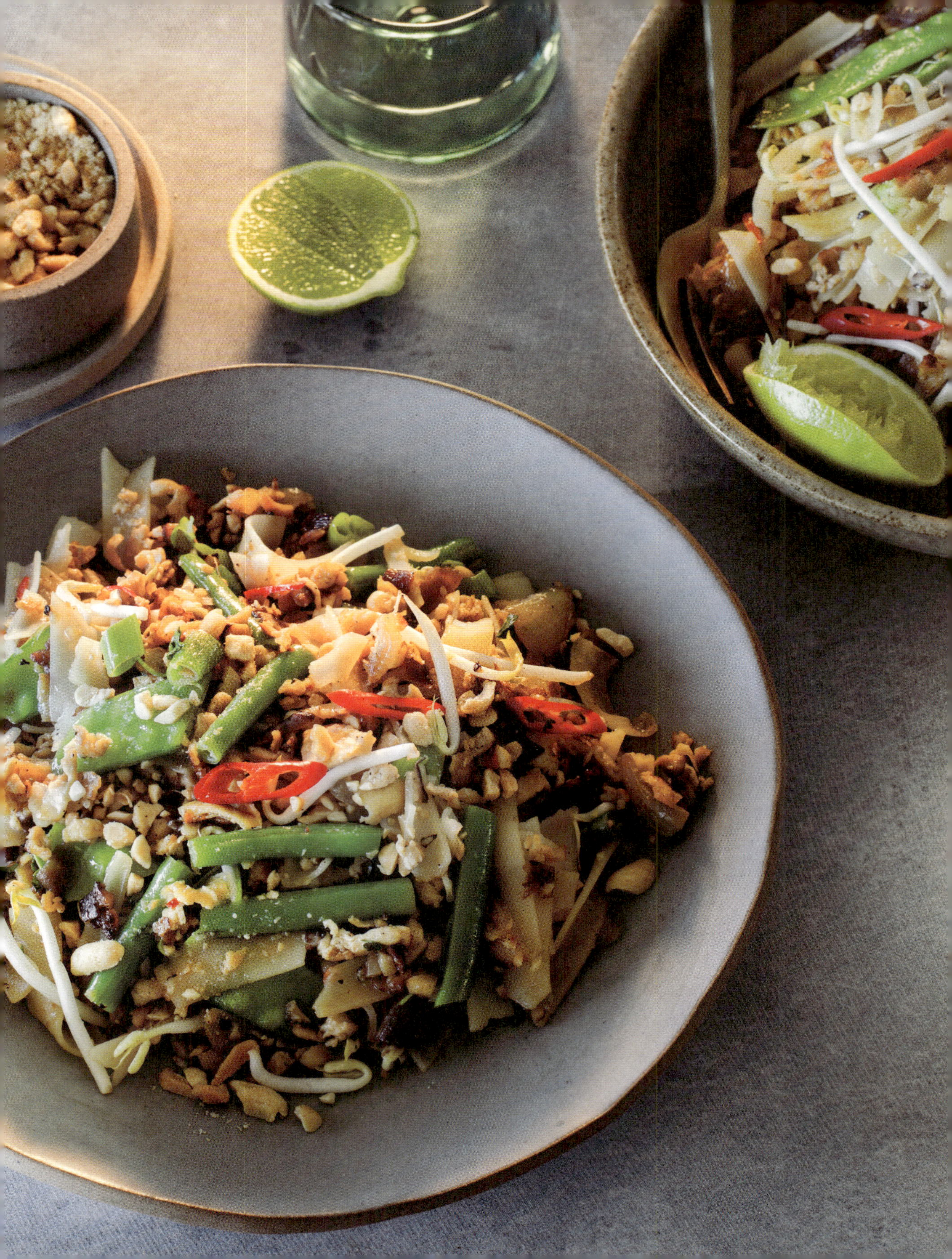

LUSH THAI GREEN CURRY

PREP 15 minutes   **COOK** 30 minutes   **SERVES** 4

My original chicken Thai green curry recipe from *Everyday Delicious* has been insanely popular — and really, who doesn't love a good green curry? Here I've worked up a splendid planty alternative, loaded with veges and all the good stuff. Roasted pumpkin and eggplant give it good flavour without going mushy — I've cut them in different sizes as they cook at different rates, so don't just hack them up any old way. This is creamy, rich and satisfying, with a zing of fresh lime and lemongrass and a crunch of nuts on the top. If you don't want to use tofu, just add a few more vegetables.

Preheat the oven to 180°C regular bake. Place the pumpkin and eggplant in a large, deep roasting tray, toss with a little oil and season with salt and pepper. Roast in the oven for about 25 minutes, or until tender.

If using the tofu, place on paper towels or a clean tea towel and season with salt and pepper. Meanwhile, in a small processor or small blender, whizz the paste ingredients along with ⅓ cup of the coconut cream to make a smoothish paste. You can also grind the paste using a mortar and pestle.

Heat a large frying pan, flameproof casserole dish or wok over a medium-low heat. Add the curry paste and cook for around 10 minutes to release the aromas, stirring frequently so that it doesn't stick. It should reduce and darken, and you should see little pools of oil bubbling up.

Add the remaining coconut cream along with the beans, bamboo shoots and kaffir lime leaf (or lime zest) and simmer gently for around 10 minutes.

Add 2 tbsp oil to a frying pan over a high heat. When hot, fry the tofu until golden all over and set aside.

Add the roasted vegetables to the curry and simmer for a few minutes.

Add the brown sugar, lime or lemon juice and tamari or soy sauce. Stir to combine and taste it; add more lime or lemon, salt, sugar or soy until it's to your taste. If it needs thinning down, which might happen if you leave it to cool and later reheat it, you can always add a little water. Just before serving, stir through the tofu and nuts.

Serve with rice and pile up with coriander and nuts. If you like it hot, you can throw on some chilli flakes or chopped red chillies, too. Squeeze a little extra lime or lemon juice over before serving.

TIPS

+ You can substitute the eggplant or butternut with shiitake or brown button mushrooms. No need to roast them; just add when the coconut cream goes in.
+ If you can find lemongrass sticks, finely mince the inner soft part of 2 stalks instead of using paste.
+ If you like baby corn, add one can (drained) to the sauce while it's simmering.

700g butternut or pumpkin, peeled and cut into 3cm chunks

1 large eggplant, cut into 5cm chunks (optional, see tips)

neutral oil (I used grapeseed)

300g block firm tofu, cut into 3cm chunks (optional)

½ cup roasted cashews (or peanuts), plus extra to serve

CURRY PASTE

3–4 big green chillies (deseeded for a milder curry, or use 3 red deseeded chillies)

2 medium shallots, peeled

3 cloves garlic, peeled

1 tbsp chopped fresh ginger

¾ cup chopped fresh coriander leaves and stalks (and washed roots if you have them)

3 tbsp peanut oil (or melted coconut or grapeseed oil)

2 tbsp Thai green curry paste (mild)

1 tbsp lemongrass paste (see tips)

2 tsp ground cumin

2 tsp vegetable or chicken-style stock powder

1 tsp salt

½ tsp black pepper

CURRY

800ml coconut cream

1 bunch green beans, halved

1 x 225g can bamboo shoots, drained and rinsed

1 kaffir (makrut) lime leaf (or use the zest of 1–2 limes)

1 tbsp soft brown sugar

1 tbsp lime or lemon juice, plus extra for serving

1 tbsp tamari or soy sauce

TO SERVE AND GARNISH

cooked rice (I like brown rice)

coriander leaves

TO MAKE IT GLUTEN-FREE

Use a GF soy sauce and stock.

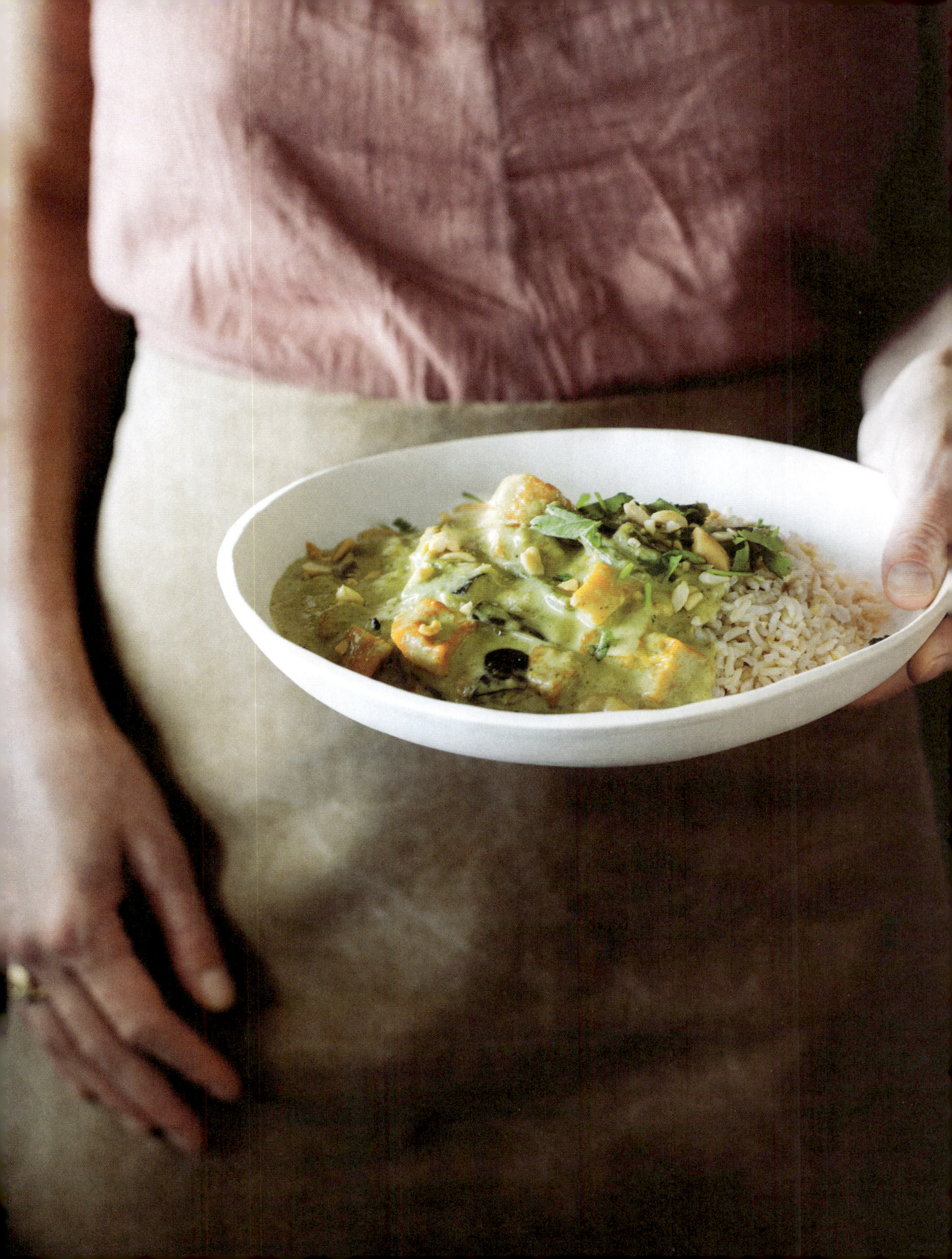

PUMPKIN & CHICKPEA CURRY

- 1kg pumpkin, peeled and cut into 3cm pieces
- neutral oil (I use grapeseed)
- 2 large onions, finely sliced
- 3 cloves garlic, crushed
- 1 tbsp finely grated ginger
- 1 tbsp ground cumin
- 1 tbsp ground turmeric
- 1 tsp ground coriander
- 1 tsp garam masala
- 1 tsp nigella seeds or black cumin seeds (optional)
- 1 x 400g can chickpeas, drained (save the liquid for another recipe)
- 1–2 cups vegetable stock
- 500ml coconut cream
- 1 tsp vegetable or chicken-style stock powder (optional)
- 2 packed cups roughly chopped fresh spinach leaves (or use baby spinach)
- 1½ tbsp lemon juice
- ½ tsp salt, or to taste
- ½ tsp finely ground black pepper, or to taste

TO SERVE
- ¾ cup chopped cashews
- cooked brown or white rice
- chopped fresh coriander

IT'S GLUTEN-FREE
Just check the stock.

PREP 15 minutes **COOK** 40 minutes **SERVES** 4

This is one of those deliciously hearty and savoury meals that you can boastfully produce at dinner time when there seemed to be nothing fresh in the fridge to use. If you don't have any pumpkin hanging around, you can sub in orange kumara (I always try to have some of that around, because it keeps well). Regular kumara or potato will work, too. Even some chopped eggplant would be a welcome addition. If you don't have any fresh herbs to add at the end, it's not a biggie.

Preheat the oven to 200°C regular bake. Spread the pumpkin pieces out on a roasting dish, drizzle with oil, season with salt and pepper and bake for 30 minutes.

Fry the cashews for the garnish in a little oil over a medium heat until golden. Set aside.

While the pumpkin is cooking, heat ¼ cup oil in a large saucepan or cast-iron pot over a medium heat. Add the onion and cook, stirring every now and then, for about 15 minutes until it has turned lovely and soft and golden. Don't try to rush this part — it creates a deep flavour base for the curry.

Add the garlic and ginger and cook, stirring occasionally, for another couple of minutes. Add the dry spices and cook for another minute, stirring often so that they don't stick and burn. Add a little more oil if it seems too dry.

Add the drained chickpeas, 1 cup of the stock, coconut cream and stock powder (if using), stir, and simmer uncovered for another 15 or so minutes until reduced slightly. If you think the curry needs thinning down at any point, stir through some more stock.

Add the roasted pumpkin, spinach, lemon juice, salt and pepper and cook for another 5 minutes until the spinach is wilted. Season to taste with more salt, pepper and lemon juice if you think it needs it.

Serve the curry on rice and garnish with the coriander and fried cashews.

TIPS

+ If you like a little heat in your curry, add some chilli powder with the other dry spices.
+ Nigella seeds have nothing to do with Nigella Lawson (unfortunately), but they taste incredible. You might need to pay a visit to a specialty food store to find them, but I always keep some on hand to use with Indian-style curries or roasted vegetables.
+ Instead of cashews, you could dry-fry ⅓ cup sliced almonds until golden.

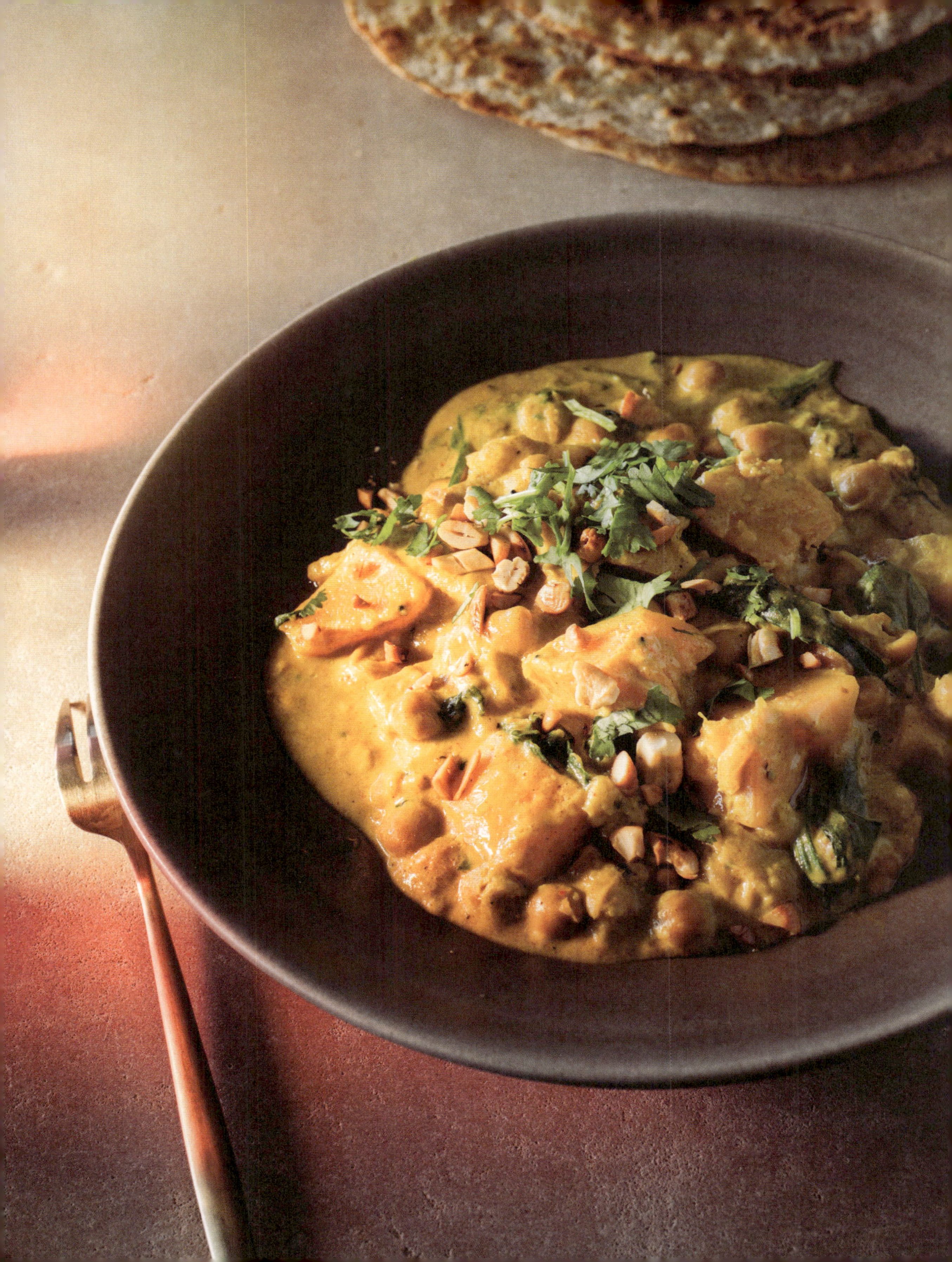

BARRIER CURRY

PREP 15 minutes   **COOK** 1 hour   **SERVES** 4–6

¼ cup grapeseed or coconut oil
2 large onions, thinly sliced
1½ tbsp finely grated ginger
4 cloves garlic, chopped
1½ tsp each ground cumin, ground coriander and curry powder
½ tsp chilli powder
2 tsp ground turmeric
½ tsp each ground white and black pepper
750ml vegetable or chicken-style stock
¾ cup dried brown lentils
4 washed medium-sized potatoes, chopped into 5cm pieces
2 large ripe tomatoes, chopped
1 tbsp lemon juice
1½ tsp garam masala
½ cup coconut cream

TO SERVE
cooked brown or white rice
lemon wedges
chopped fresh parsley or coriander
warmed roti or pita bread (optional)

TO MAKE IT GLUTEN-FREE
Ensure that you use a GF stock.

I threw this recipe together (just casually) when holidaying on Great Barrier while I was pregnant with Sky, and it was one of the very first recipes I wrote up for this book. Out there it's a bit of a drive to the shop for supplies, so we often rely on what we have on hand in the pantry (until we get the organic vege and fruit box delivery, then it's like Christmas). It's a special curry — it's filling, nutritious and tastes divine. Anything with potato in it has my heart, and all the ingredients in here work together perfectly to create an immensely satisfying meal. For something different, try serving it with wild rice if you can find it. Delicious in either summer or winter.

Heat the oil in a deep-sided frying pan or flameproof casserole dish over a medium-low heat. Add the onion and cook, stirring frequently, for about 15 minutes. You want the onion to go golden and mushy — it will shrink down a lot. This is where a lot of the flavour and sweetness in the curry comes from.

Add the ginger and garlic and cook for another few minutes.

Add the cumin, coriander, curry powder and chilli and stir for a minute.

Add the turmeric, peppers, stock, lentils and chopped potatoes. Stir, cover with a lid and simmer on a low heat for 30–40 minutes, stirring every now and then, until the lentils and potatoes are tender and the sauce has thickened. If you need to add more liquid or simmer longer, go for it.

When it's the right consistency, add the tomatoes and simmer for another few minutes. Stir through the lemon juice, garam masala and coconut cream and season to taste with salt and pepper. At this point, you can either add more coconut cream and stock if you think it needs to be thinner, or keep simmering if you want it to be thicker.

Serve over the rice with a squeeze of lemon, a scattering of fresh herbs and roti or pita bread, if you like.

TIPS

+ If you like your curry to have a bit of heat, add more chilli powder.
+ If you can't find lovely red ripe tomatoes, use a handful of halved cherry tomatoes instead.
+ Stir some chopped spinach through in the last few minutes of cooking if you have some on hand.
+ If you have coconut yoghurt you could dollop some of this on when serving.

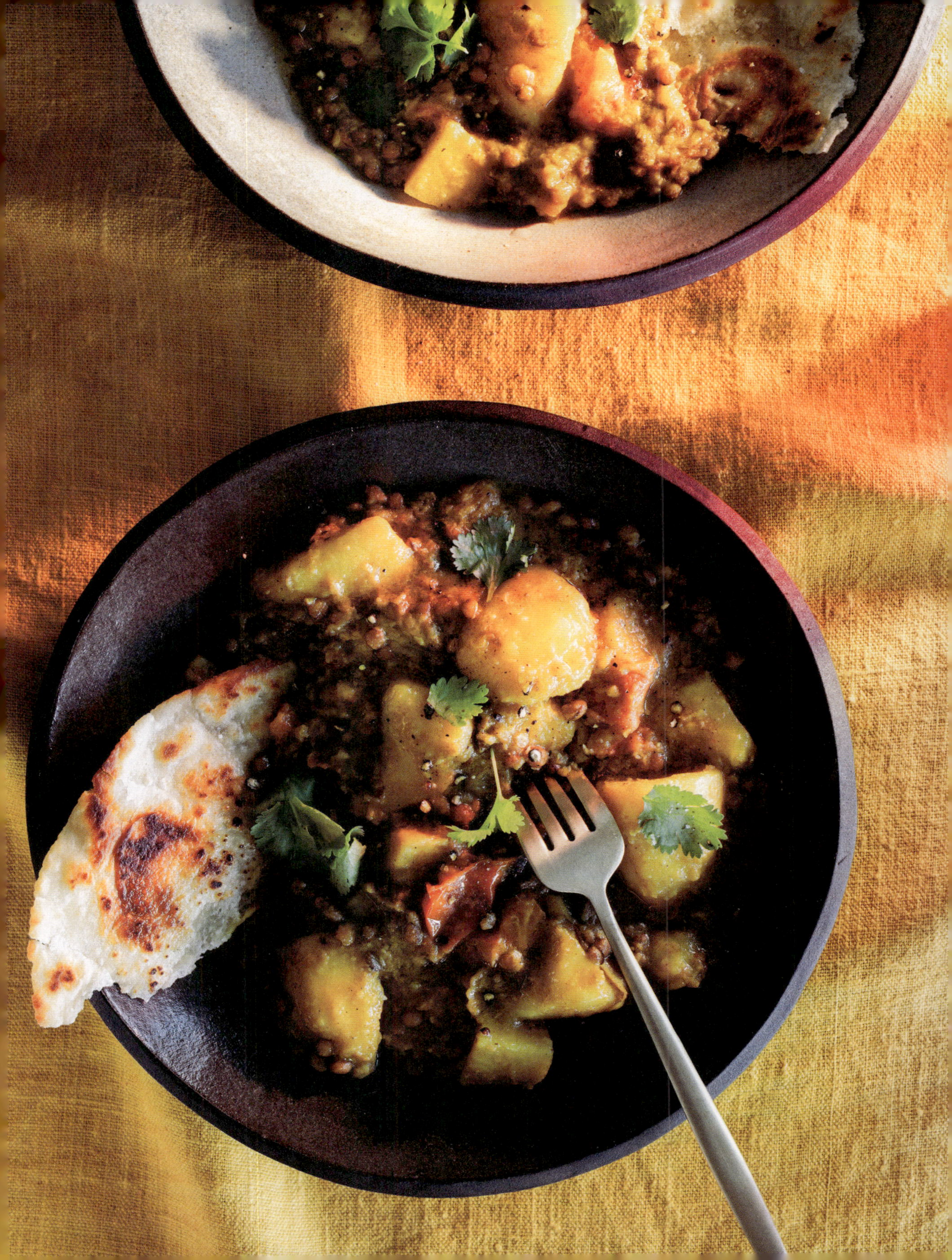

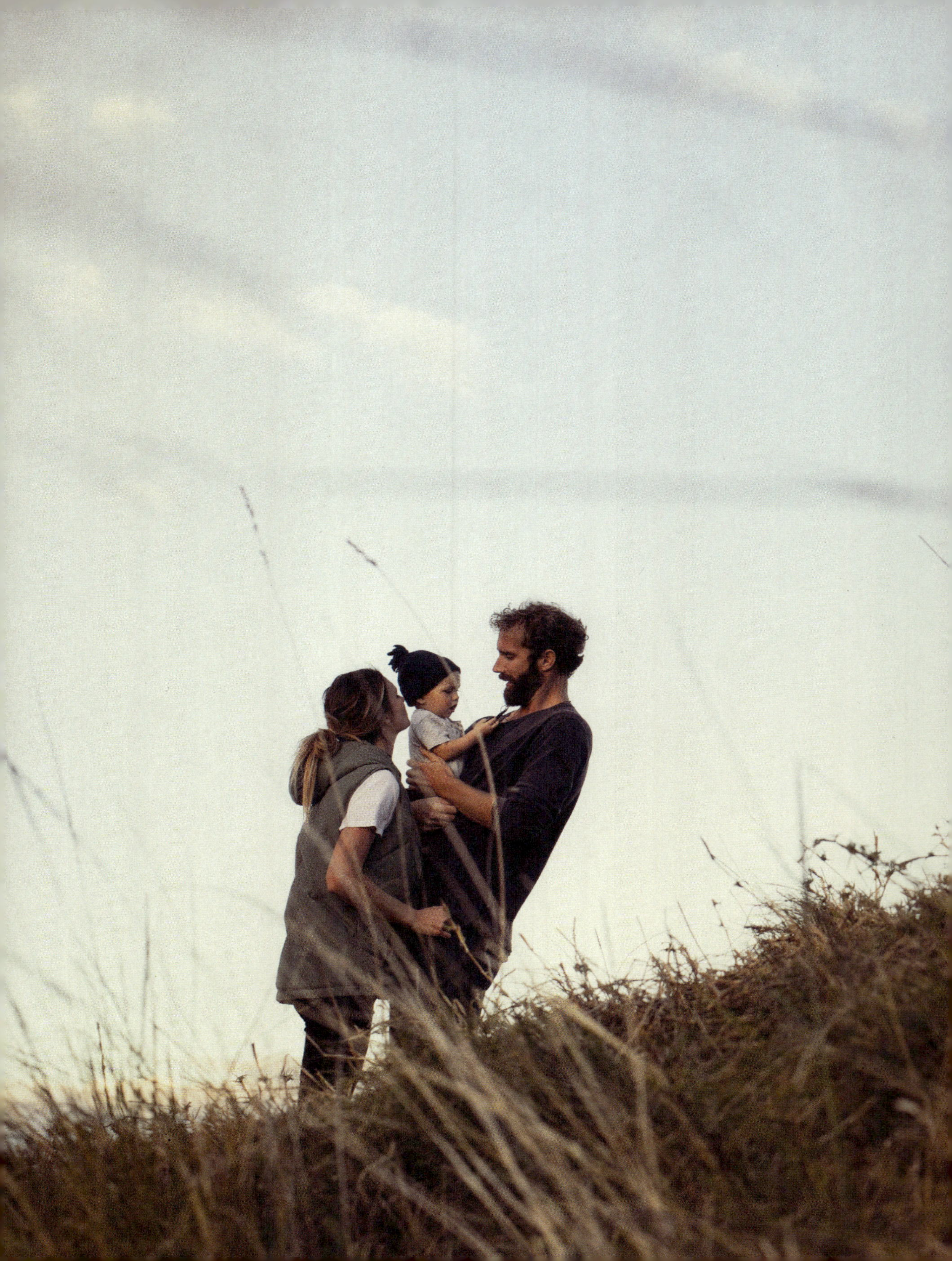

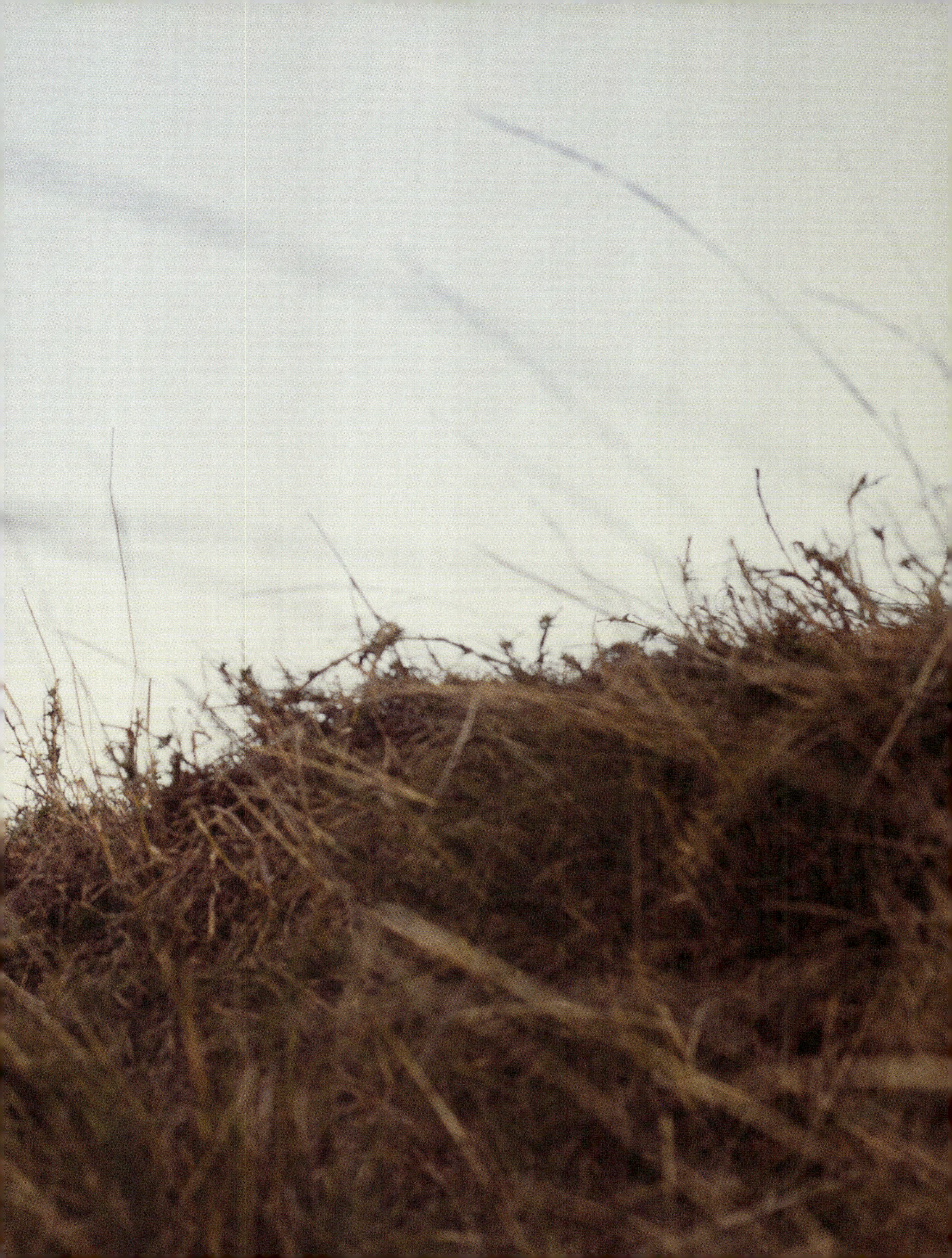

SUNDAY ROAST PIE

PREP 1 hour   **COOK** 45 minutes   **SERVES** 4–6

1kg pumpkin
1–2 medium kumara (or potatoes)
2 onions, peeled and cut into eighths
2 whole bulbs garlic
1 stalk rosemary, leaves chopped
¼ cup extra virgin olive oil
200g shiitake or brown button mushrooms
1 tbsp tamari or soy sauce
¾ cup frozen peas, defrosted a little

SAUCE
¼ cup neutral oil
¼ cup plain flour
2½ cups plant-based milk
3 tsp vegetable or chicken-style stock, dissolved in 3 tbsp boiling water
1 tbsp nutritional yeast
2 tsp Dijon mustard
¼ tsp finely ground white pepper
¼ tsp finely ground black pepper

TO ASSEMBLE
500g dairy-free puff pastry (rolled 5mm thick if need be)
¼ cup canned chickpea liquid (aquafaba), for brushing
sesame seeds, for sprinkling

TO MAKE IT GLUTEN-FREE
Use GF pastry, stock, flour and tamari.

TIPS
+ If you're not a fan of mushrooms, just leave them out — or roast a quartered cauliflower with the pumpkin.
+ You can make these as little individual pot pies in ramekins with pastry tops (and bottoms if you like). Bake for 35 minutes.

When I created this recipe I had a good old roast dinner in mind — tender, golden roasted pumpkin and kumara, sweet caramelised onions and juicy peas drenched in a healthy amount of white sauce seasoned up to the eyeballs. Now imagine all that cosily encased in a cloak of golden, crispy pastry . . . oh yes, it's a real banger of a meal that will satisfy the heftiest of roasty cravings. And it's not limited to dinner — I quite like it cold for a cheeky snack, or packed up into a lunch out on the boat or on a picnic, or even popped in a lunchbox.

Preheat the oven to 180°C fan-bake (190°C regular bake).

Peel and deseed the pumpkin and cut into roughly 4cm chunks. Peel and chop the kumara the same way. Place both in a large, deep roasting tray along with the onions (break them up a bit first), garlic bulbs and rosemary. Drizzle with oil and season generously with salt and pepper. Toss it all together with your hands, then roast in the oven for 45 minutes.

Slice the mushrooms into halves or quarters, then add to the tray along with the tamari or soy sauce and roast for another 15 minutes.

To make the sauce, place the oil and flour in a medium-sized saucepan over a medium-low heat and cook for a few minutes, stirring so that it doesn't colour. Remove from the heat and slowly pour in the milk, whisking all the time. Add the dissolved stock, nutritional yeast, mustard and peppers (you probably won't need salt as the stock is salty, but taste it to check anyway). Place back over a medium heat and stir constantly for a few minutes until thickened.

If your pan with the sauce is big enough, add all the roasted veges to it — or transfer everything to a large mixing bowl. Squeeze the garlic flesh out of the skins.

Add the peas to the rest and stir to combine. If you wanted to add some baby spinach or sautéed chopped regular spinach, now would be the time.

Line a pie or baking dish with about two-thirds of the pastry, bringing it all the way up and over the sides. Add the filling, brush the edges of the pastry with water, and top with a pastry lid. Press down around the edges to seal. Brush with aquafaba, cut a couple of steam holes, and sprinkle with sesame seeds.

Bake for about 45 minutes, or until the pastry is golden brown. You can brush with another layer of aquafaba halfway through cooking, if you like, to make it extra golden.

Serve with seasonal greens or a fresh salad.

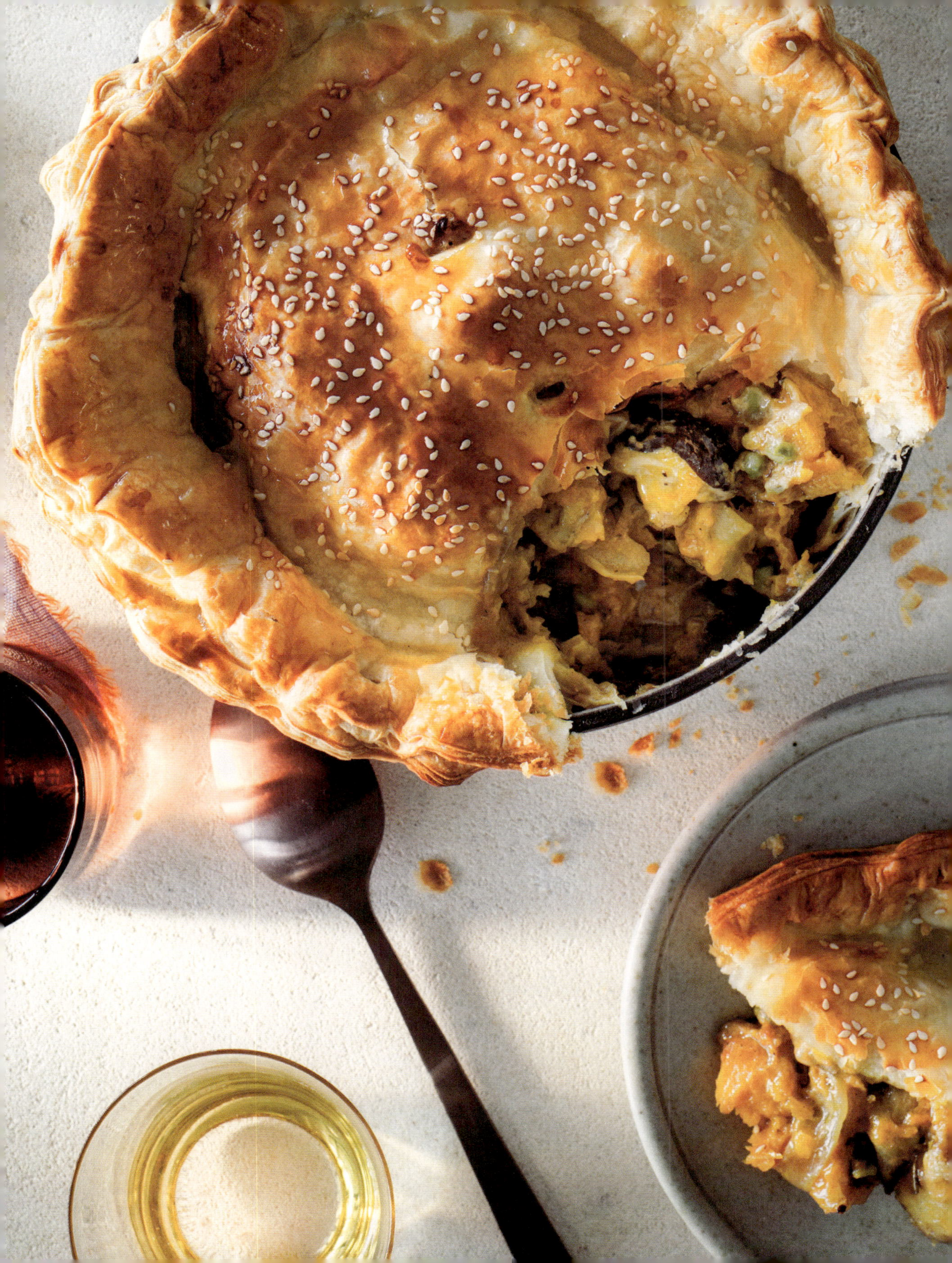

FIRESIDE COTTAGE PIE

PREP 45 minutes   **COOK** 30 minutes   **SERVES** 6–8

One chilly autumn evening, we were mildly disheartened at the sad state of the contents of our fridge but both felt like something homey and comforting. Douglas had a hankering for a meat-free cottage pie, and I thought that sounded like a bloody good idea because everyone loves cottage pie! Especially me. So he went about cooking the potatoes while I muddled the filling together as I went. It all came together into this really quite kick-ass dish — as we sat there by the fire tucking in, we realised we'd nailed it. And it happened to be the same day that we bought our little house in the country, so there are lots of happy vibes jammed into this one. Mum made it for me when Sky was first born, and boy, it went down a treat! If your family doesn't like mushrooms, chop them very small so they aren't noticed (you could pulse them to small pieces in a food processor).

Preheat the oven to 200°C fan-bake (210°C regular bake) and have a medium-sized baking dish ready.

Chop the mushrooms — some small, with some larger pieces for texture if your family is okay with mushrooms. Chop and use the stalks, too.

Place the olive oil in a large flameproof casserole dish that (ideally) has a lid. Set over a medium heat and add the onion and celery. Cook, stirring every now and then, for about 10 minutes until softened. Add the mushrooms and cook for another 5 minutes or so until softened.

Add the garlic and herbs and cook for another few minutes. Add the remaining filling ingredients. Stir, then cover and simmer very gently for about 30 minutes until the lentils are tender, stirring a few times as it cooks. It should thicken up nicely. If you don't have a lid, you will need to simmer for longer and perhaps add more liquid. Season the mixture with salt and pepper to taste.

While the lentil mixture is simmering, cut the potatoes into halves or quarters, depending on their size. Place in a large saucepan of salted cold water, bring to the boil and simmer until tender — 20 minutes or so. Drain well. Add back to the pan along with the dairy-free spread or coconut oil and smash roughly — I just use a wooden spoon. Season well with salt and pepper.

Scatter the lentil mixture with half the Plant Parmesan (if using). Top with the potato in an even layer, then scatter with the remaining Plant Parmesan.

Toss the bread pieces in a bowl with a good glug of olive oil. Scatter on top of the potato and season with salt and pepper. Bake for about 30 minutes, or until the filling is bubbling and the top looks crunchy and golden.

Serve with your choice of green veges or a salad.

FILLING

- 400g Portobello or fresh shiitake mushrooms
- 2 tbsp olive oil
- 2 onions, finely chopped
- 1 large stalk celery, finely chopped
- 2 cloves garlic, crushed
- 2 tbsp chopped fresh herbs — oregano, rosemary, sage, thyme (or use 1½ tsp dried oregano)
- 1 cup uncooked brown lentils, rinsed
- 2 cups vegetable stock
- 1 x 400g can chopped tomatoes
- 3 tbsp tomato paste
- 1 tsp vegetable, chicken-style or beef-style stock powder
- ½ tsp kelp powder (optional, or use 1 tsp soy sauce)
- ½ tsp finely ground black pepper

TOPPING

- 1.25–1.5kg Agria potatoes, peeled or scrubbed
- ¼ cup dairy-free spread or unflavoured coconut oil
- ¼ cup Plant Parmesan (optional, see page 196)
- few slices good-quality bread, chopped into small pieces
- extra virgin olive oil

TO MAKE IT GLUTEN-FREE

Use GF bread, stock and soy sauce.

TIPS

+ You can use 2 drained cans of lentils if you need to save on time; you won't need as much liquid. Start with 1 cup of stock and add more if needed.
+ Feel free to add some grated dairy-free cheese to the topping, too.

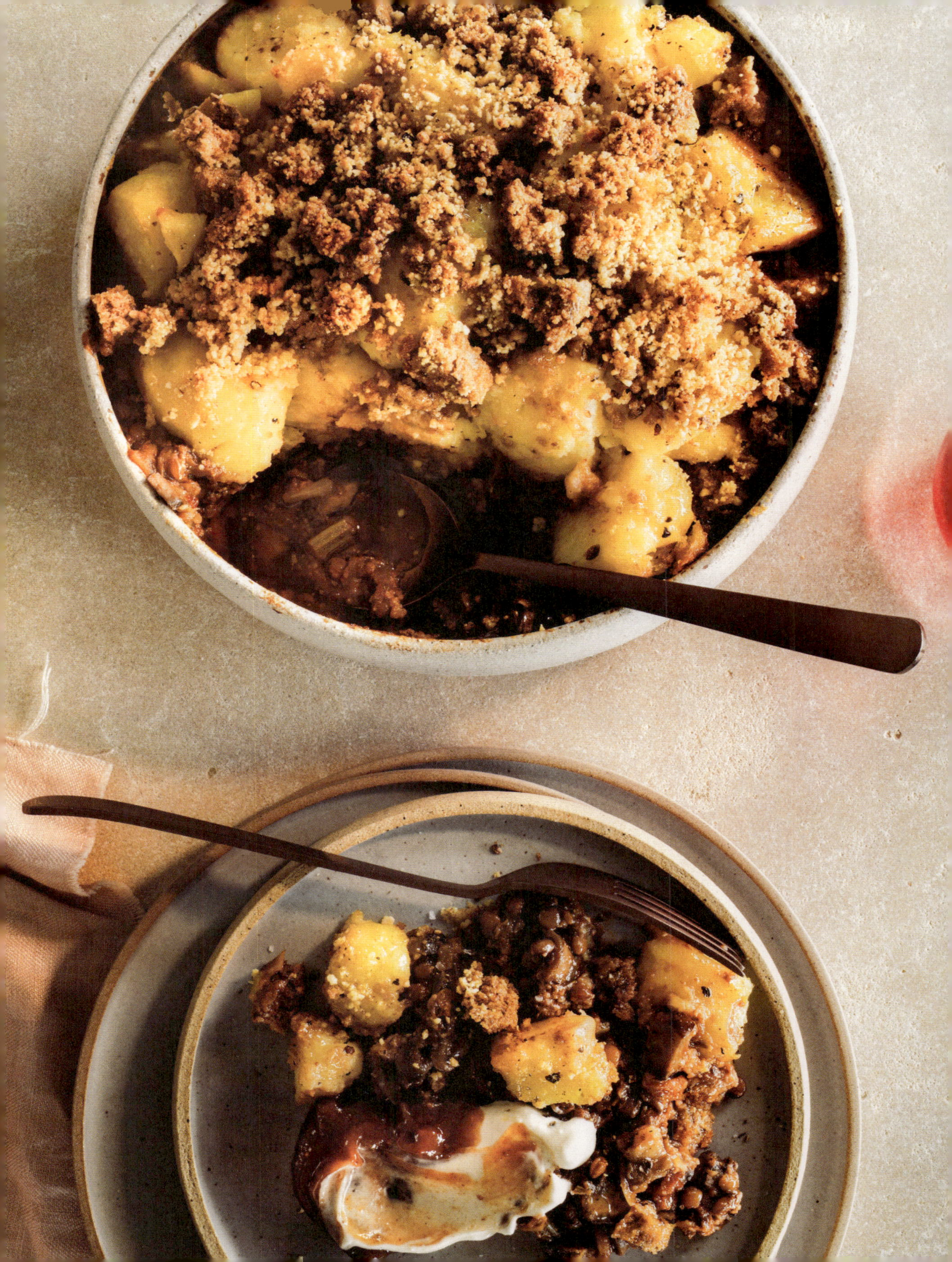

EATLOAF

PREP 1 hour   **COOK** 45 minutes   **SERVES** 10

½ cup dried brown lentils (or use 1 x 400g can)
1 large kumara (about 450g), peeled and cut into 3cm chunks
extra virgin olive oil
1 large onion, chopped
300g shiitake or Portobello mushrooms, roughly chopped
4 cloves garlic, crushed
1 stalk rosemary, leaves very finely chopped
1 cup raw walnuts
1 cup raw sunflower seeds
½ cup rolled oats or breadcrumbs
5 tbsp tomato paste
1 tbsp miso paste (or use 1 tsp Vegemite or Marmite)
2 tsp vegetable stock powder
1 tbsp tamari or soy sauce
1½ tsp salt
1 tsp finely ground black pepper
½ tsp kelp powder (optional)

GLAZE
¼ cup tomato sauce
¼ cup BBQ sauce (or use extra tomato sauce)
2 tbsp malt vinegar
2 tbsp brown sugar

TO MAKE IT GLUTEN-FREE
Ensure that your oats/breadcrumbs, stock powder, miso paste, soy sauce, BBQ sauce and tomato sauce are GF. Use apple cider vinegar instead of malt vinegar.

TIPS
+ If you can find dried shiitake mushrooms, use 80g and soak in warm water until soft. Drain, chop finely and add to mixture.
+ You can shape the loaf freehand on a baking tray lined with baking paper, which means you get more glazed surface, but you won't get the chewy outside bits.

It's meatloaf, without the meat! I originally created this superb recipe for Christmas lunch because it was something I could make ahead and heat up when we were ready to go. The result was splendid. The texture is softer, less heavy than the tradish version, and it's packed full of flavour. The glaze makes it perfect — sweet, salty, tart and glossy, it's like a classy version of tomato sauce on a sausage. Well, a plant-based sausage, that is. This loaf can be served hot, warm or cold, even in a sandwich with a good splurt of your favourite sauce. You can also fry thick slices cut from a cold loaf the next day.

Preheat the oven to 180°C fan-bake (190°C regular bake) and line a baking tray with baking paper.

Rinse the lentils, place in a medium-sized saucepan and cover with plenty of salted water. Bring to the boil, then simmer until tender — about 25 minutes — and drain. (If using canned, just drain them.)

Arrange the kumara on a baking tray and drizzle all over with olive oil. Season with salt and pepper and toss to combine. Cover with foil. Bake for 25 minutes, or until tender.

Add ¼ cup oil to a large frying pan or flameproof casserole dish over a medium heat. Add the onion and cook for 10 minutes, stirring occasionally, until soft and gooey. Add the mushrooms, garlic, rosemary and a pinch of salt and cook, stirring, until the veges have reduced right down and the mushrooms are tender — about 10 minutes. Leave to cool slightly.

Place the nuts and seeds in a large food processor and pulse until you have a chunky crumb. Transfer to a large mixing bowl along with the oats/breadcrumbs, tomato paste, miso, stock powder, tamari or soy sauce, salt and pepper, and kelp powder (if using).

Tip the kumara, lentils and cooked mushroom mixture into the food processor and pulse until you have a slightly chunky mixture — not a paste, but processed enough to stick together well. Scrape down the sides a couple of times as you go to combine it better. Add to the bowl with everything else and scrunch to mix evenly with your hands.

Press the mixture into the loaf tin and smooth out the top. Combine the glaze ingredients in a small bowl and brush generously over the top of the loaf.

Bake for 50 minutes, glazing again once or twice during cooking.

Leave to cool in the tin for 15–20 minutes, then slice very gently with a sharp knife. Or it can be stored, well sealed, in the fridge until you need it — reheat at 170°C for 20 minutes or so. It's easier to slice when it's cooler.

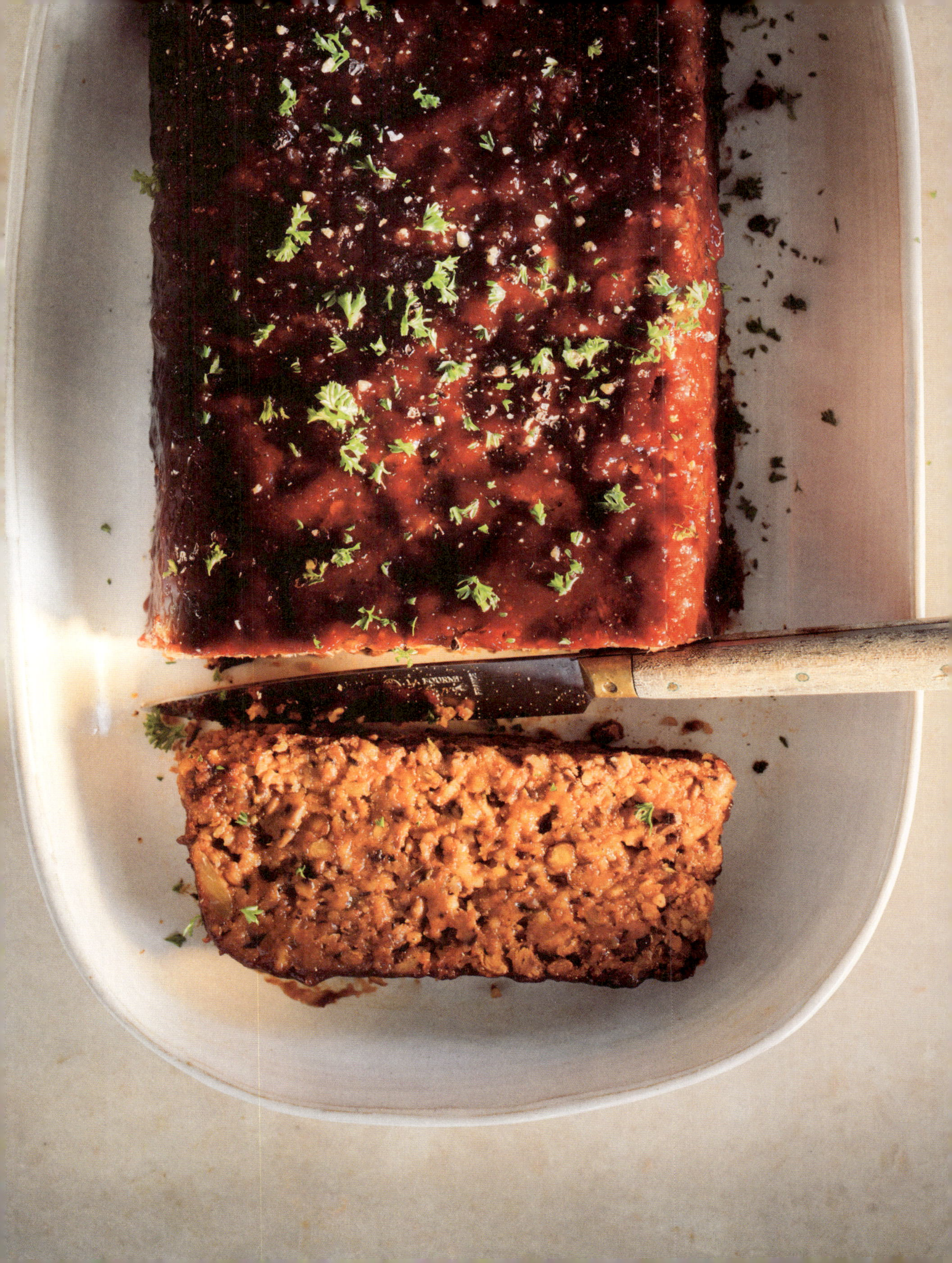

SOFT TACO FIESTA

MEXICAN FILLING

2 x 500g cans young green jackfruit

⅓ cup mild chipotle sauce (or a hotter one if you like things spicy)

3 tbsp tomato paste

3 cloves garlic, crushed

1 tbsp paprika

2 tsp onion powder (optional)

2 tsp mild smoked paprika

2 tsp vegetable stock powder (or a cube of chicken-style stock)

1 tsp ground cumin

1 tsp dried oregano

2 tbsp brown sugar

2 tbsp neutral oil

1½ cups water

SLAW

2–3 cups very finely chopped cabbage

⅓ cup plant-based mayo or aïoli (see page 182)

TO SERVE

soft tortillas

plant-based aïoli (see page 182)

smashed avocado

finely sliced red onion

chopped fresh coriander

squeeze of fresh lime or lemon juice

TO MAKE IT GLUTEN-FREE

Use GF chipotle sauce, stock and tortillas.

PREP 30 minutes, plus marinating time **COOK** 30 minutes **SERVES** 4

This is another meal that's on heavy rotation at our place. First, because it's diabolically tasty; and second, because it's a cinch to whip up on a weeknight. Smoosh up a couple of cans of jackfruit and fry it up with some juicy flavourings, pile it on a warmed tortilla with some creamy slaw, tangy onion, loads of creamy avo and aïoli, and add a zesty hit of citrus and a few splottles of hot sauce. Oh, and coriander because it's the best. Plonking everything in the middle of the table is a fun and simple way to serve dinner so that people can get involved. The more mess, the better!

Drain the jackfruit in a colander, then rinse thoroughly under running water. Take each piece and squash it with the flat side of a large knife to squish it out and break it up a bit. Any big, tough core pieces can be chopped up a bit.

Place the jackfruit shreds and chunks in a mixing bowl and add the remaining filling ingredients except the oil and water. Mix to combine and set aside for 20 minutes if you can, for the flavours to infuse (or up to 2 days).

Put the oil in a medium-sized saucepan over a medium-high heat. When hot, add the jackfruit mixture and fry, stirring frequently, for about 5 minutes until starting to turn golden. Add the water, reduce the heat to medium-low, and simmer until most of the liquid has evaporated and you're left with a nice thick mixture to stuff tacos with. This may take 15–20 minutes. Season to taste with salt — you'll need at least 1 teaspoon. Set aside, keeping it warm.

To make the slaw, combine the cabbage with the mayo or aïoli and season with salt and pepper to taste.

I like to flash-fry the tortillas in a dry frying pan over a high heat after quickly dipping them in water — or just follow the heating instructions for the particular type of tortillas you are using for best results. If you have a gas hob, a quick dip over the flame to get some charring is nice, too.

Serve the tortillas with the jackfruit, slaw and your choice of toppings. I'd go for all of them, plus hot sauce/Tabasco, because that's how I roll.

TIPS

+ If you can't find chipotle sauce, you can leave it out — but it's worth hunting down and most supermarkets now stock it in the condiments aisle.
+ To make it super-quick and easy, you can use a good-quality taco seasoning mix with the jackfruit in the place of the other filling ingredients (still use the oil and water though).
+ For the best-tasting red onion, place the very thin slices in a small bowl and add a big pinch of salt, a squeeze of lemon juice or a splash of vinegar, and a pinch of sugar. Leave for 10 minutes, then squeeze and serve.

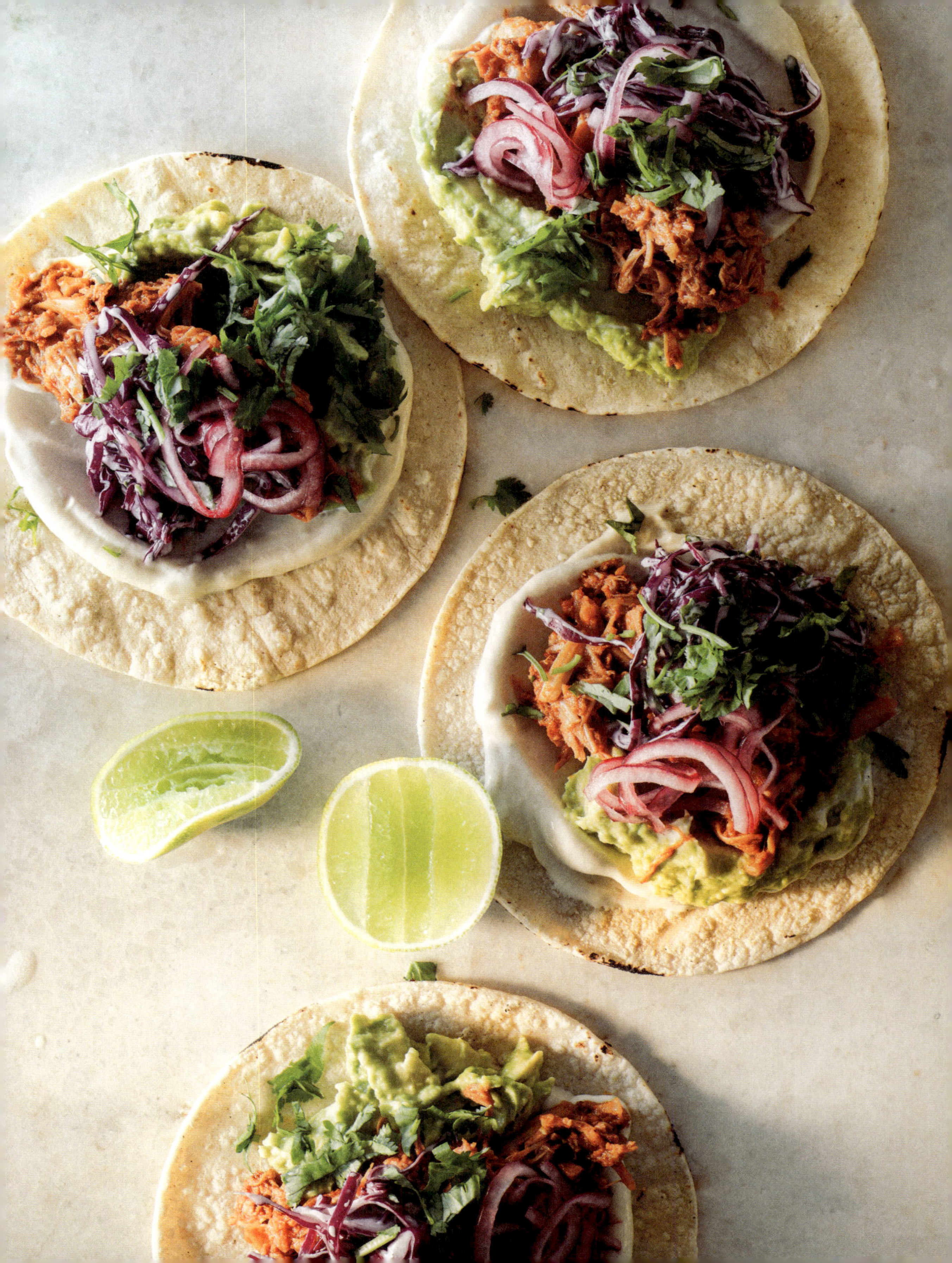

ASIAN-STYLE NO-MEATBALLS

½ cup brown rice
grapeseed oil, for frying
200g tofu, grated (organic is best)
200g mushrooms, chopped into 1cm dice (I like fresh shiitake)
1 large eggplant, chopped into 2–3cm pieces
1 tsp sesame oil
4 cloves garlic, crushed
1 tbsp grated fresh ginger
2 tbsp plain flour
½ tsp salt
½ tsp finely ground black pepper
2 tbsp chopped fresh chives, plus extra to serve

SAUCE
¾ cup water
1 tbsp cornflour mixed in 3 tbsp water
¼ cup sweet chilli sauce
2 tbsp soy sauce
2 tbsp brown sugar
½ tsp Chinese five-spice
¼ tsp finely ground black pepper

TO SERVE
cooked noodles or potatoes
chopped fresh chives or coriander (optional)
Asian greens, broccolini or green beans

TO MAKE IT GLUTEN-FREE
Use GF flour, and tamari instead of soy sauce.

PREP 15 minutes   **COOK** 35 minutes, plus 30 minutes to chill
SERVES 4–5

Making plant-based 'meatballs' can be a real pain in the butt when you don't have the meat protein to help them stick together during cooking. This recipe relies on rice to hold everything in a lovely shape — and it works beautifully. Texturally they're lighter and not as chewy, but they have bags of flavour — especially when coated in my glossy, tangy sauce. Sure to be a family-pleaser; we love them at our place. You can make the balls in advance and just fry them up when you're ready to go. You can use the flesh of a small cooked kumara in place of the eggplant, in a pinch.

Cook the brown rice in a small saucepan of salted water until tender, then drain and set aside.

Heat 1 tablespoon oil in a frying pan or flameproof casserole dish over a high heat. When hot, add the grated tofu with a good pinch of salt and a crack of pepper. Cook, stirring frequently, for about 10 minutes until the tofu is golden and starting to go a bit chewy. Tip onto a plate and set aside.

Add another tablespoon of oil to the pan along with the sesame oil and place over a medium-high heat. Add the mushrooms and cook for 5 minutes or so, stirring frequently. Add the eggplant and 2 tablespoons water, and cook for another 5–10 minutes until the veges have gone soft and lost some moisture — the eggplant should be quite mushy. Add the garlic and ginger and cook for another couple of minutes.

Add the cooked rice, flour, salt and pepper and cook for another couple of minutes. It's okay if it looks a bit strange at this point — the flour will help bind it.

Tip the mixture into a food processor and process briefly, until it's turned slightly gummy and comes together easily but isn't a paste — you still want some nice pieces of mushroom in there for texture. Add the tofu and chives and pulse to just combine. Season to taste with more salt and pepper if you need to.

Roll into balls slightly smaller than a golf ball and arrange on a tray lined with baking paper. Refrigerate for about 30 minutes to firm them up (or overnight).

Stir all the sauce ingredients together in a little jug ready for later.

To cook the balls, heat a little oil in a pan over a medium-high heat, add the balls (in batches if need be) and fry until browned all over. When all the balls are browned, put them all back in the pan, stir the sauce again and pour it in. Cook over a medium heat for a few minutes until it's thickened up nicely.

Serve the no-meatballs and sauce over noodles or potatoes with fresh chives or coriander on top if you want, and some greens on the side.

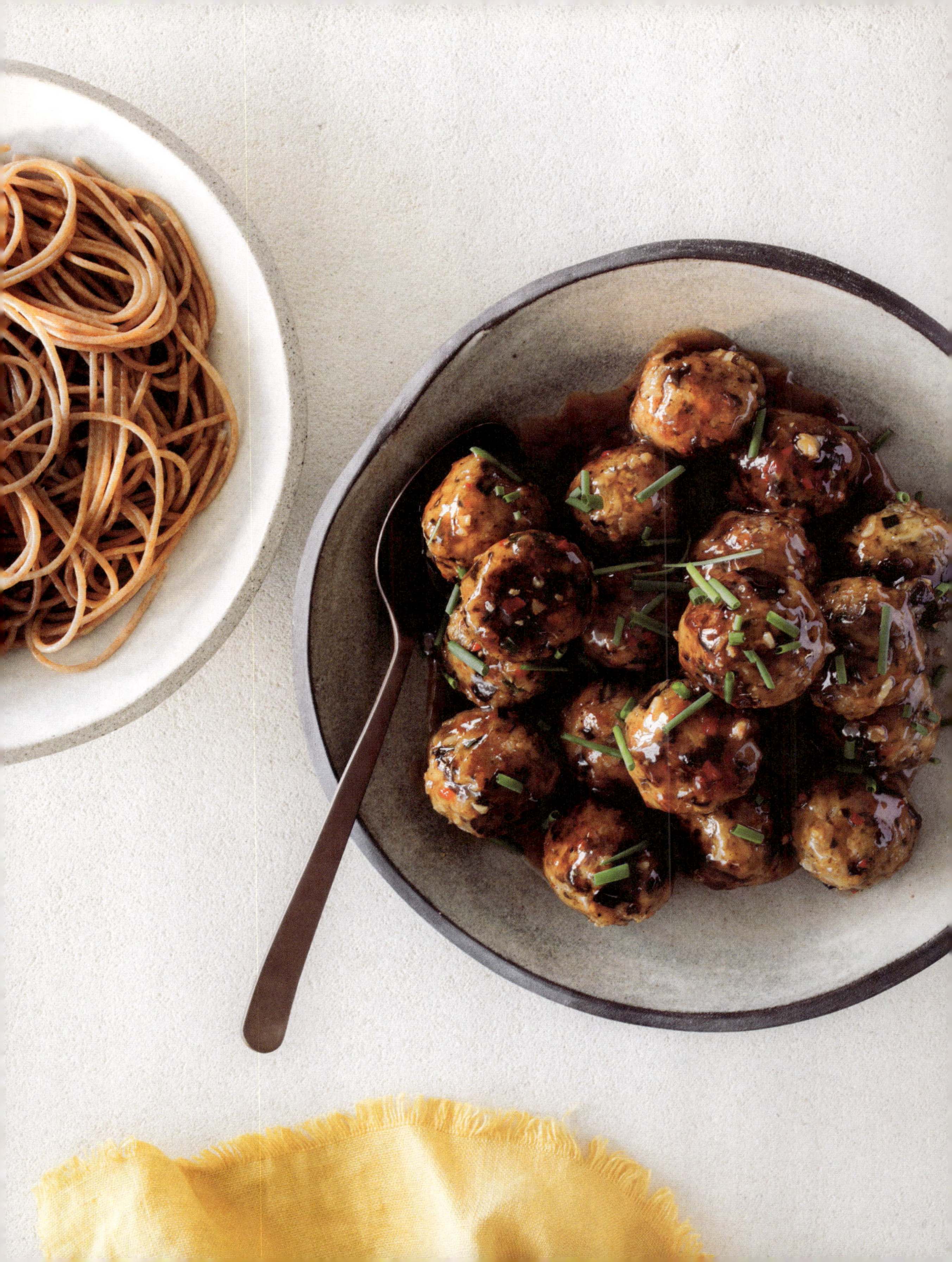

THAT MOROCCAN DISH

PREP 20 minutes   **COOK** 45 minutes   **SERVES** 4–5

¼ cup extra virgin olive oil
2 onions, sliced
4 cloves garlic, chopped
1 tbsp freshly grated ginger
1 tbsp ground turmeric
2 tsp each ground cumin, coriander and paprika
1 tsp mixed spice
½ tsp finely ground black or white pepper
1 x 400g can lentils, drained (or cook your own)
1 x 400g can chickpeas, drained
1½ cups vegetable or chicken-style stock
1 x 400g can chopped tomatoes
2 tbsp honey (or use maple syrup or brown sugar, to taste)
½ cup dried apricots, quartered (or use dates or prunes)
½ cup Sicilian or Kalamata olives (optional)
2 tbsp finely chopped preserved lemon (or zest of 1 lemon)
2 tsp lemon juice

TO SERVE

cooked couscous, brown rice or quinoa
freshly chopped coriander or parsley (or both)
⅓ cup chopped toasted pistachios or sliced almonds (optional)
plant-based aïoli (see page 182), or coconut yoghurt with a squeeze of lemon
lemon wedges

TO MAKE IT GLUTEN-FREE

Serve with rice, quinoa or potatoes and make sure that your stock is GF.

'I'd go back to a restaurant for that,' Douglas yelled out as he went back for a third helping of this the first time I made it. Oh yes, chickpeas — aka garbanzo beans, which I think is a much cooler name, we should all start using it — are awesome. We eat lots of them. Packed with protein so they make a meal, they're also high in fibre and iron — great to welcome into your food fabric (in ways other than just hummus). They take on the flavour of anything you add; a good simmer with some spices works wonders, as in this dish. First-time eaters could be a little suspicious, but if you pile enough aïoli, herbs and nuts on top, you should be right.

Add the oil to a large frying pan or flameproof casserole dish over a medium heat. Add the onion and cook, stirring frequently, for about 10 minutes, until lovely and soft and golden. Add the garlic and ginger and cook, stirring, for another few minutes.

Add the spices and cook for another minute, stirring so the spices don't stick.

Add the remaining ingredients and stir to combine. If you have a lid, cover and simmer for about 20 minutes, then remove the lid and continue to simmer until reduced to a thick sauce suitable for serving over couscous. Or just simmer with the lid off the whole time, adding more liquid if you need to.

At this point, season to taste with salt — you may need ½ to 1 teaspoon. You can also add more honey, lemon juice and/or pepper until the balance of flavours is to your liking.

Serve the curry over your cooked couscous, rice or quinoa, scatter with herbs and pistachios or almonds (if using), and dollop with a good spoon of aïoli or lemony coconut yoghurt. An extra little squeeze of lemon, and you're good to go!

TIPS

+ Add a pinch of chilli flakes if you like some spiciness.
+ If you can find preserved lemon at your supermarket, it's very yummy, with an intense lemony flavour. You only use the rind and pith, not the flesh.
+ You can use another can of chickpeas in place of lentils if you like — I would mush the second can up a bit.

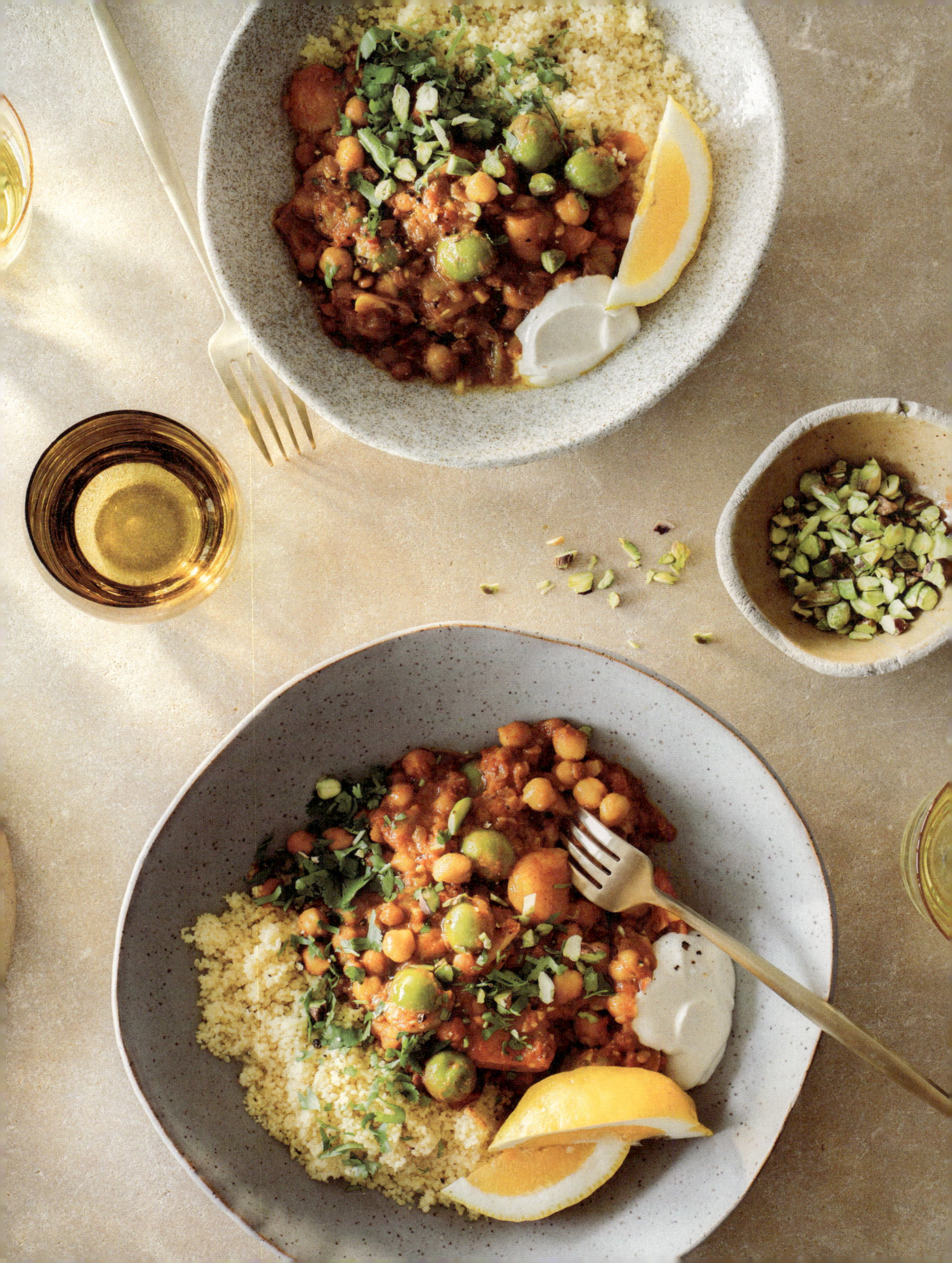

SAMOSA STUFFED POTATOES

4–5 large floury potatoes (I like Agria)

olive oil, to coat potatoes

¼ cup coconut oil (or use grapeseed)

2 onions, finely chopped

2 tsp finely grated ginger

1 tsp black or yellow mustard seeds (optional)

3 cloves garlic, crushed

1 tbsp curry powder

2 tsp ground turmeric

1 tsp ground coriander

½ tsp garam masala

½ tsp chilli flakes (optional)

⅓ cup coconut cream

¾ cup just-cooked peas

2 tbsp finely chopped fresh coriander or parsley

2 tsp lemon juice

TO SERVE

coconut yoghurt or plant-based aïoli (see page 182)

chopped coriander or parsley

chutney or relish

squeeze of lemon (optional)

IT'S GLUTEN-FREE

PREP 25 minutes   **COOK** 1 hour   **SERVES** 4–5

I adore a well-made vegetable samosa — they're one of my favourite things to eat (the recipe in *Homemade Happiness* is the greatest!) What *isn't* my favourite thing, though, is how time-consuming they are to make. I can't just casually whip up 30 little folded and deep-fried pastry pockets for a weeknight dinner; just not gonna happen, mate. This dish, however, gives you all the deliciousness of the samosa flavour, the creamy potato and the fresh pop of peas without all the effort.

Preheat the oven to 200°C regular bake and line a baking tray with baking paper.

Wash the potatoes, scrubbing them to remove any dirt if need be. Dry them, then coat with olive oil and sprinkle with salt. Prick each one a few times with a fork. Arrange on the baking tray and bake for 45 minutes to 1 hour, depending on how big your potatoes are (see tips). Allow to cool slightly.

While the potatoes are cooking, prepare the delicious spiced mixture. Add the coconut oil to a frying pan over a medium-low heat. When hot, add the onion, ginger and mustard seeds (if using) and a pinch of salt and cook, stirring, for about 10–15 minutes, until the onion is turning a lovely deep golden and has gone a bit mushy.

Add the garlic, curry powder, turmeric, ground coriander, garam masala and chilli flakes (if using) and cook for another 5 minutes, stirring constantly so that the spices don't stick. Add the coconut cream, stir through and simmer for 5 minutes or so until reduced right down.

When the potatoes are cool enough to handle, slice the tops off lengthways. Using a spoon, carefully scoop most of the flesh out of the potatoes, leaving a wall of potato there to hold it together.

Add the potato flesh to the pan with the onion and spices, along with the peas, fresh herbs and lemon juice. Stir/mash to combine but leave some chunks. Taste and season with salt and pepper.

Pile the filling back into the potatoes, replace them on the baking tray and bake for another 10 minutes or so to heat through.

Serve the potatoes with a dollop of coconut yoghurt or aïoli, extra fresh herbs, chutney or relish of your choice and a squeeze of lemon if you like.

TIPS

+ A fork should easily pierce through the potatoes when done. Or use a small paring knife and pierce one from the top — it should go through easily and come out without lifting the potato back up with it.
+ If you can be bothered, you can fry the potato skins from the tops in a neutral oil until crispy and serve them with the samosa potatoes!

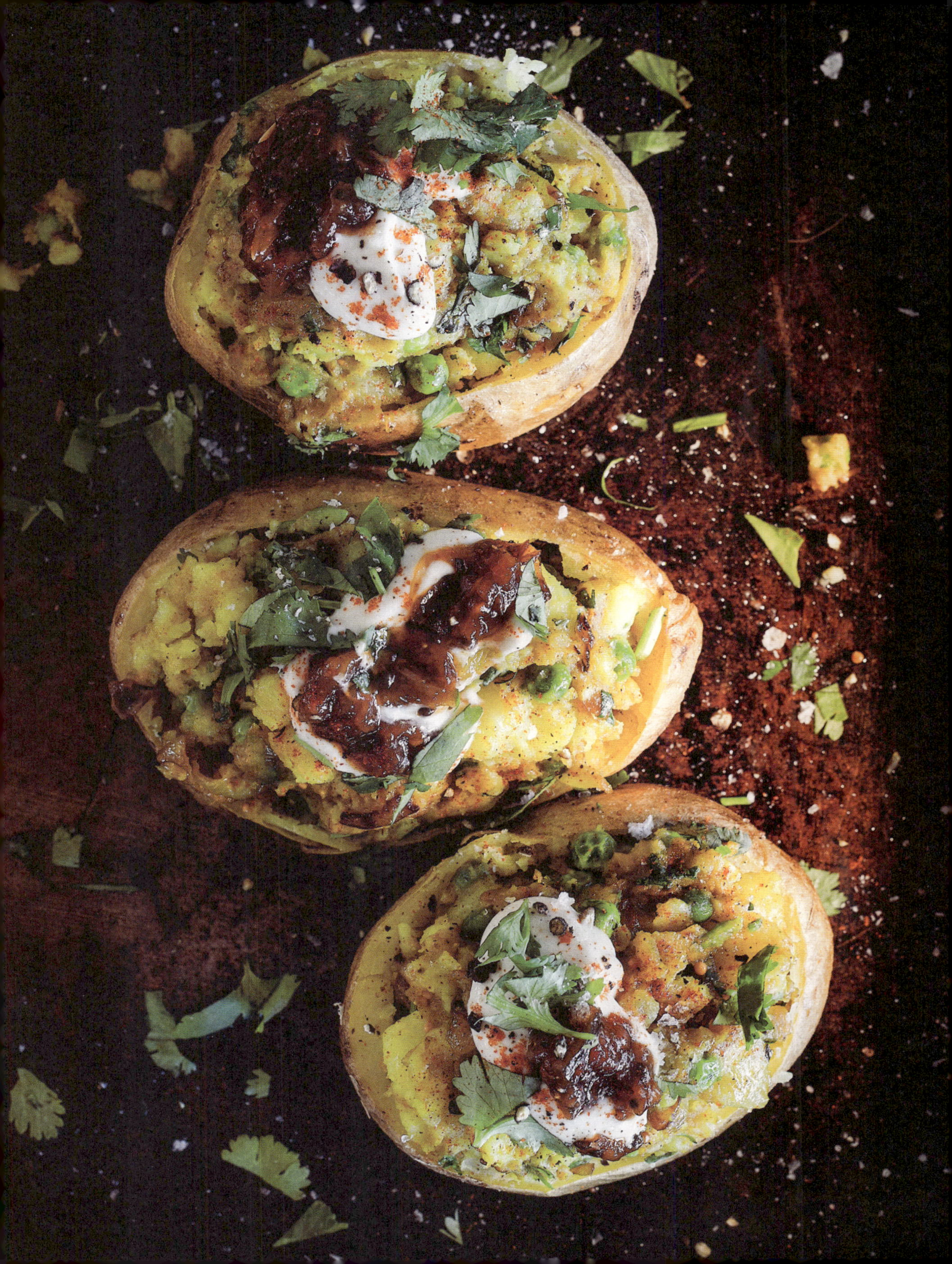

CRISPY TOFU BURGERS

- 2 x 300g blocks firm tofu (organic is best)
- ½ cup plant-based milk
- ¼ cup plant-based mayo or aïoli (see page 182)
- ½ cup plain flour
- 1½ cups dried breadcrumbs
- neutral oil, for frying (I used grapeseed)

SAUCE
- ½ cup sweet chilli sauce
- 2 tbsp soft brown sugar
- 2 tsp soy sauce
- 1 tsp sesame oil
- 2 cloves garlic, crushed
- zest and juice of 1 lime (or ½ lemon)

SLAW
- ¼ large red or green cabbage, finely shredded
- 1 large carrot, grated
- ⅓ cup finely chopped roasted peanuts
- ⅓ cup plant-based mayo or aïoli (see page 182)
- ¼ cup chopped fresh coriander

TO SERVE
- burger buns or plain fresh buns
- plant-based mayo or aïoli (see page 182)

TO MAKE IT GLUTEN-FREE
Ensure that your breadcrumbs, flour, buns and soy sauce are all GF.

PREP 40 minutes **COOK** 15 minutes **SERVES** 4–5

I have to be honest and say that, at least for now, I'm done with vege patties in burgers. I'm a bit of a burger purist and to me the texture is always a bit lacking. (Of course the vege patties in *Eat* are delectable, but you've already got that recipe.) So for this book I've chosen to forge ahead with other insanely delicious and interesting fillings to mix things up a bit. Tofu never looked so good!

Slice the tofu into either two or three slabs, depending on how thick you want the patties.

Mix the milk and mayo in one shallow bowl, place the flour in another, and the breadcrumbs in a third bowl. Arrange side by side on the benchtop. Have a clean board or plate ready to put the crumbed tofu patties on.

Season the tofu patties generously on both sides with salt and pepper. Gently take a patty and dip it first in the flour, dusting off the excess gently, then in the milk mixture, then coat it with the breadcrumbs. If you want them really crispy, you can dip again in the milk mixture and coat in another layer of breadcrumbs. Repeat with the remaining tofu. If you can, refrigerate uncovered for 30 minutes so that the coating firms up a bit.

To make the sauce, combine all the ingredients in a small bowl and season with salt and pepper. Set aside.

To make the slaw, combine all the ingredients in a large mixing bowl and season to taste with salt and pepper.

Heat about 1cm oil (or enough to come halfway up a patty) in a medium-sized frying pan over a medium-high heat. When it's nice and hot (the tip of a wooden spoon handle dipped in should bubble when it's ready), add a few tofu patties and fry for a few minutes until deep golden and crispy on each side. Set aside to drain on a wire rack set over paper towels while you fry the rest.

If you're using gluten-free buns, you may want to grill them just before serving; if you're using nice soft buns, you may not need to.

To assemble, layer the burger up with the bottom bun, mayo or aïoli, a tofu patty, slaw, sauce and top bun. I like to season with extra salt and pepper too (naturally). Squish down and enjoy!

TIPS

+ If you prefer a thicker sauce, you can simmer it very gently in a small saucepan for a few minutes, then allow to cool. You can also add the juice of 1 orange for more tang if you're doing it this way.
+ If you can't be bothered crumbing the tofu (sometimes I can't), just dust the slabs in well-seasoned flour and fry on a high heat until crispy — it's still amazing.

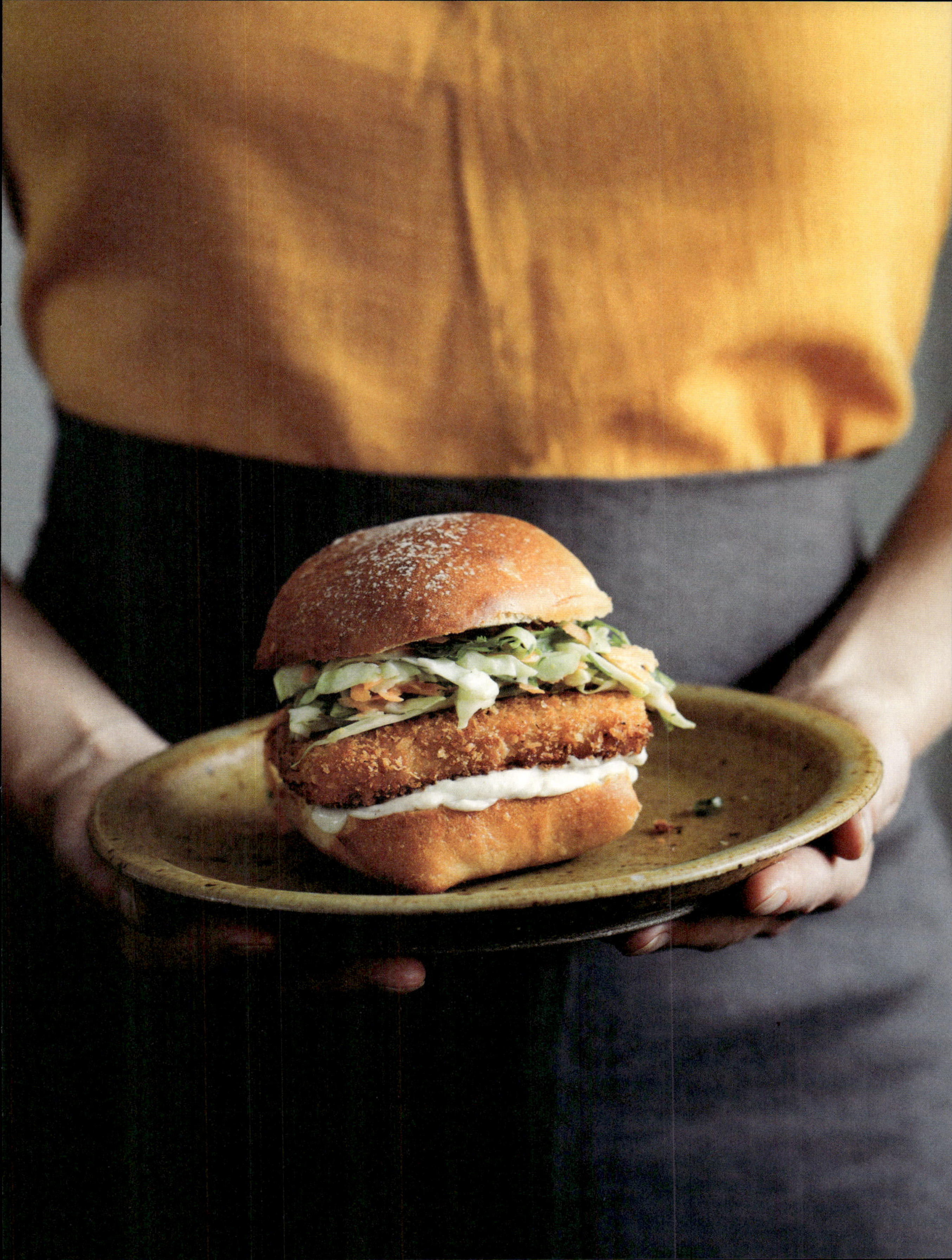

BBQ BURGERS WITH CRISPY ONION RINGS

PREP 15 minutes   **COOK** 1 hour   **SERVES** 4–5

Look at the state of these bad boys. They're so delectably good that we ate the actual burgers made for this photo even though they'd been sitting out for half a day in 30°C heat! They had wilted a bit but were still insanely delicious, so just imagine what they're like fresh, hot and crispy, dripping with luscious sauces and creamy aïoli. Old mate jackfruit really flaunts it in this recipe — everyone will be fooled. Fruit in a burger might seem weird but it works, so just embrace it and pile in!

Drain the jackfruit pieces in a colander and rinse well with cold water. Set aside.

Heat 1 tablespoon oil in a medium-sized frying pan over a medium heat. Add the onion and a pinch of salt and cook, stirring occasionally, for about 10 minutes until soft. Add the garlic and cook for another minute or so.

Add the drained jackfruit pieces to the pan, along with the BBQ sauce, stock, tomato paste and chilli (if using). Stir to combine and simmer for about 30 minutes, or just until the liquid has reduced right down. Now you can refrigerate it until you need it.

Just before serving, make the onion rings. Stir the flour, sugar, baking soda, baking powder and salt together in a medium-sized mixing bowl. Add the beer or water, aquafaba and oil, and stir with a fork until only just combined — lumps are fine.

Heat 1–2cm oil in a frying pan over a medium-high heat. When hot enough (the tip of a wooden spoon handle should bubble when it's ready), use tongs to dip an onion ring in the batter and gently lower into the hot oil — do as many as will fit comfortably in the pan. Cook until golden and crispy on both sides (a few minutes), then drain on a wire rack set over paper towels on the benchtop.

Before serving, fry the jackfruit mixture until hot. If it's still in the same pan you cooked it in, just turn the heat up and stir occasionally — a bit of browning on the bottom is fine.

You can choose to grill the buns with cheese and dairy-free butter on them, or just have them uncooked.

To assemble, stack all the components together (including the onion rings) and dig in!

TIP

+ The jackfruit mixture keeps for a couple of days in the fridge if you need to make it in advance. If it has dried out a bit, just add a little water when you fry it up before serving.

PULLED BBQ FILLING

2 x 450g cans young jackfruit in brine
neutral oil, for frying
1 large onion, finely chopped
4 cloves garlic, crushed
1½ cups good-quality BBQ sauce
1 cup vegetable stock
1 tbsp tomato paste
pinch chilli flakes (optional)

ONION RINGS

1 cup plain flour
1 tsp sugar
½ tsp baking soda
¼ tsp baking powder
1½ tsp salt
250ml beer or water
3 tbsp canned chickpea liquid (aquafaba), or plant-based milk
2 tbsp neutral oil, plus extra for frying
1 large onion, sliced into 1cm rings

TO ASSEMBLE

burger buns
sliced dairy-free cheese
dairy-free butter (optional)
plant-based aïoli (see page 182)
lettuce leaves
sliced gherkins
sliced tomato
sliced or smashed avocado (optional)
chipotle sauce, tomato sauce or Sriracha sauce

TO MAKE IT GLUTEN-FREE

Ensure that your buns, flour, BBQ sauce, stock and beer are all GF.

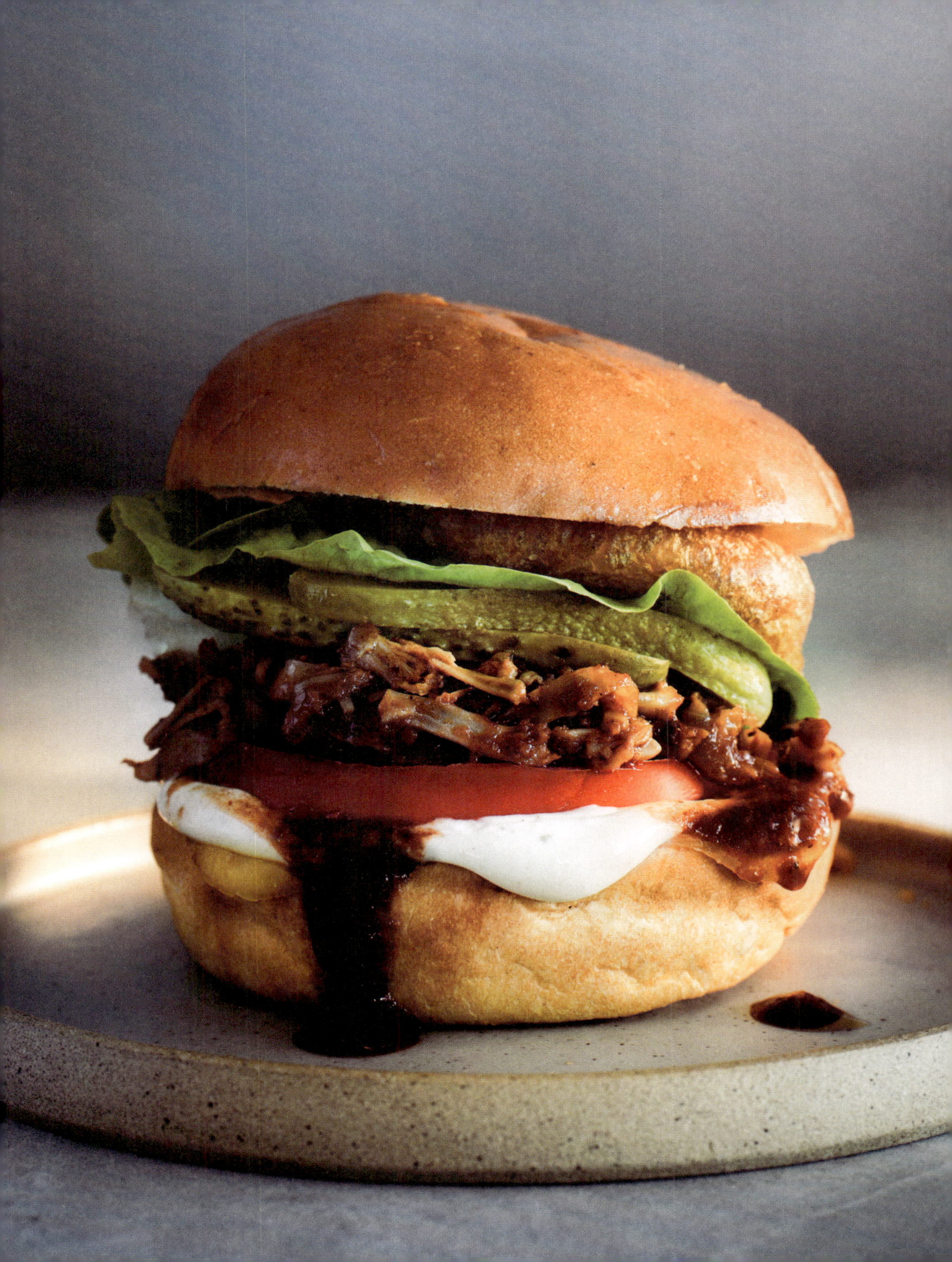

NOT DOGS

PREP 15 minutes **COOK** 1 hour **SERVES** 4

SAUSAGES
6–8 medium-sized carrots
3 cups vegetable stock
2 tbsp brown sugar
1 tbsp tomato paste
1 tbsp miso paste
2 tsp apple cider vinegar
3 cloves garlic, chopped
1 tsp smoked paprika
1 tsp salt
½ tsp ground black pepper
neutral oil, for frying

CARAMELISED ONION
2 tbsp olive oil
1 large onion, sliced
½ tsp salt
½ tsp sugar

TO SERVE
hot dog buns, warmed
tomato sauce
American mustard
plant-based mayo or aïoli (see page 182)

TO MAKE IT GLUTEN-FREE
Use GF burger buns or bread, and make sure that your stock and tomato paste are GF.

You have to love these just for the novelty factor. I mean, how delicious do they look — and it's a friggin' carrot in a bun. That's right — a carrot. I think I'm in love! I served these as an entrée when I had my folks over for dinner (so classy, I know), and it may have been the wine but they all reckoned it tasted like the real thing. I can't take credit for the idea but I have developed my own special brining mixture, which is where you get the savoury flavours of a real frankfurter (without the dodginess). With enough onions, mustard, aïoli and ketchup in there it tastes so legit.

Peel the carrots, then use the peeler to round off the ends so they look as much like frankfurter sausages as possible.

Place the carrots in a saucepan together with the remaining sausage ingredients except the oil, and set over a medium-low heat. Simmer until the carrots are completely cooked through. How long you need will depend on the size of your carrots — mine took about 45 minutes on a low simmer. You don't want any crunch left in the carrots, or they will be too much like carrots.

Leave the carrots to cool in the liquid. If you don't need them straight away, refrigerate them in the liquid until you do (up to a few days). They actually taste better after a day anyway.

To make the caramelised onion, place the olive oil and onion in a small frying pan over a medium-low heat. Cook, stirring occasionally, for about 5 minutes until softened. Add the salt and sugar and cook for another 10 minutes or so until starting to caramelise.

When you're ready to serve, drain the sausages on paper towels. Add a splash of neutral oil to a frying pan over a medium-high heat. When nice and hot, briefly fry the sausages, being careful not to break them, until they are hot and seared.

Serve the sausages in warmed buns along with onion, aïoli, tomato sauce and mustard.

TIPS
+ Choose carrots that don't taper very much, to make it easier to shape them (and make less waste).
+ To warm the buns, cover with foil and heat in a 150°C oven for 5–10 minutes.

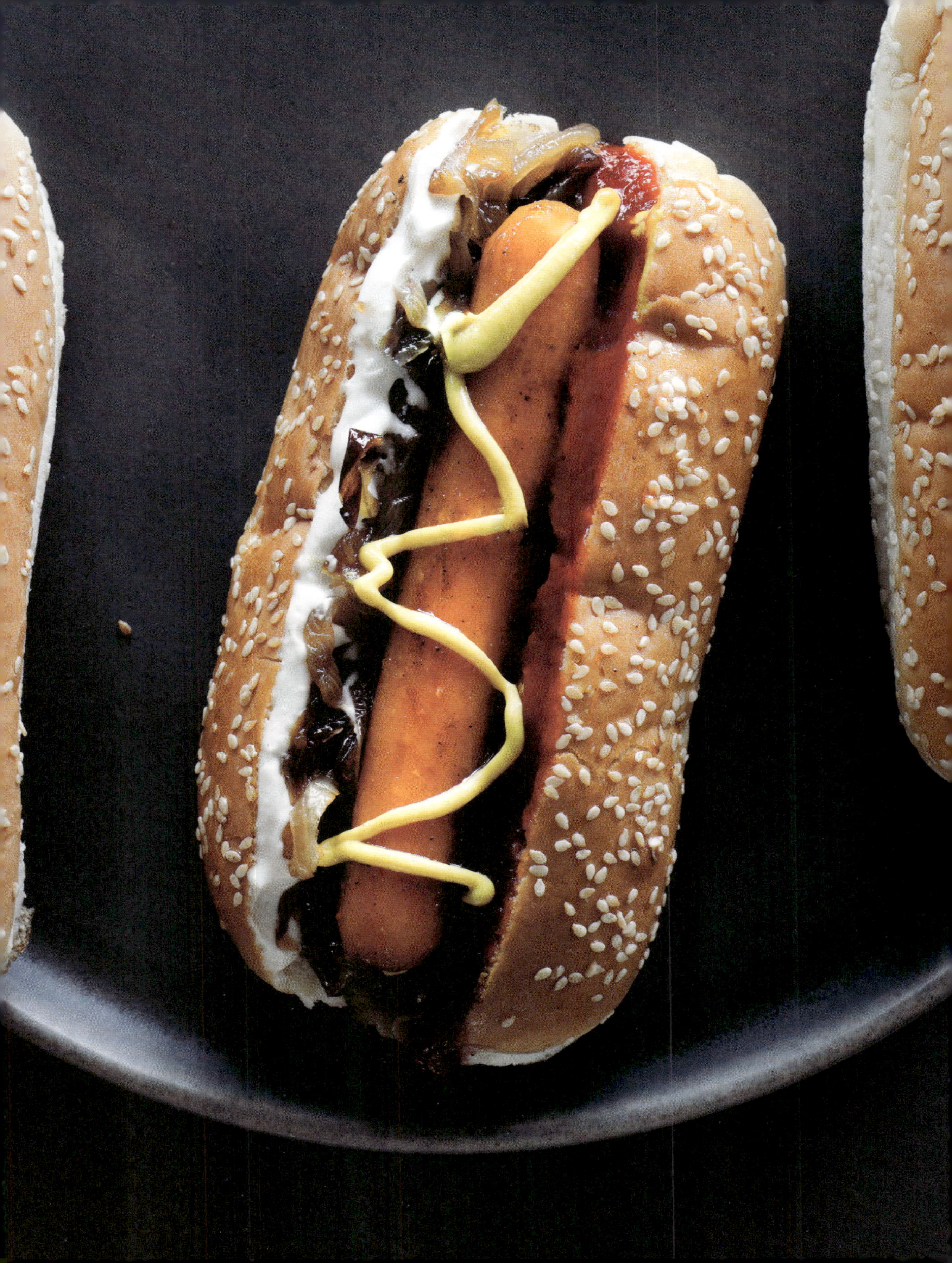

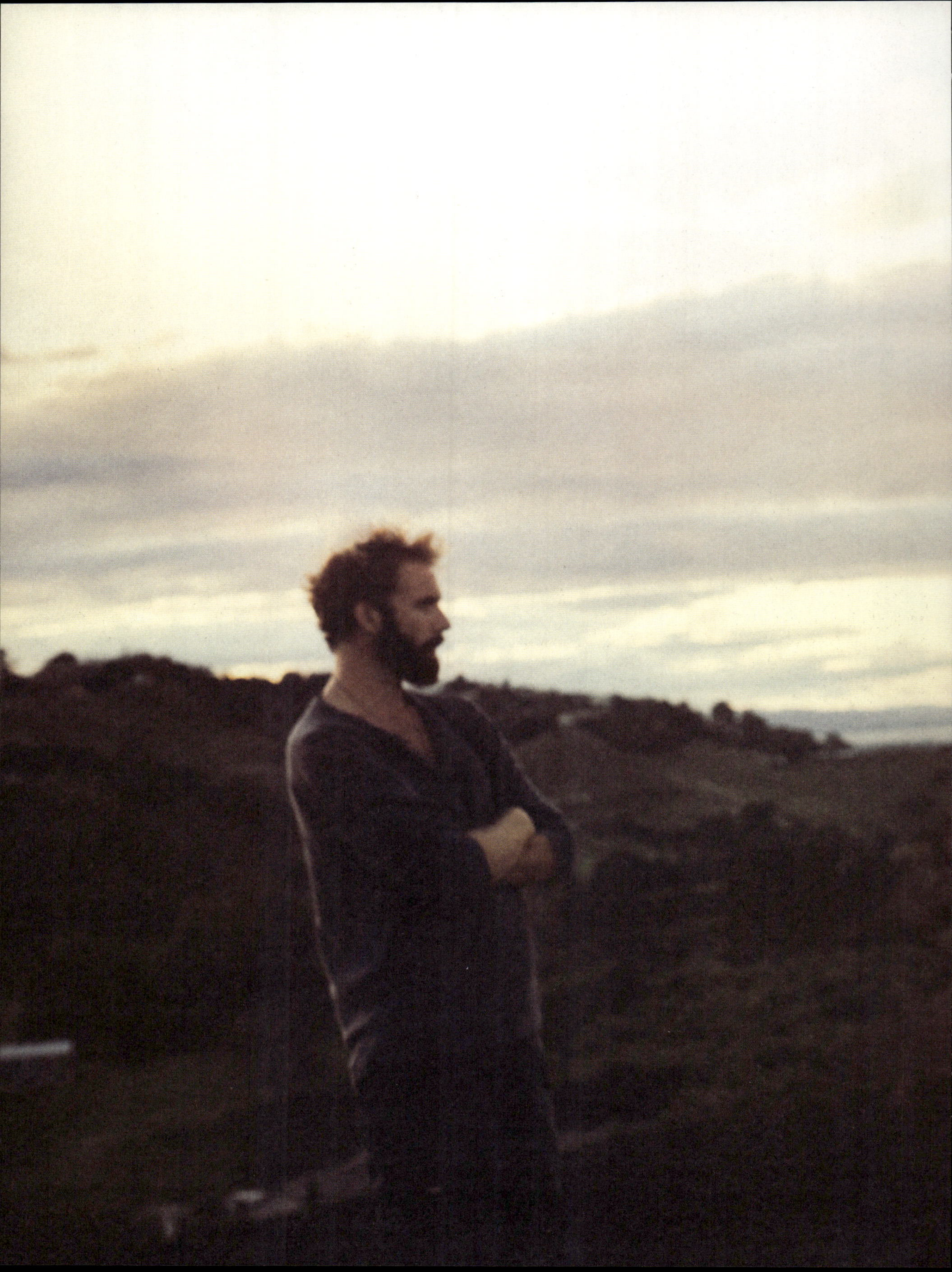

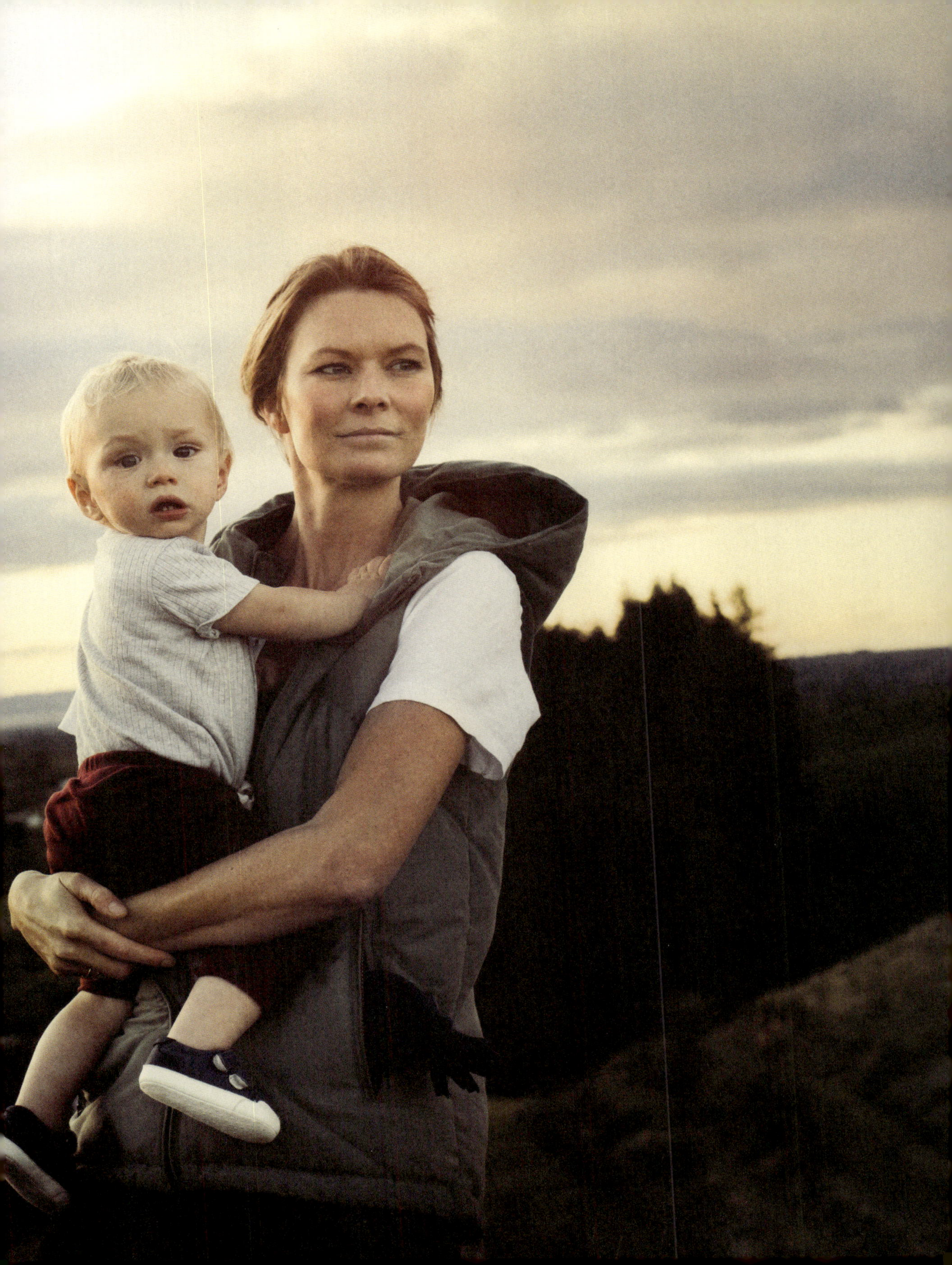

FRENCH ONION SOUP

SOUP

8 large onions (about 1.5–2kg)
¼ cup unflavoured coconut oil or grapeseed oil
½ tsp salt
1 tsp sugar
5 cloves garlic, finely chopped
1 tbsp fresh thyme leaves
½ cup white wine
¼ cup port or brandy (optional)
5 cups beef-style stock (see tips, or vegetable stock)
½ tsp finely ground black pepper
¼ tsp ground white pepper

TOASTIES

1 cup cashews, soaked in just-boiled water for 15 minutes
¼ cup water
2 tbsp nutritional yeast (optional)
½ tsp salt
8 small or 4 large slices good-quality bread
fresh thyme leaves, or chopped parsley
olive oil, for drizzling

TO MAKE IT GLUTEN-FREE

Use GF stock and bread.

TIPS

+ At the supermarket I buy a stock labelled 'beef-style', which is plant-based. It's good for a dark colour and a rich flavour — look for one containing 'real' ingredients. But any good-quality vege stock will do — preferably one in a carton.
+ If you don't have time to make the cashew cheese, you can grill dairy-free cheese slices on the toasties instead.

PREP 10 minutes   **COOK** 1 hour 15 minutes   **SERVES** 4

The French onion soup I tasted in France blew my mind with its exquisite, deep, heart-nourishing tastiness. I thought I had my work cut out for me creating a plant-based version because the tradish one usually credits a good meaty stock and a thick wedge of melted Gruyère cheese for being so rich and satisfying. However, the real flavour hero here is the mass of onions. It's nothing short of a miracle to see how a giant pile of them, all bitter and raw, reduces into a thick mass of caramelised, jammy goodness. It requires a little patience, but really it's very easy — and undeniably good.

Peel the onions, halve them top to bottom and slice them about 5mm thick (or you can use the slicer attachment on your food processor to save time). You will have a massive pile of onions!

Ideally you'd use a large, deep flameproof casserole dish for this, but a good, heavy-based soup pot would do. Place your pot over a medium-low heat, add the oil and onions, and cook, stirring every now and then, for about 15–20 minutes until the onions have softened.

Add the salt and sugar and continue to cook over a medium-low heat for another 30 minutes or so. You'll find that the onions start to turn a deep golden-brown colour. Don't be tempted to turn the heat up if it looks like nothing is happening. Stir regularly, or the onions will catch and burn — but not constantly.

Add the garlic and thyme and cook for another 15 minutes or so. You'll end up with a brown mush, 2 cups' worth at most.

Add the wine and port or brandy (if using) and let it bubble up to deglaze the pot of any caked-on goodness on the base and sides.

Add the stock and peppers and stir to combine. Simmer for another 10 minutes or so until the flavours have infused. Season to taste with salt and more pepper if it needs it.

To make the toasties, preheat the oven grill to medium. Drain the cashews and place in a high-speed blender or bullet blender along with the water, nutritional yeast and salt, and whizz until it's pretty smooth. You can use a food processor for this; it will just take a lot longer to get smooth. Season your cashew cheese with salt and pepper to taste.

Grill the bread slices on one side until lightly browned, then turn over and spread with some cashew cheese and top with a few fresh thyme leaves or chopped parsley. Drizzle with olive oil, season generously with salt and pepper and grill for a few minutes until bubbling — keep an eye on it so that the bread doesn't burn.

Ladle the soup into warmed bowls. Serve the toasties either on top of the soup (where it will soften), or next to it if you prefer crusty bread.

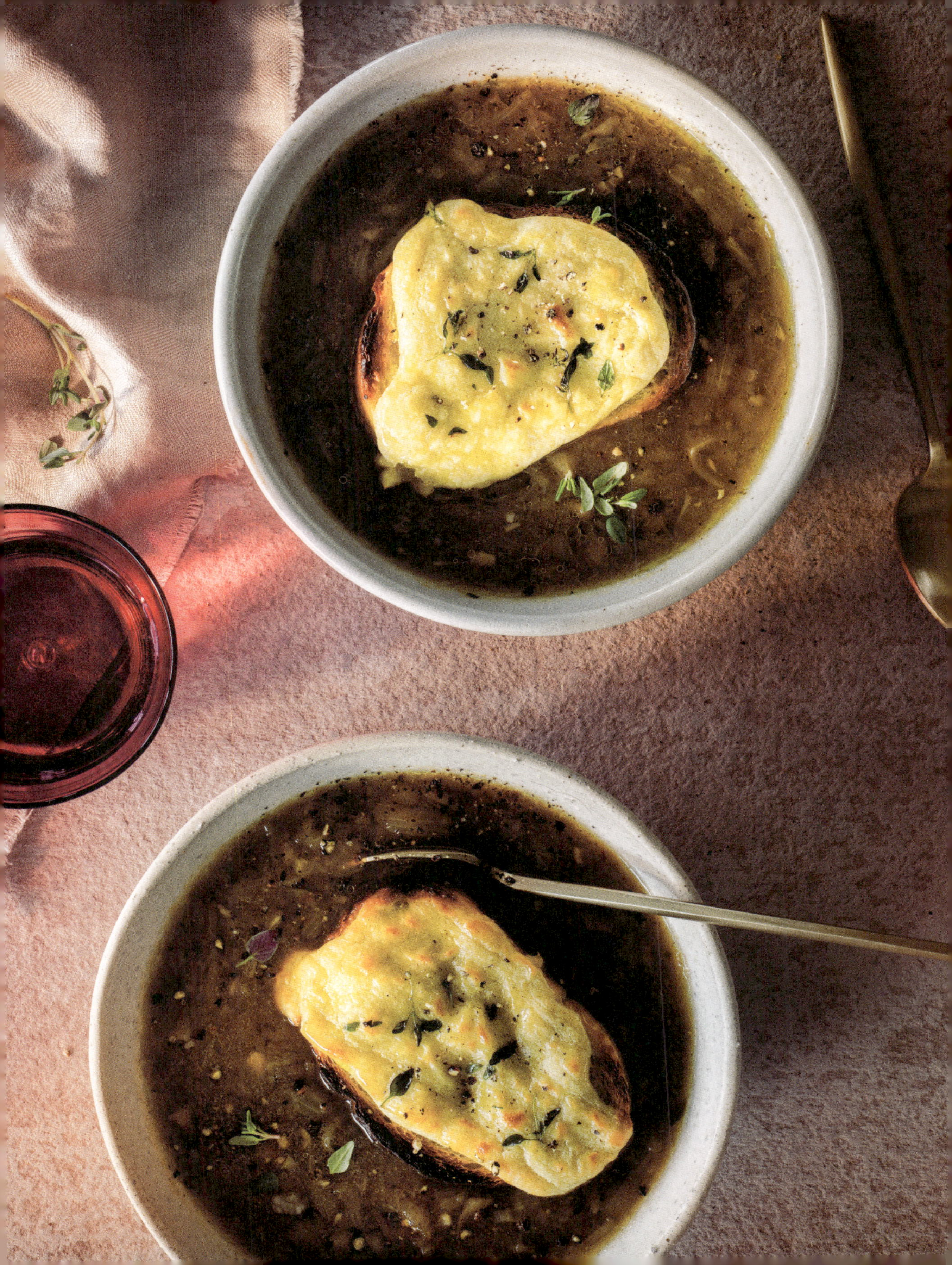

COCONUT & LEMONGRASS BROTH

- 1 x 300g block tofu, cut into 2–3cm chunks
- 2 stalks fresh lemongrass (or 2 tbsp lemongrass paste)
- grapeseed oil, for frying (or use coconut oil)
- 2 large cloves garlic, finely chopped or grated
- 1 tbsp finely grated ginger
- 1–2 red chillies, seeds scraped out, finely chopped
- 2 tsp ground turmeric
- 1 x 400ml can coconut milk
- 500ml vegetable stock
- 1 cup chopped button mushrooms (or use a drained 225g can of bamboo shoots)
- 250g cherry tomatoes, halved
- 100g sugar snap peas or snow peas
- ¾ cup whole raw cashews
- 250g dried thin egg-free noodles
- 1 tbsp tamari (or use soy sauce)
- 1 cup roughly chopped fresh coriander (Thai basil or Vietnamese mint would be nice too)
- 1 cup mung bean sprouts (optional)
- 1 large lime (or 1 medium lemon)

TO MAKE IT GLUTEN-FREE
Ensure your noodles, soy sauce and stock are GF.

PREP 15 minutes **COOK** 20 minutes **SERVES** 3–4 as a light meal

This is a fresh, bright, flavoursome meal that will fill your heart with sunshiney goodness. The mushrooms are optional because I know a lot of people don't like them — you could sub them with bamboo shoots if you preferred. It's a quick and simple dish to prepare without having to make a curry paste, and sure to be a crowd-pleaser.

Arrange the tofu chunks on a few layers of paper towels with an extra paper towel on top.

If you're using fresh lemongrass, strip the tough outer layer off the stems and set aside. Mince the tender inner part.

Add 2 tbsp of the oil to a large saucepan over a medium-low heat. Add the minced lemongrass (or the paste), garlic, ginger and chilli. Cook, stirring, for about 5 minutes until fragrant.

Stir in the turmeric then add the coconut milk, stock, mushrooms (or bamboo shoots) and the lemongrass leaves (if you have them). Bring to a gentle simmer, stirring frequently, for a couple of minutes.

Add the tomatoes, sugar snap or snow peas and cashews and turn off the heat.

Cook the noodles according to packet directions, drain and set aside. Have some nice big soup bowls at the ready.

Heat a little oil in a frying pan over a high heat. Season the tofu all over with salt and pepper and fry until golden all over. Drain on paper towels.

Heat the broth just so it's hot, add the tamari, taste and season with more salt and pepper if you like.

Divide the noodles between bowls and add a little fresh coriander. Ladle the broth over top. Top with the fried tofu chunks, mung bean sprouts (if using) and remaining coriander. Finely zest a little lime or lemon zest over each bowl and give each a squeeze of juice.

TIPS

+ To ramp up the greens, you could stir through some chopped spinach to wilt.
+ Feel free to add more coconut milk or stock if you need more sauce when it comes to dishing up.
+ You can add a little maple syrup or brown sugar if you like the broth a little sweeter.

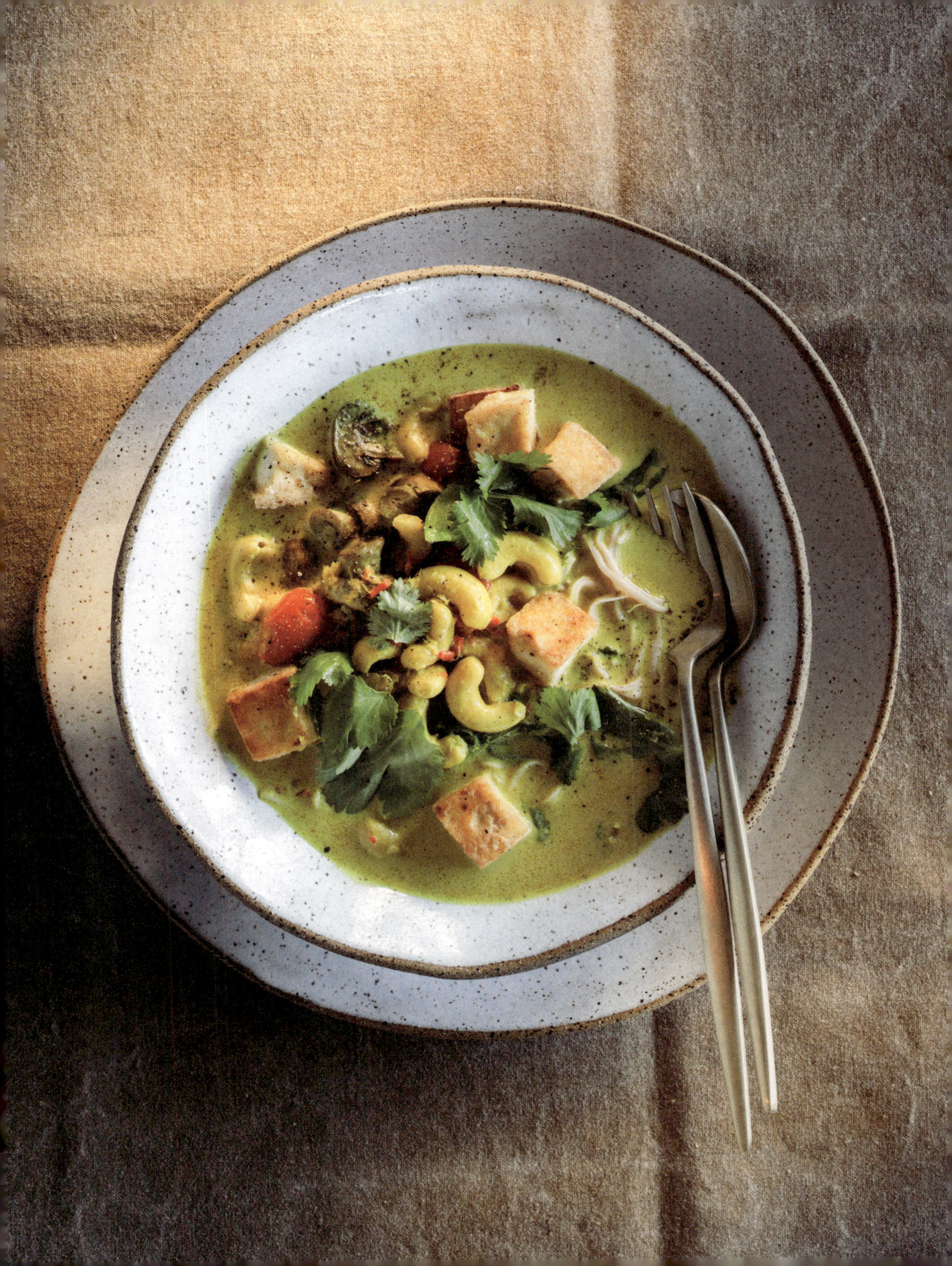

ÜBER-TASTY JAPANESE NOODLES & CRUNCHY TOFU

PREP 15 minutes   **COOK** 30 minutes   **SERVES** 4

This dish looks like something you might get from a restaurant, but it's easy and quick to make and is rammed with amazing flavour. Fresh shiitake mushrooms are wonderful — such great meaty texture and umami flavour. You can get them at the supermarket now, but if you can't find them, use Portobello instead. If you can't be bothered crumbing the tofu, just give the pieces a quick dust with well-seasoned flour and sear in a pan with a little oil, and it will still be delish.

Slice the tofu into roughly 3cm pieces. Lay them on a few stacked pieces of paper towel and place a few more paper towels on top, to draw some of the moisture out.

Put a soup pot or large saucepan over a medium heat. Add the grapeseed oil, sesame oil, ginger, garlic and mushrooms. Cook for 5 minutes or so until the mushrooms are starting to soften up nicely.

Add the stock, mirin, soy sauce, Chinese five-spice, star anise and pepper. Stir briefly, then cover and simmer gently for about 20 minutes until the flavours have infused.

While the broth is simmering, season the tofu pieces all over with salt and pepper. Whisk the mayo and milk together in a small bowl. Place the flour in a second bowl and the crumbs in a third bowl. Dip each piece of tofu first into the flour, then into the mayo mixture, then into the crumbs to coat (see tips). Set aside.

Heat ½ cm depth of oil in a frying pan over a medium-high heat. When hot, add the tofu pieces and fry until crispy and dark golden brown on all sides. Set aside on a wire rack or paper towels to drain while you serve up the soup.

When ready to serve, add the noodles straight into the simmering pot and cook for the time given on the packet (see tips). Add the greens with a few minutes to go.

To serve, ladle the soup into bowls, top with the tofu pieces and sprinkle with coriander, chives or spring onion.

TIPS

+ You can make the broth ahead of time, then reheat it before adding the noodles and greens. Or you can cook the noodles and greens separately, drain and pile into bowls and ladle the broth over the top.
+ Udon noodles would also be nice in this dish.
+ To make the tofu extra crunchy, you can do two dips in the mayo/milk mixture and crumbs.

TOFU

2 x 300g blocks firm tofu (organic is best)
¼ cup plant-based mayo (see page 182)
¼ cup plant-based milk
½ cup plain flour
1½ cups panko or breadcrumbs
grapeseed or sunflower oil, for frying

BROTH

2 tbsp grapeseed oil
1½ tsp sesame oil
2 tbsp finely grated ginger
4 cloves garlic, chopped
300g fresh shiitake or Portobello mushrooms, cut into large chunks
6 cups vegetable stock
¼ cup mirin (or 2 tbsp rice wine vinegar and 1 tsp sugar)
2 tbsp soy sauce
1 tsp Chinese five-spice
2 whole star anise (optional)
½ tsp finely ground black pepper
280–300g dry soba noodles
1–2 bunches Asian greens (like pak choy, or use spinach), large leaves roughly chopped
chopped fresh coriander, chives or spring onion, to serve

TO MAKE IT GLUTEN-FREE

Use GF noodles, breadcrumbs, flour, stock and soy sauce.

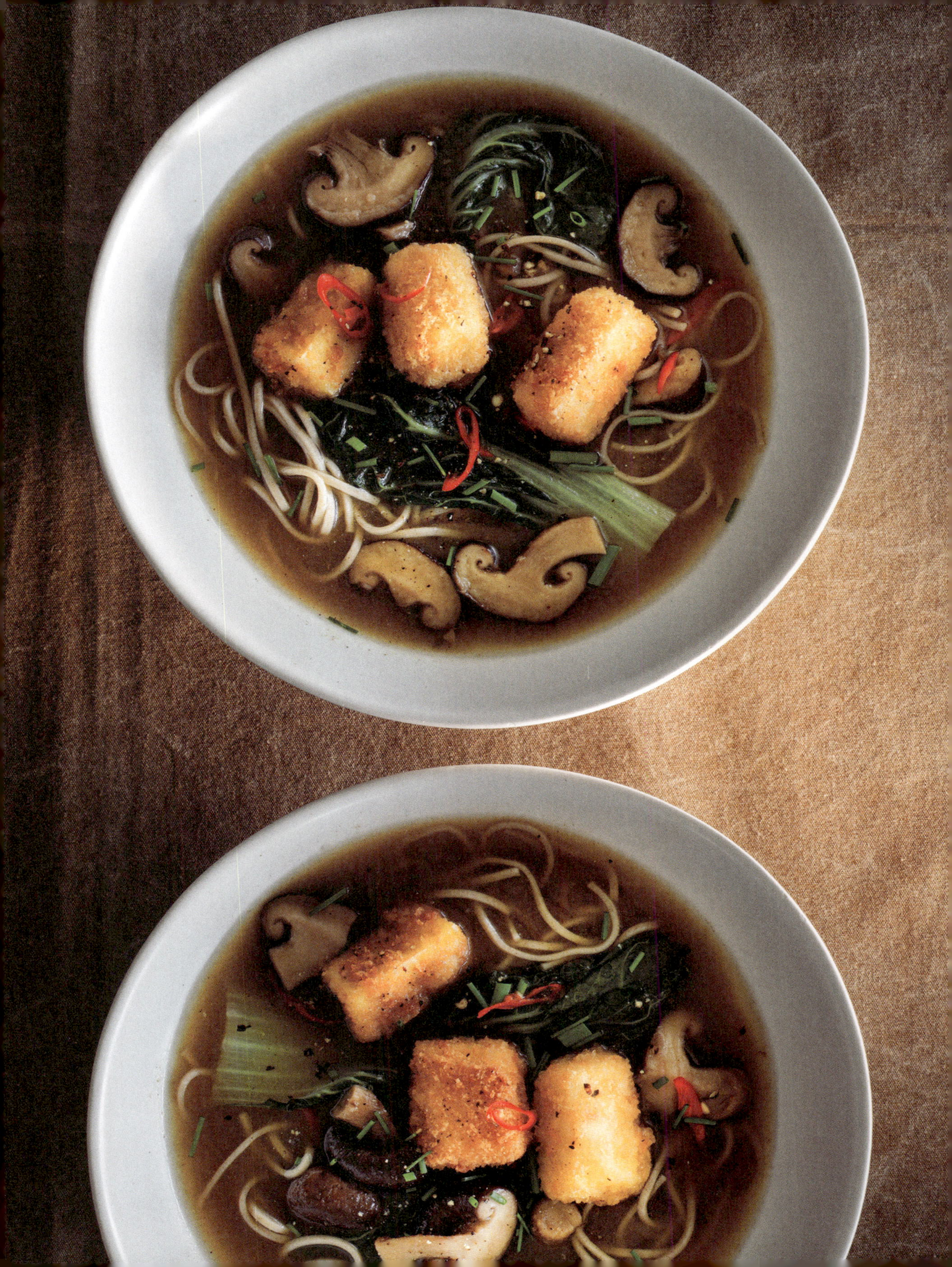

CREAMY MUSHROOM SOUP

PREP 15 minutes, plus 30 minutes soaking time   **COOK** 30 minutes
SERVES 4 as a light meal

SOUP

1 cup raw cashews

3 tbsp unflavoured coconut oil or grapeseed oil

4 shallots, peeled and quartered (or use 1 medium-sized onion)

4 large cloves garlic

1 tbsp fresh thyme leaves

750g Portobello mushrooms, roughly chopped

1½–2 cups vegetable or chicken-style stock

1½ tbsp nutritional yeast

1½ tbsp lemon juice

1 tsp salt

½ tsp finely ground black pepper

3 cups rice or soy milk

TASTY MUSHROOM MORSELS

1 tbsp grapeseed oil

100g fresh shiitake mushrooms (or use brown buttons), sliced

3 tsp tamari or soy sauce

½ tsp smoked paprika

2 tsp maple syrup

TO MAKE IT GLUTEN-FREE

Use a GF stock.

TIP

+ Fry some finely torn or chopped bread in olive oil until crunchy and scatter on as croutons, if you like.

Mushroom soup is one of those unglamorous affairs that tastes a million times better than it looks. And I'm okay with that. The humble mushroom has a special place in my heart. Although I never liked them as a kid, all of a sudden in my late teens I realised what I'd been missing out on when they started appearing in creamy pastas and sauces. Now we're never without mushrooms in the fridge and they go in everything — Portobellos and shiitakes act as our modern-day meat. A soup is a lovely way to enjoy the unique savoury flavour of mushrooms, and this one is not only rich and satisfying but also super creamy. Best served with some crunchy toast or garlic bread.

Place the cashews in a heatproof bowl and cover with just-boiled water. Leave to sit for at least 30 minutes, or as long as you have.

To make the mushroom morsels, heat the oil in a small frying pan over a medium heat. Add the mushrooms and cook, stirring, for about 5 minutes until softened. Add the tamari or soy sauce, smoked paprika and maple syrup and cook for a few more minutes to caramelise. Season with pepper and set aside.

To make the soup, heat the oil in a large saucepan over a medium-low heat. Add the shallots and cook, stirring, for about 15 minutes until golden but not browned.

Add the garlic and thyme and cook for another few minutes to soften the garlic. Add the mushrooms and cook for another 10 minutes or so, stirring occasionally, until the mushrooms have started to break down and soften.

Place the drained cashews in a high-speed or bullet blender together with the stock, nutritional yeast, lemon juice, salt and pepper. Whizz until silky smooth.

Add the cashew mixture to the mushrooms along with the milk and stir to combine. Cook, stirring, for a few minutes until heated through and the mushroom is cooked.

Remove from the heat and purée using a stick blender or a standard blender (you may have to put it in the blender in batches, and never blend hot liquids!).

Return the soup to the pan, taste it and season with extra salt, pepper or lemon until it's to your liking. You can also play with the consistency — if you think it's too thick, add a little more milk.

Serve the soup in bowls with some mushroom morsels. I also like to add a dollop of aïoli (see page 182) and a scattering of fresh herbs.

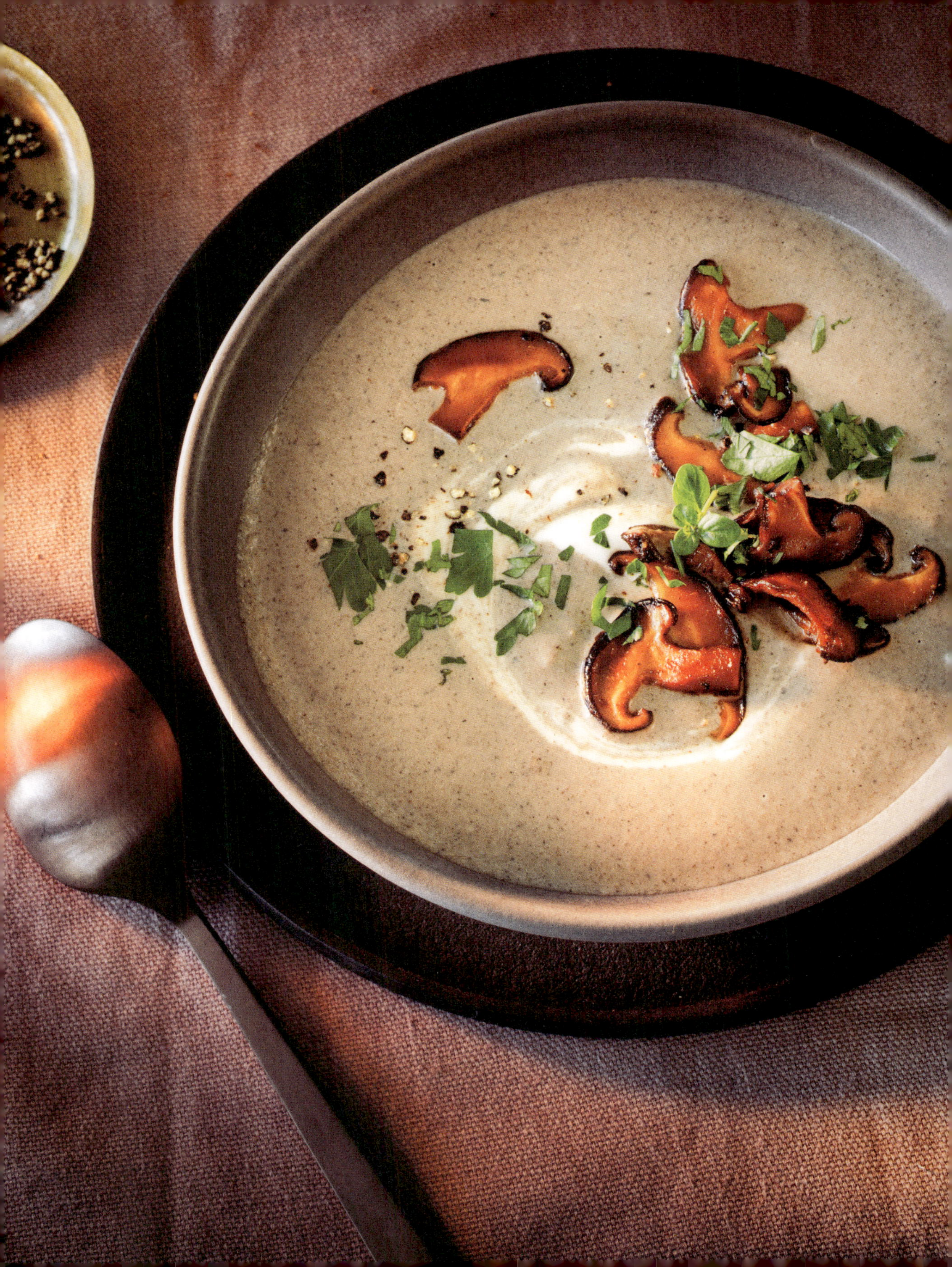

RAMEN

GOLDEN GARLIC OIL

½ cup neutral oil

10 cloves garlic, finely chopped (not crushed)

CHILLI OIL

½ cup neutral oil

1½ tbsp chilli flakes

BROTH

6 cups beef-style or chicken-style stock (see tips; or use vegetable stock)

200g finely sliced Portobello mushrooms

2 ripe tomatoes, sliced (optional, but good for flavour)

5 thin slices fresh ginger

2 tbsp soy sauce

1 tbsp miso paste (optional)

2 tsp brown sugar

1 tsp Vegemite or Marmite

½ tsp kelp powder (optional; see page 231 for more info)

½ tsp finely ground black pepper

TO SERVE

180g dried ramen or thin wheat noodles

¼ cup chopped chives or spring onions

TO MAKE IT GLUTEN-FREE

Omit the Vegemite/Marmite and use GF noodles, stock, soy and miso paste.

PREP 20 minutes   **COOK** 10 minutes   **SERVES** 4 as a light meal

I used to love buying those cheap, imported spicy ramen noodles in a cup, where you poured boiling water over them and then slurped up a storm. They were sooo good with sooo much flavour (and salt and MSG, probably!). I wanted to create a homemade version that was easy yet still a flavour-bomb, like getting a big hug from the inside. This broth is bursting with umami flavours and as tasty as anything. Ramen is pure comfort food that you can whip up any old time and not feel bad about (it's especially good after a big night or on a cold winter's day). The flavoured oils are what makes it really delectable; they're totally addictive and you'll want to spoon them over everything.

To make the garlic oil, heat the garlic and oil in a small saucepan over a medium-low heat, stirring every now and then, until the garlic turns fragrant and golden. It may take about 10 minutes. Keep a close eye on it — if it turns dark brown, it will be bitter, and you will have to discard it and start again. When the garlic is golden, immediately pour into a small bowl and set aside.

To make the chilli oil, place the chilli flakes in another small bowl. Pour the oil into the same pan you cooked the garlic in and heat over a medium heat for a few minutes. When nice and hot (a drop of water should spatter when dropped in), pour the oil over the chilli flakes. Set aside.

Place all the broth ingredients in a medium-sized saucepan and set over a medium-high heat. Bring to the boil, then simmer for about 10 minutes until the mushrooms have shrunk right down in size. Drain through a fine-meshed sieve into a bowl. Discard the solids (see tips) and return the liquid to the saucepan along with 2 teaspoons of the garlic oil and 1 teaspoon of the chilli oil. Set aside until ready to serve. (You probably won't need extra salt, so don't add any without tasting first.)

Cook the noodles according to the packet directions, then drain.

To serve, divide the noodles among serving bowls. Ladle over the broth. Spoon in chilli oil to taste, then the golden garlic oil with the little pieces of fried garlic — they're the best! Scatter with spring onion or chives and dig in.

TIPS

+ Beef-style and chicken-style stocks are available at most supermarkets, and there's no meat in them.
+ You can add the cooked mushrooms back to the soup instead of discarding, if you like, but it's also fine to leave them out.
+ To make this more of a meal, you could add some Asian greens or spinach to the strained broth, and fry a grated block of tofu until crispy and sprinkle it over the top.
+ You can keep leftover garlic oil and chilli oil in a well-sealed container or jar in a dark, cool place for a few weeks.

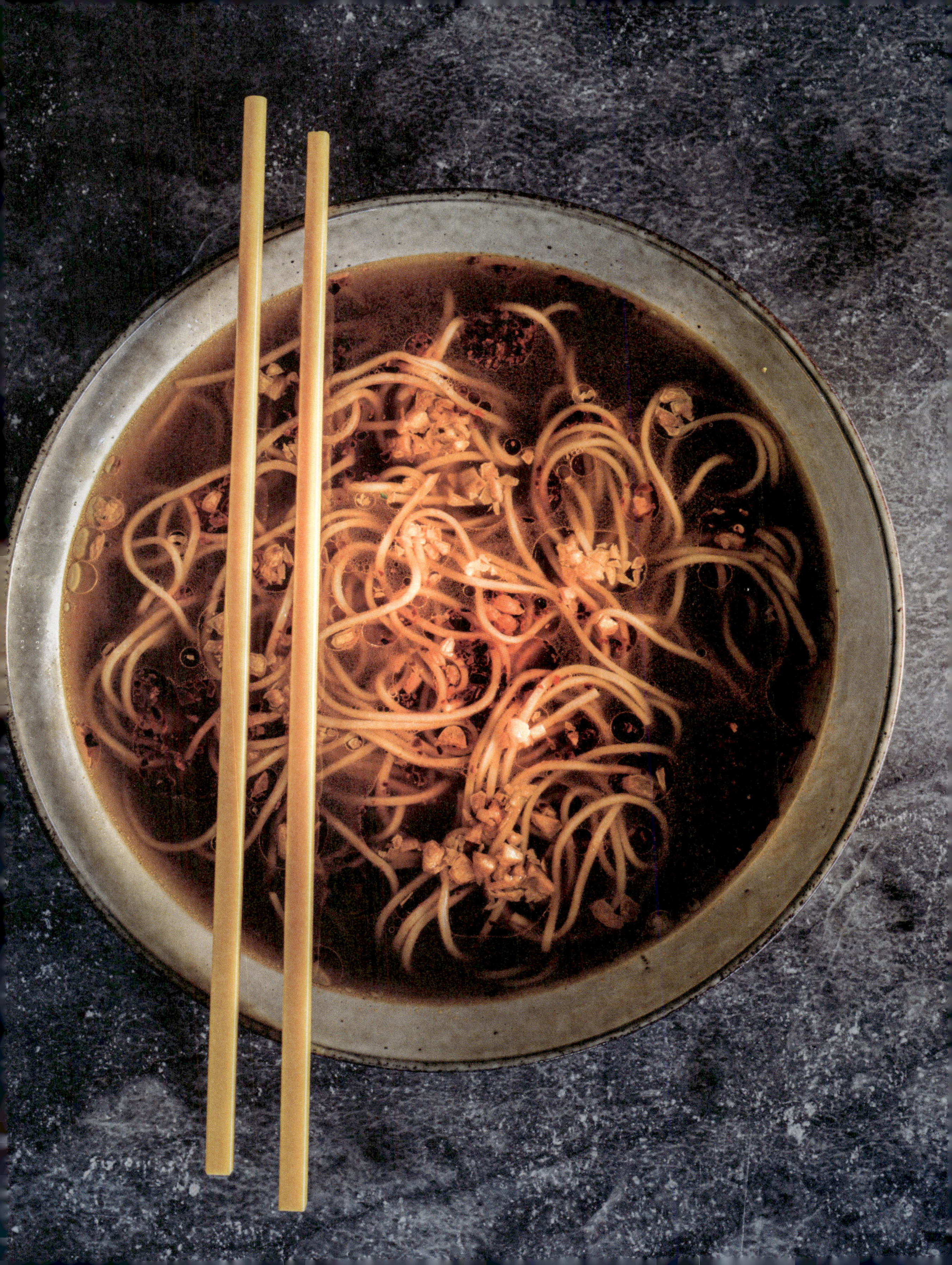

SUMMER VEGETABLE MEDLEY

- 2 fresh sweetcorn cobs, peeled
- 1 x 400g can whole tomatoes, drained
- 3 tbsp extra virgin olive oil
- 1 large onion, finely chopped
- 1 large clove garlic, crushed
- 200g fresh spinach, leaves only, roughly chopped
- 1 x 400g can cannellini beans, drained and rinsed
- 1½ cups vegetable stock, plus more if needed
- 2 medium courgettes, very thinly sliced
- finely chopped fresh parsley, to serve

PREP 15 minutes **COOK** 20 minutes **SERVES** 3–4 as a light meal

What the fig is a 'medley', you might ask . . . well, I didn't know what else to call this dish. It's not a soup, and 'stew' is a rather clumsy word. No matter what you call it, though, this is one of my favourite summer (or autumn) dishes. It just looks like a few chopped veges but has such beautiful flavours and delicate textures, and the veges sing with simplicity and deliciousness. With the cannellini beans, it's also filling. The key is to not overcook the veges — just until each one is bright and tender.

Using a sharp knife, run the knife down each sweetcorn cob to slice off the kernels. Set aside.

Drain and quarter the tomatoes, removing any white end-bits.

Heat the olive oil in a large saucepan or medium-sized soup pot over a medium-low heat. Add the onion and garlic and cook, stirring, for about 7 minutes until soft and fragrant.

Add the tomatoes, spinach and cannellini beans. Cover with the stock, increase the heat to medium and simmer for a few minutes, stirring once or twice, until the vegetables are just tender.

Add the sliced courgette, cover and simmer for another 30 seconds or so until the courgette is only just tender. Remove from the heat and season to taste with salt and pepper. Scatter with parsley and serve immediately with some nice crusty bread (garlic pitas are nice).

TIPS

+ If you have access to really nice, ripe red tomatoes that are full of flavour (especially homegrown ones), use 4 of these instead of the can. (I'd remove the skins first — cover briefly in just-boiled water, allow to cool slightly, then peel.)
+ You can use chard or silverbeet in place of spinach if you like.

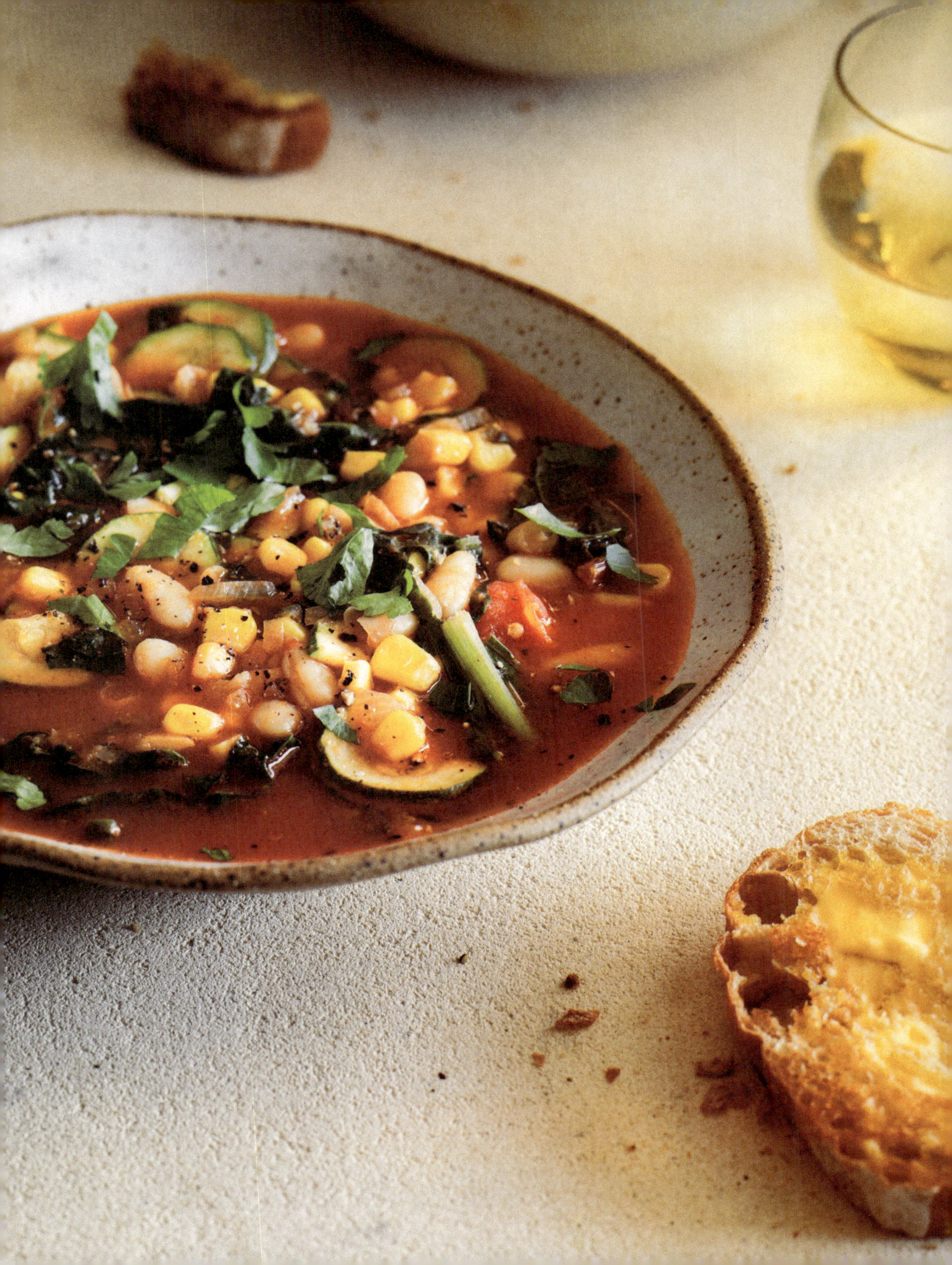

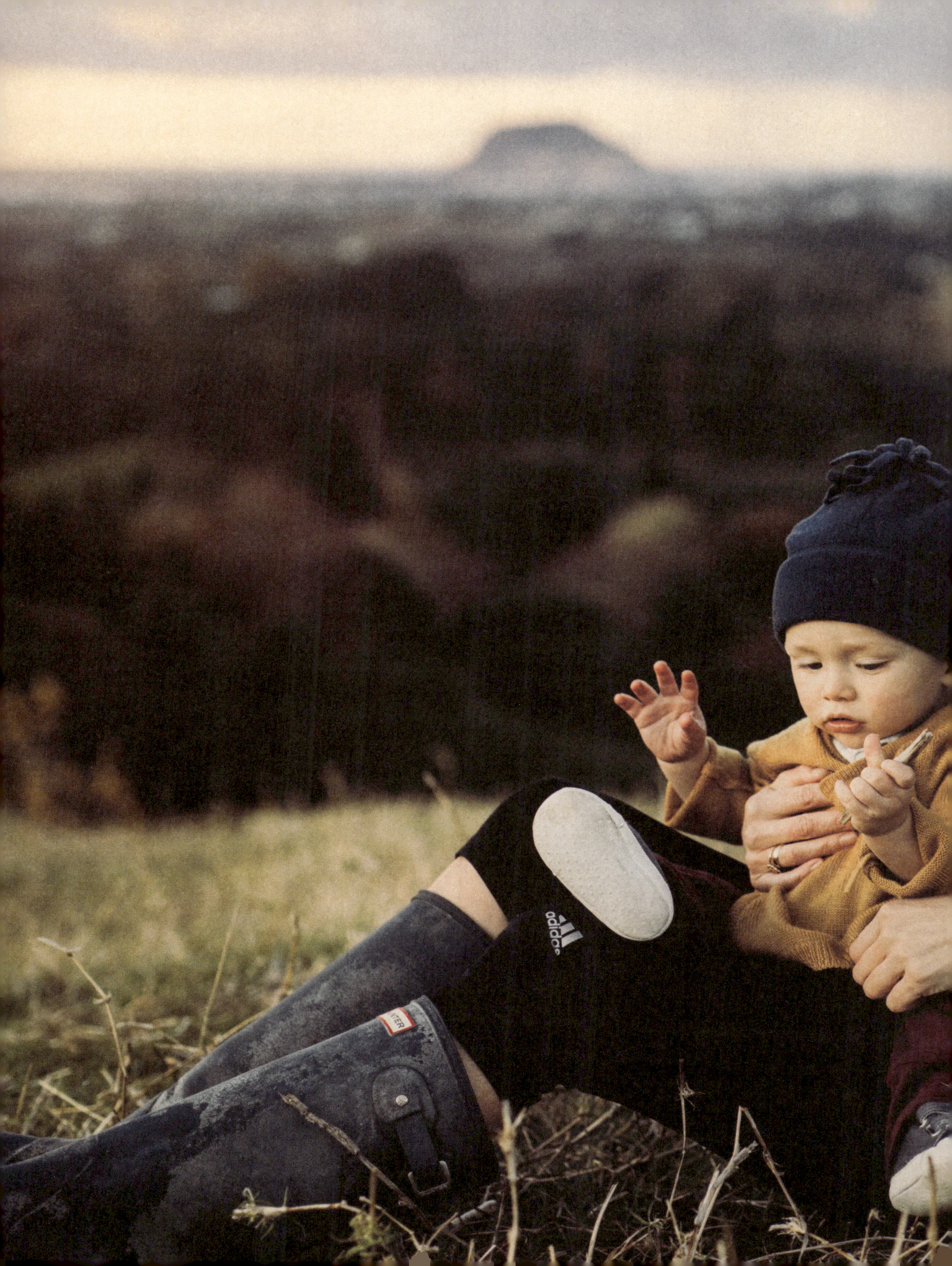
adidas

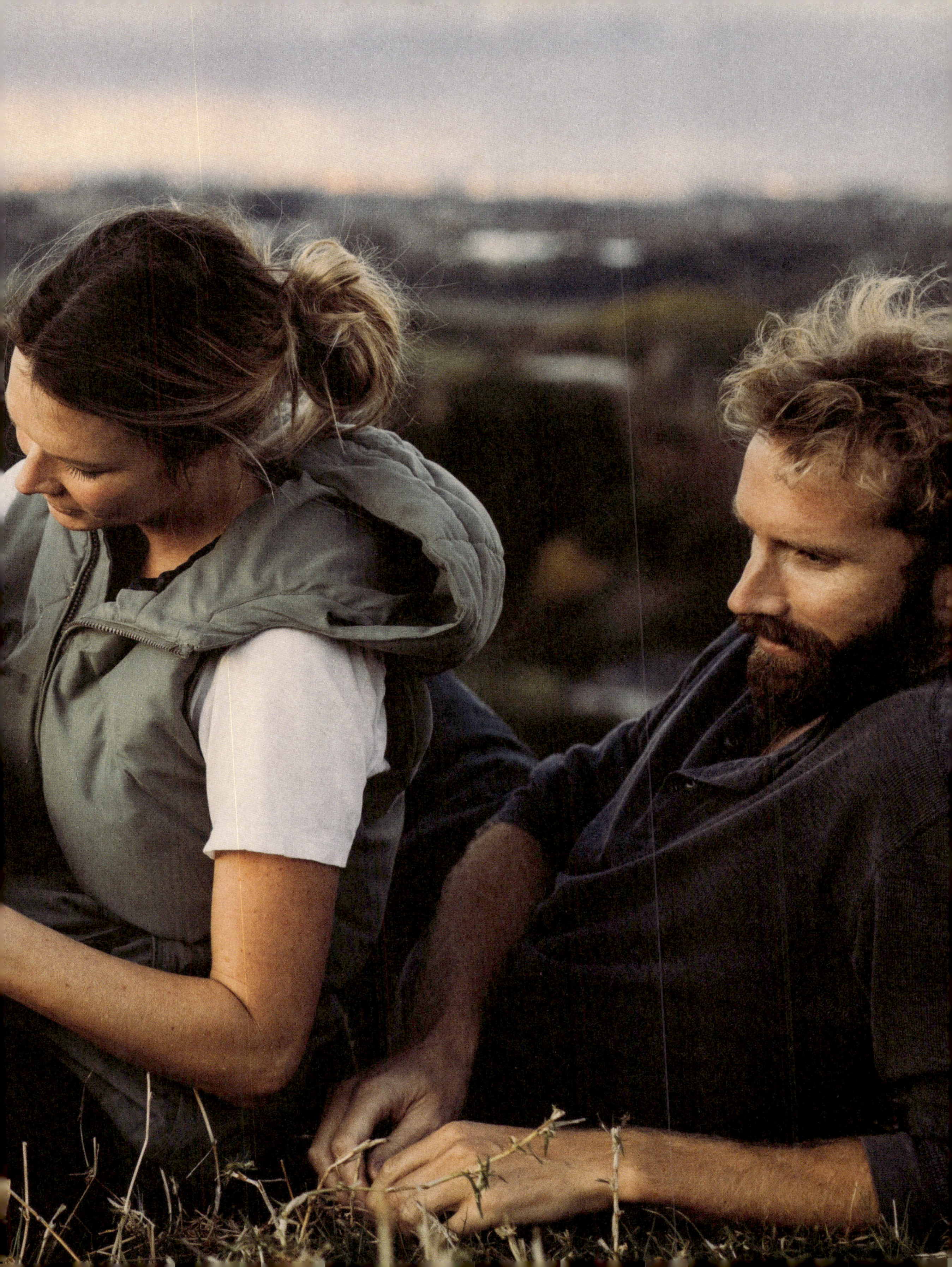

HEFTY GREEN SALAD

DRESSING

juice of 1 orange
3 tbsp extra virgin olive oil
1½ tbsp honey (or use maple syrup or brown sugar, to taste)
1 tbsp lemon juice
2 tsp tahini
small clove garlic, crushed
¾ tsp salt
½ tsp finely ground black pepper

SALAD

1½ cups frozen shelled edamame beans (see tip)
1 cup pumpkin seeds
1 tbsp tamari
2 large avocados, sliced
2 stalks celery, finely sliced
1 telegraph cucumber, finely sliced
2 large pears, finely sliced
2 spring onions, finely sliced (or use ¼ red onion)
1 cup alfalfa or mung bean sprouts
lettuce leaves
mesclun, baby spinach and/or rocket, if you like

—

IT'S GLUTEN-FREE

PREP 25 minutes **SERVES** 3–4 as a light meal, 5–6 as a side

This salad can easily be served as a meal by itself, especially when the weather is warmer, or as a side if you want a really robust meal or something to take to a BBQ or pot-luck. It is bursting with the goodness and fillingness of avocados, bean sprouts, edamame beans and pumpkin seeds. And the dressing is SO damn good. Tahini is like a butter made from ground-up sesame seeds, and it packs awesome flavour and creaminess into the dressing.

—

To make the dressing, whizz everything in a little blender or whisk in a small bowl until creamy. Set aside.

Bring a saucepan of water to the boil, add the frozen edamame beans and boil gently for about 5 minutes. Drain and rinse under cold water. Set aside.

Toast the pumpkin seeds in a dry frying pan over a medium-high heat for a couple of minutes, shaking the pan to cook them evenly until smelling toasty and just starting to turn golden. Turn off the heat, add the tamari and shake it around until the tamari has evaporated.

Place all the remaining salad ingredients in a bowl along with the pumpkin seeds and edamame beans. When ready to serve, add the dressing and toss it through.

—

TIPS

+ Edamame beans can be found in the freezer section of most supermarkets. If you can't find them, you can leave them out or use snow peas, plus extra of the other ingredients.
+ Feel free to add as many sprouted things as you can find — we love sprouted mung beans, sunflower seeds and salad sprouts.

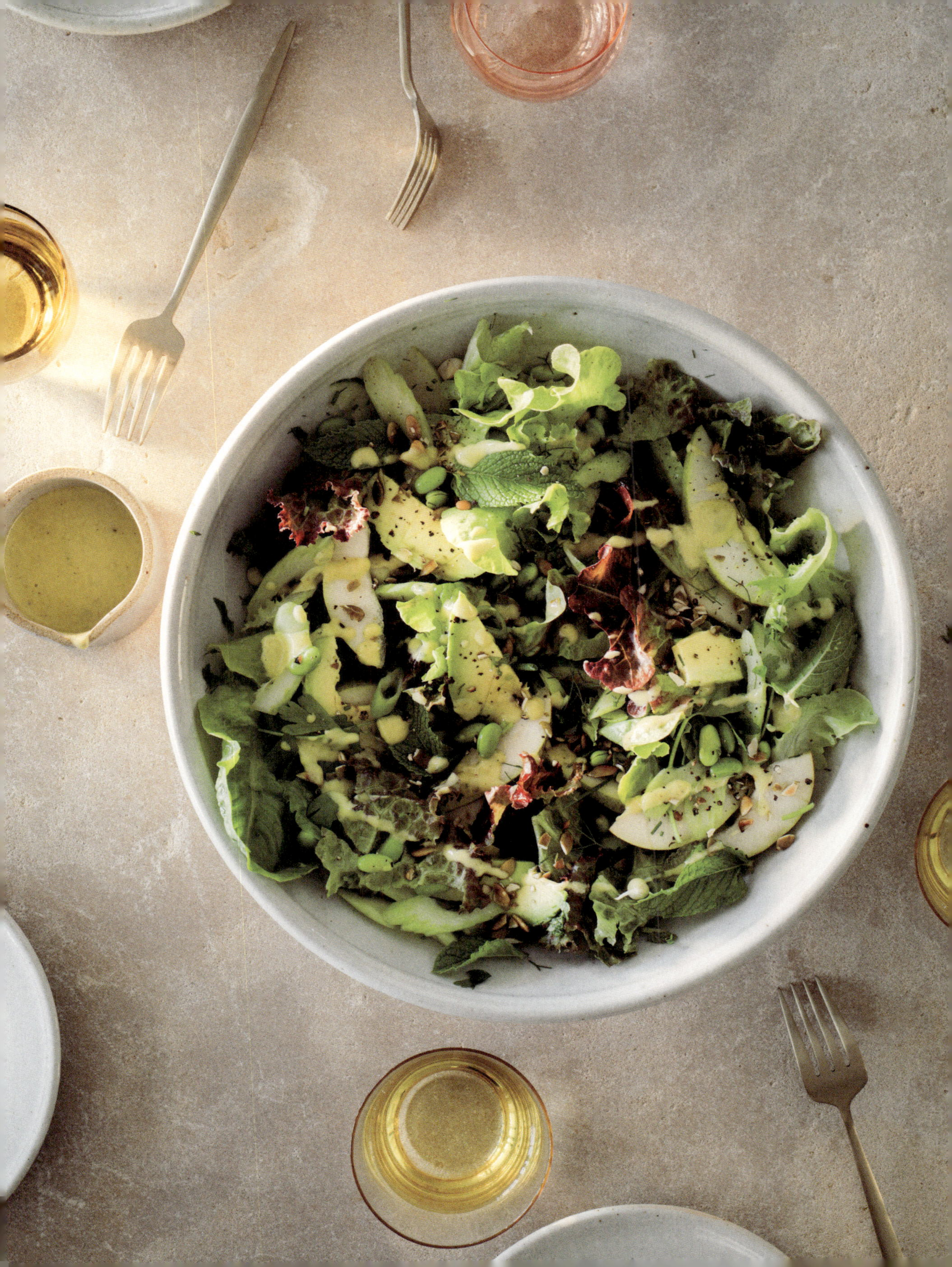

POTATO SALAD

1.5kg Agria potatoes
½ cup plant-based mayo or aïoli (see page 182)
¼ cup chopped fresh herbs (I used parsley and mint)
1 tsp dried dill (or 1 tbsp chopped fresh)
1 clove garlic, crushed
2 tsp lemon juice
2 tsp capers (optional)
1 tsp salt
½ tsp finely ground black pepper
2 large stalks celery, finely chopped
3 gherkins, chopped (optional)

PREP 15 minutes   **COOK** 25 minutes   **SERVES** 4–5 as a side

It's no secret that potatoes are one of my favourite foods in the whole world — we buy them in huge quantities. I usually cook some up to keep in the fridge ready to be eaten in whichever fashion takes our fancy — perhaps fried up with some salt and olive oil for breakfast, or turned into a salad like this one. Whoever told you eating potatoes is going to make you fat is wrong, so if you've been avoiding them out of fear it's time to welcome them back into your life. They're actually very good for you (helpful for the lymphatic system, apparently, with loads of vitamins and minerals). This salad is a corker — creamy, crunchy, zesty, heavenly. And it tastes even better the next day. Goes well with anything, at any time, warm or cold.

Peel the potatoes and cut into halves or quarters, depending on the size. You want them about 5–6cm, still nice and chunky.

Add to a large saucepan of cold salted water, bring just to the boil and simmer gently until tender — about 25 minutes. Drain and allow to cool until warm rather than hot.

Combine the mayo or aïoli, herbs, garlic, lemon juice, capers (if using), salt and pepper in a small bowl.

Transfer the potatoes to a large bowl and add the celery, gherkins (if using) and mayo mixture. Toss to combine (I use clean hands for this — but that's just me). Either serve straight away or keep covered in the fridge until the next day.

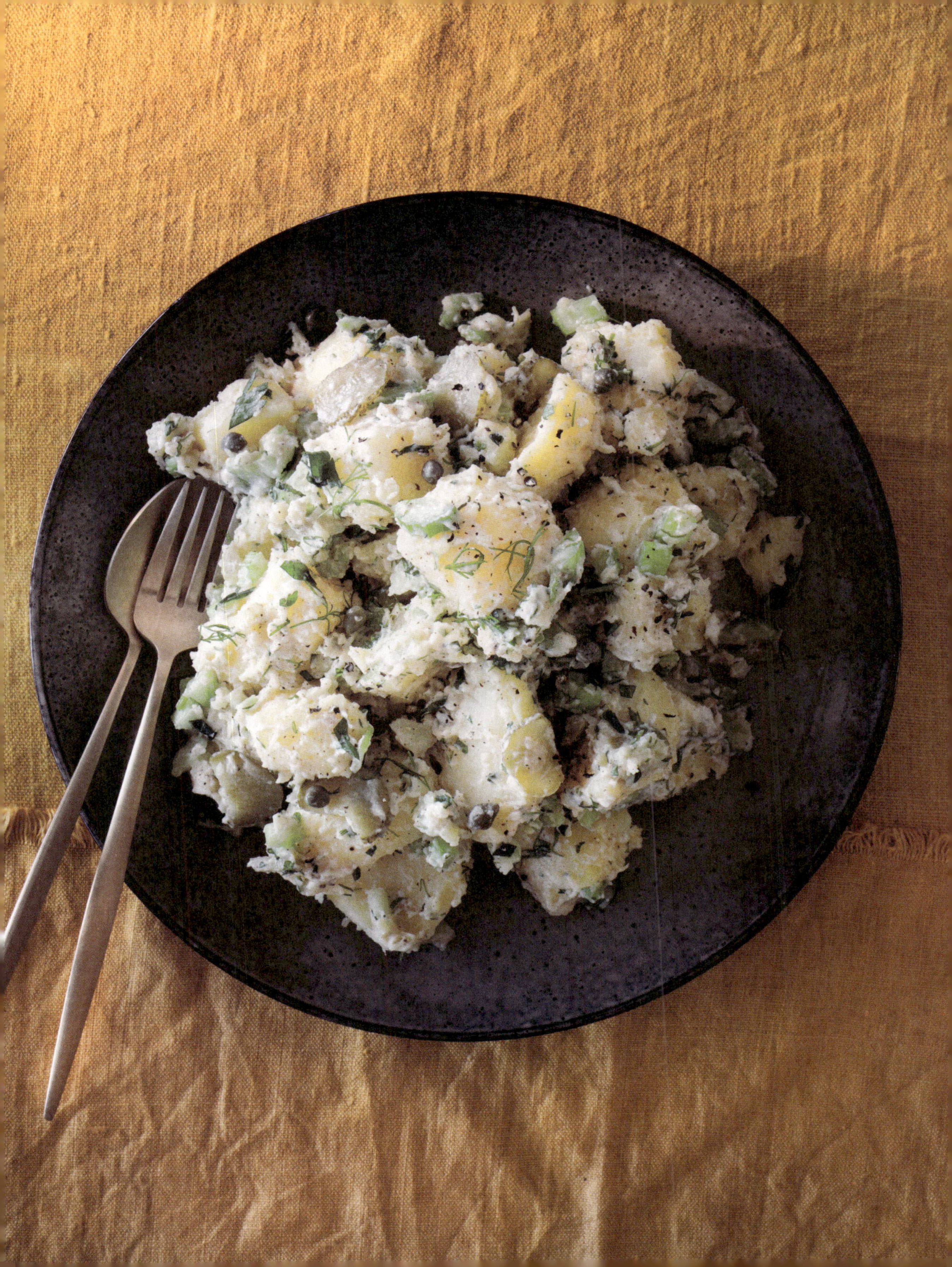

MOROCCAN ROASTED CARROT & QUINOA SALAD

1.5kg carrots, peeled

1 whole bulb garlic

2 tsp whole cumin seeds

pinch chilli flakes

⅓ cup extra virgin olive oil

¼ cup honey, warmed if necessary to thin (or use ⅓ cup maple syrup)

1½ cups quinoa

3 cups vegetable stock

2 tsp ground turmeric

2 segments preserved lemon (or zest of 1 lemon)

zest and juice of 1 orange

½ cup raisins, sultanas or chopped dried apricots

¾ cup sliced or chopped almonds (or pine nuts, or a mixture)

1 tsp very finely grated ginger

juice of ½ lemon

¾ cup chopped fresh coriander

IT'S GLUTEN-FREE

PREP 20 minutes **COOK** 1 hour 10 minutes
SERVES 4 as a light meal, 6 as a side

This was another dish that I created by accident when basically all I had left in the kitchen was the things in this ingredients list. While sometimes just using what you have can be a bit of a fail, at other times it can work an absolute treat — and let me tell you, this was a real winner. It's a whole meal on a tray: the carrots go lovely and sticky and caramelised, and the orange freshens it all up to make it sing.

Preheat the oven to 160°C regular bake.

Cut the carrots lengthways into thin sticks, at most 1.5cm thick at the fattest end. Place on a large baking tray (or two smaller ones) along with the garlic bulb, and scatter with the cumin seeds and chilli flakes. Season generously with salt and pepper. Drizzle the olive oil and honey over and toss to combine everything evenly. Arrange in an even layer and bake, uncovered, for 1 hour.

While the carrots are cooking, cook the quinoa according to the packet directions but use stock instead of water, and add the turmeric. Set aside once cooked, keeping it warm.

Prepare the preserved lemon by scraping out and discarding the flesh and membrane. Finely chop the rind and set aside.

After an hour is up, the carrots should look kind of shrunken and be starting to caramelise. Remove the garlic bulb and turn the heat up to 180°C. Add the orange zest and juice, chopped preserved lemon, raisins or other dried fruit, nuts and ginger to the carrot tray. Toss it all around a bit and bake for another 10 minutes until the nuts are just toasty. Leave to cool slightly.

Place the quinoa in a large serving bowl and add the carrot mixture as well as all the cooking juices from the tray. Squeeze in the roasted flesh from the garlic. Add the lemon juice and chopped coriander and mix gently to combine. Serve hot, or at room temperature if preferred.

TIPS

+ Steam 300–500g of green beans to add if you like — or throw in some wilted spinach.
+ If you love olives, you could chop up some green or Kalamata olives and mix them through too.
+ If you don't have liquid stock for the quinoa, you can make it up with powdered stock in water.

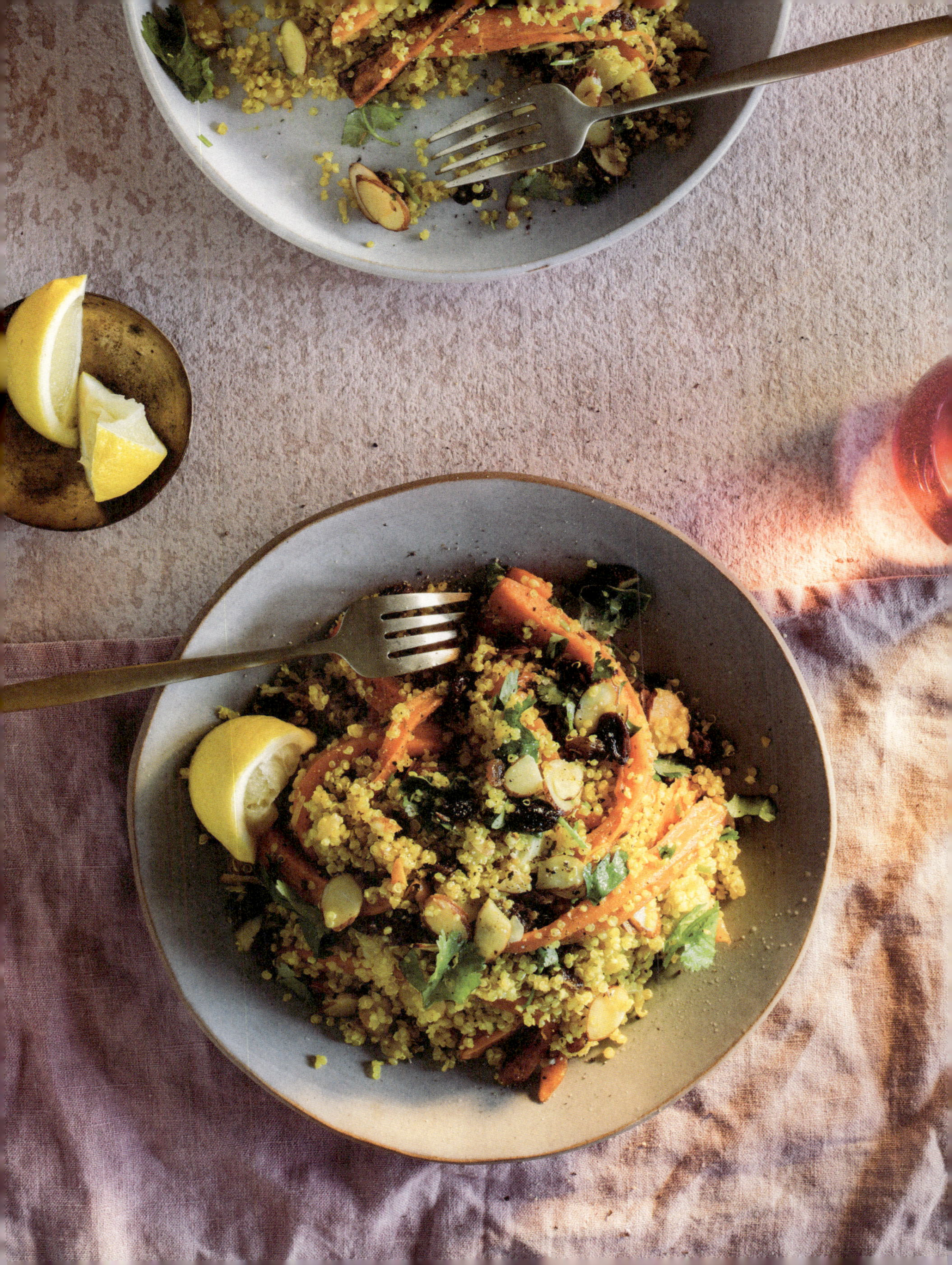

NOODLY PEANUT SLAW

PREP 20 minutes   **SERVES** 4 as a light meal, 6 as a side

Maybe I did something a bit outrageous when I first added noodles to a slaw — but hey, it happened, because I'm obsessed with noodles. I just can't get enough of them, I even eat them plain (have done ever since I was little). Anyway, here they add a pleasingly filling chomp to a fresh crunchy salad; it feels like you're getting more substance in every bite. You can serve this as a grunty side dish (great for a shared lunch or a BBQ bring-a-plate), or enjoy it as a light meal by itself in summer like we do (along with some minted new potatoes if you feel like it). The dressing is bangin'; the whole thing works together as a colourful, flavourful and textural delight.

___

DRESSING

- 2 tbsp good-quality peanut butter (smooth or crunchy)
- ¼ cup plant-based aïoli or mayo (see page 182)
- 1 small clove garlic, crushed
- 1 tbsp brown sugar
- 2 tsp sesame oil
- 2 tsp tamari or soy sauce
- 2 tsp apple cider vinegar
- zest and juice of 1 lime
- ½ tsp ginger juice (see tips)
- ½ tsp salt
- ¼ tsp finely ground black pepper

SALAD

- 100g vermicelli noodles (or any egg-free noodle)
- 1 cup frozen shelled edamame beans
- ½ cabbage (red, Savoy or green, or a combo)
- 2 medium-sized carrots, peeled and grated or julienned
- 1 cup mung bean sprouts
- 1 stalk celery, finely sliced
- ¾ cup roughly chopped roasted peanuts, plus extra for serving
- ¼ cup raisins or sultanas
- ⅓ cup chopped coriander leaves and stalks, plus extra for serving
- 2 tbsp toasted sesame seeds (optional)

Place the dressing ingredients in a small jug or mixing bowl and whisk to combine. Set aside.

Soak the noodles in just-boiled water according to the packet directions, drain and set aside.

Put the edamame beans in a small saucepan, cover with just-boiled water and simmer for about 5 minutes, until tender and bright. Drain and rinse under cold water. Set aside with the noodles.

Remove the inner core piece of the cabbage and slice the outer leaves very thinly. Place in a very large mixing bowl together with the edamame beans, noodles, carrot, bean sprouts, celery, peanuts, raisins or sultanas, and coriander.

Add the dressing and toss everything to combine (I just use clean hands — it's easier to control the overflow).

Serve the salad on a platter or in a bowl, topped with the extra peanuts and coriander, and sesame seeds if you like.

___

TIPS

+ Edamame beans are a young version of soy beans — they're a complete protein source, with all the amino acids you need as well as folate and vitamin K. You should be able to find them in the frozen section at your supermarket, but if not then use peas instead.
+ Any leftovers keep well in the fridge for a day or so — the flavours intensify and soak into the cabbage (yum).
+ Aside from the cabbage and carrot, you can be quite flexible with what you put in this salad — as long as it's fresh and crunchy (thinly sliced fennel and capsicum would work well).
+ To make ginger juice, finely grate fresh ginger and squeeze out the juice.

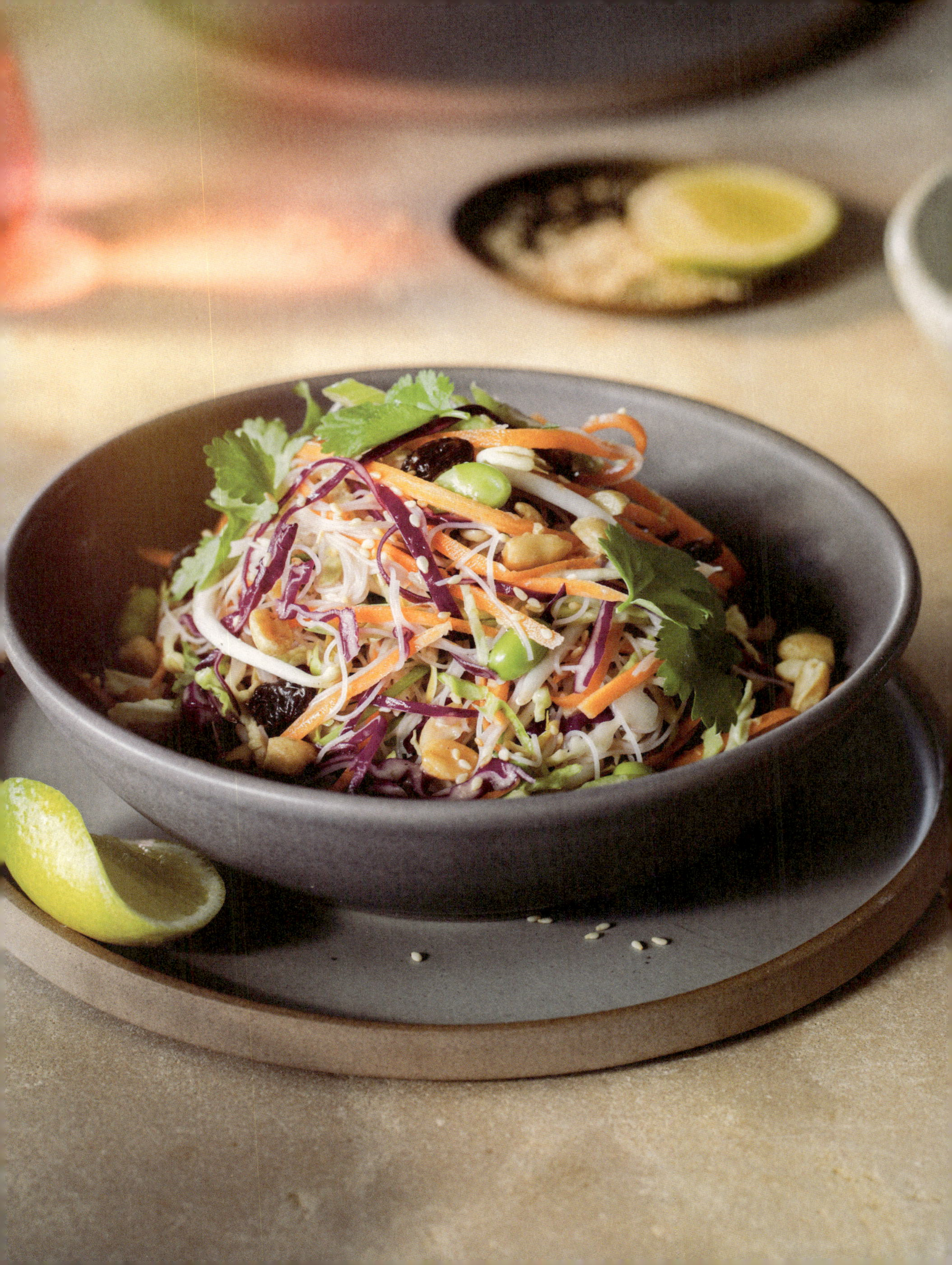

WARM BROCCOLI, KUMARA & AVOCADO SALAD

PREP 35 minutes   **SERVES** 4 as a meal, 6 as a side

700g purple-skinned kumara, peeled and cut into 3cm chunks
6 tbsp extra virgin olive oil
3 tbsp sunflower seeds
3 tbsp pumpkin seeds
¼ cup buckwheat groats (or use finely chopped roasted almonds)
400g broccoli, cut into small florets and stems peeled and thinly sliced
zest of 1 lemon
1 clove garlic, crushed
½ cup olives (stuffed green, Kalamata, Sicilian)
3 tbsp white wine vinegar
1 tsp toasted cumin seeds (optional)
1–2 large avocados, peeled, stoned and diced into 2cm pieces
small handful coriander sprigs

IT'S GLUTEN-FREE

This recipe was given to me by Ray McVinnie, a true culinary genius and one of my main cooking mentors on my post-*MasterChef* journey. There's really nothing he doesn't know about food. This salad is so much more than just the sum of its parts, and a good example of how the right combination of humble ingredients can result in a meal that delivers flavour, texture and looks awesome, too. Of course, for me anything with kumara in it is going to be a winner. Here, the toasty little seeds and buckwheat make each mouthful a crunchy moment of happiness. You should be able to find buckwheat at the supermarket — just ask.

Preheat the oven to 200°C regular bake and line a shallow oven tray with baking paper.

Place the kumara in the oven tray and add 2 tablespoons olive oil. Season generously with salt and pepper. Mix very well (I just use my hands), then spread out into a single layer and place in the oven for 30 minutes, or until the kumara is tender and browned.

Meanwhile, toast the seeds and buckwheat groats separately. Heat a dry pan over a moderate heat, add the sunflower seeds and toast, stirring frequently, until beginning to brown. Remove from the heat and cool in a bowl.

Do the same with the pumpkin seeds, toasting them until they pop and brown. Add to the sunflower seeds.

Lastly, put the buckwheat groats into the dry pan and toast until just darkening in colour. (If using almonds, omit this step.) Add to the seeds and set aside.

Bring a saucepan of salted water to the boil, then add the broccoli. Boil gently for 2 minutes, then drain well.

Transfer the still-warm kumara and broccoli into a salad bowl and add the seeds and buckwheat, along with the lemon zest, garlic, olives, remaining oil, vinegar and cumin seeds (if using). Mix well to combine.

Taste and season with more salt and pepper. Transfer everything to a serving platter or large bowl.

Serve scattered with avocado and coriander.

TIPS

+ The original recipe stated 1 avocado, but if (like me) you love avo and you want the salad bulked up a bit, use two.
+ I like serving this with a big dollop of aïoli (see page 182) on the side for extra creamy deliciousness.

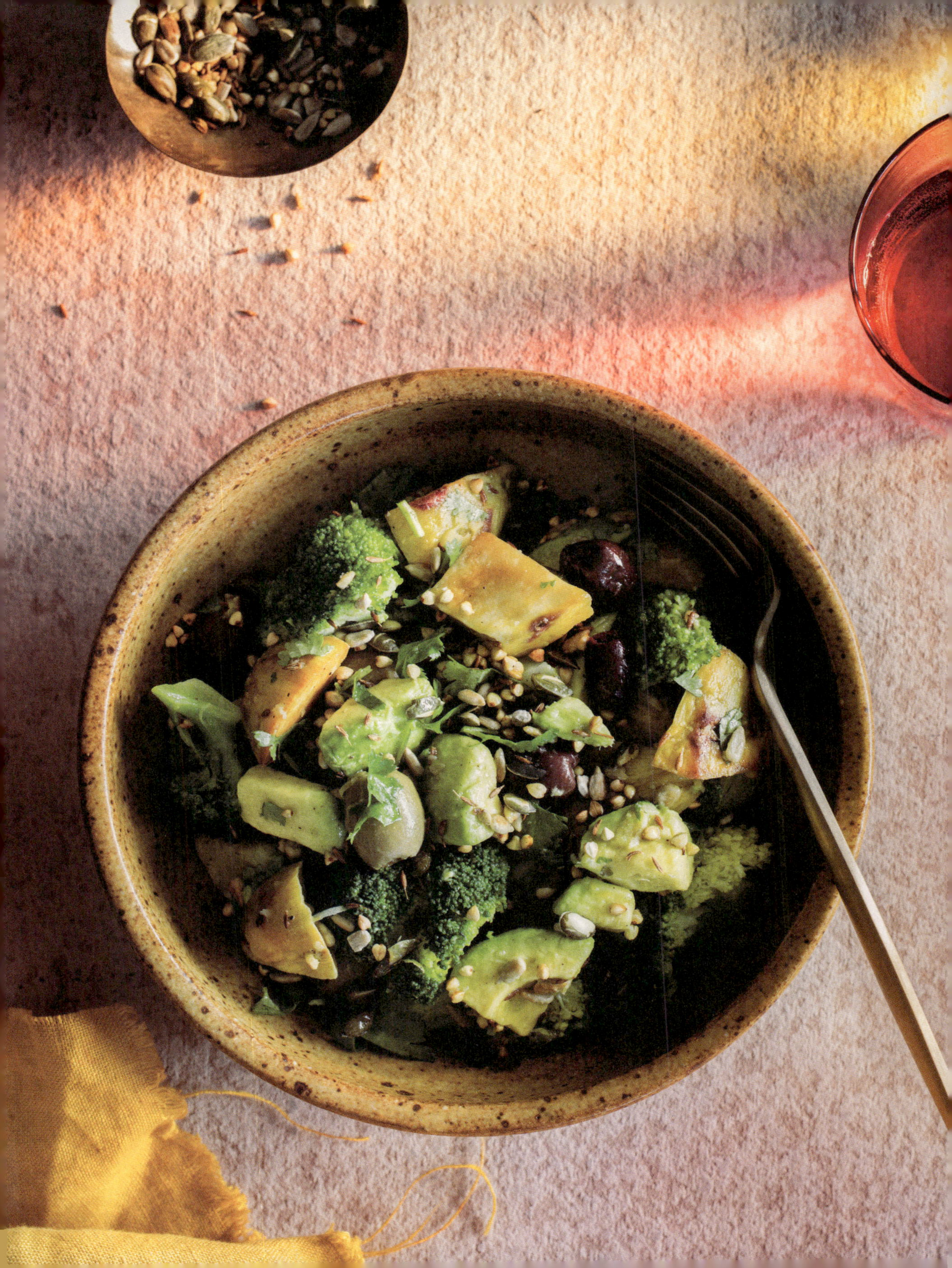

MAUMAU'S STRAWBERRY SALAD

DRESSING

1 tbsp balsamic vinegar
1 tbsp brown sugar
1 tbsp extra virgin olive oil
1 clove garlic, crushed
¼ tsp salt
¼ tsp fine black pepper

SALAD

1 medium-sized red onion
¼ tsp salt
¼ tsp sugar
1 tsp red or white wine vinegar, or lemon juice
1 telegraph cucumber
1 punnet juicy red strawberries
1 head lettuce (or use 2 baby cos lettuces)
1 cup alfalfa sprouts
2 large ripe avocados, thinly sliced
½ cup basil leaves, roughly torn
½ cup chopped walnuts

PREP 20 minutes   **SERVES** 2 as a main, 4–5 as a side

Me and my best mate Andrea call each other Maumau (long story that goes back to us being hilariously awesome choir geeks at high school) . . . anyway, used to make a version of this salad for our Sunday lunches when we were in our early twenties, when we'd drink cheap bubbly and watch movies we'd already seen too many times (*Titanic*, *Seven*, *Troy* and *The Little Mermaid* were staples). Ah, such excellent memories — and such a delicious salad. It's amazing as a side or as a light meal along with breads and things. Load it up with as much avo as you like — you literally can't have too much (I live on the stuff).

Whisk all the dressing ingredients together in a little bowl until the sugar is dissolved. Set aside until ready to use.

Peel the red onion and slice very thinly with a sharp knife. Place in a small bowl with the salt, sugar and vinegar or lemon juice. Toss to combine and leave to sit for at least 10 minutes to pickle.

Use a peeler to carve large strips out of the cucumber flesh, stopping when you reach the seeds. Set the strips aside (discard the very outer skins).

Cut the strawberries into quarters. Season with a little salt and pepper and set aside.

Tear the lettuce into pieces. Arrange in a large bowl or on a platter and layer with the cucumber strips, sprouts, pickled red onion, avocado, strawberries, basil and walnuts. Give it a crack of black pepper.

Just before serving, drizzle the dressing over the salad. It will make it look all murky if it sits there too long — you could even get people to dress their own salads if you're worried about it.

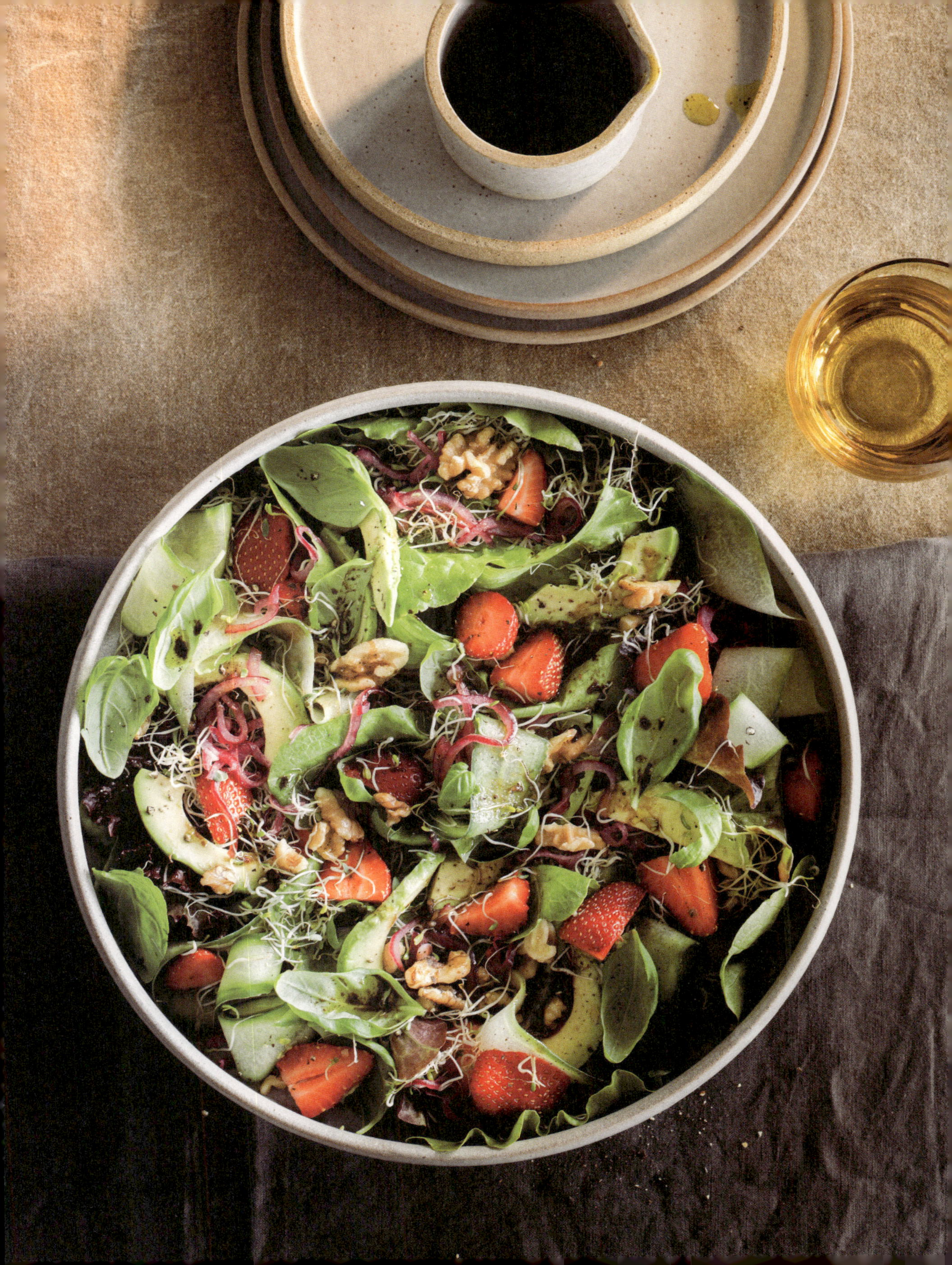

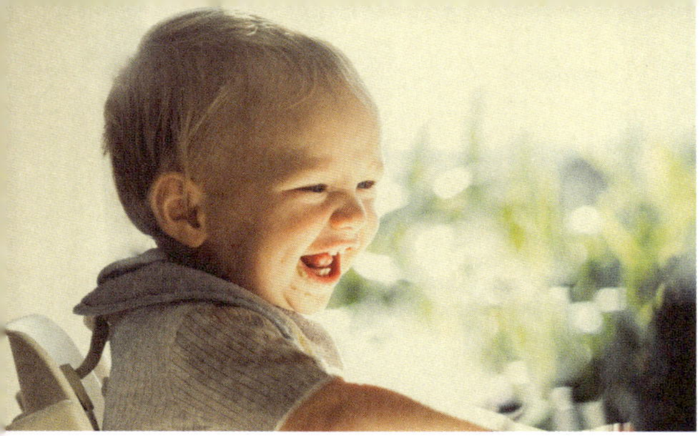
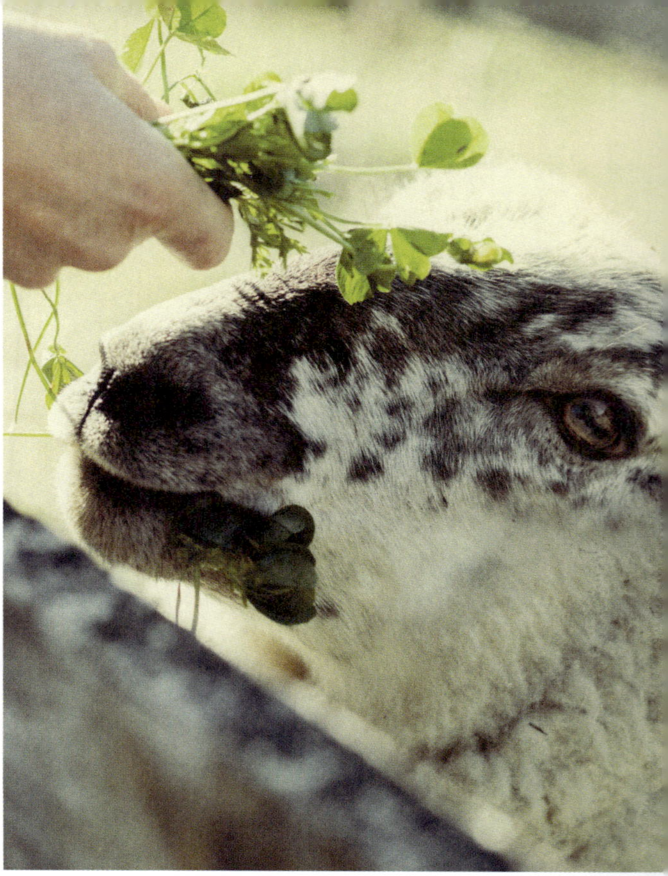
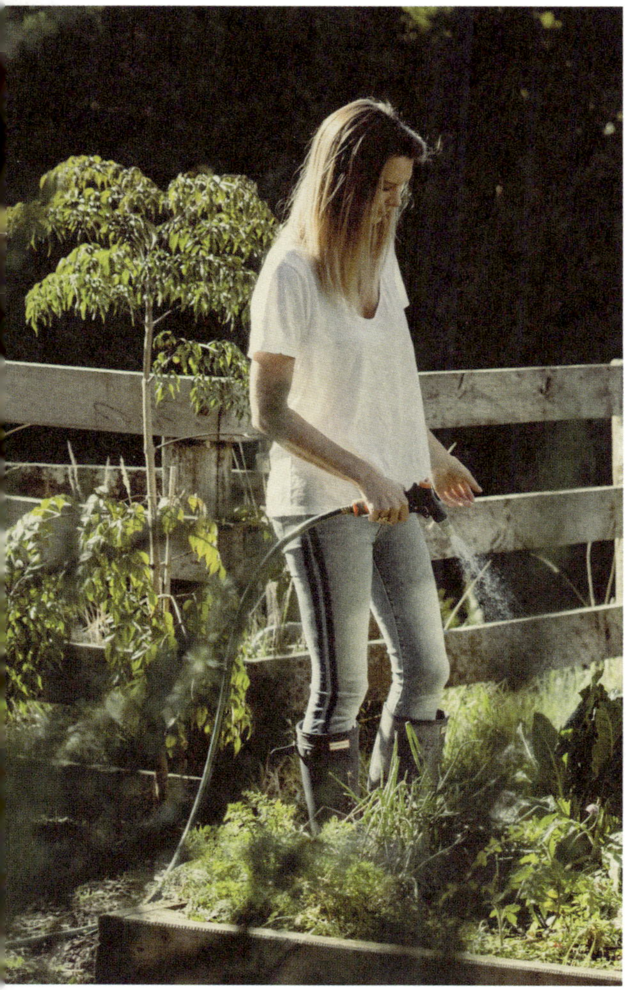
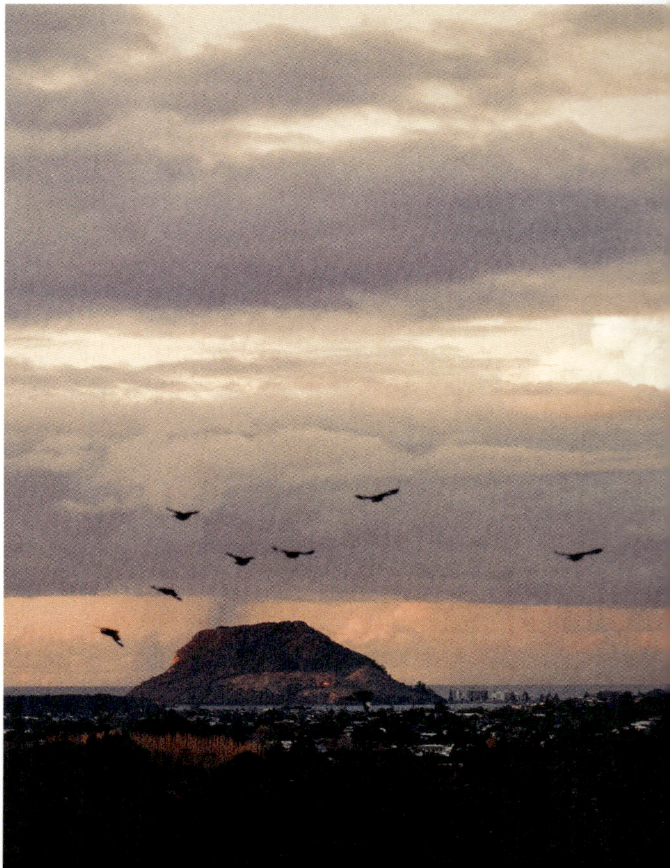
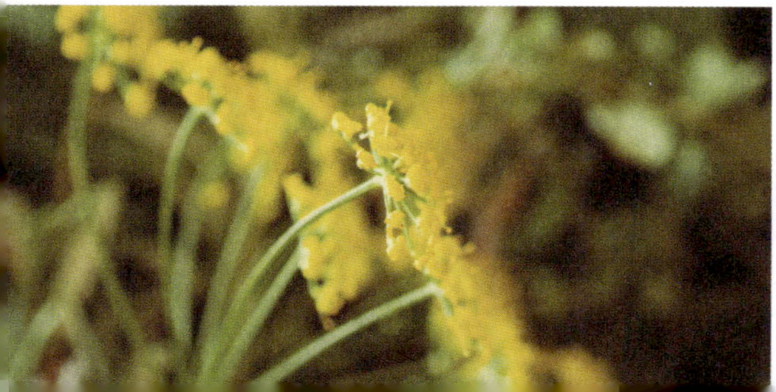

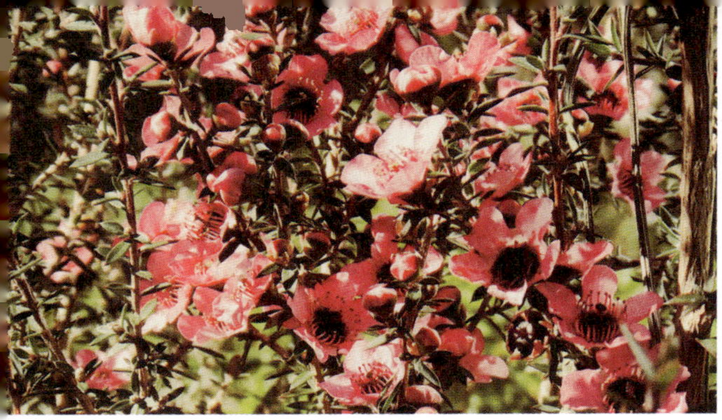
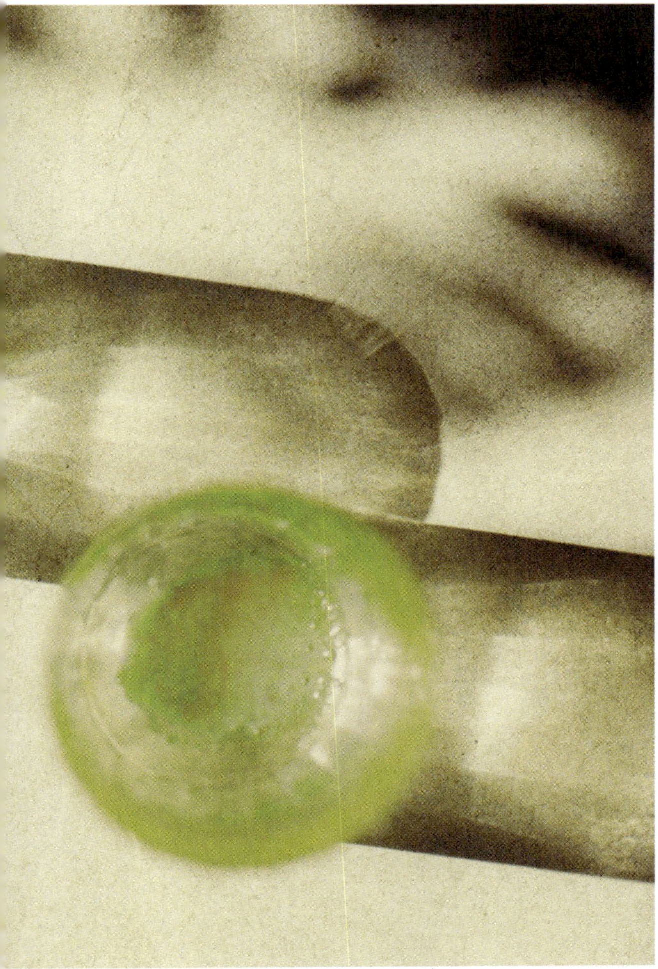
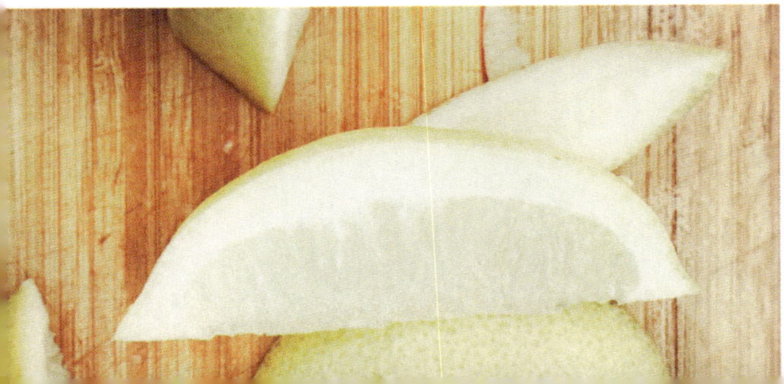
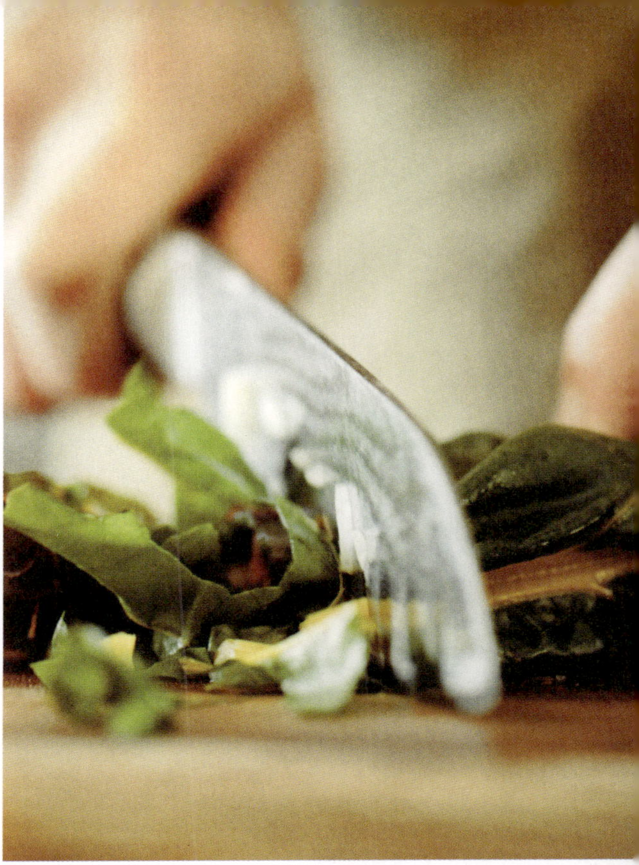
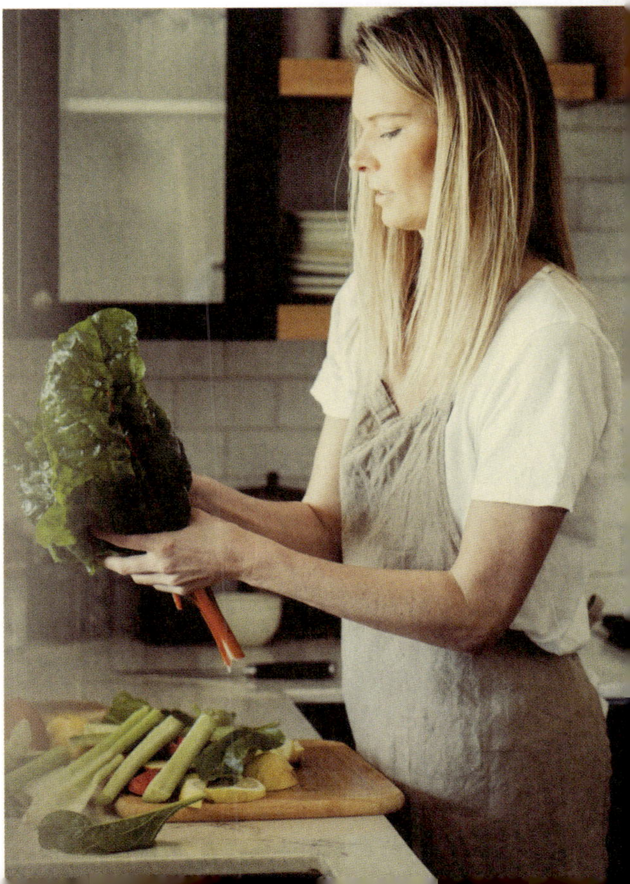

LOVELY LETTUCE CUPS

PREP 30 minutes **SERVES** 4 for a light meal, or 7 as a nibble (12–15 pieces)

My friend (and, appropriately, fellow *MasterChef* winner) Aaron Brunet made these some years ago at the height of my carnivorousness, and I remember being blown away that something made purely of plants could be so tasty. He very kindly offered up the recipe for this book so that I could share it with you guys too. Aaron has an undeniable gift for flavours and textures — you'll see what I mean when you try these little beauties. They're fresh and fragrant as well as savoury and satisfying. Each layer adds a note to the overall song: crunchy lettuce base, fragrant mint and basil, rich walnut mince, sweet fruity salsa, creamy cashew, and tastebud-tingling toppings of lime, salt and chilli. Awesome for a light meal or as an appetiser for a crowd.

To make the mince, place all the ingredients in a food processor and pulse just enough to clump together. Don't over-blend, or you'll make walnut butter!

Combine the salsa ingredients in a bowl, and season to taste with salt and pepper.

To make the cashew cream, place all the ingredients in a high-speed blender or bullet blender and whizz until smooth, scraping down the sides once to catch any lumps. You can also use a food processor, but it will take longer and you'll need to scrape down the sides several times.

To assemble, lay out the lettuce leaves (some larger and some smaller is fine). Pop one or two mint leaves and a basil leaf on each.

Add a decent base layer of walnut mince (about a tablespoon, more on larger lettuce leaves), then a spoonful of salsa and some avocado.

Top with:

a dollop of cashew cream
a sprinkle of paprika
a tiny pinch of salt
a few drops of fresh lime juice
a garnish of coriander and basil
a slice of fresh chilli (to taste, optional).

Serve immediately.

TIPS

+ You can make double the amount of walnut mince and freeze leftovers — it's great as a wrap filling for school lunches.
+ The cashew cream keeps in the fridge for a week. Use it like sour cream to dollop on soups or as the base for a creamy salad dressing.
+ Instead of the cashew cream you can use the aïoli on page 182.

WALNUT MINCE
1 cup raw walnuts
1 tbsp tamari or soy sauce
1 tsp cumin seeds
¼ tsp ground black pepper
¼ tsp chilli powder (optional, to taste)

SALSA
8 cherry tomatoes, chopped
½ yellow capsicum, chopped
1 golden kiwifruit, finely chopped (or use green kiwifruit, mango or pineapple)
¼ cup chopped fresh coriander
¼ tsp salt

CASHEW CREAM
¾ cup raw cashews
⅓ cup cold water
¼ tsp salt
2 tbsp lemon juice
zest of ¼ lemon

TO ASSEMBLE
2 x baby cos lettuces (12–15 leaves)
fresh mint leaves
basil leaves
1 avocado, finely chopped
paprika
1 lime (or lemon), cut into wedges
fresh coriander, chopped
1 red chilli, finely sliced (optional)

TO MAKE IT GLUTEN-FREE
Ensure that your soy sauce is GF.

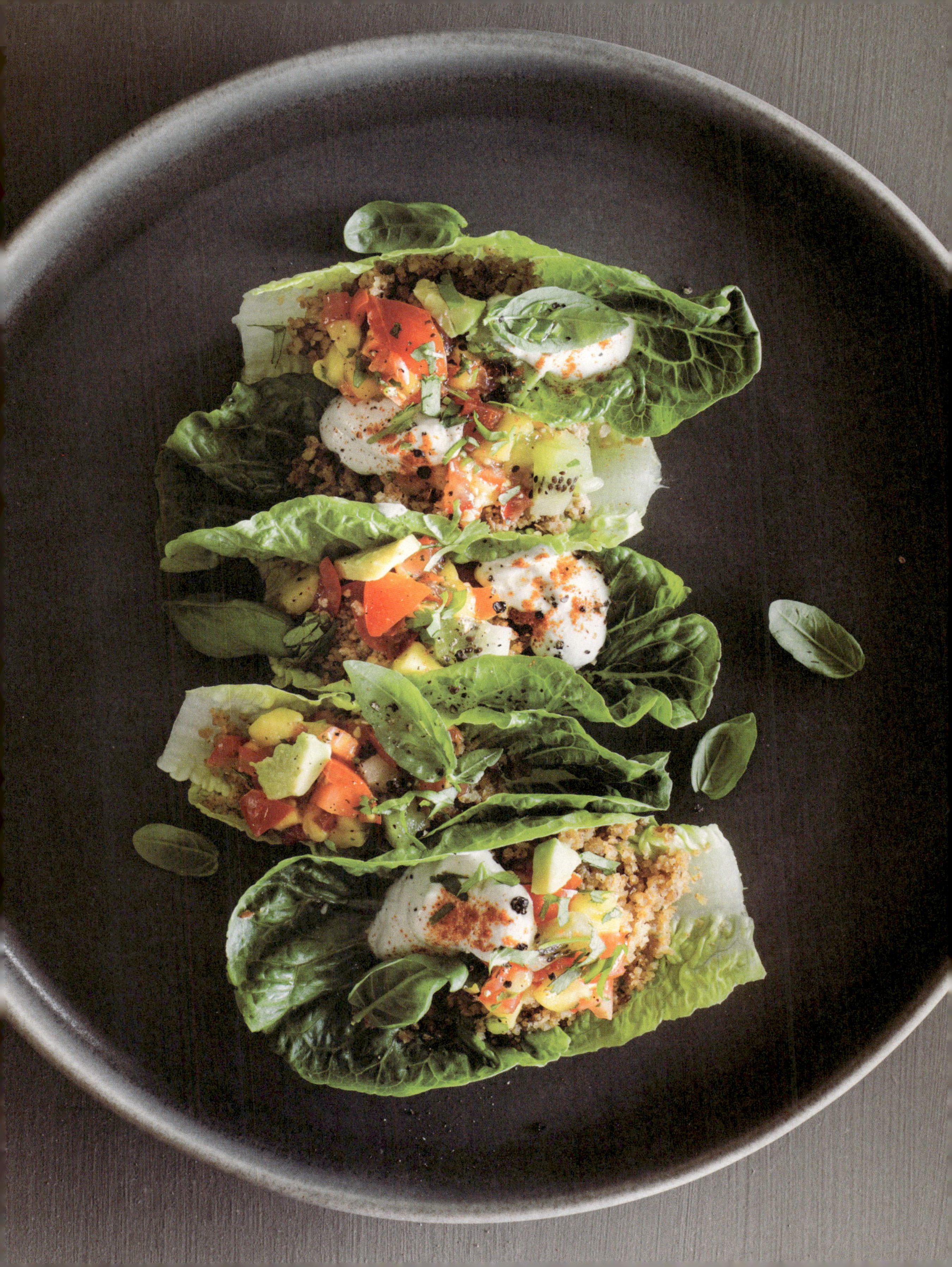

GRILLED SWEETCORN

SMOKY SAUCE
¼ cup plant-based mayo or aïoli (see page 182)
2 tsp lemon juice
2 tsp paprika
½ tsp mild smoked paprika
1 clove garlic, crushed
½ tsp salt
¼ tsp finely ground black pepper

TO FINISH AND SERVE
4–5 cobs fresh sweetcorn
¼ cup chopped fresh coriander
lemon or lime wedges
chilli flakes or Tabasco sauce

PREP 15 minutes   **COOK** 15 minutes   **SERVES** 4–5 as a side

It was summertime as I was testing this book, and we all know that in summer sweetcorn is in abundance and remarkably cheap. I couldn't go past this classic, much-loved Mexican street food (even though I haven't been to Mexico yet. It's on the bucket list; in the meantime a homemade corn fiesta will have to suffice). This is awesome as a side dish, or as a delicious lunch or light dinner served with an avocado-laden salad or salsa. Sweet, spicy, salty, zingy and magnificently juicy. All the good things, with minimal effort required.

───

Preheat the grill to medium and have a roasting tray lined with baking paper ready.

To make the smoky sauce, combine all the ingredients in a small bowl. Set aside.

Remove the husks from the corn. Bring a large saucepan of water to the boil, add the corn and simmer until the kernels are bright yellow and cooked through (about 10 minutes). Drain.

If you have a gas hob, you can sear the corn a little on the outside by using tongs to hold the cobs in the flame. It will only take a couple of minutes.

Arrange the cobs on the roasting tray and brush generously all over with the mayo mixture (reserve some for serving).

Grill for 5 minutes, or until golden and bubbling.

To serve, scatter with fresh coriander, lime or lemon juice, chilli flakes or Tabasco sauce, and extra mayo.

───

TIP

+ If you're having a BBQ, you can soak the corn cobs, still in their husks, in water for 30 minutes, then BBQ them over a medium heat for 10 minutes until cooked. Remove the husks and grill cobs on the BBQ to sear them a little before finishing off with the smoky sauce.

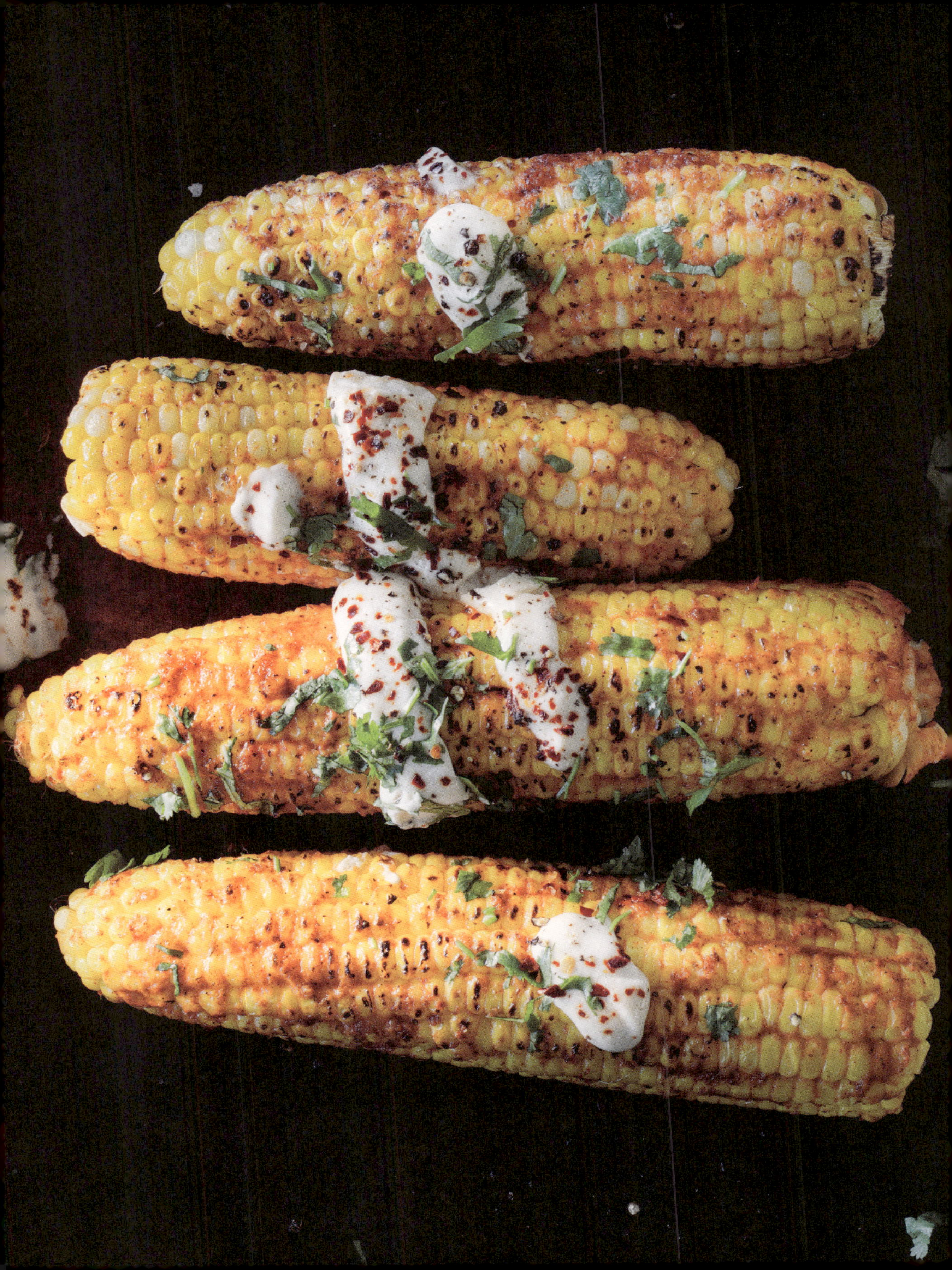

FESTIVE STUFFED MUSHROOMS

½ cup pine nuts (70g bag)
¾ cup brown rice
12–14 medium-sized Portobello mushrooms
olive oil
1 tbsp fresh thyme leaves
2 onions, finely chopped
4 big cloves garlic, chopped
1 stalk rosemary, leaves very finely chopped
⅓ cup roughly chopped raisins or sultanas
¼ cup Plant Parmesan (see page 196; or use 2 tbsp nutritional yeast flakes)
1 tsp vegetable stock powder
squeeze of lemon juice
¼ tsp finely ground black pepper

TO SERVE
plant-based aïoli (see page 182)
chopped fresh parsley or chives

TO MAKE IT GLUTEN-FREE
Ensure that you use a GF stock powder.

PREP 30 minutes   **COOK** 30 minutes   **SERVES** 4 as a light meal, 8 as a side

There's a saying floating around that 'life's too short to stuff a mushroom'. Whoever coined *that* phrase has clearly never enjoyed a good stuffed mushroom (probably been burned by some tragic recipe served up in the '60s). Done well, a stuffed mush is a tasty, 'meaty' tidbit with endless flavour combination options. Here I've gone with something a little Italian. I served these on Christmas Day for my family — I made the stuffing in advance, then cooked them just before serving. They were a hit, and there were quite a few requests for the recipe (always a sign that you've had a win). You can make them in giant Portobello mushrooms for a more gutsy meal, or in smaller ones for finger food. Just adjust the number and cooking time accordingly.

Preheat the oven to 180°C regular bake and line a baking/roasting tray with baking paper.

Lightly toast the pine nuts in a small, dry frying pan until golden, shaking the pan to toast them evenly (don't take your eyes off them!). Set aside.

Simmer the rice in a medium-sized saucepan of water until very tender (I like to add a couple of teaspoons of stock powder for flavour). Drain and set aside.

Remove the stalks from the mushrooms. Finely chop the stalks and set aside.

Arrange the stalk-less mushroom caps gill-side up on the baking tray and drizzle with a little olive oil. Scatter with the thyme leaves. Season with salt and pepper and roast in the oven for 10 minutes.

While the mushrooms are roasting, add 3 tablespoons olive oil to a medium-sized frying pan over a medium-low heat. Add the onion and cook, stirring, for about 10 minutes until soft. Add the pine nuts, chopped mushroom stalks, garlic and rosemary and cook for another 7–10 minutes until very soft and starting to caramelise a little.

Add the cooked rice, raisins or sultanas and Plant Parmesan and cook for a few more minutes.

Remove the mushrooms from the oven and tip any juices in the roasting tray into the rice mixture, then cook for a minute or so to dry it out. Stir through the lemon juice and pepper, and season with salt to taste.

Pile the filling on top of the mushrooms in nice little heaps, then bake for another 15–20 minutes.

To serve, dollop each mushroom with aïoli and sprinkle with fresh herbs.

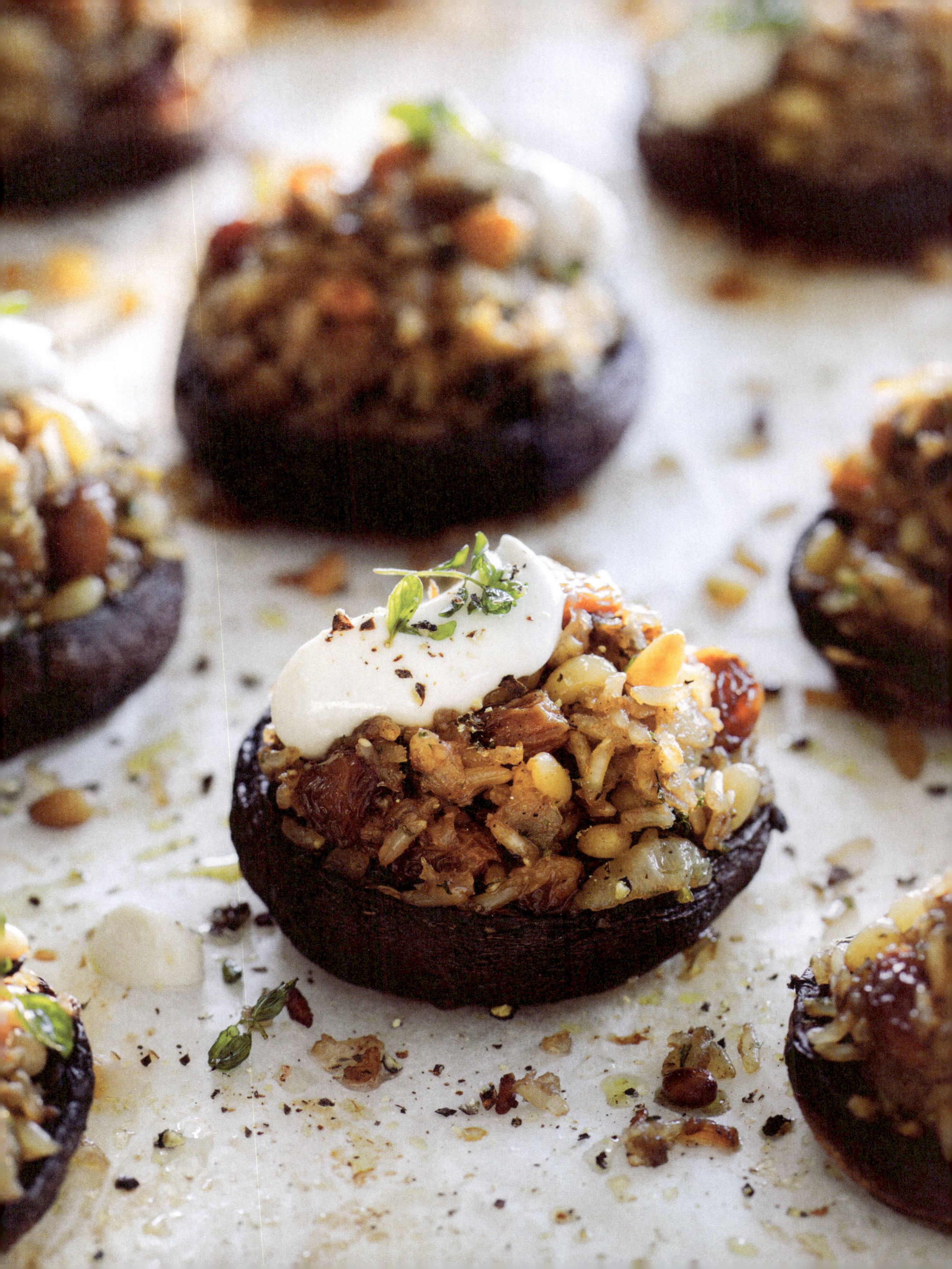

CRISPY SWEET & SOUR CAULIFLOWER

PREP 30 minutes **COOK** 30 minutes **SERVES** 4 as a light meal, 8 as a nibble

Crispy deep-fried cauliflower with a sticky, tasty sweet and sour sauce . . . it's definitely worth the hassle of labouring over a pan of hot oil when you fry this one up. Awesome for a snack while you're watching the rugby, or as nibbles with drinks with your mates, or even as a naughty Saturday-night dinner. Just make sure you serve it up straight away, because the crispiness doesn't last long. And remember — it may be deep-fried but at the end of the day it's still cauliflower, and you're still eating veges, which is a win!

To make the sauce, add the oils to a medium-sized saucepan over a medium-low heat. Add the ginger and garlic and cook, stirring all the time, for 1 minute. Add the remaining sauce ingredients and stir to combine. Increase the heat to medium and cook, stirring constantly, for a few minutes until it has thickened up. Take off the heat and set aside.

To make the batter, place the flour, baking powder, baking soda, salt and pepper in a bowl. Add the water and stir with a fork until combined, but not totally smooth. Lots of little lumps are good because they make the best crispy bits when cooked.

Add the oil to a medium-sized saucepan over a medium-high heat and leave it to heat up for 5 minutes or so. To check if it's ready for frying, dip the handle of a wooden spoon or the tip of a wooden chopstick into the oil — if it starts bubbling steadily, then the oil is hot enough for frying (see tips).

Place a wire rack on top of some paper towels on the benchtop, for the cauliflower to drain on when cooked.

You'll need to do the cauli in a few batches. One by one, using tongs, dip as many pieces of cauliflower as will fit in the pan into the batter, then very carefully drop into the oil. Cook for a few minutes, until deep golden brown and crunchy. Transfer to the rack while you cook the rest.

To serve, you can either toss the cauli in the sauce *just* before serving (it will go soggy quickly), or have everyone spoon a little sauce onto their cauli or dip it into a bowl of sauce.

TIPS

+ Serve as a meal with noodles or rice, and steamed greens of your choice.
+ Try to get a good-quality soy sauce or one with reduced salt; some of the cheaper ones are pretty thick and way too salty and can blow out the sauce.
+ If you have a thermometer, the oil needs to be around 180–190°C.

SAUCE

1 tbsp sesame oil
2 tsp neutral oil
3 cloves garlic, crushed
2 tsp finely grated ginger
1½ cups pineapple juice (or use water)
¼ cup brown sugar
¼ cup soy sauce (a low-salt one if possible)
3 tbsp sweet chilli sauce
2½ tbsp cornflour mixed with ¼ cup water
3 tsp rice vinegar (or use lemon juice)
¼ tsp finely ground black pepper

BATTERED CAULI

1 head cauliflower, cut into small florets
1½ cups plain flour
1 tsp baking power
½ tsp baking soda
1½ tsp salt
¾ tsp finely ground black pepper
1½ cups cold water
500ml grapeseed or sunflower oil, for frying

TO MAKE IT GLUTEN-FREE

Use a GF flour blend without raising agent added and 1¾ cups water.

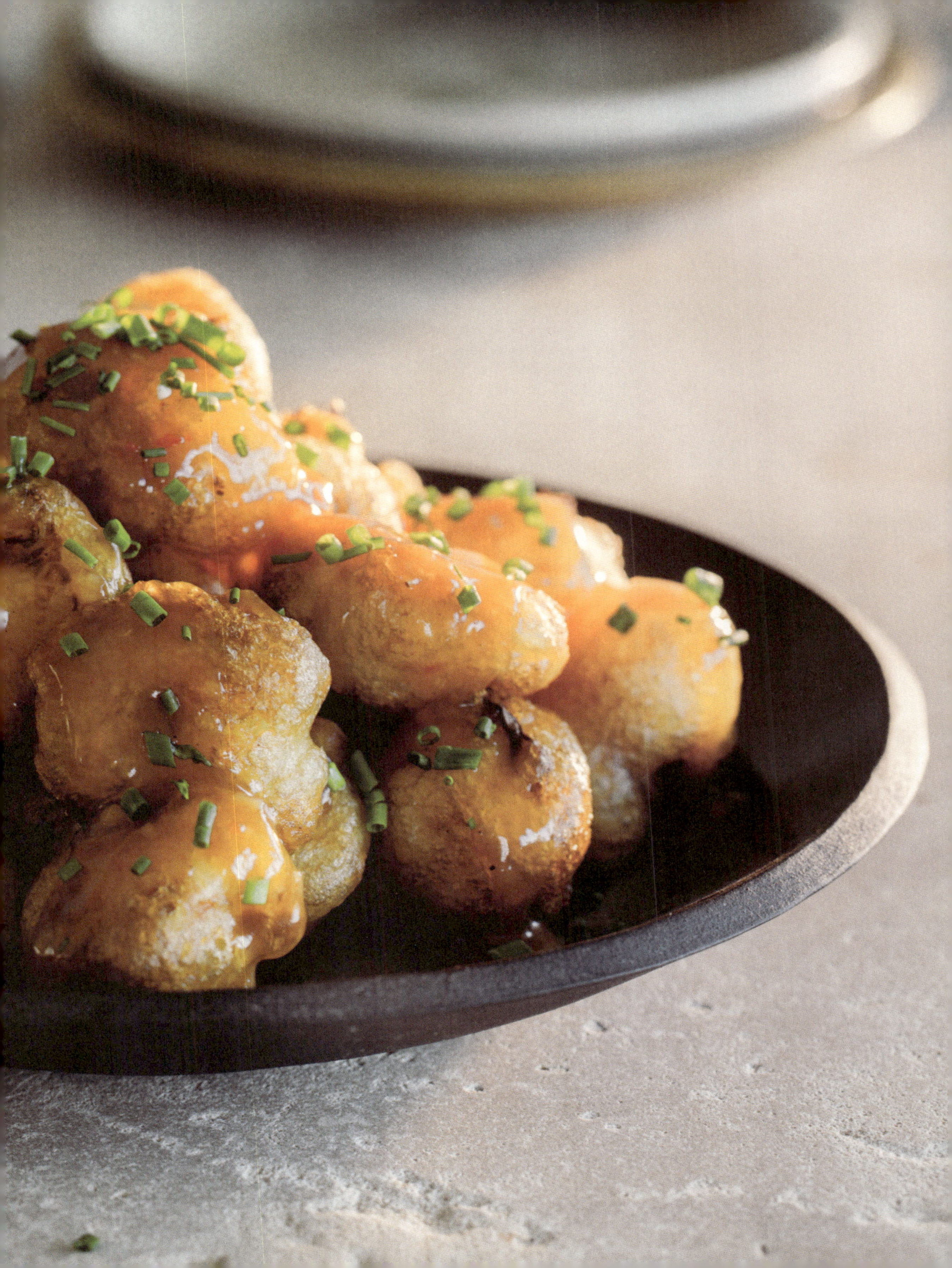

MAYO SALAD SAMMIES

CREAMY FILLING

1 x 400g can chickpeas (keep the drained liquid for another recipe)

⅓ cup finely chopped red onion

2 sticks celery, finely chopped

½ cup plant-based aïoli or mayo (see page 182)

3 tbsp chopped fresh herbs (parsley, chives, dill)

2 tsp Dijon mustard

2 tsp lemon juice

1 tsp nutritional yeast

½ tsp dried tarragon or dill

pinch finely ground black pepper

pinch finely ground white pepper

TO ASSEMBLE

bread of your choice, or pita pockets or wraps

lettuce leaves

sliced avocado

alfalfa sprouts

sliced cucumber

PREP 10 minutes   **MAKES** 4–5 sandwiches

I love a good creamy mayo sandwich for lunch. If I'm being a bit naughty, this filling goes on soft, fresh white bakery bread (as you can see). Or for something more nourishing, my homemade bread or a warmed wholemeal pita pocket. The slightly mushed chickpeas add texture and creaminess, as well as making for a much more filling sammie. And the crunchy little pops of celery and fresh herbs work with the mustard and lemon to counter the lush aïoli. A great one for a packed lunch. The filling works in wraps, too.

Place the chickpeas in a mixing bowl and mash until no whole ones remain, but it's not a total mush. Add the other filling ingredients and stir to combine. Add more lemon, salt, herbs or pepper to taste. You could even add a little more aïoli or mayo if you're feeling luxurious.

Assemble into a sandwich with a generous amount of filling, stacked up with the other ingredients.

The filling keeps in the fridge for a couple of days in an airtight container.

TIPS

+ You can mix it up with any soft herbs you have on hand — a little basil or tarragon would be nice, too.
+ The creamy filling is also great on toast.

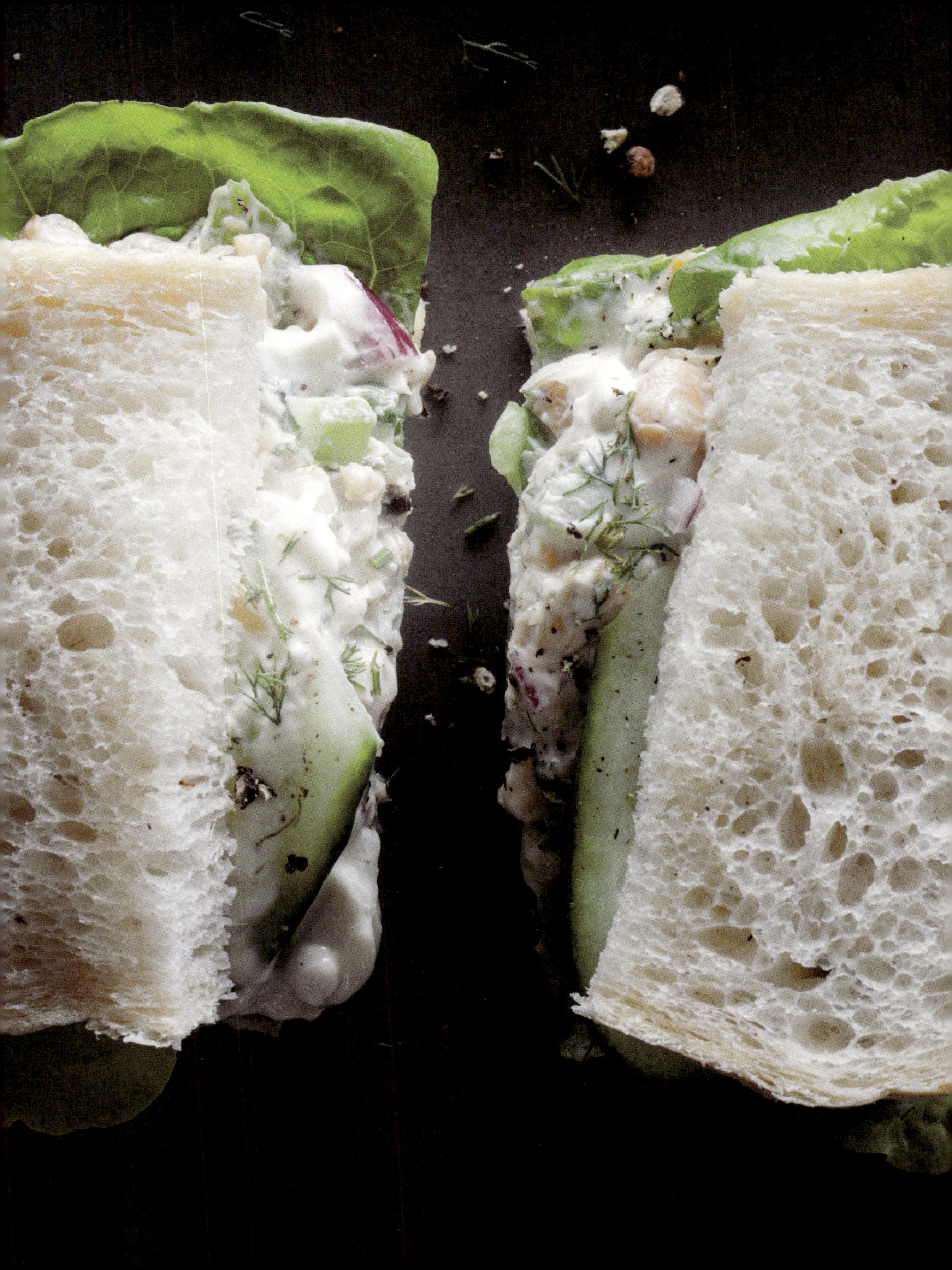

SNAUSAGE ROLLS

PREP 30 minutes, plus 20 minutes to chill   **COOK** 45 minutes
SERVES 4 as a meal, 8 as a snack

FILLING

⅓ cup each brown lentils and French green lentils (or ⅔ cup brown lentils), rinsed

3 cups vegetable or chicken-style stock (or use stock powder and water)

1 large onion, roughly chopped

2 stalks celery, roughly chopped

1 large carrot, peeled and roughly chopped

200g Portobello or shiitake mushrooms (or a mixture)

4 cloves garlic, crushed

3 tbsp extra virgin olive oil

3 tbsp tomato paste

½ cup walnuts, whizzed to a crumb

2 tsp vegetable or chicken-style stock powder

½ tsp fennel seeds

½ tsp cumin seeds

2 tsp soy sauce or tamari

1 tsp paprika

½ tsp curry powder

½ tsp finely ground black pepper

¼ cup plain flour

TO ASSEMBLE

350g rolled dairy-free flaky puff pastry

¼ cup canned chickpea liquid (aquafaba)

1 tbsp sesame or poppy seeds

TO MAKE IT GLUTEN-FREE

Use GF flour, pastry, stock and soy sauce.

Sausage rolls will always be über-cool, no matter what anyone says. They're always the first to be nabbed at a morning tea, classily dressed-up with a generous splurt of store-bought tomato sauce . . . crispy, juicy little taste bombs. No animals were harmed in the making of these beauties, but I have to say I massacred a few plants. But happily, the result is utterly delish. You can either make little mini rolls for a party or finger-food, or serve them larger like this as part of a meal with potatoes and salad or veges. Not a sausage, a snausage!

To make the filling, simmer the lentils in the stock until just tender — about 25 minutes. Drain and set aside.

Place the onion, celery, carrot, mushrooms and garlic in a food processor and pulse until chopped quite finely but not mushy.

Heat the oil in a frying pan over a medium heat. Add the chopped veges and cook, stirring, for 15–20 minutes, until they have reduced right down to a soft golden mush.

Add the drained lentils and remaining filling ingredients except the flour, and stir to combine. Cook for another 5 minutes or so over a medium heat. If it seems a little dry, add more tomato paste and a little water and cook a bit more.

Add the flour and stir through. Remove from the heat and leave to cool down to room temperature (or put in a bowl in the fridge to speed it up).

Line a large baking tray with baking paper.

To assemble, lay the pastry sheet/s out on a clean floured benchtop (or roll your own to about 5mm thick). Arrange the cooled filling in a neat log (about 6cm wide) lengthways down the middle. Fold up both sides of the pastry snugly (you might have a big overlap, but that's okay — pastry is yum). Brush a little water on both parts where the pastry joins. Place seam-side down on the lined baking tray and refrigerate for 20 minutes or so to firm up.

Preheat the oven to 180°C fan-bake (190°C regular bake).

Slice the chilled log into hearty chunks using a bread knife and a light sawing motion. Brush the rolls all over with the aquafaba and prick the tops a couple of times with a knife. Sprinkle with sesame or poppy seeds.

Bake in the lower half of the oven for around 45 minutes, or until the pastry is dark golden brown and puffy. Serve with a dollop of tomato sauce, relish or chutney.

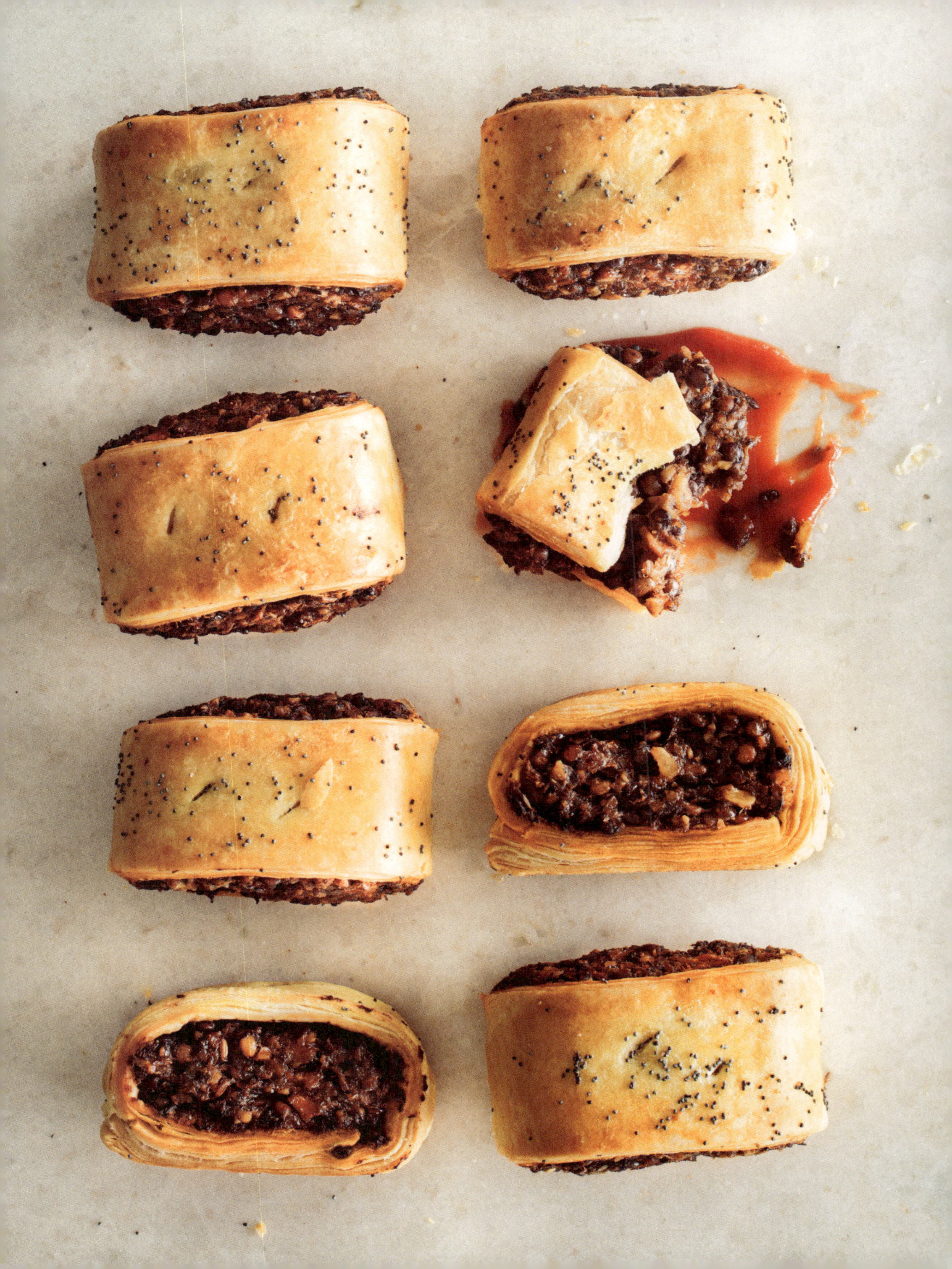

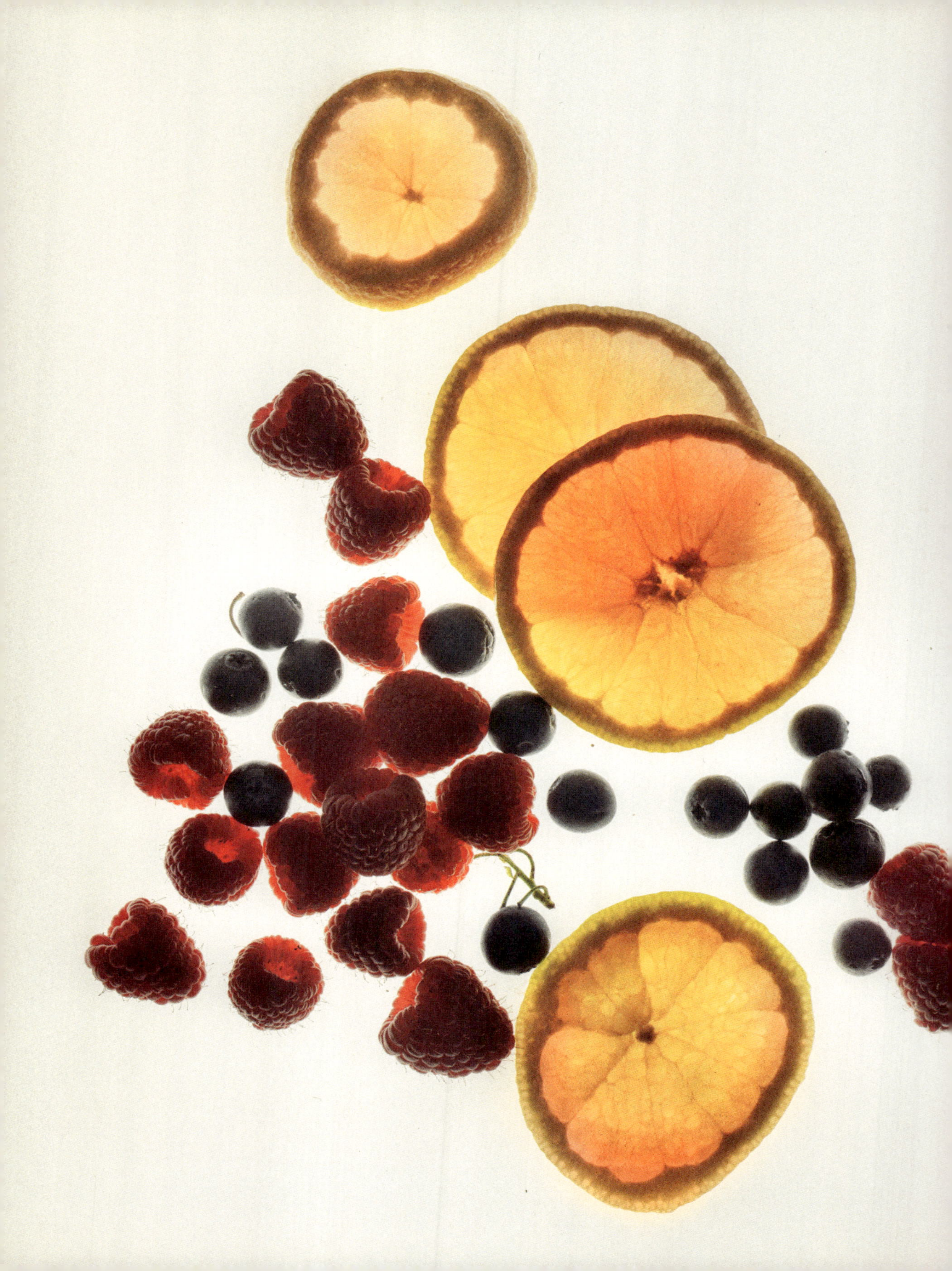

SWEETS

It wouldn't be a Chelsea cookbook without baking and desserts now, would it? Here you'll find a lifesaving assortment of some of our most beloved classics, which I've 'plantified' (think caramel slice and Snickalicious), as well as some excellent new delicacies in the form of cakes, fudge, chocolate, ice cream and gelato, cheesecakes, truffles, meringues and donuts. Happily for many of you, most of these recipes are naturally gluten-free or can easily be made that way. Yep — it's delectably dangerous and so, so good.

VANILLA CELEBRATION CAKE

CAKE

2 cups plain flour
1½ cups ground almonds
½ tsp salt
2 cups rice or other milk
1 cup caster sugar
⅔ cup grapeseed oil
1 tbsp vanilla bean paste or vanilla extract
zest of 2 oranges
zest of 2 lemons
2 tsp baking soda
2 tsp apple cider vinegar

ICING

½ cup dairy-free spread
2 cups icing sugar
2 tsp vanilla bean paste (or use vanilla extract)
1 tsp orange or lemon zest (optional)
1 tbsp plant-based milk (if needed)

TO FILL AND TOP

fresh berries
raspberry or strawberry jam
icing sugar (optional)

TO MAKE IT GLUTEN-FREE

Use a GF flour mix without raising agent added, then add 1 teaspoon of baking powder to the flour mixture (see tips).

PREP 10 minutes plus cooling and decorating   **COOK** 30–35 minutes
MAKES 1 two-layer 20cm cake (or 1 larger cake)

You guys kept asking me for a vanilla version of my Crazy Italian Chocolate Cake from *Scrumptious*. In other words, you wanted a cake that was dairy- and egg-free (and easily made gluten-free), but wasn't a chocolate cake and wasn't a fail. It took me ages to get it right, but finally here it is! It reminds me of my Sweet Pea Cake from *Eat* — it has a similar subtle citrus flavour but is denser, almost like a friand . . . moist and luscious. It can be dressed up into a magnificent work of art, like here, or covered in coloured icing for a kid's birthday cake. I used two of my Chelsea Winter tins, and they were perfect! Don't go any larger than 22cm or your cakes will be too flat. (See tips on page 126 for making different-sized cakes.)

Preheat the oven to 180°C regular bake and line two 20cm baking tins with baking paper right up the sides (I just use one piece smooshed in).

Place the flour, almonds and salt in a large mixing bowl and stir with a whisk to combine. Make a well in the centre.

Put the milk, sugar, oil, vanilla and zests in another, smaller mixing bowl and whisk gently for 30 seconds or so to help dissolve the sugar. Add this to the dry mixture and stir very gently with a whisk again until you have a smooth batter.

Place the baking soda in a very small bowl or small cup. Add the vinegar and stir briskly — it will froth up straight away. Immediately add it to the cake batter (scrape it all out with a spatula), then gently fold it into the batter with the spatula until it's evenly incorporated.

Scrape the batter evenly between the two tins. Bake for about 30–35 minutes, or until a skewer poked in comes out clean. Cool in the tins for 5–10 minutes, then transfer to a wire rack to cool completely.

To make the icing, place the dairy-free spread in a mixing bowl (or use your cake mixer and paddle attachment) and beat for 30 seconds until pale and fluffy. Sift in the icing sugar half a cup at a time, beating well after each addition, until you have a light, fluffy icing. Add the vanilla and zest (if using) and beat in. You can beat in the milk if the icing seems a little stiff.

Recipe continued on next page

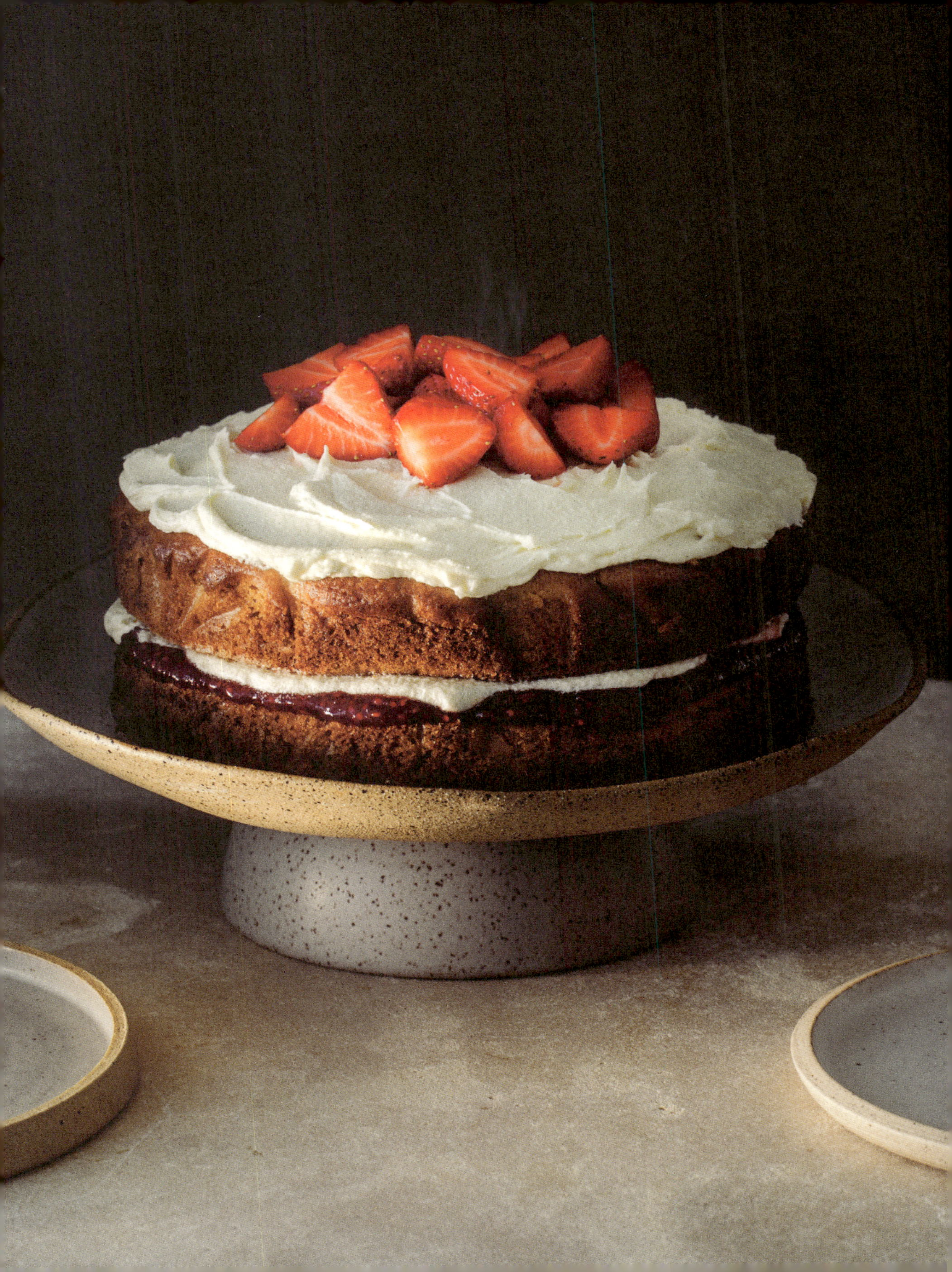

VANILLA CELEBRATION CAKE continued

To assemble, turn the bottom cake upside-down (so that the two flat sides will meet in the middle and make the cake more stable). Spread the top (flat) side of the bottom cake with a thin layer of jam. Spread the bottom side of the top cake with icing — not too much icing or jam in the middle, though, as you don't want it too squidgy when you cut it — and place it on top of the bottom cake.

Spread the remaining icing out on top of the cake and scatter with fresh berries. Dust with icing sugar, if using.

Keeps at room temperature in an airtight container for a couple of days.

TIPS

- When making a gluten-free cake, I find that only using 1⅔ cups flour (rather than 2) works best. The gluten-free cake is also best eaten the day you make it.
- To make one larger 23–24cm cake, use one large tin and adjust the temperature to 160°C with a cooking time of around 1 hour 15 minutes.
- If you just want one smaller cake, halve the ingredients and use one 20cm tin — I ice it and don't bother with the jam.
- If berries are out of season (although you can usually find blueberries), you can top this with freeze-dried fruit, orange and lemon zest, fresh flowers, or passionfruit pulp/syrup.
- The vanilla bean paste is really yummy for the icing and is worth the special purchase. You could also scrape the seeds out of vanilla pods. But normal vanilla extract is fine too.
- If you can't eat almonds, you can substitute ½ cup coconut flour for the almond meal. The texture won't be as good, though.

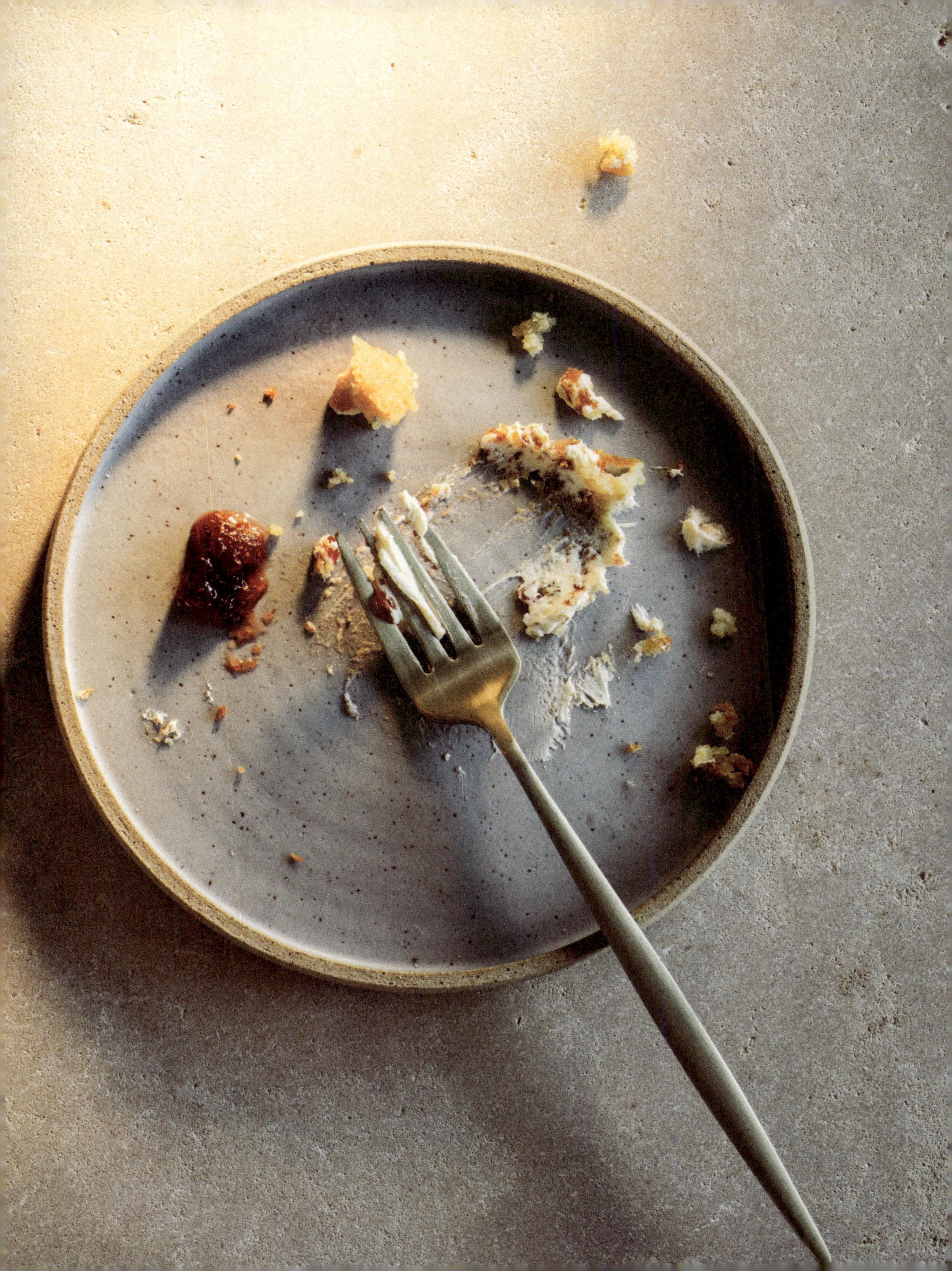

OREO CHEESECAKE

PREP 30 minutes, plus 6+ hours soaking time and 7+ hours to freeze
SERVES 10

Well hello, handsome! Have you ever seen anything so luxuriously edible in your life? If you're like me and you're a sucker for Oreos (I ate an embarrassing amount while I tested the recipe — and yes, Oreos are plant-based), this dessert will have you fizzing, especially as it looks like you're serving up a giant Oreo! Also, five whole packets of cookies go into this, which makes it legit. Because you serve it frozen, you can make it ahead of time (up to a month) — just make sure it's extremely well-wrapped in its tin.

Place the cashews in a large heatproof bowl and cover with just-boiled water. Leave for 6 hours to soak (overnight is even better). Drain and rinse.

Line the base and sides of a 22–23cm springform tin with baking paper.

Place the base ingredients in a food processor and whizz until you have a fine crumb. Tip into the tin and press into an even layer (easiest with wet fingers or a spatula).

Place the drained cashews, coconut cream, coconut oil, icing sugar, vanilla and salt in a blender (a food processor works, but a blender is ideal). Process or blend until silky smooth — this could take 1–5 minutes, depending on how good your machine is. Transfer to a bowl and fold through the chopped Oreos.

Pour the mixture on top of the base, cover and freeze for about 2 hours before adding the chocolate topping.

Place the chocolate and coconut cream in a heatproof bowl sitting over a saucepan with a little simmering water in the bottom (don't let the bowl touch the water). Leave it until the chocolate has nearly melted, then stir until smooth. Spread gently over the cheesecake in an even layer, then arrange overlapping Oreos around the outside and crumble some up in the middle.

Cover and freeze again for 4–5 hours, or overnight, to set. When you're nearly ready to serve, take the cheesecake out of the freezer and let it sit for 30 minutes or so to soften before you cut into it.

TIP

+ The cheesecake will hold up in the fridge once defrosted.

BASE
2 x 137g packets Oreos
2 tbsp coconut oil

FILLING
2½ cups raw cashews
1 cup coconut cream
½ cup melted coconut oil
1 cup icing sugar
1 tbsp vanilla bean paste (or vanilla extract)
¾ tsp salt
1 x 137g packet Oreos, very finely chopped

TOPPING
100g dairy-free eating chocolate, chopped
100ml coconut cream
2 x 137g packets Oreos

TO MAKE IT GLUTEN-FREE
You can find GF 'Oreo-style' biscuits at most supermarkets these days. They're often called something like 'choc creme' or 'cookies and cream'.

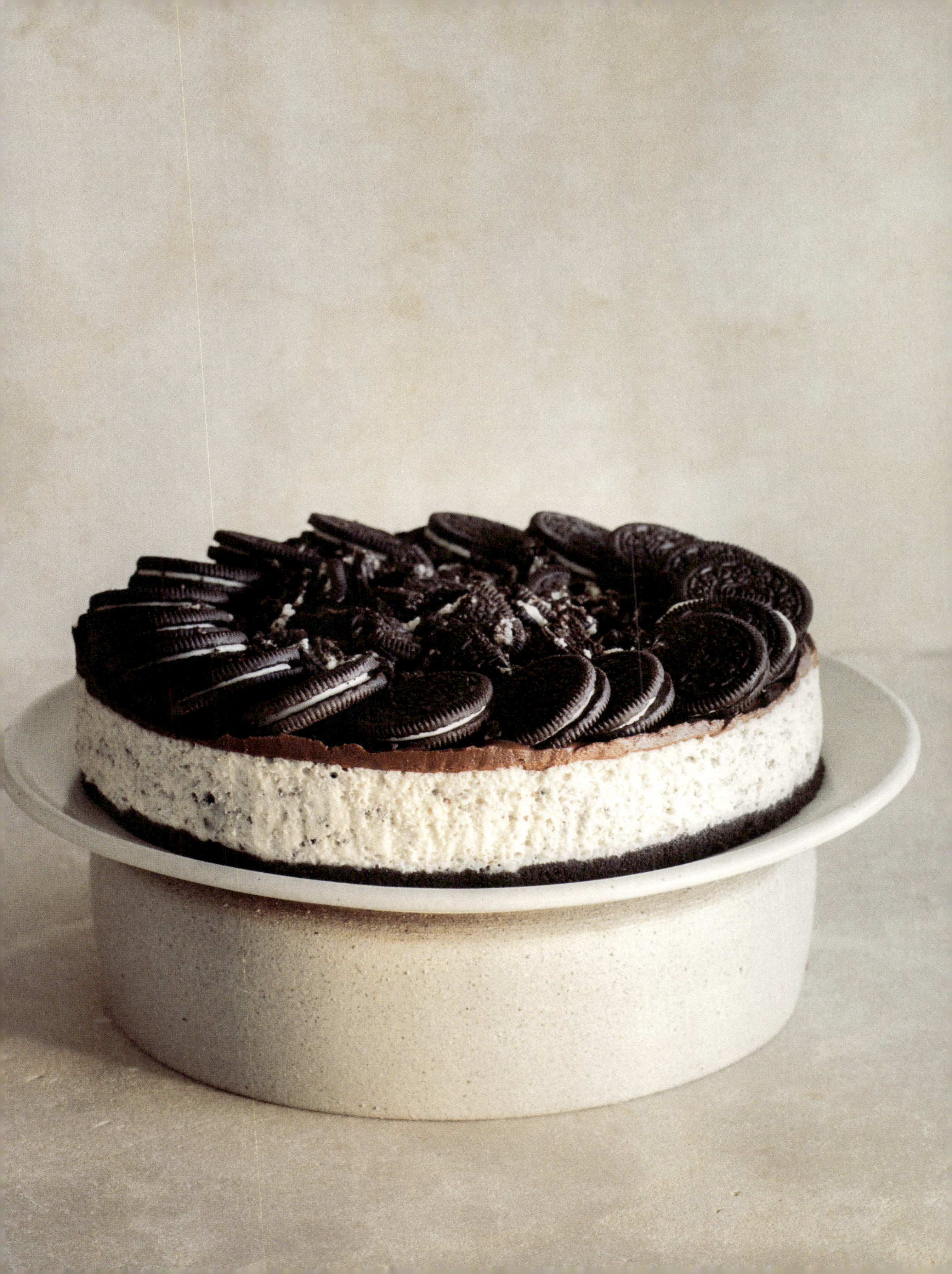

CARROT CAKE

CAKE

⅔ cup soft brown sugar or caster sugar

¾ cup grapeseed, rice bran or sunflower oil

½ cup canned chickpea liquid (aquafaba)

¼ cup plant-based milk

2 tsp vanilla extract

1 tsp apple cider vinegar

½ tsp salt

1½ cups plain flour

1 tsp baking soda

½ tsp baking powder

2 tsp ground cinnamon

½ tsp ground ginger

¼ tsp ground cloves

¼ tsp ground nutmeg

¾ cup ground almonds

1½ cups peeled and grated carrot

⅓ cup raisins or sultanas

¼ cup chopped walnuts (optional)

ICING AND GARNISH

½ cup dairy-free spread

1¼ cups icing sugar

zest of 2 lemons

2 tbsp lemon juice

¼ tsp salt

1 tbsp just-boiled water

chopped pistachios, walnuts or pumpkin seeds

TO MAKE IT GLUTEN-FREE

Use a GF flour mix without raising agent added

PREP 20 minutes **COOK** 45 minutes **MAKES** one 21–22cm cake

A perennial favourite always welcome at any occasion, carrot cake is both majestic and humble at the same time. Whoever thought of putting a grated root vegetable in a cake can enjoy a hearty figurative pat on the back from me! It's lightly spiced, with flecks of walnut and the odd juicy raisin floating around in there. The icing will surprise and delight you because it tastes pretty much like traditional cream cheese icing. All in all, a big win, because you'd never know this cake was egg- and dairy-free. Best of all, you just chuck everything in and stir the batter. I usually make it with gluten-free flour, and it works a treat.

Preheat the oven to 180°C regular bake. Line the base and sides of a 21–22cm round cake tin with baking paper (I just chuck a whole piece in and flatten/scrumple it up the sides).

Place the sugar, oil, aquafaba, milk, vanilla, vinegar and salt in a medium-sized bowl and stir with a whisk to combine.

Sift the flour, baking soda, baking powder and spices into a large mixing bowl. Add the almonds and stir to combine, then make a well in the middle and scrape the wet mixture in. Fold until evenly combined. Add the carrot, raisins and walnuts, if using, and fold them through.

Scrape the mixture into the tin, smooth it out and bake for about 45 minutes, or until a skewer poked in comes out clean. Cool in the tin for 10 minutes, then remove and leave to cool completely on a wire rack.

To make the icing, beat the spread and icing sugar in a bowl for a few minutes until light and fluffy. Add the lemon zest, juice, salt and a little boiled water, and beat again briefly until smooth. You can add a little more water if you like it a bit thinner. It may not go completely smooth, but that's okay. Let it cool to room temperature, then spread on top of the cooled cake. Sprinkle with pistachios, walnuts or pumpkin seeds.

Keeps for a few days in an airtight container at room temperature.

TIP

+ This cake isn't huge, so make sure you use the correct size of tin. If you like, you can double the mixture to make 2 x 21cm cakes and stack them with extra icing in the middle. Or, if you need a whopper of a cake for a special occasion, make one large cake using a 24cm tin.

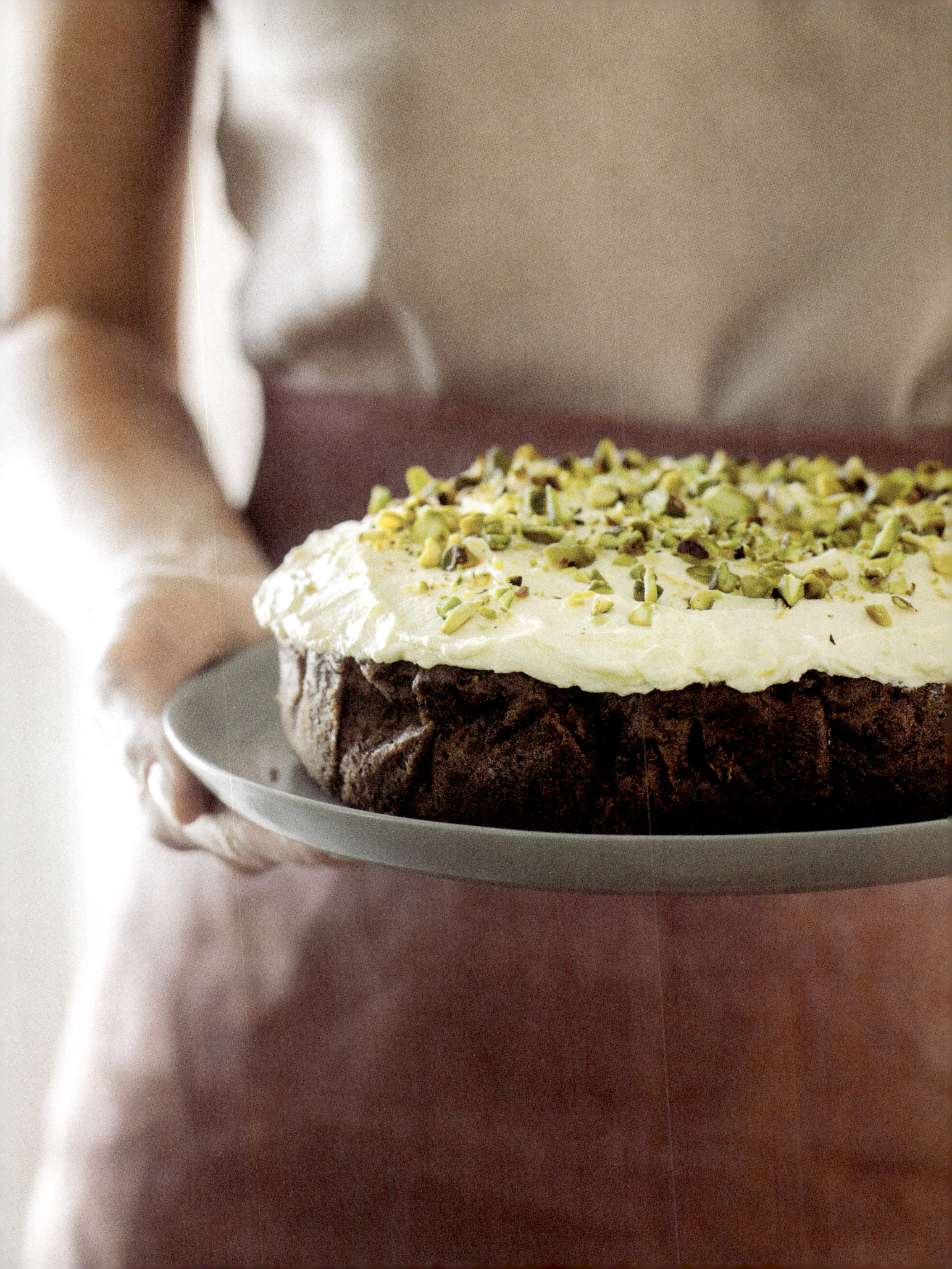

SNICKALICIOUS CHEESECAKE

PREP 45 minutes, plus 4+ hours to set **SERVES** 12

Oh lord, what have I done . . . I've taken my world-famous Snickalicious Slice, made it plant-based and then turned it into a cheesecake so it's even more magnificent than it already was. It tastes just like the slice, but more . . . desserty. I even put caramel popcorn on top, because everything is better with caramel popcorn! The only person I've encountered who *doesn't* love this is Douglas, because he thinks that peanut butter in sweet things is gross (clearly, he needs professional help). Anyway, you're gonna love this — it's simple to make, super-impressive to all, and holds up really well out of the fridge.

Place the cashews for the filling in a heatproof bowl, cover with boiling water and let sit for at least 20 minutes, then drain.

Line the base and sides of a 23cm springform cake tin with baking paper.

Place the base ingredients in a food processor and whizz on high for 20 seconds or so until it clumps together — I find that tilting the processor a bit helps it mix up more evenly and not stick to the sides. Tip into the tin and press down (using slightly wet fingers) into an even layer. Refrigerate.

Tip the drained cashews into a high-speed blender (or the large cup of a bullet blender) and add the coconut cream, coconut oil and just-boiled water. Whizz until it's silky smooth. You may have to stop and start, scrape the sides, and tilt and shake the machine a bit to get it going — even add a little more water. Just be patient and do what you have to!

Scrape the cashew mixture into a large mixing bowl and add the peanut butter, icing sugar, lemon juice, vanilla and salt. Beat with an electric mixer for a minute or so until smooth. Scrape the mixture onto the base, smooth it out evenly and freeze for at least 1 hour to firm up a bit before adding the topping.

To make the topping, place the first measure of chocolate and coconut cream in a heatproof bowl sitting over a saucepan with a little gently simmering water in the bottom (don't let the bowl touch the water). Stir until smooth, then spread out over the cheesecake. Scatter with popcorn if you want to, and sprinkle with chopped chocolate. Return to the freezer for 3 hours, or overnight, to finish setting.

Defrost for an hour or so (in the tin is fine) before serving, and slice with a sharp knife. It's a bit awkward slicing with the popcorn, but you'll manage.

Once defrosted, you can store the cheesecake in the fridge for a few days. You can also freeze it in the tin, very well wrapped, for up to a month. To be honest, it's pretty nice served frozen, too — leave it out to soften just a little before tucking in.

BASE
- 1¼ cups ground almonds
- 1¼ cups desiccated coconut
- ⅓ cup roasted peanuts
- 2 tbsp cocoa
- 2 tbsp brown sugar
- 2 tbsp peanut butter
- 2 tbsp coconut oil
- ¼ tsp salt

FILLING
- 2½ cups raw cashews
- ¾ cup coconut cream
- ½ cup melted coconut oil (I use flavourless)
- 2 tbsp just-boiled water
- 1 cup smooth peanut butter
- 2 cups icing sugar
- 2 tbsp lemon juice
- 2 tsp vanilla extract
- ½ tsp salt

TOPPING
- 150g dairy-free chocolate (I used 50% cocoa solids)
- 150ml coconut cream
- 1 cup caramel popcorn (optional; look for one with no dairy)
- ½ cup finely chopped dairy-free chocolate, for sprinkling

IT'S GLUTEN-FREE
Just check your popcorn and peanut butter.

TIPS
+ A cheap peanut butter works best for this recipe, as they aren't as oily as the fancy ones.
+ You can use a good-quality food processor for the nuts — but you might have to whizz on high for about 10 minutes.

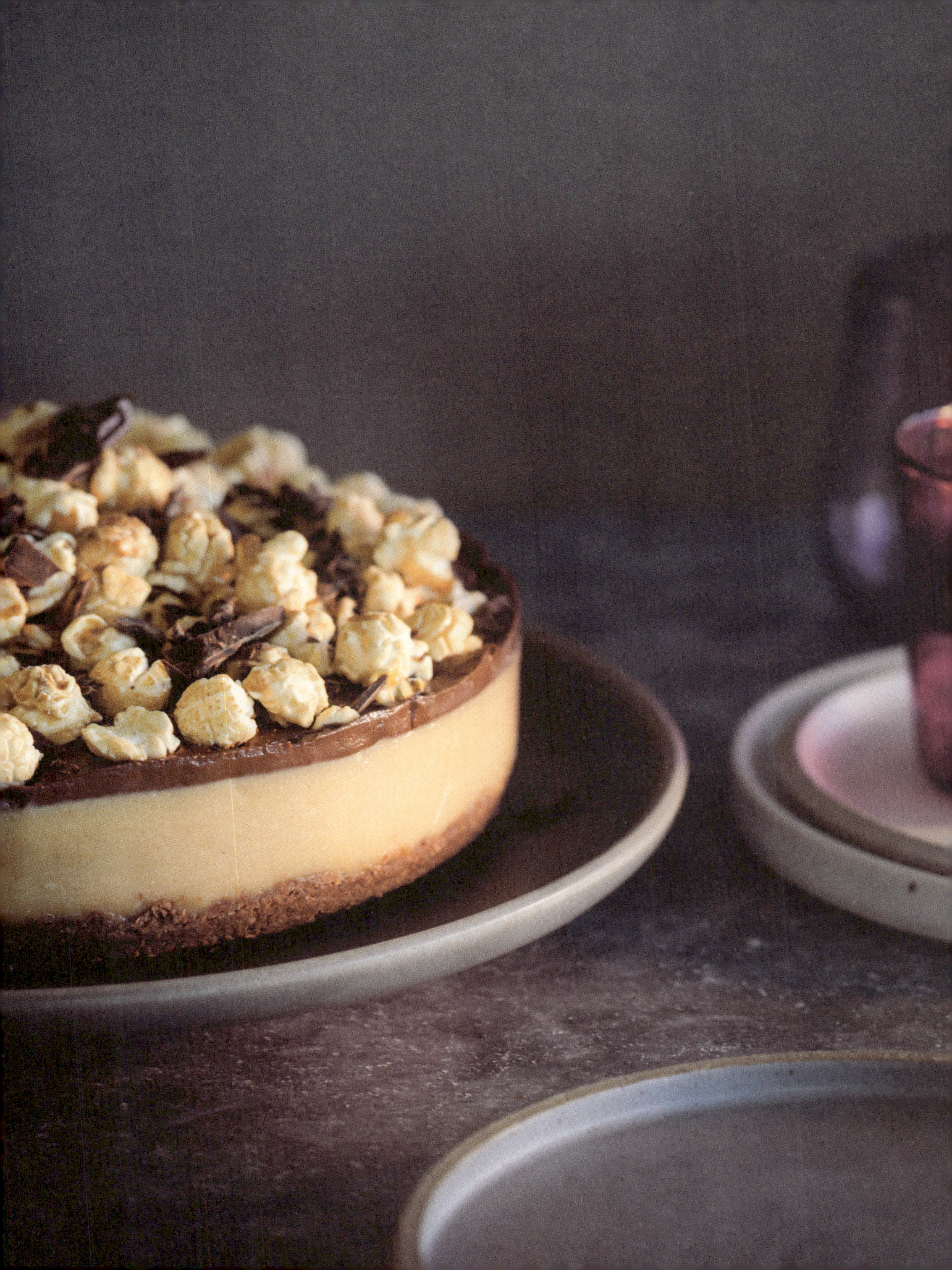

SPICED PEAR VELVET CAKE

PREP 20 minutes **COOK** 1 hour **SERVES** 12

This recipe is inspired by one from Jordan Rondel, aka The Caker. Jordan and I did our first book tour together way back in the *At My Table* days. She's so cool, so beautiful — and a very clever baker. This recipe proves it . . . it's vegan and gluten-free, yet you'd never know it. It's called a velvet cake because the baking soda and vinegar react to give the cake a gorgeous, pillow-soft, velvety texture. It's actually quite a grown-up cake, I think. Humming with warming cinnamon and spice and topped with juicy pears, serve it with a dollop of coconut yoghurt on the side and a cup of coffee, and you'll be winning.

CAKE
- 2 cups gluten-free flour mix (without raising agent)
- 1½ cups ground almonds
- 1 cup soft brown sugar (or coconut sugar)
- 1 tbsp ground ginger
- 1 tbsp ground cinnamon
- 1 tsp mixed spice
- ½ tsp salt
- 2 cups rice or soy milk
- ⅔ cup grapeseed or sunflower oil
- 2 tsp vanilla extract
- 2 tsp baking soda
- 2 tsp apple cider vinegar
- 2 small ripe pears, peeled, cored and cut into slices

TOPPING
- 2 tbsp icing sugar
- ½ tsp ground cinnamon
- fresh edible flowers (optional)

TO SERVE
- coconut yoghurt
- warmed jam (blackberry or raspberry is good)

IT'S GLUTEN-FREE
But you can use regular flour if you like.

Preheat the oven to 180°C regular bake and line a 23–24cm cake tin with baking paper over the base and up the sides (or use two tins for a layer cake with jam — see tips).

In a large mixing bowl (or in the bowl of an electric mixer), combine the flour, ground almonds, sugar, spices and salt. Make a well in the centre and add the milk, oil and vanilla, and stir with a whisk to combine evenly.

In a very small bowl, combine the baking soda and vinegar (it will froth up immediately) and straight away add this to the cake mixture. Stir again until combined.

Scrape the batter into the tin and arrange the pear slices in a ring around the edge of the cake, putting a couple of pieces in the middle. Bake for 45 minutes, or until springy to the touch, golden in colour and a skewer poked in comes out clean. Allow the cake to cool for 10 minutes before removing from the tin and leaving to cool on a wire rack.

Combine the icing sugar and cinnamon in a small bowl. Using a mesh sieve, dust the mix over the cooled cake. Decorate with fresh flowers if using.

Serve with a dollop of coconut yoghurt and a spoonful of warmed jam. Store in an airtight container in a cool, dry place for up to 2 days.

TIPS
+ To make a very pretty two-layer cake, use 2 x 21.5cm cake tins and only cook the cakes for 30–35 minutes. Layer them up with jam and coconut yoghurt in the middle.
+ You can use ½ buckwheat and ½ gluten-free flour mix (or replace the gluten-free flour mix entirely with buckwheat flour) for a lovely nutty, earthy flavour more true to Jordan's original recipe.
+ The pears are also interchangeable for any fruit you prefer (apples work well).

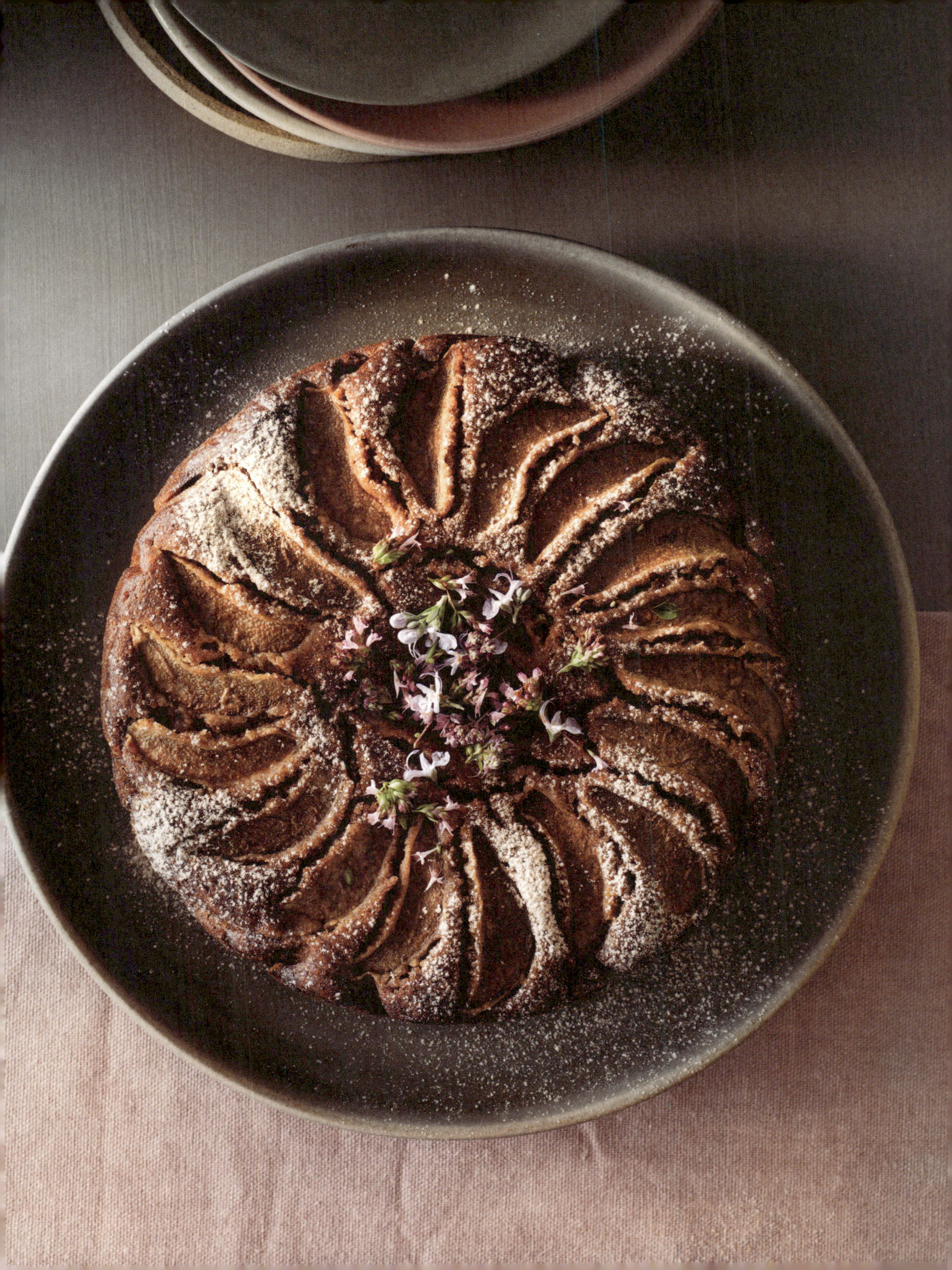

CHOCOLATE BANOFFEE PIE

PREP 1 hour 15 minutes, plus 5+ hours to chill **SERVES** 8

This is one hell of a dessert — all layered up with rich chocolate on the base, followed by date caramel, fudgy bananas and cool creamy custard, and festooned liberally with crumbled-up banana chips, chocolate and walnuts. Definitely next level. Okaaaay, I know I've complained about dates disguised as caramel before, but that was for caramel slice, which is different. Velvety butterscotch for the drizzle and dates for the base layer really are the perfect solution — sweet and gooey!.

Line the base and sides of a 24cm cake tin with baking paper.

Put the dates for the base and the caramel in a heatproof bowl and cover with just-boiled water. After 5 minutes, take 6 out for the base, leaving the others in for another 5–10 minutes. Drain, keeping some liquid for later.

To make the base, put all the ingredients (including the 6 softened dates) in a food processor and blitz until you have a fine crumb, scraping down the sides if need be. Press into the base of the tin, and then go up the sides about 4–5cm. Be quite firm. Refrigerate.

To make the chocolate layer, microwave the chocolate in a glass or ceramic bowl in the microwave on high for 1 minute. Stir well, then add the coconut cream and microwave for another 30 seconds. Stir until smooth, then scrape onto the base and smooth out in an even layer, making sure it goes about halfway up the sides, too. This will seal the base and stop it going soggy. Refrigerate until firm.

To make the caramel layer, put the drained dates in a food processor with 3 tablespoons of the soaking water and the cashew butter (if using), vanilla and salt. Whizz until you have a paste. Spread evenly on top of the set chocolate and refrigerate.

To make the custard cream, place all the ingredients in a medium-sized saucepan, whisk to combine and cook over a medium heat, stirring constantly with a whisk, for about 5 minutes until nice and thick. Scrape into a bowl, press a round of baking paper on the top so that a skin doesn't form, and refrigerate until it turns into a firm, jelly-like mass. When set, remove the baking paper and beat or whisk until it has a smooth, soft pudding consistency.

Slice the bananas, coat in a little lemon juice and arrange on top of the caramel layer in an even layer.

Scrape the creamy custard mixture on top of the bananas and smooth out a little, leaving some whippy bits. Refrigerate for a few hours to set, or overnight.

Just before serving, sprinkle generously with the chopped walnuts, chocolate and banana chips. If you like, drizzle with butterscotch too.

Keep any leftovers in the fridge. It's best eaten within a day or so.

BASE
6 pitted dates
1¼ cups ground almonds
1 cup chopped walnuts
1 cup desiccated coconut
¼ cup coconut oil
1 tsp vanilla extract
pinch salt

CHOCOLATE LAYER
125g dark chocolate, chopped (50% cocoa solids or higher is often dairy-free)
⅓ cup coconut cream

CARAMEL LAYER
1 cup pitted dates
2 tsp vanilla extract
1 tbsp cashew butter (optional)
pinch salt

CUSTARD CREAM
500ml rice or soy milk
¼ cup coconut oil, melted
¼ cup custard powder
⅓ cup caster sugar
2 tsp vanilla bean paste (or use extract)
pinch salt

BANANA LAYER
2–3 ripe bananas
squeeze of lemon juice

TOPPINGS
¾ cup chopped walnuts
½ cup chopped dark chocolate
½ cup banana chips (optional)
drizzle of my Butterscotch (see page 142; optional)

IT'S GLUTEN-FREE

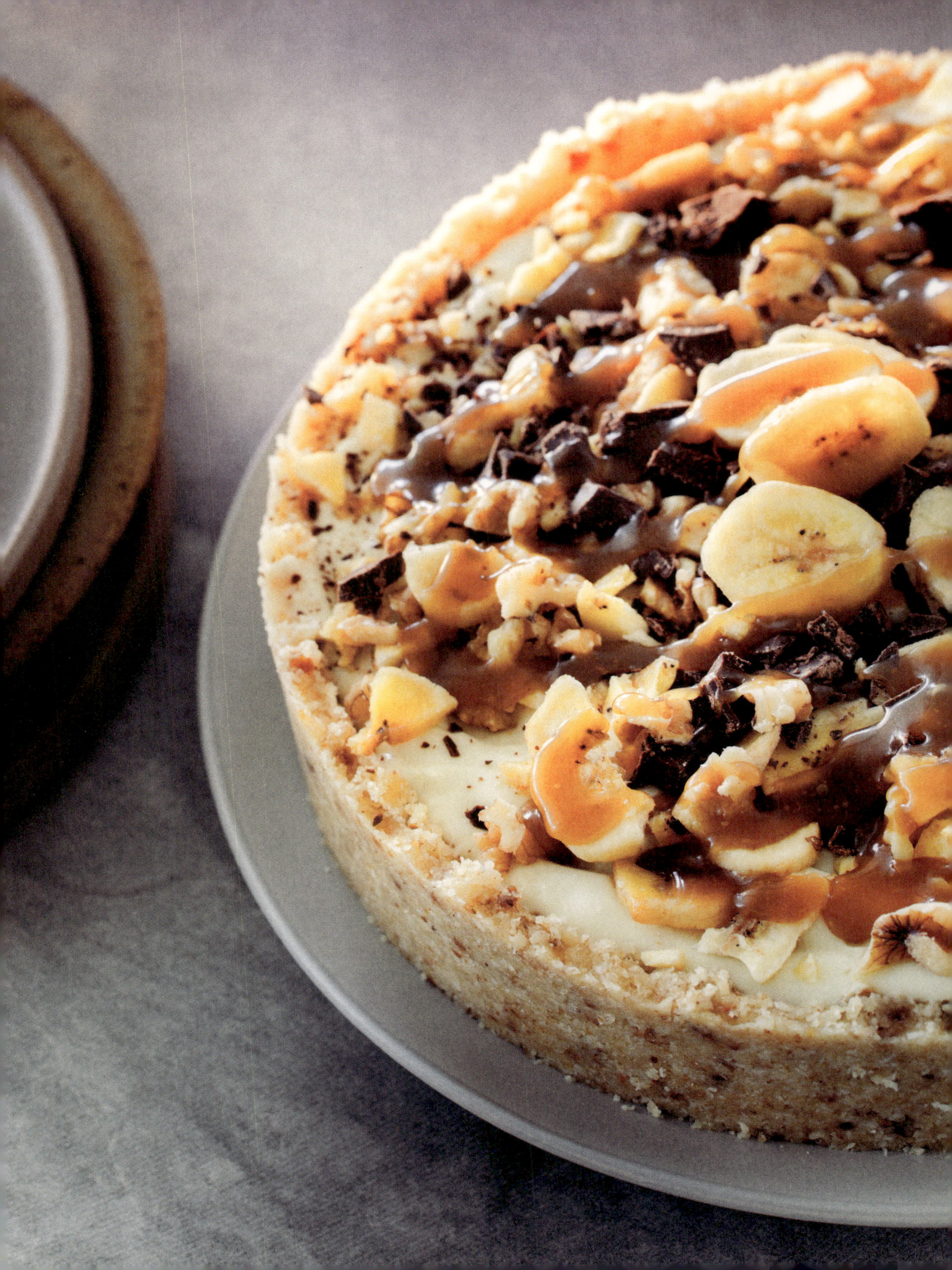

CHOCOLATE CHEESECAKE

BASE
5 pitted dates
1 cup raw cashews
1 cup ground almonds
1 cup desiccated coconut
¼ cup coconut oil, softened
1 tsp vanilla extract or paste
½ tsp salt

FILLING
400g dairy-free dark chocolate, chopped (I used 50% cocoa solids)
1¼ cups coconut yoghurt
1 x 400ml can full-fat coconut cream
1 large ripe avocado (optional)
¼ cup coconut oil
1 tsp vanilla extract
¼ tsp salt
⅓ cup canned chickpea liquid (aquafaba)
good-quality dark cocoa, for dusting

IT'S GLUTEN-FREE

TIPS

+ You can dress the cheesecake with fresh berries if they're in season, or use chocolate shavings or shards for some texture.
+ If you can't find coconut yoghurt at your local supermarket, use another can of coconut cream (look for the one with the highest fat content) and 2 tbsp lemon juice. If you have access to dairy-free cream cheese, you can use this instead of the coconut yoghurt.

PREP 40 minutes, plus 4 hours to set   **SERVES** 12

I'd like to dedicate this recipe to stylist Victoria Bell, seeing that during the photoshoot she became mildly obsessed with this dessert (in the manner of Sméagol and the One Ring). I created this recipe years ago, wanting to give people with intolerances to dairy, eggs and gluten the chance to eat a big, rich, delicious, chocolatey, celebrationy cheesecake without the pain. So it was one of my first tentative forays into plant-based cooking way before it was such a big part of my life. This has been such a popular recipe; it's always a hit on the Christmas table! Use the avocado if they're in season, cheap and perfectly ripe — otherwise you can leave it out.

Line the base and sides of a 23cm round springform tin with baking paper.

Soak the dates in hot water for 10 minutes, then drain.

Place the dates in a food processor along with the other base ingredients and whizz to a sticky crumb. (I find that tipping the processor up on its side a little so it's on an angle helps it all mix up better and not stick to the sides.)

Scrape the mixture into the tin. With wet hands, firmly press it into the base of the tin in an even layer. Refrigerate while you make the filling.

Place the chopped chocolate in a heatproof bowl sitting over a saucepan with a little simmering water in the bottom (don't let the bowl touch the water). Leave until just melted, stirring every now and then. (Or, you can microwave it in a glass or ceramic bowl — on high for 1 minute, then stir, then keep heating in 30-second bursts followed by stirring until it's nice and smooth.) Let the bowl sit on the benchtop for 15 minutes until it's cooled a bit.

Place the coconut yoghurt, coconut cream, avocado flesh (if using), coconut oil, vanilla and salt in a food processor and whizz until smooth, scraping down the sides as necessary. Transfer to a large mixing bowl.

One-third at a time, stir the chocolate mixture into the coconut cream mixture with a whisk.

Lastly, pour the aquafaba into a clean medium-sized bowl. Beat with an electric beater or whisk until firm peaks form. Stir one-quarter of the foamy aquafaba through the chocolate mixture to aerate and loosen it. Add the remaining aquafaba and fold gently with a spatula until evenly incorporated.

Scrape the mixture out on top of the base, smooth out, then cover and refrigerate for at least 4 hours until set. You could also freeze it at this point, well wrapped, for up to 2 months.

Just before serving, undo the spring on the tin and gently move the cheesecake to a serving plate. Remove the paper and dust with cocoa.

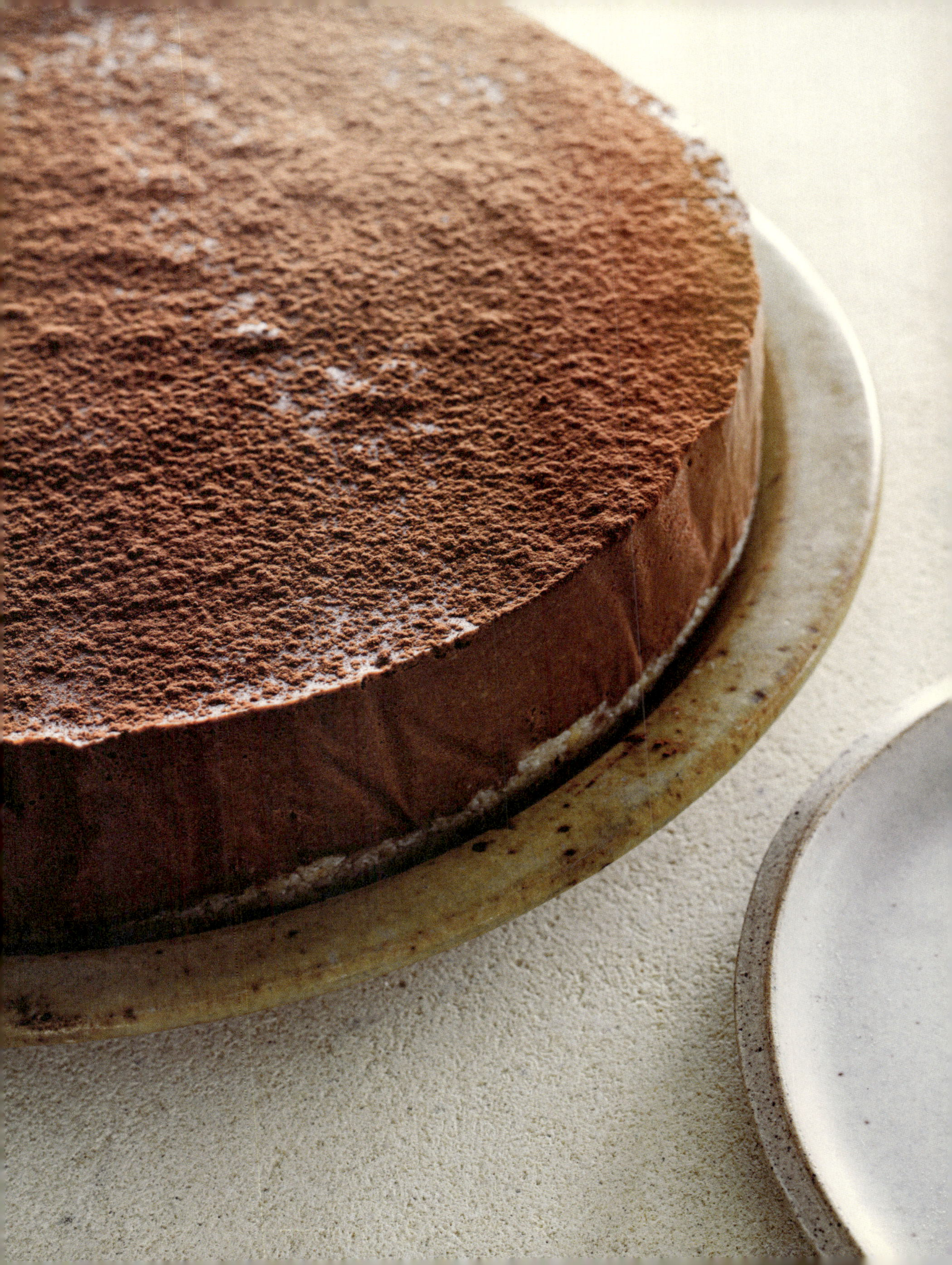

JELLYTIP CHEESECAKE

RASPBERRY JELLY TOPPING

500g bag frozen raspberries
½ cup caster sugar
2 tsp lemon juice
2 tsp raspberry essence
4 tbsp chia seeds

BASE

150g plant-based biscuits (I used Nice biscuits)
⅓ cup desiccated coconut
2 tbsp cocoa powder
3 tbsp coconut oil
3 tbsp maple syrup
1 tsp vanilla extract
¼ tsp salt

CREAMY VANILLA FILLING

3 cups raw cashews
1 cup full-fat coconut cream
1¼ cups icing sugar
⅓ cup lemon juice
½ cup coconut oil, melted
2 tbsp vanilla bean paste (or use extract)
1 tsp salt
zest of 2 lemons

CHOC TOPPING

100g chopped dairy-free chocolate, plus extra for sprinkling
100ml coconut cream
1–2 punnets fresh raspberries (optional)

TO MAKE IT GLUTEN-FREE

Use a GF biscuit for the base.

TIP

+ If you don't have chia seeds, you can stir a slurry made from 3 tbsp cornflour mixed with 3 tbsp water through the cooked raspberry mixture to make it jammy and thick.

PREP 1 hour, plus 6+ hours soaking time and 7+ hours to freeze
SERVES 8–10

I can't even tell you how good this is. It was one of the first ideas that popped into my mind as a dessert for *Supergood*, but it's taken me many iterations and trials to get it right. I was determined to deliver a perfect blend of layers of creamy vanilla, tart raspberry jamminess and chocolate. It's a veritable feast for both the eyes and the taste buds, and I'll wager it'll go down an absolute treat on any special occasion that warrants such a magnificent centrepiece for the table.

Place the cashews for the filling in a large heatproof bowl and cover with just-boiled water. Leave for 6 hours to soak (overnight is even better). Drain and rinse.

To make the raspberry jelly topping, put the berries, sugar, lemon juice and essence in a saucepan with a good pinch of salt and simmer over a medium-low heat for about 10 minutes, until reduced a little. Remove from the heat and stir through the chia seeds. Set aside to cool completely.

Line the base and sides of a 21–23cm springform tin with baking paper.

Place the base ingredients in a food processor and whizz on high until you have a nice fine crumb (tilting the processor sometimes helps it blend better). Tip it out into the tin and flatten into an even layer.

To make the creamy vanilla filling, place the drained cashews in a blender (or you can use a food processor, but a blender is best) along with the remaining ingredients, except the lemon zest. Blend on high speed until the mixture is silky smooth. (In a food processor, depending on how powerful it is, this may take quite a while — more than 5 minutes even.) Scrape the sides a couple of times to avoid any lumps, and fold through the lemon zest. Scrape it out into the tin on top of the base, and smooth out.

Freeze for 1–2 hours until it's firmed up a bit, then spread the raspberry topping over the top. Cover again and return to the freezer for 4–5 hours, or overnight, to finish setting.

To make the choc topping, microwave the chocolate and coconut cream in a Pyrex or ceramic bowl for 1 minute. Stir until smooth. Leave to cool slightly, then pour over the frozen cheesecake and smooth out in an even layer. Cover and either freeze or refrigerate until ready to serve.

Defrost the cheesecake fully before serving (in the fridge is best). Top with fresh raspberries, if using. I like to sprinkle over some extra chopped chocolate as well, for added crunch. Keeps for a couple of days in the fridge once defrosted, or you can freeze the cheesecake (unadorned) for up to a month — just make sure it's tightly sealed so it doesn't taste like the freezer.

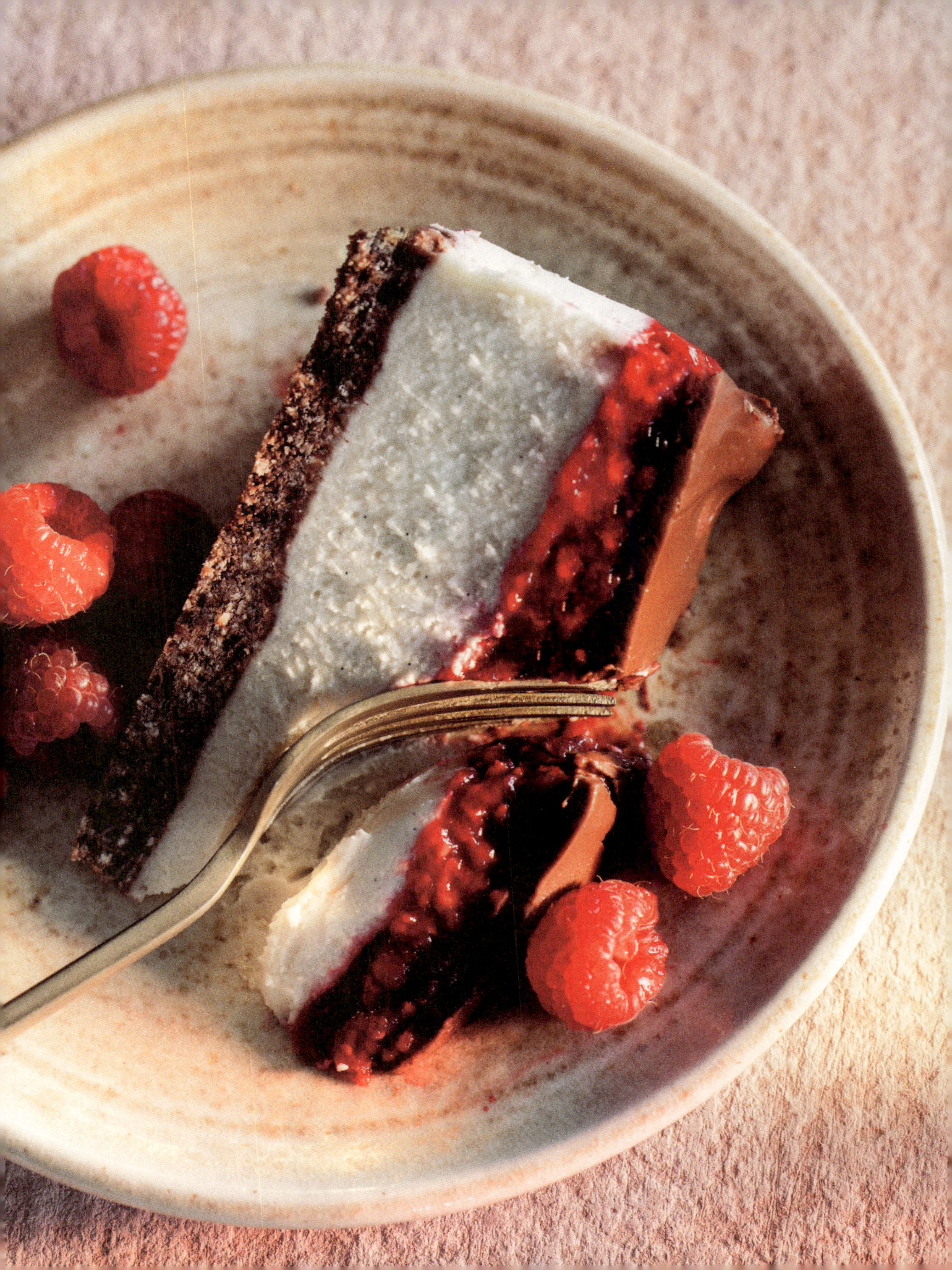

BUTTERSCOTCH

⅓ cup dairy-free spread
⅔ cup soft brown sugar
2 tbsp golden syrup
¼ tsp salt
⅓ cup coconut cream (I used Kara, the one in the tetrapack)
1 tsp vanilla extract

IT'S GLUTEN-FREE

PREP 15 minutes   **MAKES** 1 cup

There's something truly pleasurable about spooning butterscotch over a dessert and watching it cascade all over the place in rich, golden ribbons. Having a jar of this on hand can be quite cheering, to say the least. If you make a cake and you want to lush it up, drizzle some butterscotch on. Take your ice cream up a notch with a deluge of this heavenly, nostalgic nectar. You could even add some to your morning coffee — I promise I won't tell.

Melt the dairy-free spread in a medium-sized saucepan over a medium-low heat.

Add the sugar, syrup and salt and stir until combined. Let it start to bubble, then time it bubbling for 3 minutes, stirring frequently.

Pour in the coconut cream and stir until well combined (be careful, as it may spatter up).

Reduce the heat to low and let it bubble slowly for another 4 minutes.

Remove from the heat and stir in the vanilla. Pour into a jar or bowl and refrigerate until ready to use. It will keep in an airtight jar in the fridge for up to a week.

TIP

+ If your butterscotch is too firm when cold, heat it back up and add a teaspoon or two of water. If you think it's too runny, heat it on a very low heat for about 5 minutes to allow some of the liquid to evaporate.

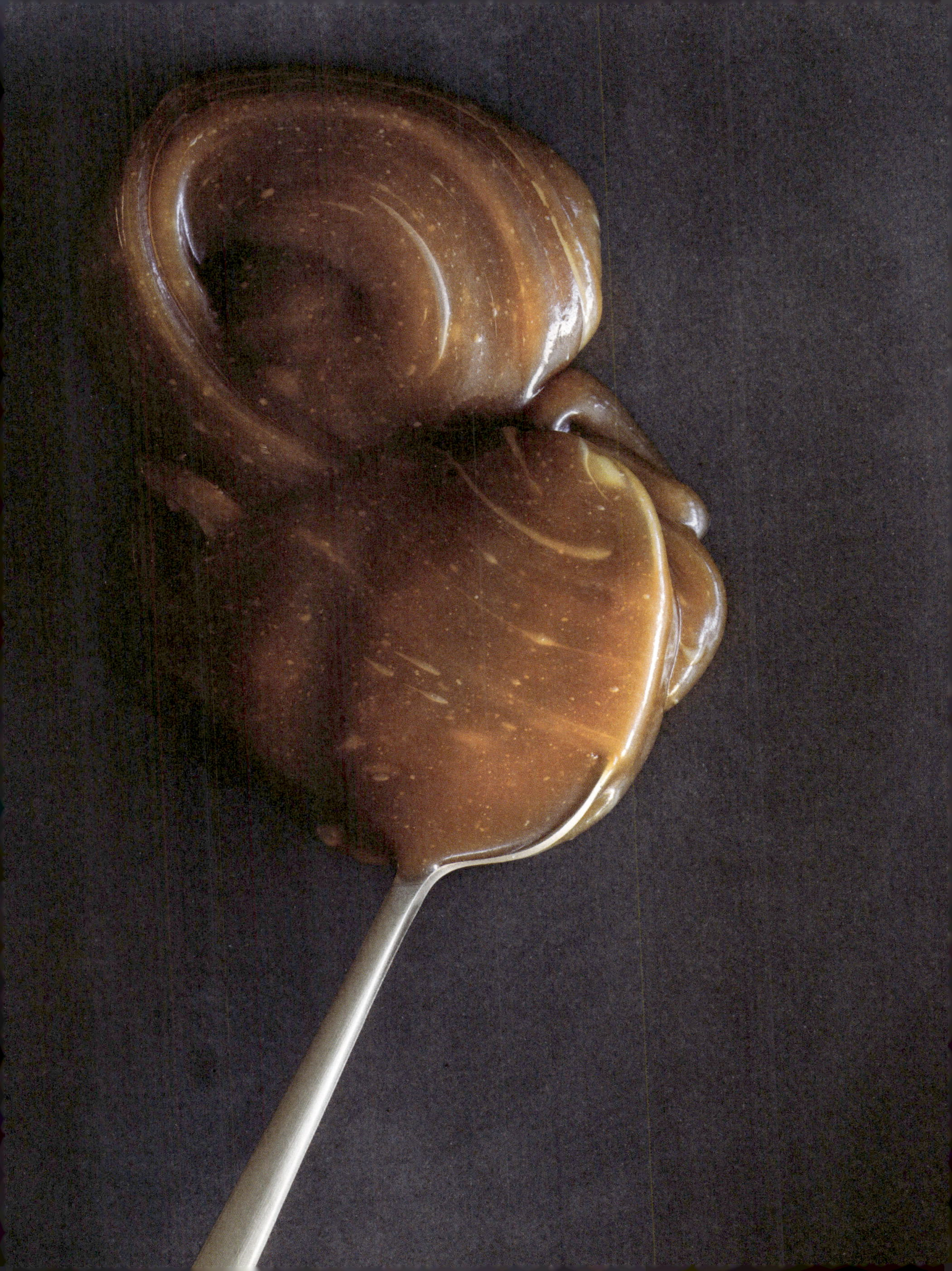

SWEET LITTLE MERINGUES

cornflour, for dusting
apple cider vinegar or white vinegar, for cleaning

MERINGUES
liquid from 1 x 400g can chickpeas (aquafaba), refrigerated
pinch salt
¼ tsp cream of tartar
1¼ cups caster sugar
1½ tbsp cornflour
1 tsp vanilla extract

TO SERVE
coconut yoghurt
fresh fruit
passionfruit pulp
icing sugar (optional)

IT'S GLUTEN-FREE

PREP 20 minutes   **COOK** 1 hour 20 minutes, plus cooling time
MAKES about 6 individual meringues

That clever wee chickpea liquid strikes again! These are actually halfway between a pavlova and a meringue (pavlovas are renowned for a marshmallowy centre, and meringues tend to be crispy and dry), though the end result will depend a little on your oven. But I have to say that using aquafaba is easier than eggs. You don't have to worry about how old they are, or try to separate them without busting the yolks (then figure out what to do with said yolks). If you want to try for one large meringue, draw a 20cm circle on the back of the baking paper and have the mixture quite high as it will spread a bit; and I cooked mine for 2 hours at 100°C. The inside won't be like a regular meringue but it will still look (and taste) cool.

Preheat the oven to 110°C regular bake and line a large oven tray (or two smaller ones) with baking paper. Dust lightly with cornflour, using a small amount in a sieve, to stop the little meringues sticking. Have the racks in the oven set ready for two trays if needed.

Start by preparing the mixing bowl you'll use (an electric stand mixer works best, but otherwise a metal, glass or ceramic bowl with an handheld electric beater is okay). Make sure it's clean and dry, then wipe it out with a paper towel and a little vinegar to make sure it's spick-and-span. Do the same to the whisk attachment or beater heads. If you have time (or the space), pop the bowl and attachment in the fridge or freezer for 10 minutes or so to cool down (this will help the meringue fluff up nicely, but it's not essential).

Carefully drain the chilled chickpea liquid (aquafaba) out of the can and into your mixing bowl along with the salt. Reserve the chickpeas for something else (see pages 54, 70 or 186).

Beat the aquafaba on medium-high speed until it's foamy, then add the cream of tartar. Keep beating until it's reached soft-peak stage. This is when the mixture forms peaks that barely hold their shape when you lift up the beater — the peaks will have their tops flopping over.

Now start adding the sugar, about 1 tablespoon at a time, beating for 15 seconds or so between each addition, until all the sugar is used up. This could take around 10 minutes. It might pay to scrape down the sides of the bowl with a spatula once or twice while you're adding the sugar.

Recipe continued on next page

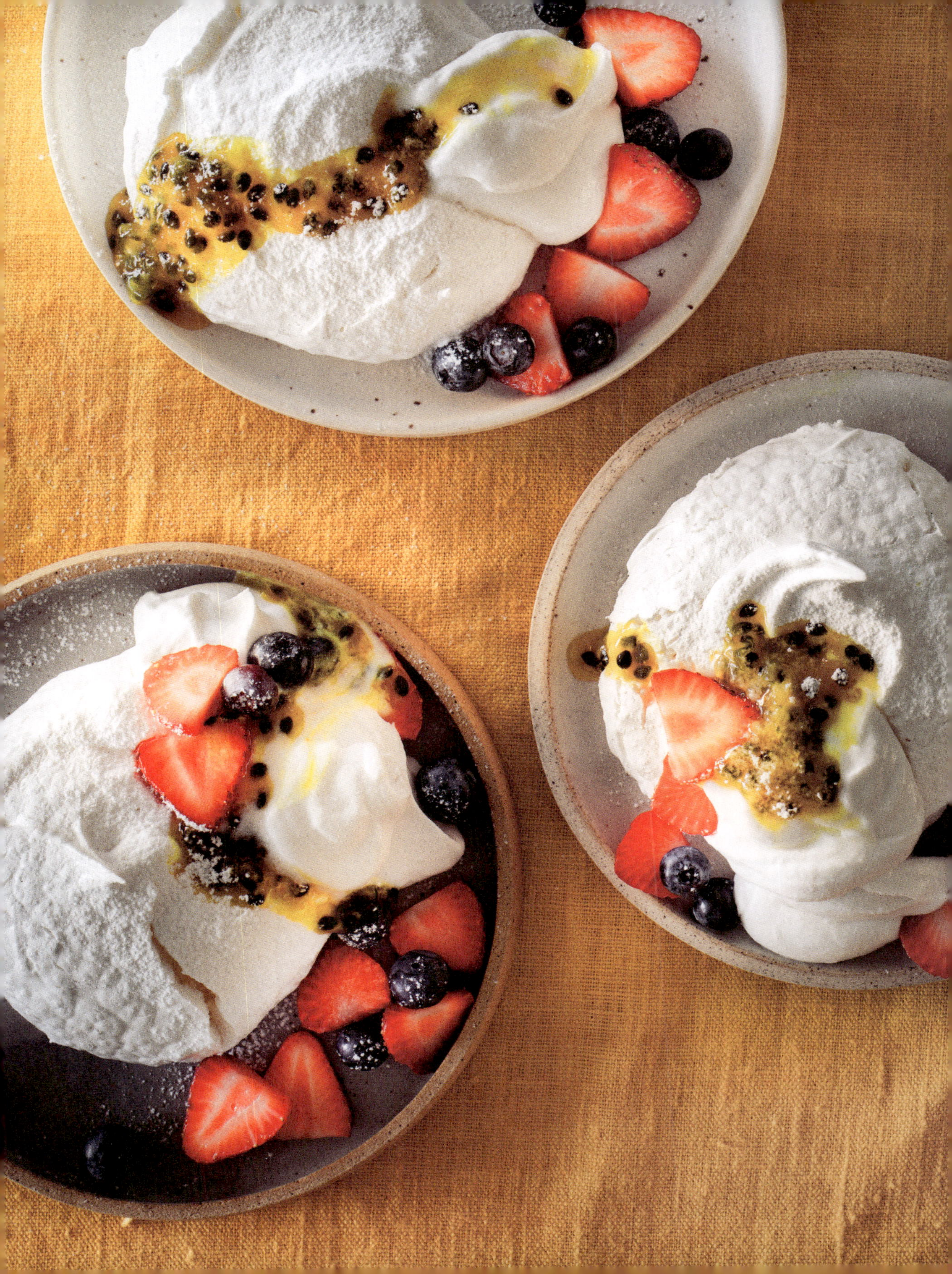

SWEET LITTLE MERINGUES continued

Once all the sugar is added, continue to beat until it has dissolved — this is important. Squidge some of the mixture between your fingers and you shouldn't feel any grit. By this time, the mixture should be thick, glossy and voluminous. It should really hold its shape. Sift in the cornflour and beat to just combine.

You can choose to pipe the meringues onto the baking paper or just freestyle it with a spoon. Make perky piles about 10cm in diameter — they will spread and puff up a little when they cook. Once I have a pile, I swirl it with the back of a dessertspoon in a circular motion to get it looking a bit like a meringue.

Bake for 1 hour and 20 minutes. When the time is up, turn the oven off without opening the door and leave the little meringues in there until they are completely cool. If you take them out early, they may be tacky and not crispy. As soon as they are out, they need to go into an airtight container so they won't go soft. They'll keep there for a couple of days.

Serve with coconut yoghurt, fresh fruit and passionfruit pulp. Dust with icing sugar, if you like.

TIPS

+ Make sure you use caster sugar not regular sugar, as the smaller granules will dissolve more quickly.
+ Cream of tartar helps stabilise the mixture and fluff it up more. It's worth finding at the supermarket, but if you don't have it use 1 tsp lemon juice instead.
+ Instead of coconut yoghurt, you can refrigerate coconut cream overnight and whip the solid cream instead (see page 225).

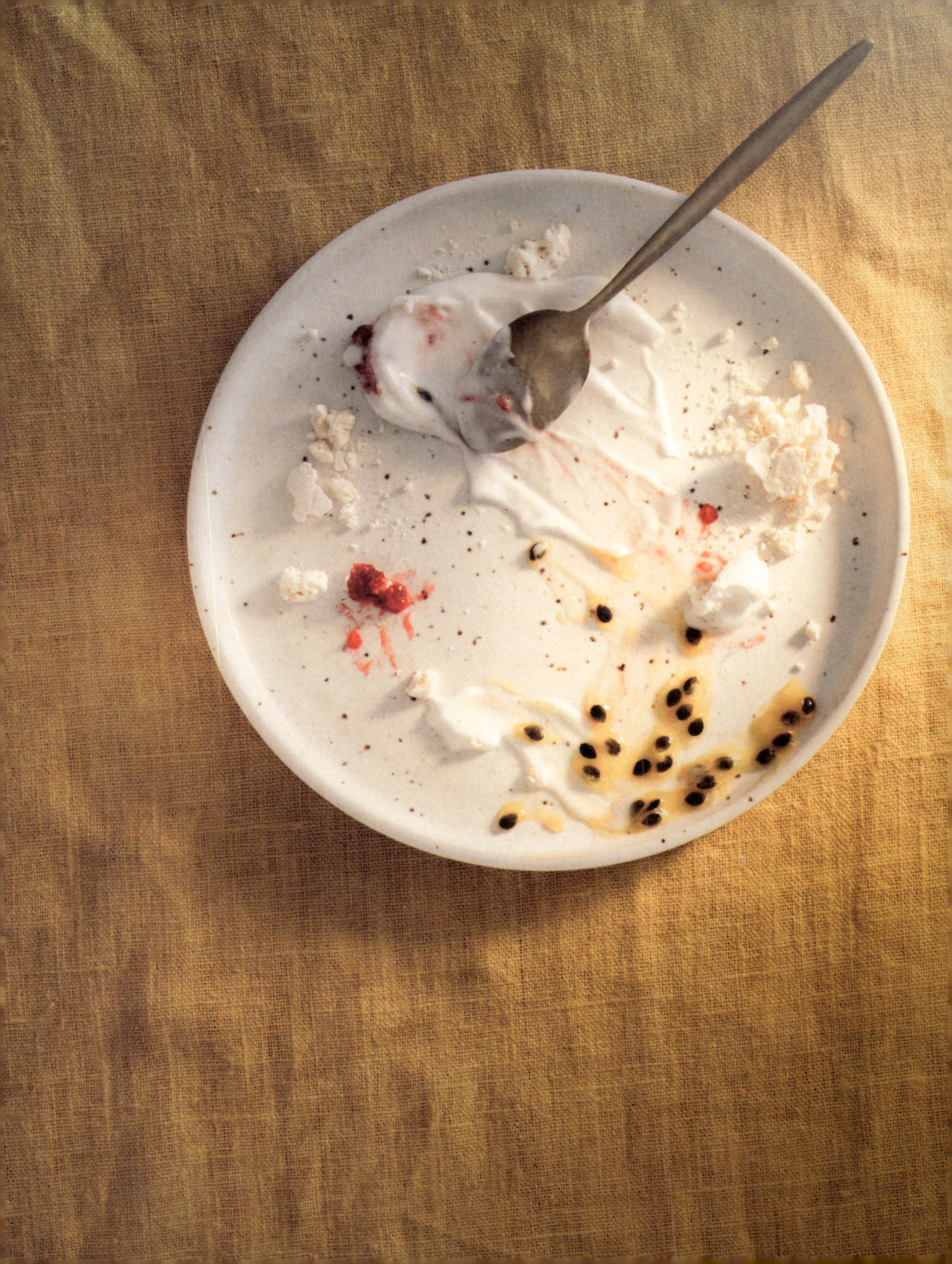

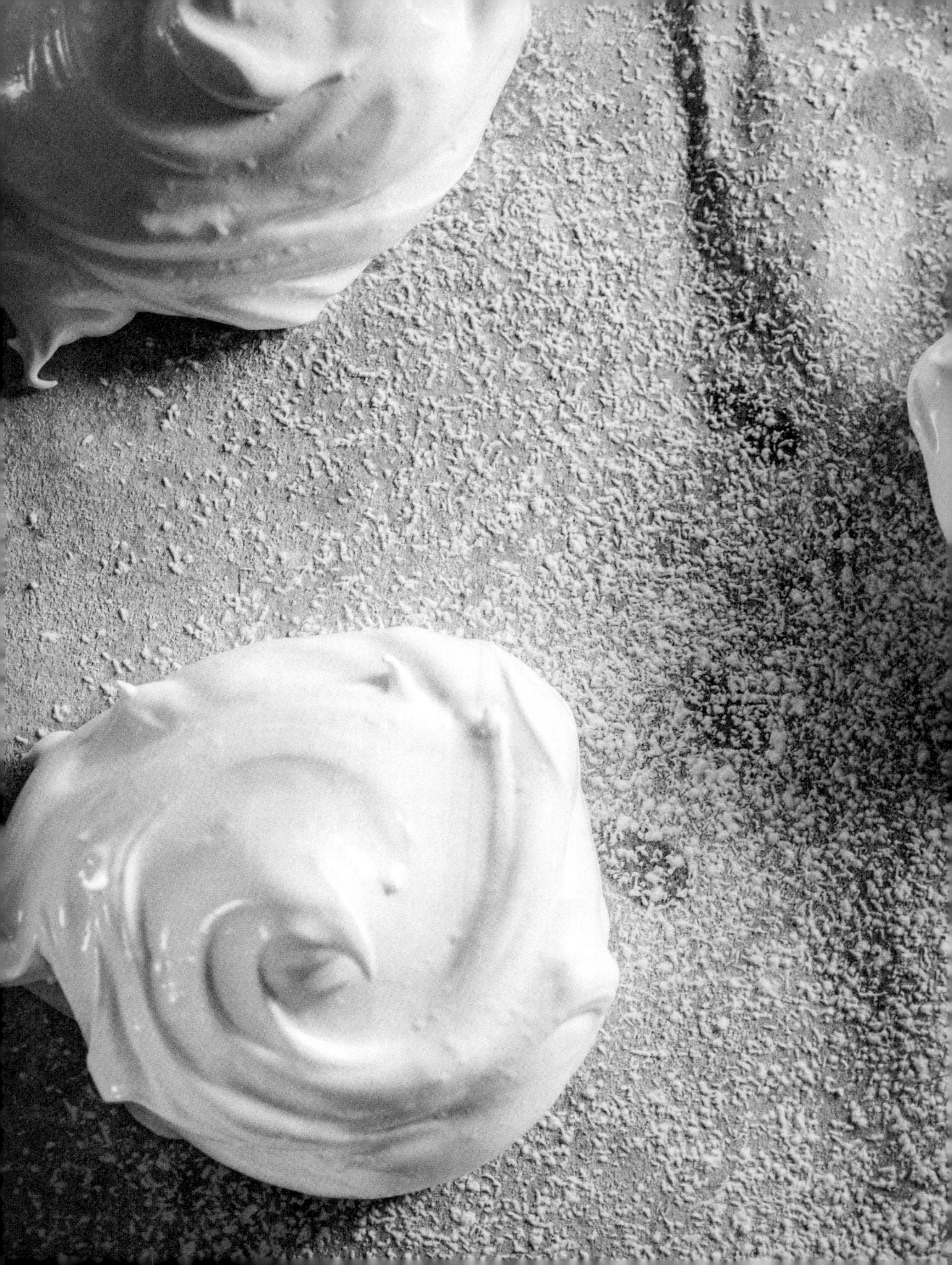

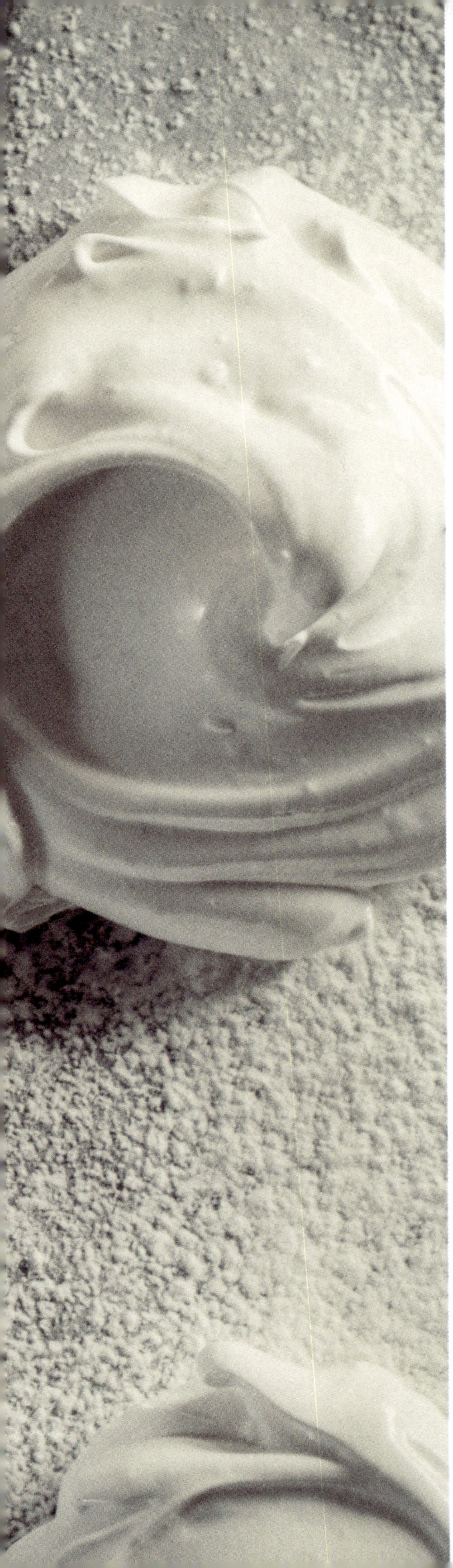
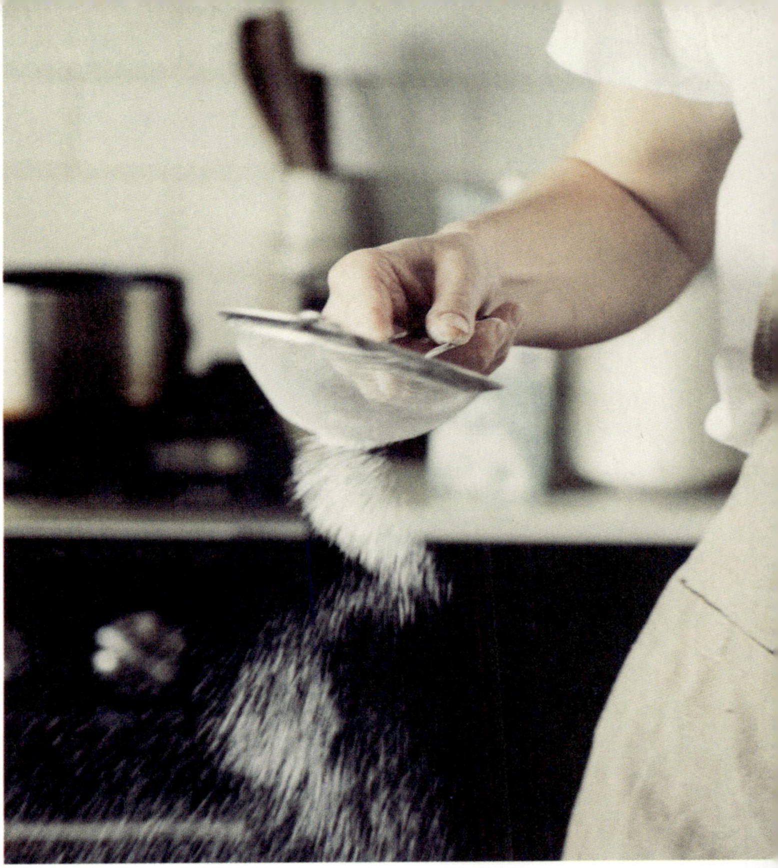
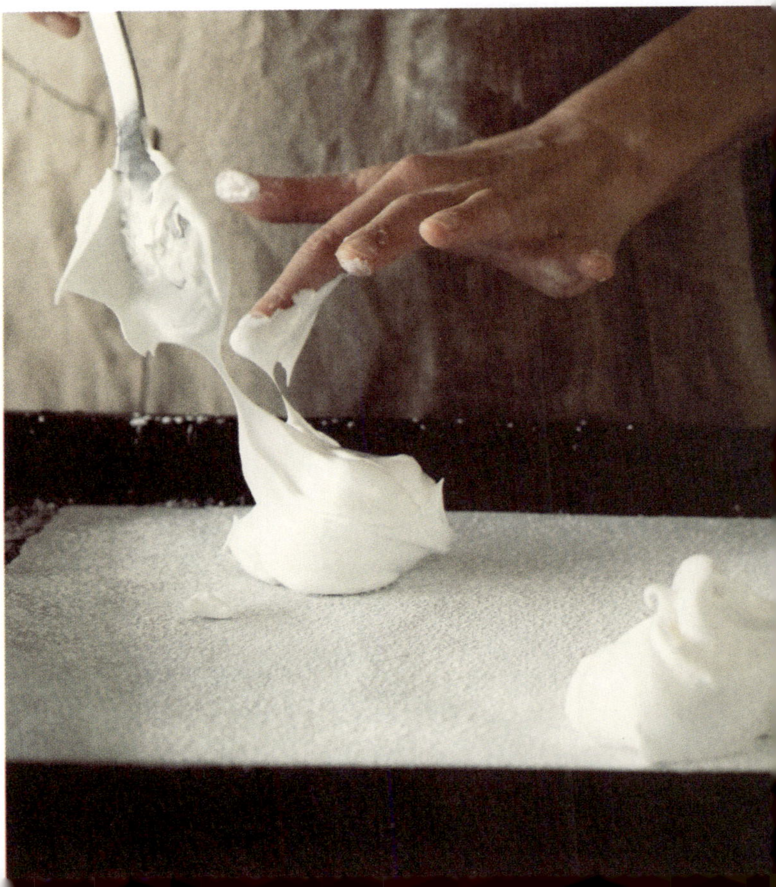

FREEDOM CHOCOLATE CHIP COOKIES

2 cups plain flour
1 tsp baking soda
¾ tsp salt
⅔ cup virgin coconut oil (at room temperature, semi-soft)
1¼ cups brown sugar
¼ cup full-fat coconut cream
¼ cup mashed ripe banana (or stewed apple, see tips)
3 tsp vanilla extract
1½ cups chunkily chopped dairy-free eating chocolate

TO MAKE IT GLUTEN-FREE
Use a GF flour blend without raising agent added. I add an extra ⅓ cup so they don't go too flat.

PREP 20 minutes, plus 30 minutes to chill   **COOK** 10 minutes
MAKES about 12–16 cookies

Welcome to the plantified version of my famous cookies! Now you can breathe easy when offering a plate of them to a crowd, knowing there's not a skerrick of egg or dairy in sight (you can make them gluten-free, too). A day after you make them, I reckon they actually taste like Cookie Time cookies. This recipe is dedicated to my friend Dave McGibbon, fellow *MasterChef* contestant, maker of giant burger cakes, pizza crammer and champion cookie-eater. Just a note — no two batches of cookies will ever look the same because there are just so many variables, so don't panic if yours seem flatter or more plump or quite different to the ones here.

Preheat the oven to 190°C regular bake (or 180°C fan-bake if you are using two trays at a time). Line one or two baking trays with baking paper. Have an oven tray in the middle of the oven (too low and the bottoms might brown).

Sift the flour, baking soda and salt into a mixing bowl and stir to combine.

Place the coconut oil, brown sugar and coconut cream in a medium-sized mixing bowl and beat (I use a handheld electric beater) until light and fluffy. Add the banana or apple, and vanilla, then beat again for 10–20 seconds. It's okay if it looks a little split.

Add the flour mixture to the creamed mixture and beat (or stir with vigour) until well combined. Stir through the chocolate.

If your dough feels firm enough, you can bake the cookies now, or cover and refrigerate for about 30 minutes. The more chilled the dough is, the less the cookies will spread; I actually like them to spread a bit.

Roll into balls a bit larger than golf-ball sized and arrange on the baking tray/s, at least 7cm apart as they will spread.

Bake in the oven for about 10 minutes — the cookies should be turning golden brown, but only around the edges, not the very middles.

Leave to cool on the tray for 10 minutes, then transfer to a cooling rack.

They will keep in an airtight container for a few days. Personally, I like them way better the next day, when they've gone soft and chewy.

TIPS

+ You can taste the banana for the first half-day after making the cookies, then it sort of disappears.
+ To make stewed apple, peel and slice a couple of apples, add slices to a small saucepan with a couple of tbsp of water over a medium heat. Cover and cook for 5–10 minutes until soft, then mash or purée.
+ You want the coconut oil the firmness of semi-firm butter — not liquid, not a hard rock.

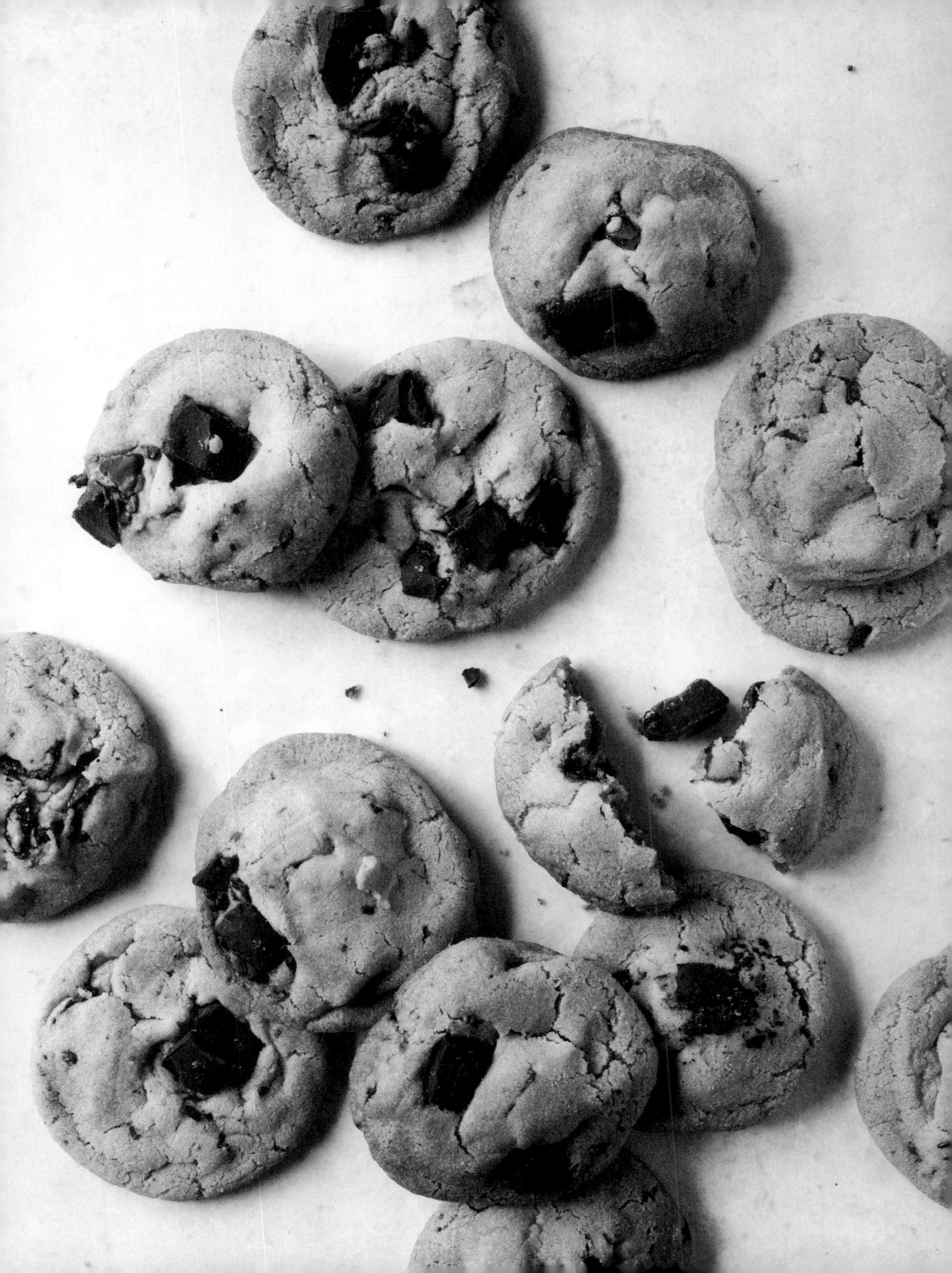

GINGER SLICE

PREP 25 minutes, plus about 1 hour to set   **COOK** 15 minutes
MAKES 24 pieces

Ain't nuttin' more classically Kiwi than the legendary ginger slice! I delight in the confused look on people's faces when I give it to them and then tell them it's plant-based. It's still sweet, buttery-tasting, luscious and super gingery. The only thing is you have to keep it in the fridge (especially in warm weather). The buckwheat is optional, but you should try it — it adds a really nice crunch and looks cool. You should be able to find it at your supermarket, just ask.

Preheat the oven to 180°C regular bake and line a 20cm slice tin with baking paper over the base and up the sides.

Place the oats, coconut, flour, buckwheat (if using) and baking powder in a large mixing bowl and stir to combine evenly.

Put the syrup, sugar, coconut oil, vanilla, ginger and salt in a medium-sized saucepan over a medium heat until just melted together. Add to the oat mixture and stir to combine.

Tip into the tin and squish it down into an even layer. Bake for 15 minutes, then allow to cool to room temperature.

To make the coconut butter for the icing, first place the desiccated coconut in a food processor. Process on high for about 10 minutes, scraping down the sides once or twice. It will be noisy, but worth it. The coconut will start out crumbly, then turn to a powder, then eventually turn into a slick, buttery paste that looks smooth when it's sitting there but will still be just a little grainy in the mouth — that's okay.

Scrape the coconut butter into a medium-sized saucepan and add the dairy-free spread, coconut oil, syrup, ginger and salt. Stir until melted, then stir in the icing sugar. Pour in the just-boiled water and stir briskly with a whisk. It should come together into a thick, spreadable icing.

Spread on the cooled base and smooth out with a spatula or the back of a warmed spoon. Sprinkle with buckwheat and crystallised ginger (if using). Refrigerate for an hour or so until firm, then slice into pieces.

Keeps for a couple of weeks in an airtight container in the fridge.

TIPS

+ You can use regular rolled oats, but the base will be a lot softer and not as chewy.
+ If you don't have a food processor and can't find coconut butter, you can make the icing by heating ¼ cup coconut oil, ¼ cup dairy-free spread and ¼ cup cashew or almond butter together with the golden syrup, ginger and salt amounts listed above. Once melted together, stir in the icing sugar — if it's a little stiff, add some just-boiled water 1 tablespoon at a time.
+ If you can find a jar of coconut butter at your local, you can use ½ cup of that instead of making your own for the icing.

BASE

1½ cups wholegrain rolled oats
¾ cup desiccated coconut
¾ cup plain flour
¼ cup buckwheat groats (optional but yum)
1 tsp baking powder
¼ cup golden syrup
¾ cup soft brown sugar
¼ cup coconut oil
1 tsp vanilla extract
2 tsp ground ginger
¼ tsp salt

ICING

2½ cups desiccated coconut
½ cup dairy-free spread
3 tbsp coconut oil
3 tbsp golden syrup
2 tbsp ground ginger
½ tsp salt
2¼ cups icing sugar
¼ cup just-boiled water

TO FINISH

2–3 tbsp buckwheat groats (optional)
few pieces finely sliced crystallised ginger (optional)

TO MAKE IT GLUTEN-FREE

Use a GF flour mix without raising agent added, and make sure your baking powder and oats are GF.

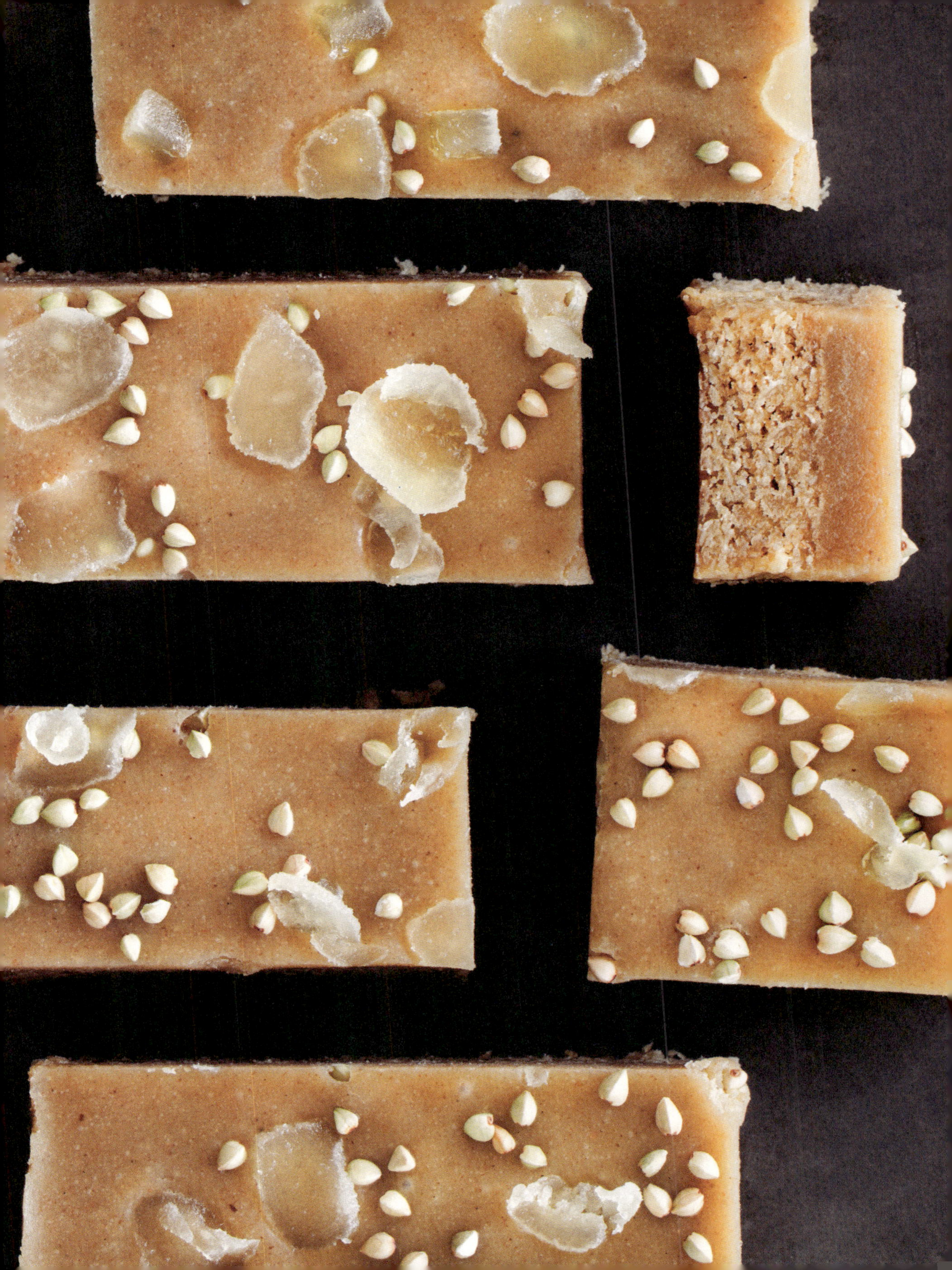

GOOEY CARAMEL SLICE

PREP 1 hour, plus 4+ hours to set   **MAKES** 24 slices

I spent a long time figuring this recipe out . . . I was determined to create a dairy-free caramel slice without having to resort to making the caramel layer out of soggy dates. I actually adore dates (they're much better for you than you think) — but dates masquerading as caramel is something I've yet to get my head around. So I created my own condensed coconut milk in place of the regular stuff. It takes a little more time, but works like a charm. If you can find canned condensed coconut milk at your supermarket, use 2 x 320g cans and add straight to the saucepan with the nut butter.

Line the base and sides of a 20cm slice tin with baking paper.

To make the caramel, place the coconut cream in a medium–large saucepan over a medium heat. Add the sugar and stir until the sugar has dissolved. Adjust the heat so that you end up with a low boil; medium–low should do it. Set a timer for 30 minutes. Stir every now and then.

While the coconut cream is condensing, make the biscuit base. Crumble the biscuits into a food processor and add the remaining base ingredients. Whizz it up until it's a really fine crumb and holds together when squished — it might need a good 20–30 seconds or so. Tip into the tin and squash it down firmly in an even layer. Refrigerate until needed.

After 30 minutes, check on the coconut cream. Depending on how big your saucepan is or how high the heat is, it may be done. When it's ready it will have reduced by half and will look thick, gloopy and be spattering a bit. Measure it — if you still have more than 2 cups of liquid, keep simmering. This is very important to ensure it sets properly. Turn off the heat.

In a small cup, mix the cornflour and water to a smooth slurry.

Add the cashew butter, dairy-free spread, brown sugar, syrup, cornflour slurry, vanilla and salt to the saucepan. Stir quite vigorously with a whisk for a minute until melted and combined. Bring to a low boil and stir for a minute until thickened nicely.

Set aside to cool for 20 minutes, then pour over the base and refrigerate again for at least 4 hours to set.

To make the topping, put the chopped chocolate and coconut cream in a heatproof bowl and microwave on high for 1 minute. Stir to combine, then if it needs more, keep heating in 30-second bursts and stirring until it's nice and smooth. Spread on top of the slice with a spatula, and refrigerate again for half an hour or so.

Slice into squares with a sharp knife. Store in an airtight container in the fridge — it'll go soft at room temperature.

CARAMEL

3 x 400ml cans full-fat (15–25%) coconut cream
1 cup sugar
2 tsp cornflour
2 tbsp water
⅓ cup cashew or almond butter (see tips)
⅓ cup dairy-free spread
¼ cup soft brown sugar
3 tbsp golden syrup
1 tsp vanilla extract
¼ tsp salt

BASE

300g plain plant-based biscuits (I used Nice biscuits)
⅓ cup dairy-free spread, melted
½ cup desiccated coconut
½ cup rolled oats
2 tbsp golden syrup
2 tbsp coconut oil, melted
1½ tsp vanilla extract
pinch salt

TOPPING

100g dark dairy-free chocolate, finely chopped
100ml coconut cream

TO MAKE IT GLUTEN-FREE

Use a plain-ish GF biscuit for the base. If you can't have oats, replace them with extra coconut.

TIPS

+ Don't use the tetrapack coconut cream for this one; it doesn't work as well as the canned variety.
+ If you have a nut allergy, try tahini instead of the nut butter.

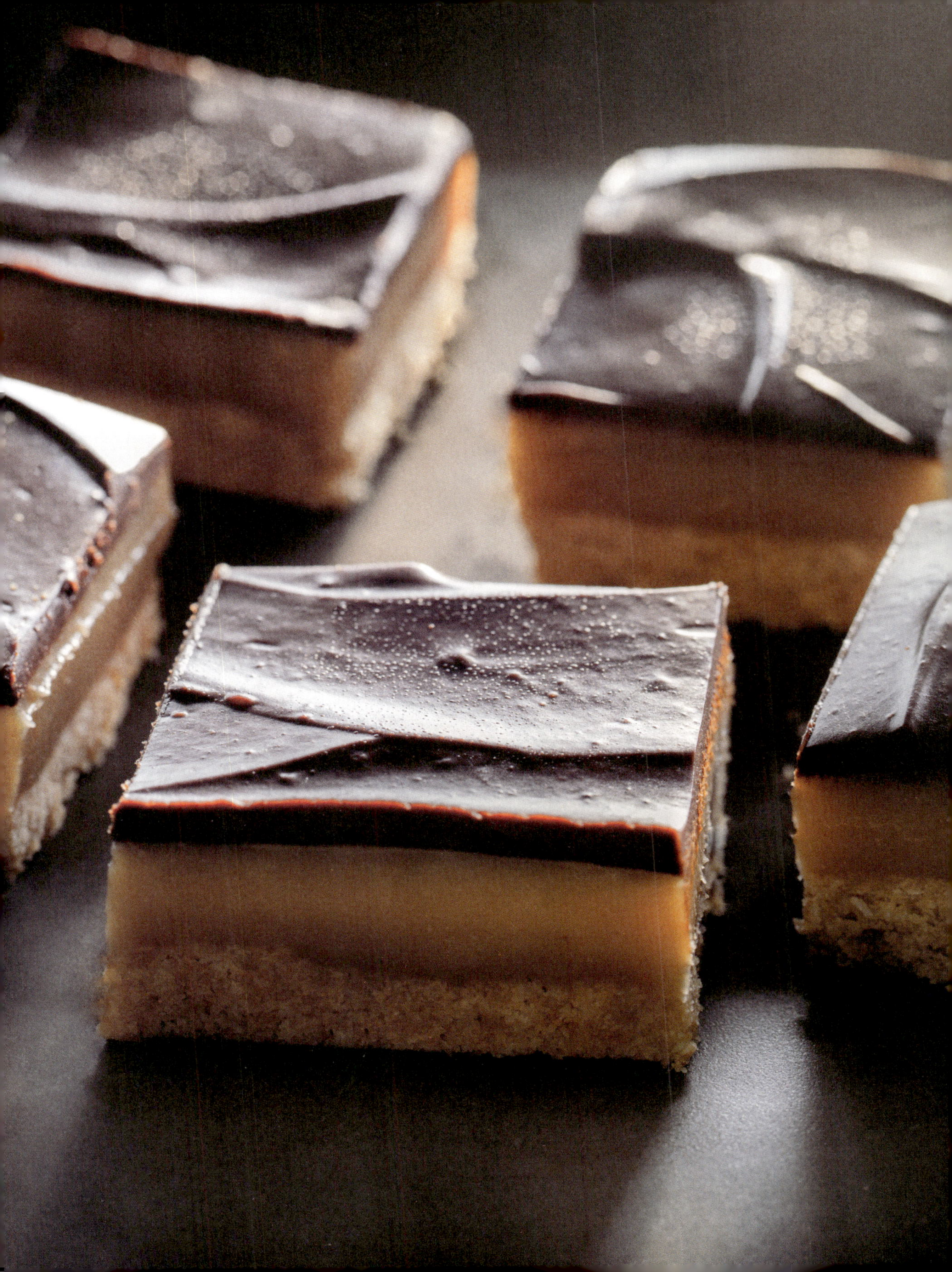

PEANUTTY RUSSIAN FUDGE

3 cups desiccated coconut
½ cup smooth peanut butter
⅓ cup coconut oil
⅓ cup honey or maple syrup
1 cup icing sugar
2 tsp vanilla extract
½ tsp salt
2 tbsp finely chopped roasted peanuts (optional)

IT'S GLUTEN-FREE

PREP 15 minutes, plus 2+ hours to set   **MAKES** 20–30 pieces

I love this stuff — it looks exactly like Russian fudge but has this epic peanutty taste explosion going on, which probably has something to do with the huge gob of peanut butter that's gone into it. Also, it's a lot easier to make without all that boiling of sugar. To get it nice and firm, we first make our own coconut butter in a food processor (a truly magic thing to watch, just you wait). Most processors should be able to handle this, but if yours doesn't you can buy coconut butter at some supermarkets, specialty food stores and online.

Line a large loaf tin with baking paper across the base and up the sides.

Put the desiccated coconut in a food processor. Process on high for about 10 minutes, scraping down the sides once or twice, until the coconut has turned into a thick, buttery liquid. It doesn't have to be silky smooth — it will still be a little grainy when it's done, but this is fine. How long it takes will depend on the quality of your food processor.

Add the peanut butter, coconut oil, honey or maple syrup, icing sugar, vanilla and salt to the food processor. Whizz until smooth (you might see some little grainy bits from the coconut but again that's okay — you don't notice them once it's set).

Scrape into the loaf tin, sprinkle with peanuts if you want, and refrigerate for 2 or more hours to set. Use the paper to lift the fudge out of the tin, then slice into pieces and keep in an airtight container in the fridge. It holds its shape pretty well out of the fridge, too.

TIP

+ Feel free to use chocolate chips in place of the chopped peanuts for the topping — or even finely chopped chocolate.

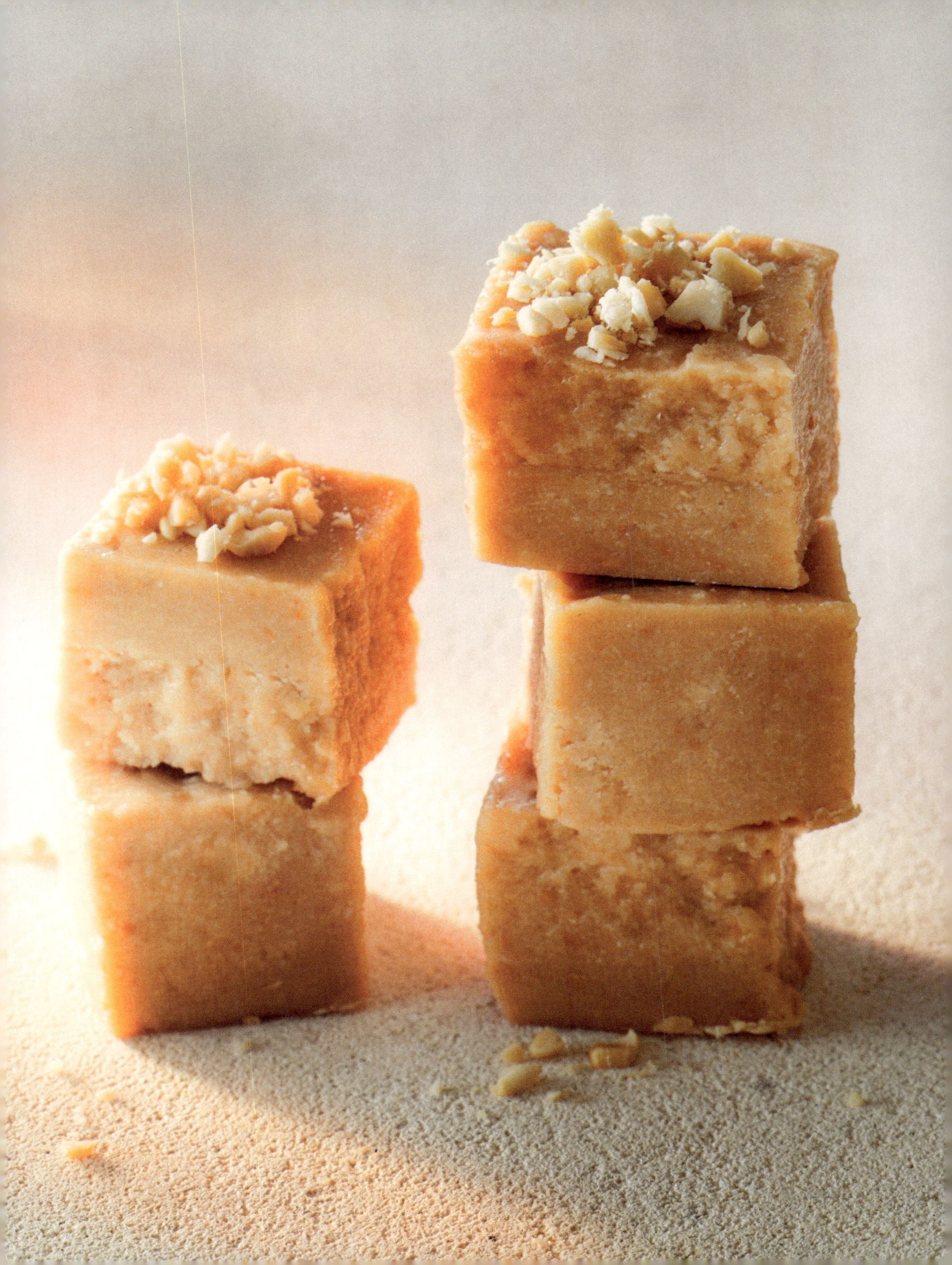

FUDGE CAKE BROWNIE

1 tbsp chia seeds
¼ cup cold water
1 cup plain flour
½ cup good-quality dark cocoa powder
1 tsp baking soda
¾ tsp salt
1 cup caster sugar
½ cup plant-based milk
⅓ cup coconut oil, melted
¼ cup almond or cashew butter, softened for 30 seconds in the microwave
2 tsp vanilla extract
200g dairy-free eating chocolate, chopped
icing sugar, for dusting

TO MAKE IT GLUTEN-FREE
Use a GF flour blend without raising agent added.

PREP 15 minutes **COOK** 25 minutes **MAKES** about 16 pieces

This brownie is decidedly decadent and rather rich! Two big ticks. Super quick and easy to whip up whenever you have a hankering for a slice of gooey, chocolatey debauchery. I like using virgin coconut oil here so that a nice subtle coconutty flavour comes through in place of butter.

Preheat the oven to 180°C regular bake. Line a 20cm x 20cm tin with baking paper over the base and up the sides.

Place the chia seeds in a little bowl with the water and give it a little stir. Set aside for 10 minutes, stirring again once or twice as it thickens.

Sift the flour, cocoa, baking soda and salt into a mixing bowl. Add the sugar and stir to combine.

Place the milk, melted coconut oil, almond or cashew butter and vanilla in another bowl and whisk briefly to combine.

Make a well in the centre of the flour mixture and add the wet mixture and the chia seeds. Stir until evenly combined. At this point it will probably look way too thick and gluggy, but fear not — this is okay. Stir through the chocolate pieces.

Scrape the mixture into the tin and smoosh out into an even layer (a wet spatula works nicely). Bake for about 20–25 minutes. The edges should have puffed up and the middle should look cooked, but the whole thing should still wobble just a tiny bit when you shake it gently.

Leave to cool in the tin for about 10 minutes, then use the paper to pull out onto a wire rack. When cool, dust with icing sugar and cut into squares.

Keeps in an airtight container for a few days — if you're lucky!

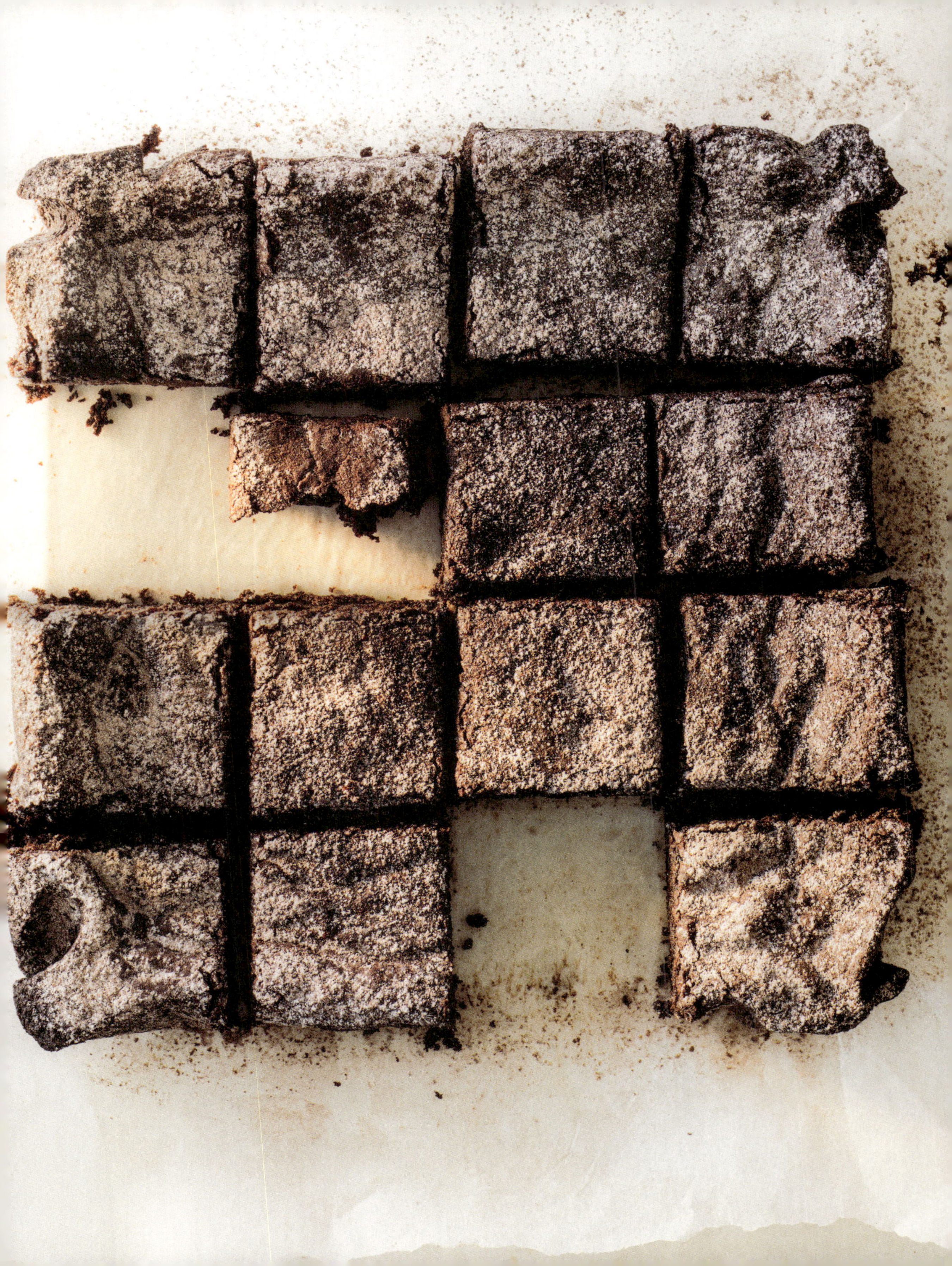

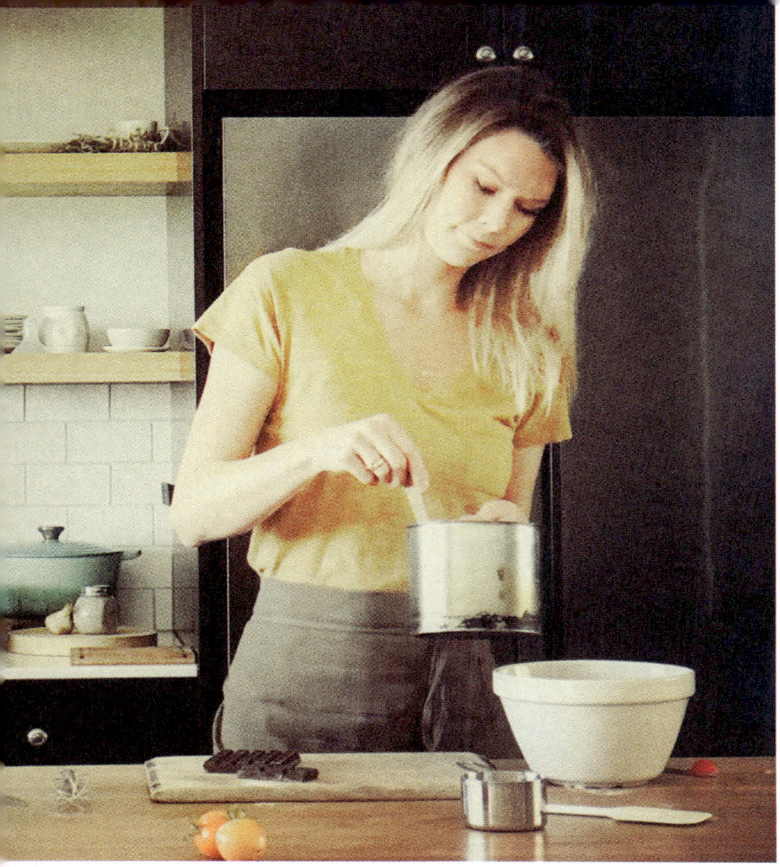
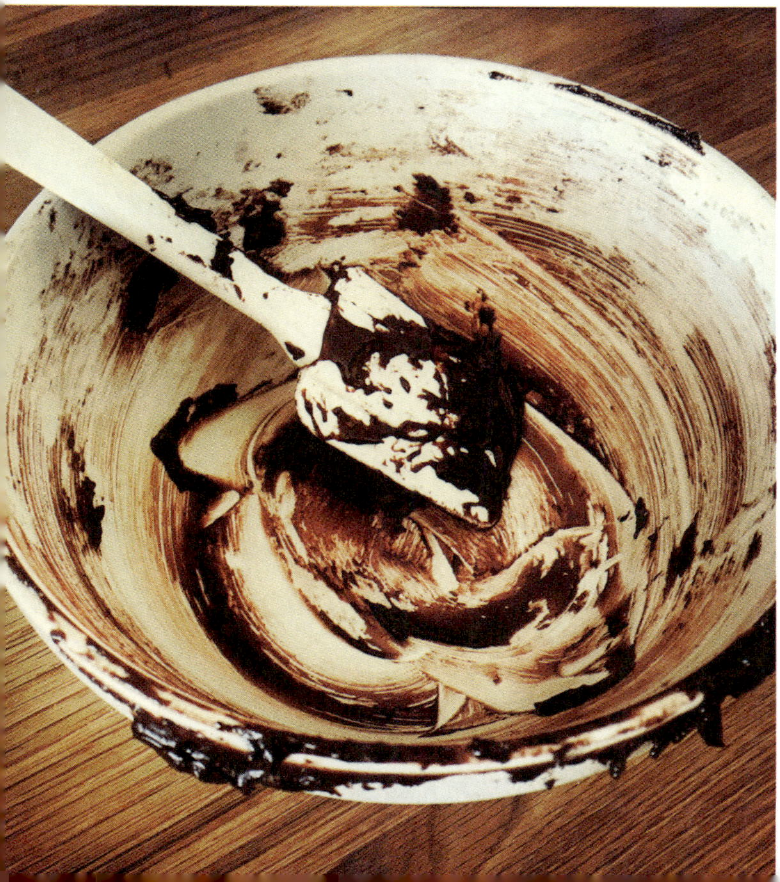
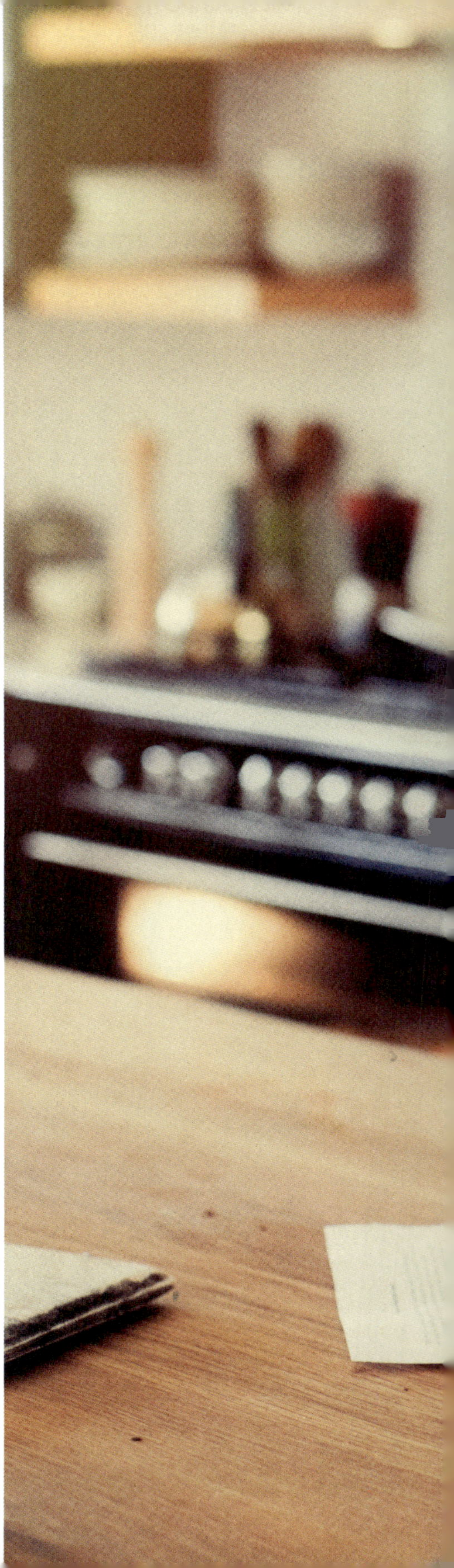

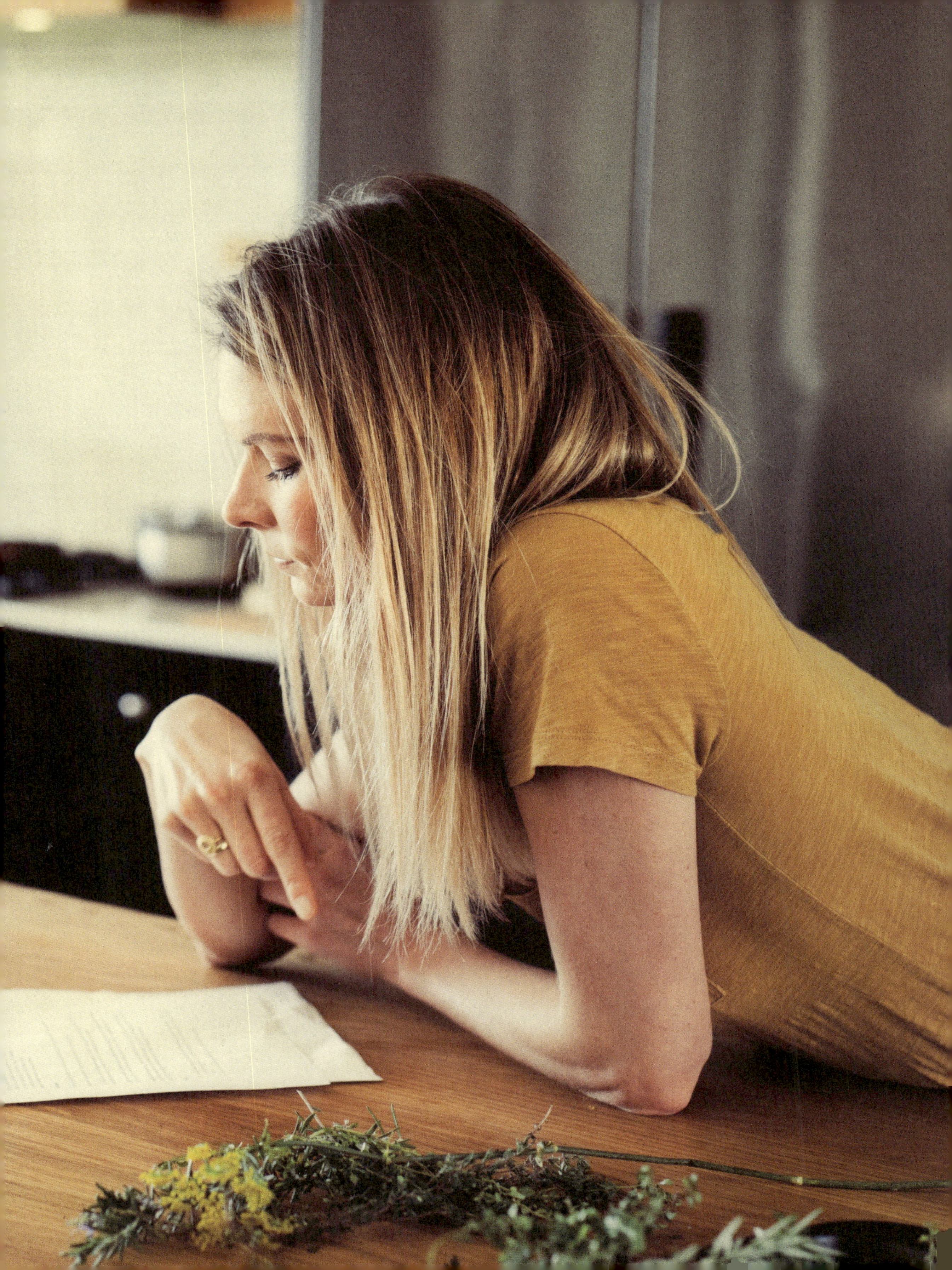

CHOCOLATE CUPCAKES & WHIPPED GANACHE ICING

1½ cups plain flour
1¼ cups caster sugar
½ cup good-quality dark cocoa
1¼ tsp baking soda
½ tsp salt
⅓ cup grapeseed or sunflower oil
1 tbsp balsamic or apple cider vinegar
3 tsp vanilla extract
1½ cups water (or cooled coffee)

WHIPPED GANACHE ICING

200g good-quality dark chocolate, chopped
½ cup coconut cream
125g dairy-free spread, at room temperature
3 cups icing sugar

chopped chocolate, to decorate

TO MAKE IT GLUTEN-FREE
Use a GF flour mix without raising agent added.

PREP 20 minutes **COOK** 30 minutes **MAKES** 12 cupcakes

Cupcakes always fill my heart with glee. When I was pregnant with Sky I was trying to stay off sugar and gluten as much as I could, but cupcakes were my Achilles heel — more than once I found myself smooshing one into my mouth as fast as I could, crumbs flying, while still trying to maintain a shred of decorum. These cupcakes are everything you want a cupcake to be: soft, moist and cakey, and piled high with an outrageously good icing made from real chocolate.

Preheat the oven to 170°C regular bake and line a 12-hole muffin tin with paper cases.

Sift the flour, sugar, cocoa, baking soda and salt into a large mixing bowl. Stir with a whisk to combine evenly.

Make a large well in the centre, and pour in the oil, vinegar, vanilla and water (or coffee). Starting in the middle, use the whisk to stir the mixture in a circular motion until it's combined to a smooth batter. Don't worry if there a few small lumps; these will disappear in the oven.

Pour the batter into the baking cups, filling to about 1cm from the top. Bake just below the centre of the oven for about 30 minutes. Cool in the tin for 10 minutes, then transfer to a wire rack to cool completely before you ice them.

To make the icing, place the chopped chocolate and coconut cream in a heatproof bowl sitting over a saucepan with a little simmering water in the bottom (don't let the bowl touch the water). Leave it until the chocolate melts, then stir gently to combine. Set the bowl on the bench to cool until lukewarm. If it's too warm, it will melt the dairy-free spread — don't let it go hard, though.

Place the dairy-free spread in a large bowl (or cake mixer). Sift in 2 cups of the icing sugar and beat until light and fluffy. Add a spoonful of the chocolate mixture and beat to combine. Add the remaining chocolate mixture and beat again to combine. Sift in the remaining icing sugar and continue to beat until smooth.

Refrigerate for an hour to set, as it will likely feel quite soft at this point. Then beat again to fluff it up just before icing.

Spoon the icing into a piping bag and ice the cooled cupcakes. (To make the swirl like I have, start in the middle and go outwards in a circle, applying quite a bit of pressure.) Finish off with some chopped chocolate.

Store in an airtight container in the refrigerator for a couple of days.

TIP

+ If you don't have a piping bag, you can use a strong resealable plastic bag with a corner snipped off, or even just spread the icing on with a knife.

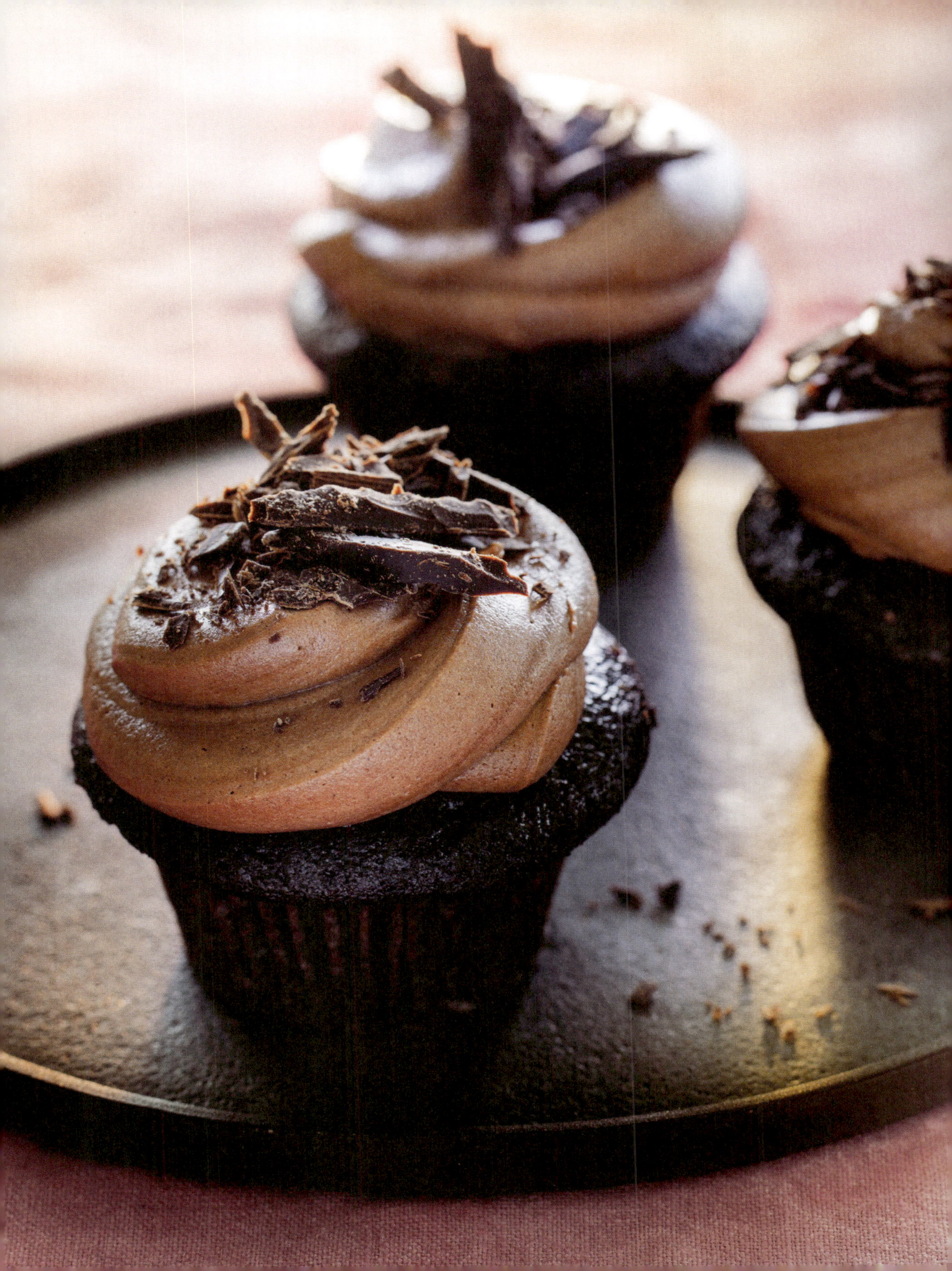

BRANBERRY MUFFINS

- 3 tbsp ground linseed (flax seed)
- 2½ cups plain flour
- 1 cup wheat bran flakes
- ¾ cup soft brown sugar
- 2½ tsp baking powder
- 2 tsp ground cinnamon
- ½ tsp salt
- 1 cup plant-based milk
- ½ cup grapeseed oil (or sunflower oil)
- 2 apples, peeled and grated
- 1 ripe banana, mashed
- 1½ tbsp apple cider vinegar or white vinegar (or lemon juice)
- 2 tsp vanilla extract
- 1 tsp baking soda
- 1 cup blueberries (defrost slightly if frozen)

TO MAKE IT GLUTEN-FREE

Use a GF flour mix without raising agent added and use ground almonds, brown rice flakes, quinoa flakes or LSA (a blend of ground sunflower seeds, linseed and almonds, available at most supermarkets) in place of the bran flakes.

PREP 15 minutes   **COOK** 30 minutes   **MAKES** 12–14 muffins

There's an idea floating around that muffins are old-school and boring, but clearly they're popular for a reason. Who doesn't love a plump, freshly baked little individual cake in a sweet paper case? So long as they aren't gluggy and bland, which these are not. Bran and blueberry is about as classic a flavour combo as you can get, although these are of course dairy- and egg-free. These aren't gluten-free because of the bran (see gluten-free note for alternatives). Perfect for a school lunchbox or morning tea.

Preheat the oven to 180°C regular bake and line a 12-hole muffin tin with paper cases. (You could just grease and flour the tin, but cleaning will be hard work!)

Put the ground linseed in a small bowl or a mug along with 7 tablespoons cold water. Stir, then set aside for 5 minutes — it will go all gloopy, a bit like egg white.

Place the flour, bran flakes, brown sugar, baking powder, cinnamon and salt in a large mixing bowl and stir to combine.

Put the milk, oil, grated apple, mashed banana, vinegar (or lemon juice) and vanilla in a medium-sized mixing bowl. Add the linseed mixture and stir to combine.

Add the baking soda to the wet mixture and stir briskly with a fork to combine.

Make a well in the dry ingredients and pour the wet ingredients in. Stir to combine evenly. Lastly, add the blueberries and fold them through.

Spoon the mixture into the paper cases (or tin) to fill them right to the top, even slightly heaped. Bake in the oven for 30–35 minutes until nice and golden.

Cool the muffins on a wire rack and bake any leftover mixture.

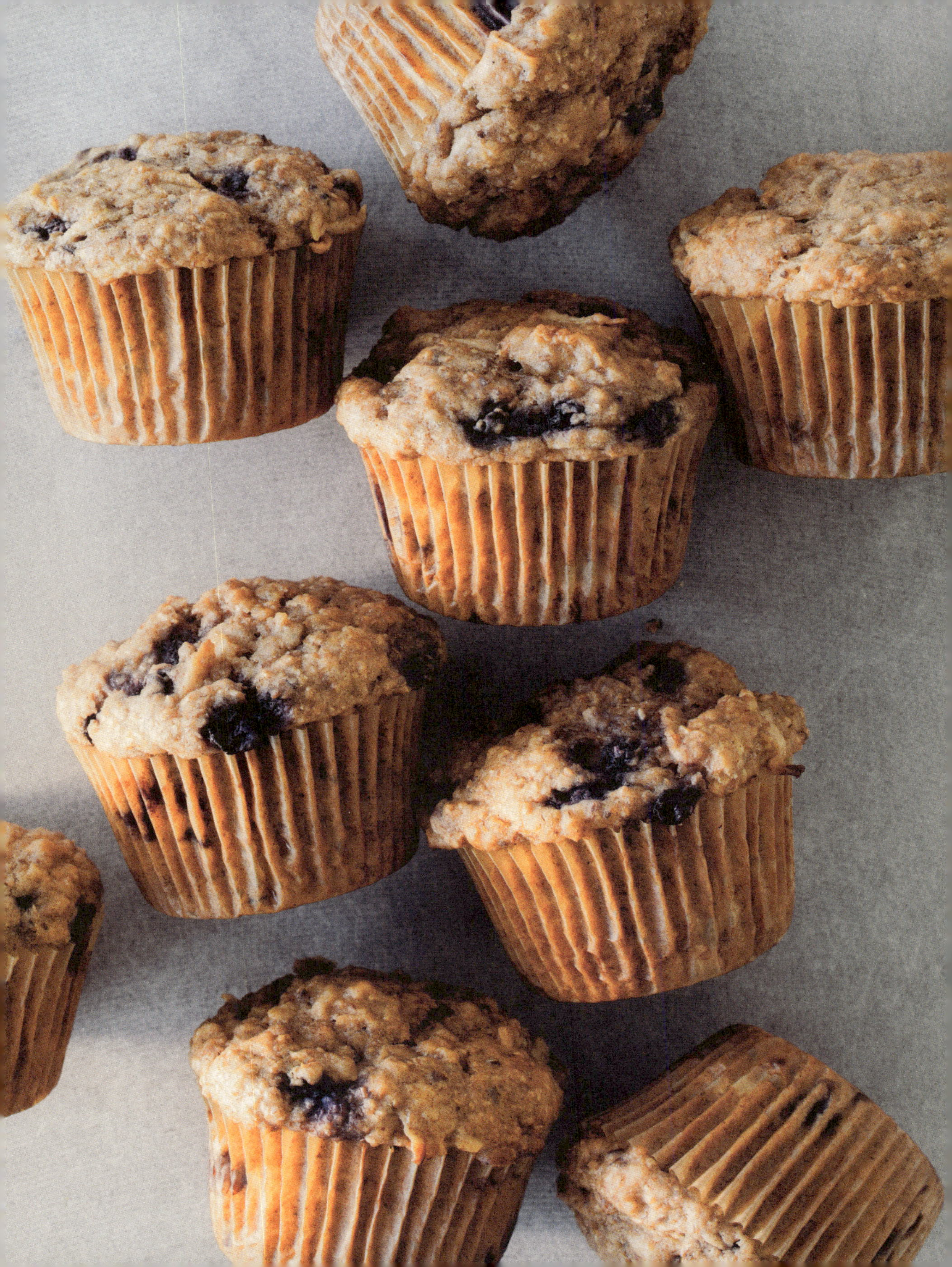

HEDONISTIC HOTCAKES

2 cups plain flour
¼ cup caster sugar
4½ tsp baking powder
¼ tsp salt
2 cups rice, soy or oat milk
4 tbsp apple cider vinegar
1 tbsp vanilla extract
coconut oil, for frying

SERVING IDEAS

maple syrup and plant-based butter (see page 190)
icing sugar and lemon
banana, berries and coconut yoghurt

TO MAKE IT GLUTEN-FREE

Use a GF flour mix without raising agent added. The mixture may be quite fluffy at first, so you can gently smooth each hotcake out in the pan with the back of a spoon, if you like.

PREP 10 minutes **COOK** 20 minutes **MAKES** 8–10 hotcakes

You'll be interested to know that I've based this recipe on one from old mate Natalie Portman, of all people (she put mini marshmallows in hers, though). It's a simple recipe and results in nice fluffy hotcakes in a jif. To be fair, they could almost double as big pikelets, too. And can I just say — get a load of this photo! These are very good hotcakes. Enjoy.

Sift the flour, sugar, baking powder and salt into a large mixing bowl and stir with a whisk to combine.

Make a well in the centre of the dry ingredients and pour in the milk, vinegar and vanilla. Stir gently with a fork until combined and mostly lump-free. The mixture will be puffy, which is what you want.

Heat a (preferably non-stick) frying pan over a medium-low heat. To test whether it's hot enough, flick a few drops of water into the pan. The drops should dance when it's ready. If your pan is a really good non-stick one, you might not need any coconut oil. Otherwise, put a teaspoon of oil into the pan, then add about ⅓ cup of mixture per hotcake. Let it cook for a minute or so, until golden brown on the bottom and little holes have appeared on the surface. Flip over and cook for another minute until cooked through.

Keep the hotcakes on a plate in a just-warm oven until ready to serve, then load up with your favourite luscious topping and hoe in like you're a hungry Homer Simpson.

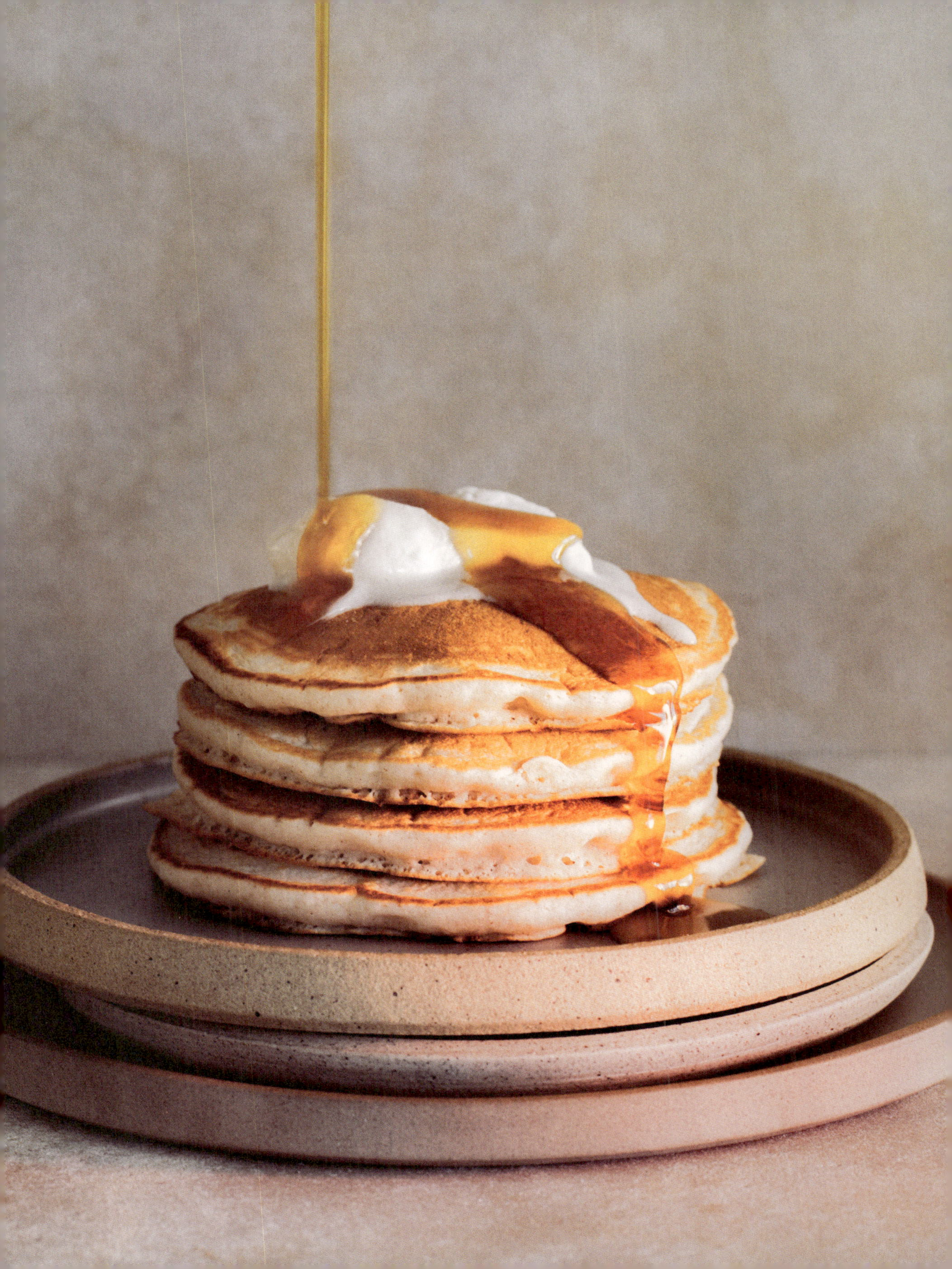

MINI SUGARED DOUGHNUTS

½ cup caster sugar
1 tbsp ground cinnamon

DOUGHNUTS
2 cups flour
3 tsp baking powder
pinch salt
¾ cup plant-based milk
⅓ cup sugar
3 tbsp canned chickpea liquid (aquafaba)
3 tbsp grapeseed oil, plus extra for frying

TO MAKE IT GLUTEN-FREE
Use a GF flour blend without raising agent added, and add 1 tbsp psyllium husk and an extra ¼ cup milk.

PREP 10 minutes **COOK** 15 minutes **MAKES** about 20 mini doughnuts

Little deep-fried morsels served hot and liberally dredged in cinnamon sugar . . . yes please! This is my version of the classic mini doughnut. Essentially they're little fried bits of cake batter, so they're a lot quicker and easier to make than regular doughnuts that require yeast, and the texture is softer and not as chewy. The key is to only drop in tiny blobs, like 2 teaspoons — any bigger and the outside will be too brown by the time the inside is cooked. Because they're so speedy to make, any time you have a hankering for some hot juicy doughnutty goodness, this recipe will be there for you.

Mix the caster sugar and cinnamon in a medium-sized bowl, ready to dunk the doughnuts in.

Sift the flour, baking powder and salt into a bowl and stir to combine. Add the milk, sugar, aquafaba and oil and stir until you have a smooth batter.

Heat about 5cm of oil in a small or medium-sized saucepan over a medium heat (it needs to be at about 180°C, if you have a thermometer). To test whether it's hot enough, poke the end of a wooden spoon in. If bubbles fizz up around the end, it's ready.

Carefully drop heaped-teaspoon-sized blobs of batter into the oil, and cook for a few minutes until lightly golden brown. They should be pale golden when they're done inside.

Carefully remove the cooked doughnuts from the oil with a slotted spoon onto some paper towels, then put them straight into the bowl of cinnamon sugar and toss to coat.

These are best eaten straight away — they're no use to anyone once they've been sitting there for a while and have gone cold, so just get stuck in!

TIPS

+ Once the cooking oil has cooled, strain it and keep it in an airtight jar in a dark, cool place for up to 3 months (the fridge is great if you have room). You can use it for other doughnuts or deep-frying recipes.
+ If you need to, you can try to reheat doughnuts in a 160°C oven for 5 minutes or so.

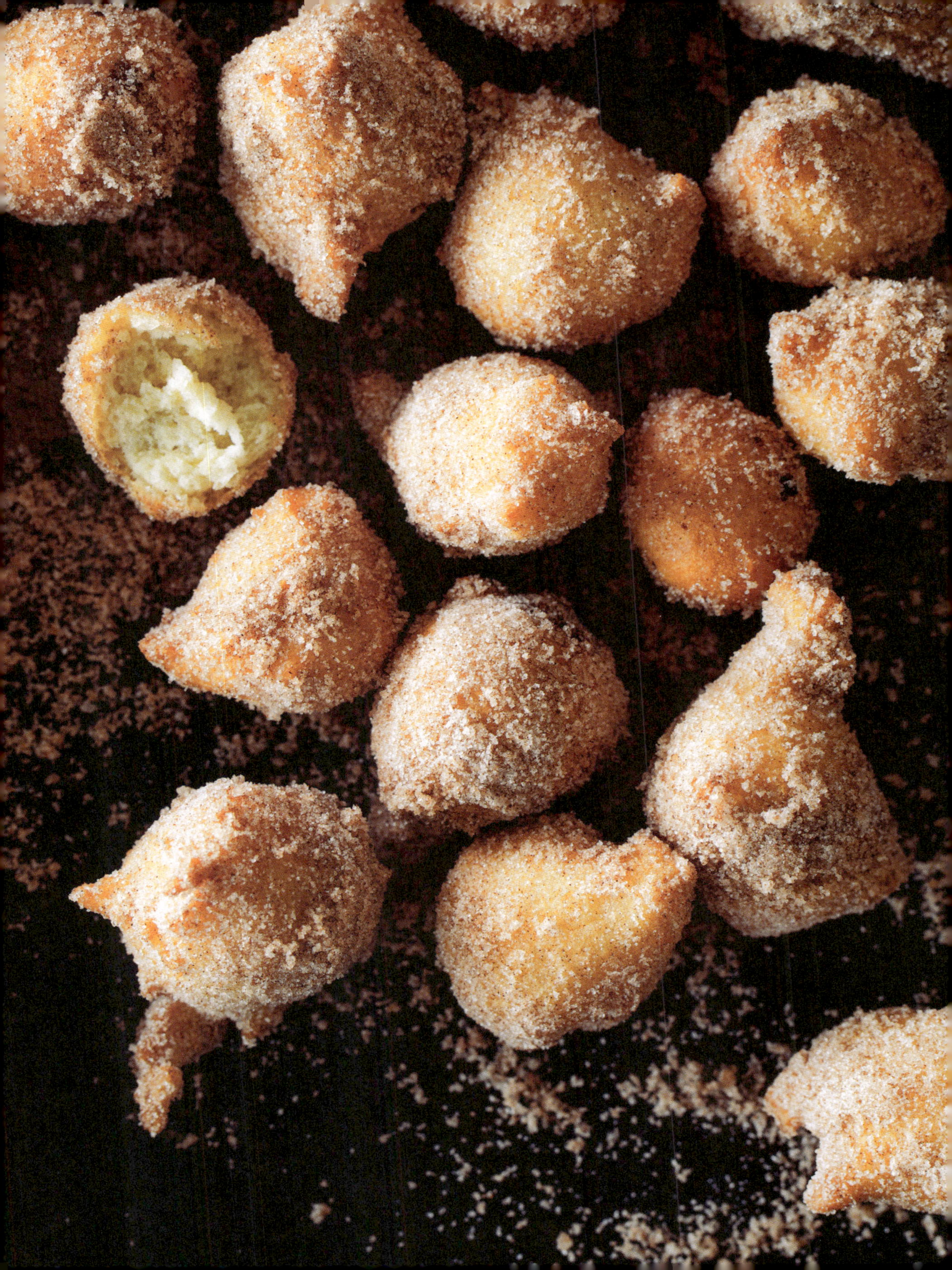

CHOCOLATE MOUSSE

200g good-quality dairy-free eating chocolate (50% cocoa solids or higher is often dairy-free)
1 tbsp just-boiled water
1 cup canned chickpea liquid (aquafaba)
1 tsp lemon juice

TO SERVE
finely chopped chocolate
dusting of cocoa powder

IT'S GLUTEN-FREE

PREP 20 minutes, plus 4 hours to set   **SERVES** 4

You've gotta love a dessert with so few core ingredients that turns out so . . . fancy. And one of those ingredients is aquafaba from a can of chickpeas. How this drab-looking liquid can morph, in mystical butterfly-like fashion, into a silky and beautiful dessert will always make my heart happy. Of course you can't taste the chickpeas — it just adds a light, airy texture to the chocolate. I'm very happy with this, because I always felt a bit weird about folding raw egg whites through mousse.

Have four small glasses or ramekins ready for the mousse, and make space in your fridge.

Chop the chocolate up finely on a clean, dry chopping board using a large, sharp knife. Transfer to a heatproof bowl (Pyrex or ceramic).

Set the bowl over a saucepan with a little gently simmering water in the bottom (make sure the water doesn't touch the bowl). Leave it there for a few minutes until you can see that the chocolate has melted quite a bit, then gently stir every now and then until smooth.

Add the just-boiled water and stir it through. Remove the bowl from the pan and leave to cool slightly while you beat the aquafaba.

Pour the aquafaba into a large, clean mixing bowl (metal, Pyrex or ceramic is best). Add the lemon juice and beat with an electric beater on high speed for a few minutes until you have a lovely thick, pillowy cloud, like meringue. When you tip the bowl upside down, the fluff should stay put.

Fold about a cup of the whipped aquafaba through the melted chocolate to aerate it.

Now, scrape the aerated chocolate mixture into the bowl containing the remaining aquafaba, and fold lightly and lovingly with a spatula until it's evenly combined — a light brown, pillowy mass. If your mixture seems a little runny at this point, don't despair; it will still set like mousse.

Ladle or pour the mixture into the prepared glasses and refrigerate for about 4 hours to set.

When ready to serve, sprinkle with finely chopped chocolate and dust with cocoa.

TIPS

+ Mixing melted chocolate with *anything* is always a bit of a gamble — sometimes you follow the instructions to a T and the end result is still a little grainy. If that happens, don't worry about it — it'll still taste awesome.
+ You can add some fresh berries on top for a refreshing pop of flavour and colour.
+ Use the leftover chickpeas to make Chelsea's Hummus (page 186), That Moroccan Dish (page 70) or Pumpkin & Chickpea Curry on page 54.

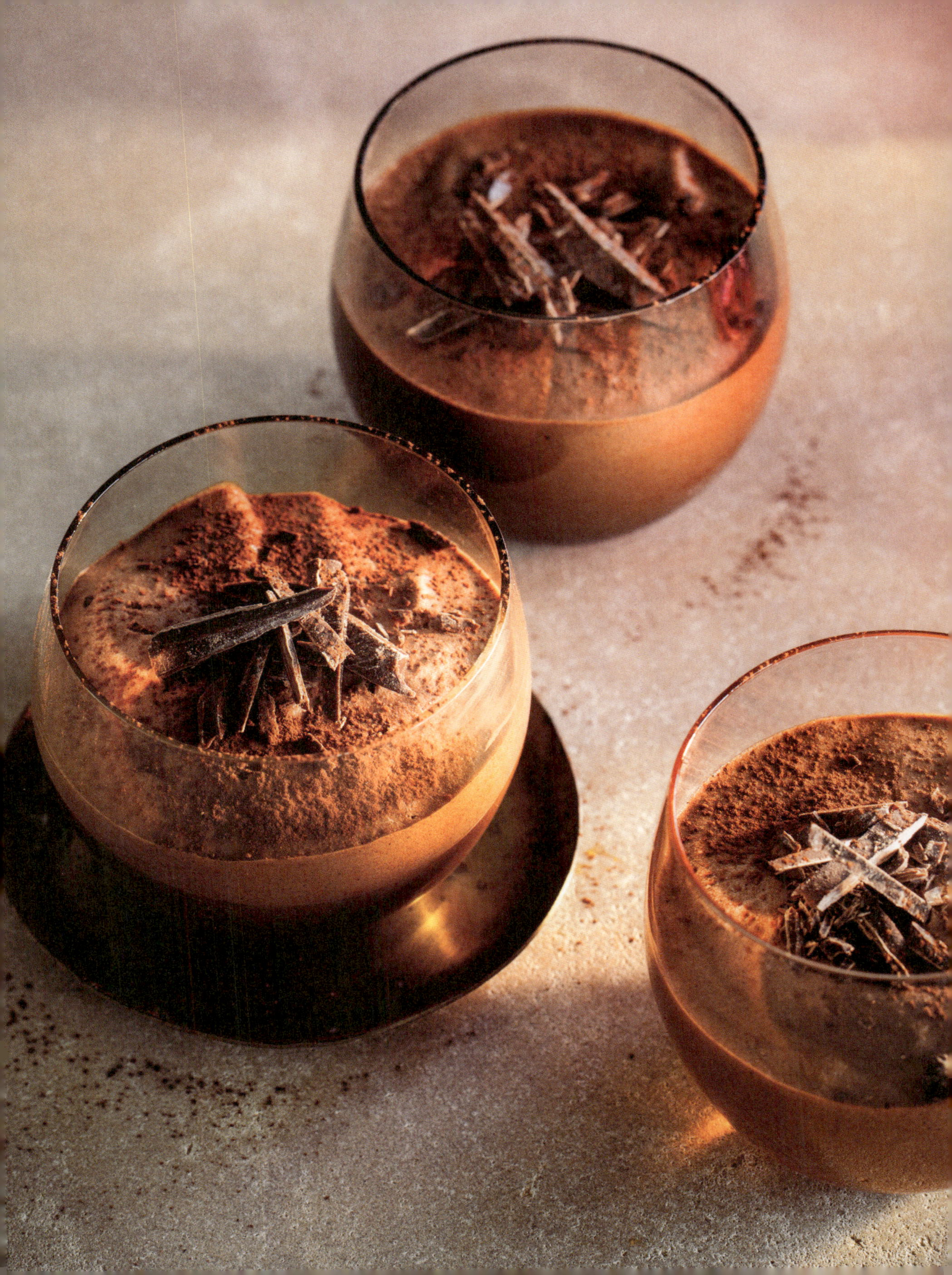

CHEAT'S CHOCOLATE

½ cup unrefined (virgin) coconut oil

5 tbsp honey (or use rice malt syrup or maple syrup)

½ cup good-quality cocoa powder, sifted

¼ cup desiccated coconut

1 tsp vanilla extract

¼ tsp salt

1 lavender flower (optional; see tips for use)

IT'S GLUTEN-FREE

PREP 10 minutes, plus 2+ hours to chill   **MAKES** 1 large bar

Who knew that making your own dairy-free (and refined-sugar-free) chocolate was so easy? I based this recipe on some gorgeously delicious chocolate I was given by a friend in Hawaii. It actually had a subtle lavender flavour as well as coconut, which sounds odd but really blew my mind — it didn't taste at all like potpourri, as you might expect it to! I've included lavender as an option to add here, but do understand that it's not everyone's cup of tea. Without it this chocolate is still beautiful; you can taste the honey, and it's as smooth as silk. You do need to keep it in the fridge, though, as it goes soft very quickly.

First, get your mould ready. I use a medium-sized loaf tin or a similar-sized plastic container and line it with baking paper — enough so that I can fold it up over the chocolate bar later. Or you can use chocolate moulds if you want to be all cool.

Place all the ingredients into a small saucepan over a low heat. Stir gently with a whisk until the mixture is melted and smooth.

Scrape into the prepared mould with a spatula and put straight into the fridge for a couple of hours. You can then either cut it into squares and keep in an airtight container, or just make grooves with a knife and break bits off when you feel like it (which will be often).

TIPS

+ If you like the flavour of lavender, and can find some in a local garden, it makes this chocolate taste extra special. Just pull the top flower bit apart into tiny little pieces and stir about ½ tsp of them through the chocolate, or sprinkle them on top before you refrigerate the bar.
+ You could add a little orange zest for an orange-flavoured chocolate, or a few drops of food-quality peppermint oil for a minty taste.

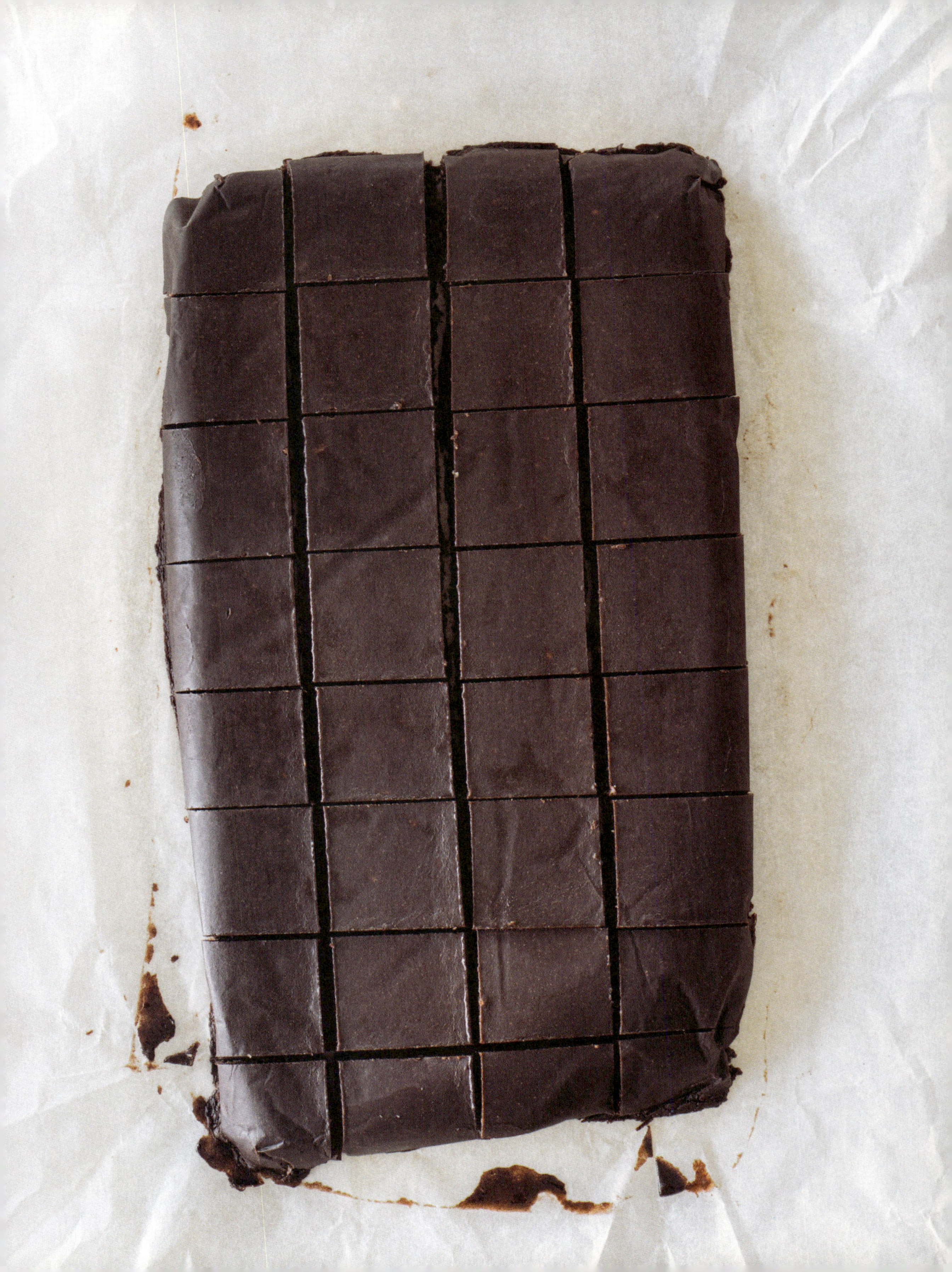

LITTLE PEANUT TRUFFLES

FILLING

250g dairy-free eating chocolate, finely chopped (I used 50% cocoa solids)

200ml coconut cream

½ cup crunchy or smooth peanut butter

2 tbsp roasted peanuts

flaky sea salt, or pink salt

COATING

250g dairy-free dark chocolate, finely chopped (I used 50% cocoa solids)

2 tbsp coconut oil or grapeseed oil

IT'S GLUTEN-FREE

PREP 45 minutes, plus 2 hours to cool and set   **MAKES** 10–12 truffles

These divine scrumlets taste as good as they look. They remind me of some outrageously fancy little morsel you might get at the poshest restaurant in town with coffee after dinner, like a *petit four*. They're not hard to make; there's just a few steps to the process. You bite into the chocolate shell through the light, silky truffle and into a little pillow of peanut butter — and the crunchy little nut is waiting there in the middle for you, a secret treat. If you're having a dinner party and can't be bothered making a dessert, just make these ahead of time and keep them in the freezer. They're rich and decadent enough to do the job.

To make the filling, place the chopped chocolate and coconut cream in a heatproof bowl and place it over a saucepan with a little simmering water in the bottom (don't let the bowl touch the water). Stir gently until melted and smooth. Remove from the heat and allow to cool slightly, then cover and refrigerate for an hour or so until it's firmed up.

Beat the chocolate mixture with an electric beater for 10–20 seconds; this will whip it up and it will seem a little fluffier and paler. More truffly. Refrigerate again for about half an hour so that it's easier to work with.

When the mixture is firmer, scoop out balls with a tablespoon measure and roll between cold, wet hands into rough ball shapes. Arrange on a baking tray lined with baking paper.

Now make a hole in each one for the peanut butter to sit in. I used a metal ¼ tsp measuring spoon I'd heated up in a mug of just-boiled water, and plunged it into each ball to gouge out a cavity. The balls don't have to stay round; it's okay if they flatten a bit as the peanut butter will round off the tops.

Dollop ½–1 teaspoon of peanut butter into each cavity. Poke in a peanut, then sprinkle with a couple of flakes of sea salt or pink salt. Freeze for 30 minutes, or more, until very firm.

To make the chocolate coating, place the chopped chocolate in a small heatproof bowl and microwave on high for 1 minute. Stir well, then heat again in 30-second bursts, stirring after each one, until completely smooth. Add the oil and stir it through.

Drop a truffle into the melted chocolate and swivel it round using a skewer or toothpick, to coat it evenly. Spear it to lift it out, hold it over the baking paper and swivel the skewer or toothpick until the truffle drops off. Repeat until they are all coated, then freeze in a well-sealed container until you're ready to eat them (they'll keep for up to 2 months).

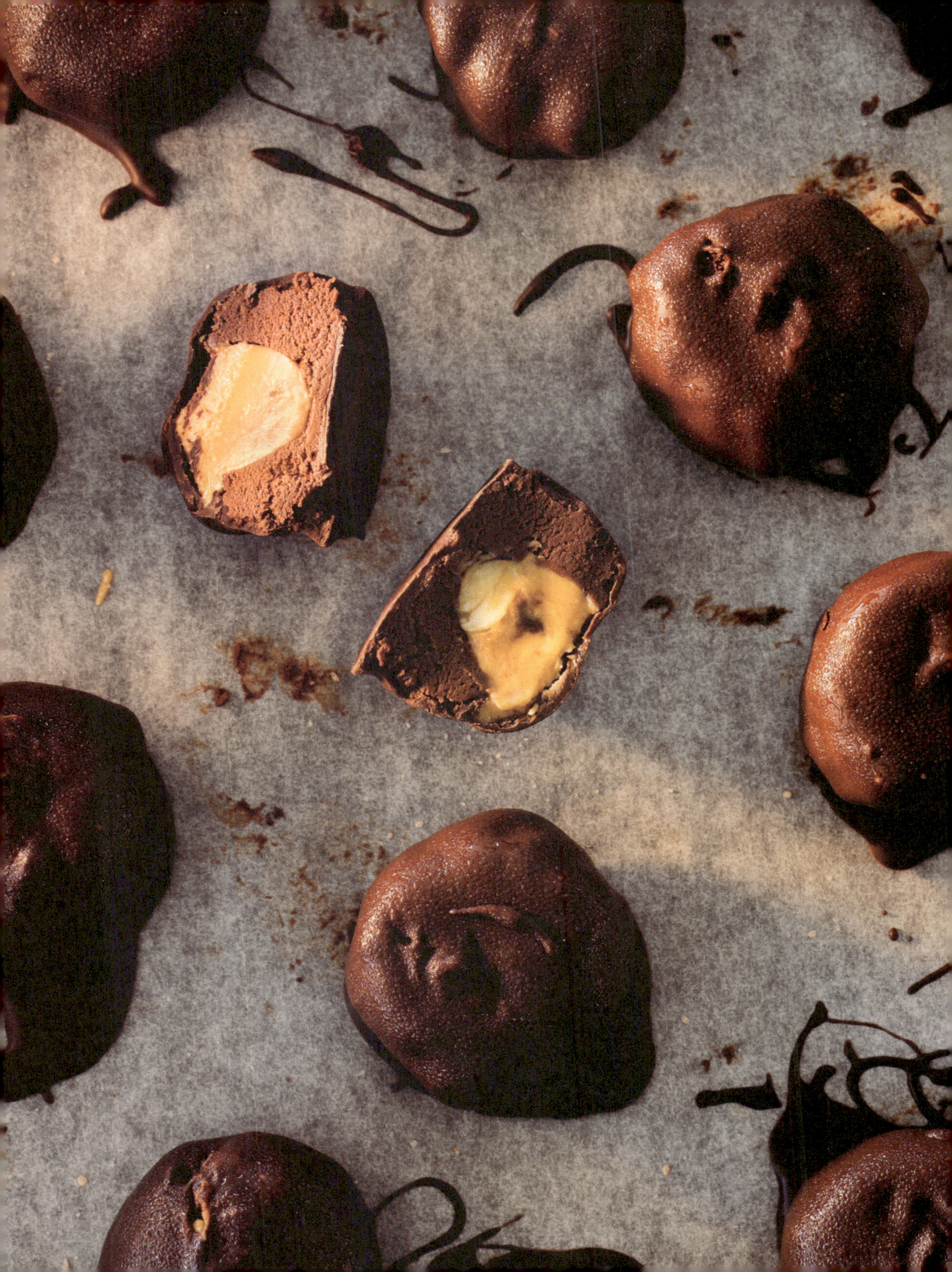

STRAWBERRY GELATO

3 large, very ripe bananas
1 punnet ripe strawberries, halved (or use 1 cup frozen)
1 tsp lemon juice
pinch salt

___

IT'S GLUTEN-FREE

PREP 5 minutes, plus 3+ hours to freeze   **SERVES** 4

This dessert is so magical. Mainly because bananas are so magical, and SO good for you. We literally buy four bunches every time we do a shop because we live on them — in smoothies, on muesli, as a snack between meals, sliced on toast with almond butter and coconut oil, mashed into baby food, or (as pictured here) blitzed into a dessert! Whizz them in a food processor when they're frozen and they take on a light, whipped, creamy texture, not unlike ice cream or gelato. If you don't have strawberries, you can just make a plain banana ice cream (use an extra banana); it's still utterly delicious.

___

Peel the bananas and slice them into 1cm chunks. Arrange on a tray lined with baking paper, along with the strawberries, and freeze until solid. Alternatively you can freeze them in a ziplock bag, but you might have to bang it on the floor to break up the banana when frozen (that's what I do!).

Place the frozen fruit in the bowl of a large food processor along with the lemon juice and salt. Process until you have a thick, creamy, gelato-ish mixture. It may be helpful to scrape down the sides once or twice as you go.

Scoop the mixture straight out of the food processor and into bowls to serve. It's best eaten straight away — it becomes rock-hard if you try to re-freeze it once it's blended.

___

TIPS

+ If you have a bullet blender you can use this instead of a food processor; you'll probably need to add 1–2 tbsp coconut cream to bring it all together.
+ You can experiment with any frozen fruit you like, keeping the bananas as a base.

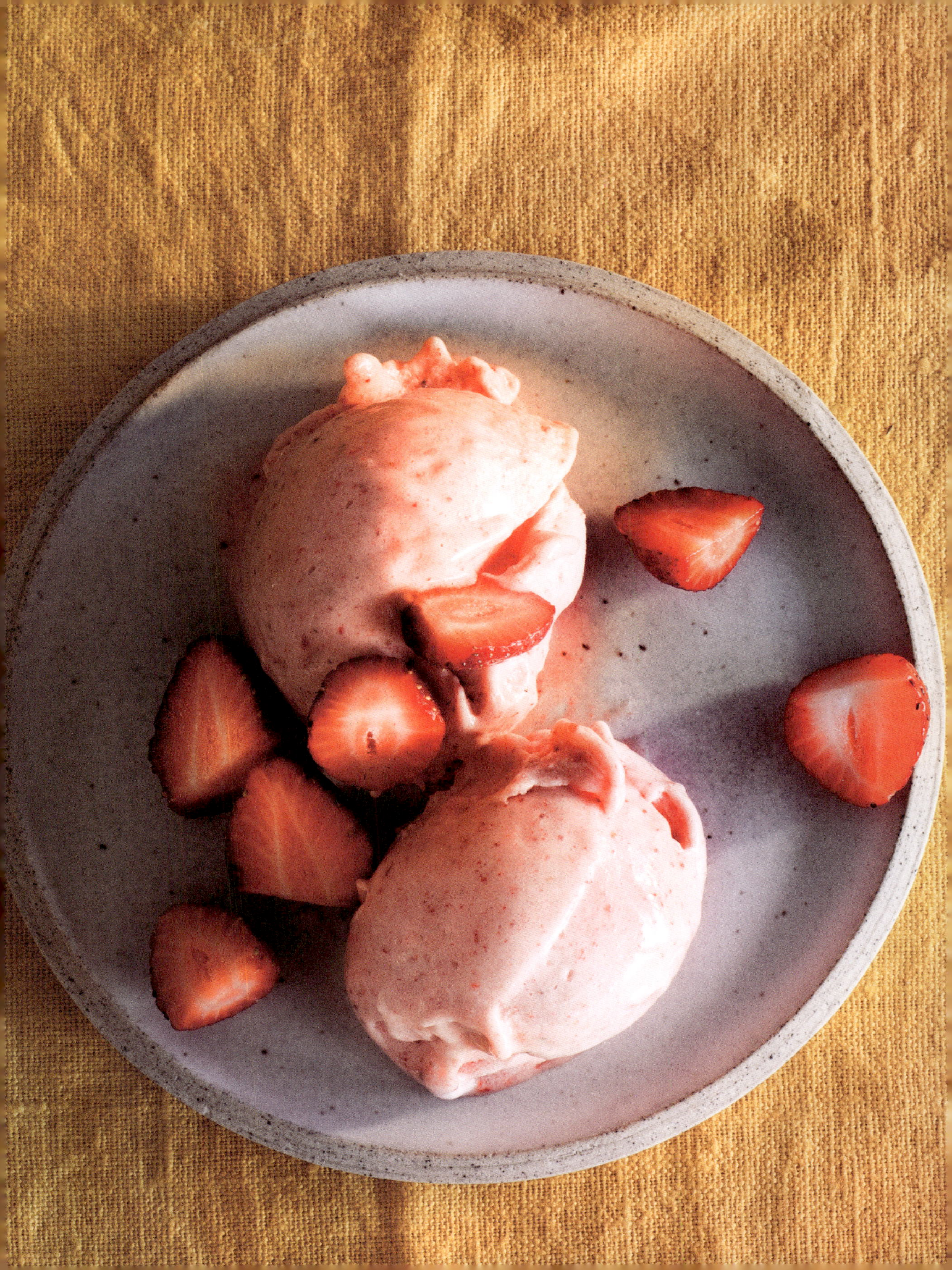

CHOCOLATE ICE CREAM

¾ cup coconut cream (or use creamy soy milk)

½ cup good-quality cocoa powder

3 tbsp grapeseed, sunflower or rice bran oil

1 tbsp vanilla extract (or vanilla paste if you want seeds)

¼ tsp salt

liquid from 1 x 400g can of chickpeas (aquafaba)

¼ tsp cream of tartar or lemon juice

¾ cup icing sugar

IT'S GLUTEN-FREE

PREP 20 minutes, plus 4+ hours to freeze   **SERVES** 4–6

Who'd have thought it — chocolate ice cream made from the liquid from a can of chickpeas. But it really works, and boy, it's a ripper. (Just as importantly, it costs SO much less than store-bought dairy-free ice cream, which can be eye-wateringly expensive.) The key is to be extremely gentle when folding the whipped aquafaba into the cocoa mixture, so the air stays in there.

Place the coconut cream, cocoa, oil, vanilla and salt in a high-speed blender or bullet blender, and blend well to combine (or use a stick blender).

Pour the chickpea liquid into a large, very clean mixing bowl and beat with an electric beater on high for 20 seconds or so, or just keep going until it's turned foamy.

Add the cream of tartar or lemon juice, then beat again on medium–high for another few minutes.

Now start adding the icing sugar a tablespoonful at a time, beating for 5 seconds in between each addition. The mixture should now be lovely and thick, voluminous and shiny, like glossy whipped meringue. It should stay put in the bowl when you turn it upside down.

Add ¼ cup of the chocolate mixture to the whipped mixture and fold in gently with a spatula.

Add half the remaining chocolate mixture and fold gently to combine, then repeat with the remaining mixture. Be gentle with this — over-mixing or being too rough can collapse the whipped mixture. Keep folding until combined evenly.

Scrape into a loaf tin or a resealable container, cover tightly and freeze for at least 4 hours.

Scoop out with a hot ice cream scoop and enjoy!

TIPS

+ For a coffee ice cream, you could add 1–2 tbsp instant coffee to the blender in place of the cocoa — or use both for a mocha flavour!
+ You could use the chickpeas to make several other dishes — Chelsea's Hummus (page 186), That Moroccan Dish (page 70) or Pumpkin & Chickpea Curry (page 54).

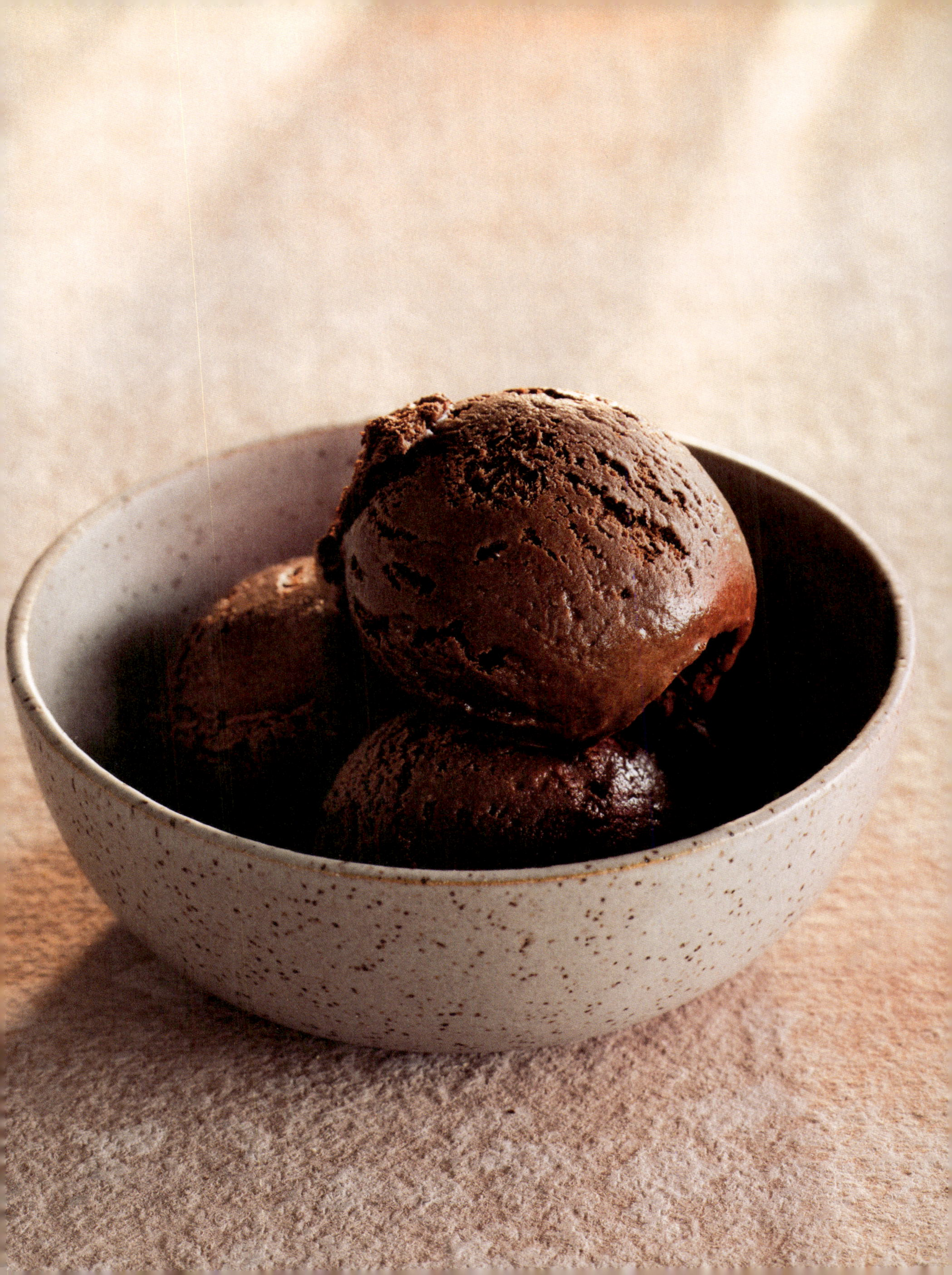

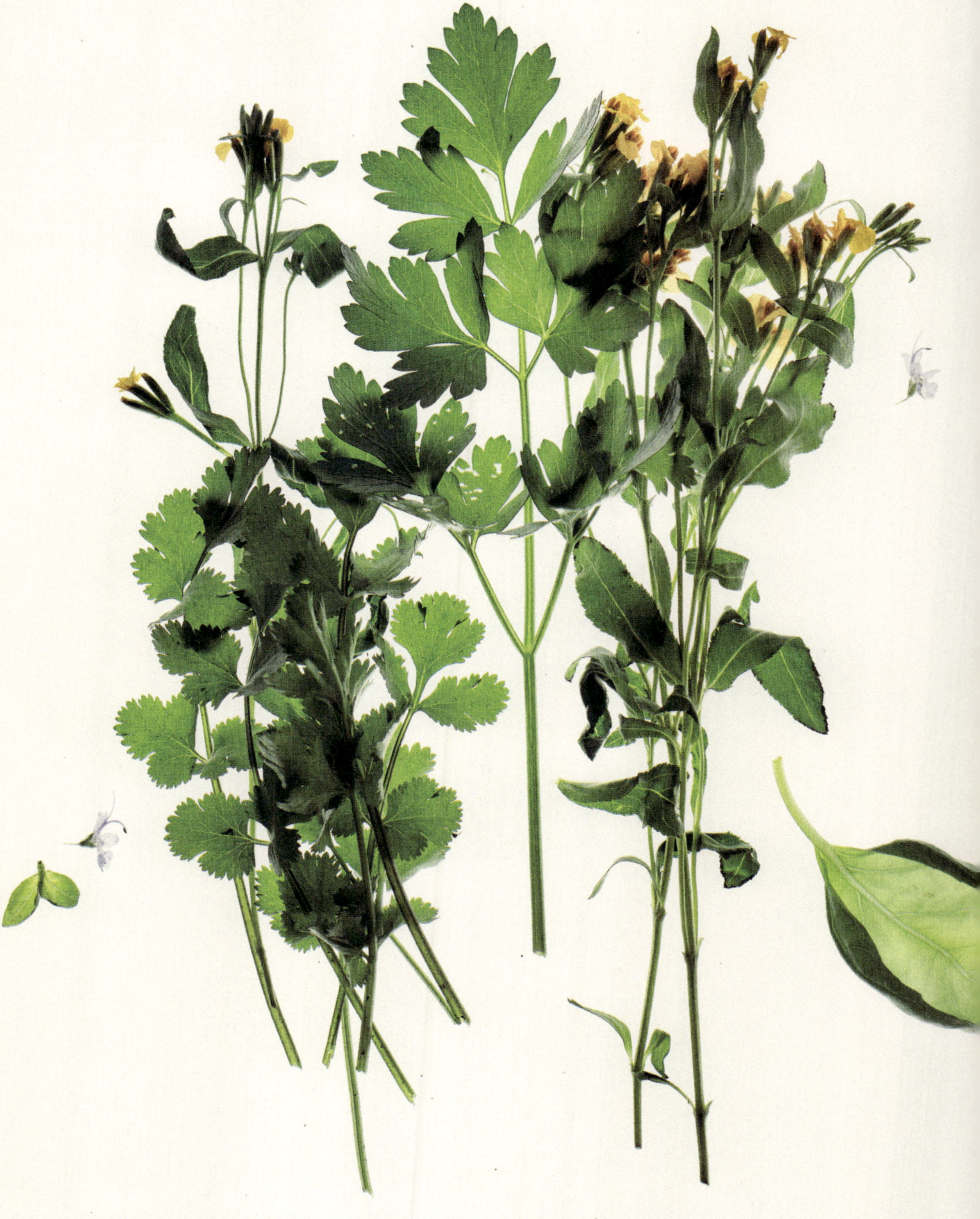

BREAKFASTS, BITS & PIECES

Here are some delicious little fridge and pantry fixtures to brighten up your life on the daily. There's just no feeling quite like the one of warm pride and satisfaction that comes with making your own goodies like aïoli, hummus, butter, feta and pesto, as well as the crackers and loaves to go with them. Also, I've shared some of our favourite breakfast staples from home; notably the greatest gluten-free muesli you could hope for, golden hash browns, one epic smoothie and luscious, vibrant juices.

CHELSEA'S FAMOUS 10-SECOND AÏOLI

1 cup grapeseed oil (or sunflower oil)
½ cup creamy soy milk (organic is best)
1 tsp Dijon mustard
1 clove garlic, crushed
1 tsp salt
¼ tsp white or black pepper
2 tsp lemon juice
1 tsp apple cider vinegar

TIPS

+ I've tried this recipe with other plant-based milks and it's just not as creamy, so I really recommend you use soy. The creamier, the better. If you can find organic as well as non-GMO, jackpot!
+ Don't try making this with extra virgin olive oil, as the flavour will be overpowering. However you can substitute ¼–⅓ of a cup of it if you like the flavour.

PREP 5 minutes   **MAKES** about 300ml

The holy grail of all things garlicky and creamy. Seriously, everyone goes nuts for it. I no longer use store-bought aïoli — this stuff is inexpensive, lightning-fast to prepare and goes with just about anything. Smeared on sandwiches and burgers, served alongside roast potatoes or veges, dolloped on just about any type of dinner for a creamy element, used as a dip for chips. We go through it at a slightly worrying rate of knots. Make a double batch if you have a few people in your household. Leave out the garlic if you want a plain but still insanely creamy aïoli.

BULLET BLENDER: You don't need to crush the garlic clove for this one. The most important thing to remember here is not to shake it up first, or it won't emulsify.

Place the oil, milk, mustard, garlic, salt and pepper in the bullet cup, twist the base on, then very gently turn it over and place it on the machine. Let it sit for 30 seconds so it separates out into layers. Only then, whizz for just a few seconds or until it turns thick and creamy. Remove the lid and stir through the lemon juice and vinegar.

STICK BLENDER: Easiest for clean up. Place the oil, milk, mustard, garlic, salt and pepper in a tall, narrow container. Your stick blender may have come with one, or use the big cup of a bullet blender, or any tall plastic container or jar (about 1 litre capacity).

Let the ingredients sit in the container for 30 seconds to settle.

Stand the blender so that it sits firmly at the base of the container, and turn it on without moving it for about 5 seconds. As the mixture starts to emulsify, gently move the blender up and down to combine the ingredients. Add the lemon juice and vinegar, give it a stir, and that's it!

BLENDER: Place the milk, mustard, garlic, salt and pepper (not the oil) in the blender and turn it on to a medium speed. Slowly drizzle in the oil in a very thin stream until it's all used up (make it very thin and slow at first, then you can speed up as you get past halfway). The mixture should thicken and emulsify into a nice creamy aïoli by the end. Add the lemon juice and vinegar and stir through.

STORAGE: Transfer to a clean glass jar (or airtight container). It keeps in the fridge for a week (if you're lucky, that is!). It doesn't freeze well.

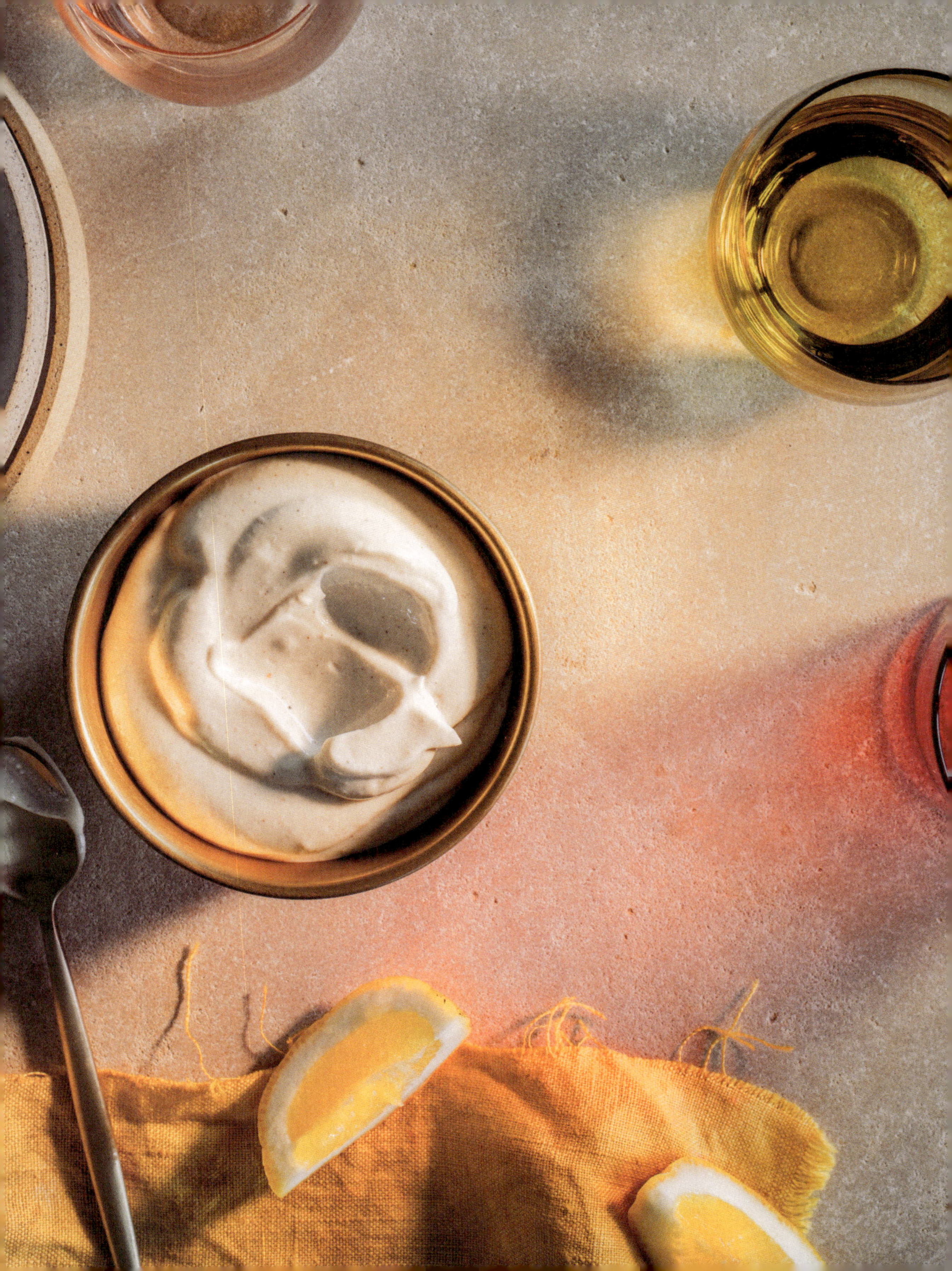

FRESH HERBY PESTO

½ cup cashews
½ cup pumpkin or sunflower seeds
1 clove garlic, crushed
2 tbsp nutritional yeast
1 tsp salt
4 cups roughly chopped fresh basil, coriander and parsley
¼ cup fresh sage, thyme and oregano leaves (optional)
1 tbsp red or white wine vinegar (or to taste)
2 tsp lemon juice (or to taste)
¼ tsp finely ground black pepper
1¼ cups extra virgin olive oil

PREP 20 minutes   **MAKES** 2 small jars

I used to think that pesto was hard to make and you needed strict ingredients to get it perfect, but really there are no firm rules. It's just about getting a nice balance of herbs and greens, creaminess from the nuts and seeds, acid and salt. And of course, cheesiness from our new friend, nutritional yeast. This is a pretty forgiving recipe — you can adjust the amount of herbs based on what you have. Like if you're a coriander fan, you can add more of this and then it'll be a great addition to Mexican-style meals. This pesto is great stirred through hot pasta, on toast with avocado and tomato, or drizzled over roast veges. And giving a jar of pesto as a gift — well, you couldn't do much better! Mainly because I find that most bought pesto tastes pretty average (and boy, it's expensive).

Place the nuts, seeds, garlic, nutritional yeast and salt in a food processor and process until fine, scraping down the sides if needed.

Add the herbs, vinegar, lemon juice and pepper, and pulse until the herbs are finely chopped. Scrape down the sides at least once so that everything is incorporated.

With the processor going on low speed, slowly add the olive oil in a thin stream until used up. Taste it — you may need more salt, or lemon, or vinegar. Keep adding until it tastes right to you. Or it may be fine just as it is!

Store the pesto in clean jars, and pour a thin layer of oil on top to help keep air out and keep it nice and green. It keeps for a week or two in the fridge (longer if you add the oil layer). You can also freeze it for up to 3 months — divide it up into little containers or ziplock bags and get it out as you need it.

TIPS

+ If you have an abundance of basil and want a basil-only pesto, by all means use that and leave out the other herbs. Same goes for coriander.
+ Of course, if you have pine nuts you can use them in place of cashews or seeds. Walnuts add a really great flavour, too.

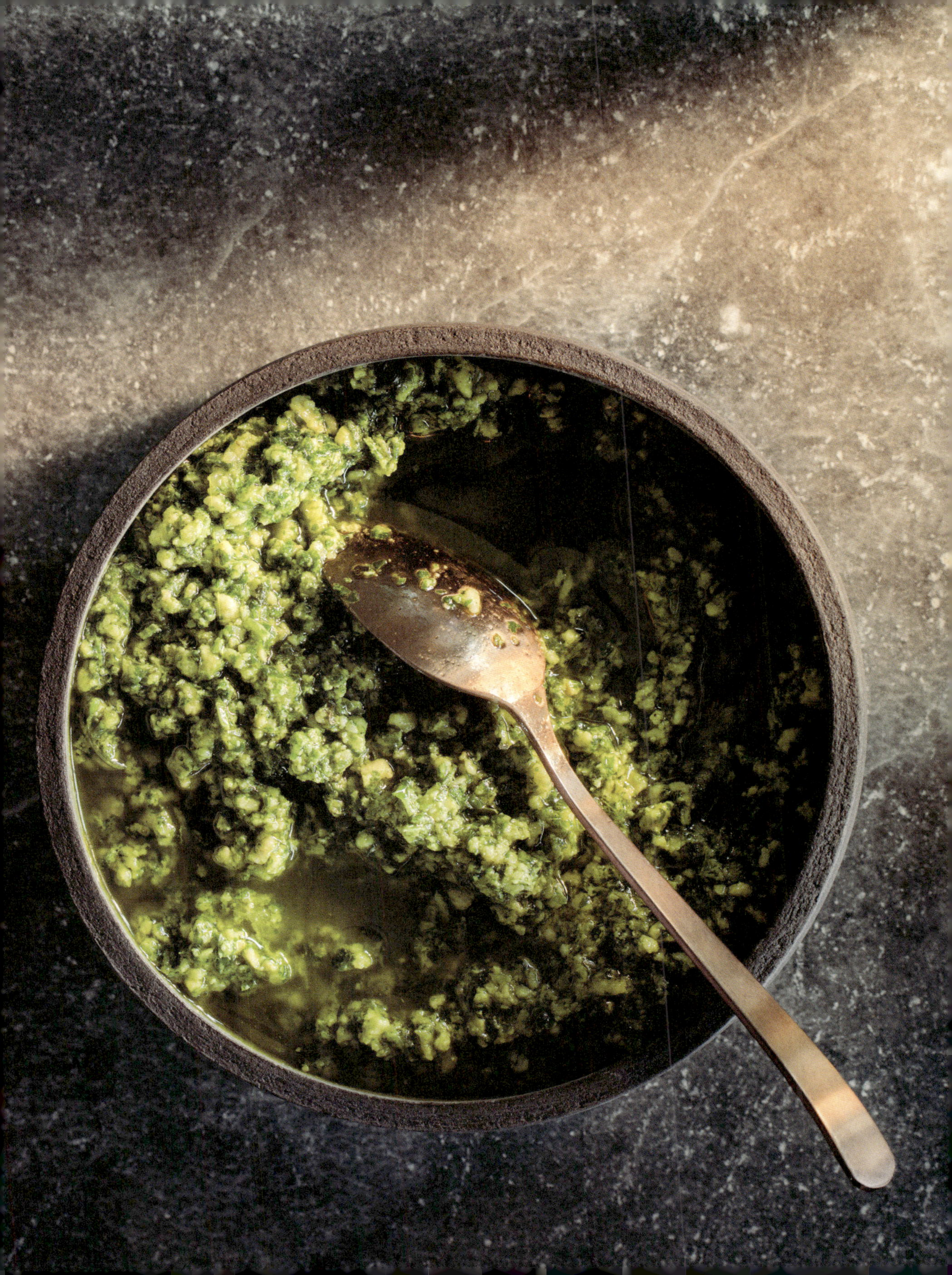

CHELSEA'S HUMMUS

2 x 400g cans chickpeas, drained (save the liquid to use in a recipe that requires aquafaba)
½ cup extra virgin olive oil
3 tbsp lemon juice
2 tbsp tahini
1–2 cloves garlic, crushed
½ tsp ground cumin (optional)
3 tbsp water
2 tsp salt

PREP 15 minutes   **MAKES** 700g

Hummus is such a magical thing — it's a rare day when there isn't a containerful in our fridge. It's a cornerstone of our diet (Sky loves it mashed through his potato), and there are so many ways to enjoy it. When a rogue hunger pang strikes, we just dig a spoonful out and eat it straight. We have it in a sandwich or on toast with avo, tomato and Marinated Feta (see page 198). In summer, I make a plate for dinner loaded with hummus, cucumber, wholemeal garlic pitas (or fried wraps), aïoli, tomatoes, coriander, grated beetroot and carrot, lemon juice and coriander — totally delicious. And it's safe to say that with all the recipes in this book that require canned chickpea liquid, you'll be making this a bit. It's so good for you that you really can't overdo it.

Place all the ingredients in a food processor and process until creamy and as smooth as you like it. Scrape down the sides a couple of times during this. Taste, and add more salt and/or lemon if you like.

If you like a roasted garlic flavour, roast a few garlic cloves in their skins at 200°C for 10 minutes, allow to cool and squeeze them in — as well as or instead of the crushed raw garlic.

TIPS

+ It's easy to save the chickpea liquid (aquafaba) for one of the other recipes in the book — it freezes well, or will keep a few days in the fridge.
+ If you're entertaining, make this rather unglamorous fella look a million bucks by smearing it artfully in a shallow bowl and topping with salt, pepper, a drizzle of olive oil, paprika, toasted cumin and coriander seeds, and fresh herbs. It goes beautifully on a platter.

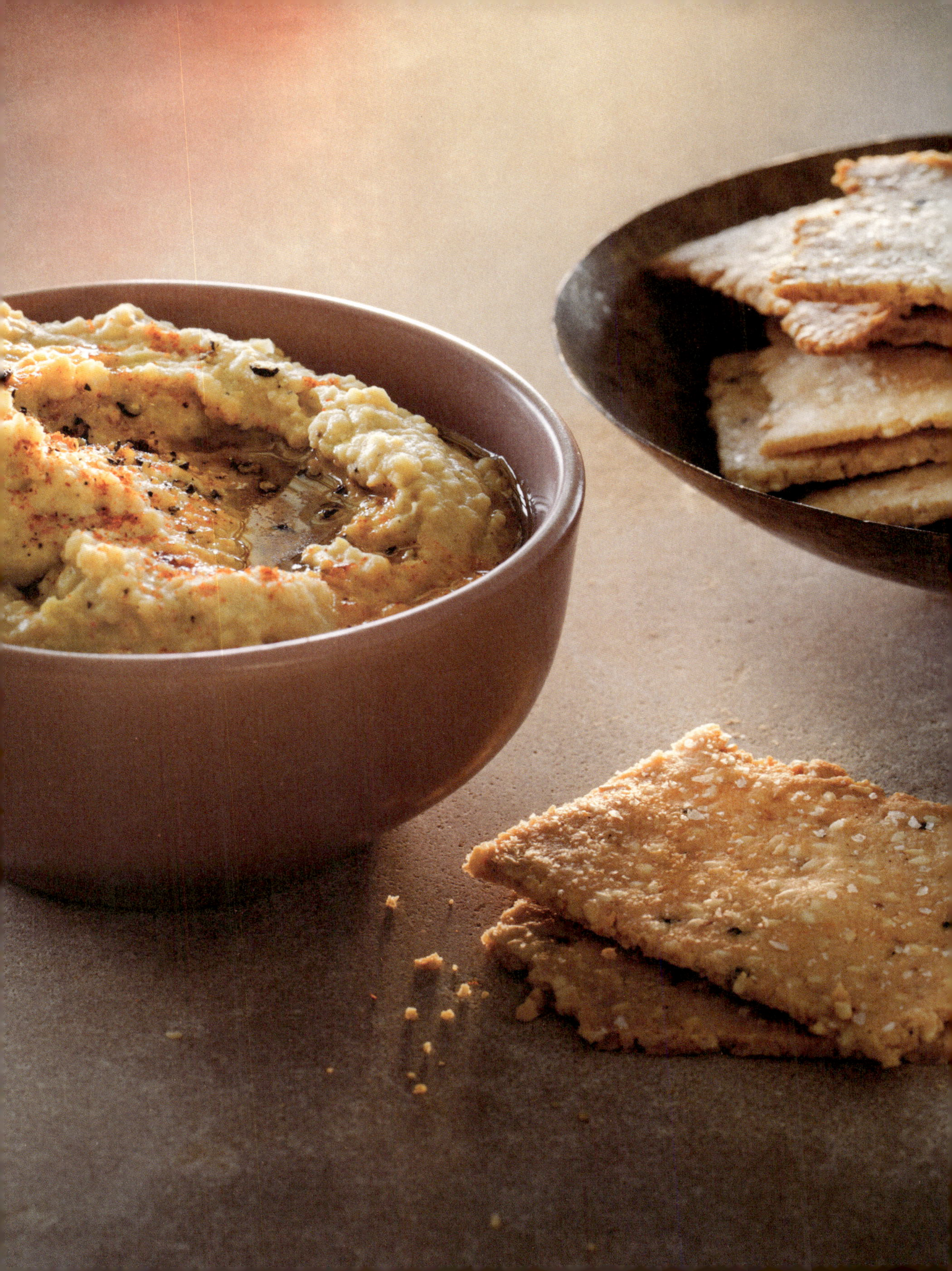

CRISPY SALTED SESAME CRACKERS

- ⅓ cup sesame seeds
- 1¼ cups ground almonds
- ¼ cup plain flour
- 3 tbsp water
- 3 tbsp unflavoured coconut oil, melted (or use extra virgin olive if you like the flavour)
- ¾ tsp salt
- ¼ tsp finely ground black pepper
- olive oil, for drizzling
- sea salt flakes, for topping (optional)
- cracked pepper, for topping (optional)

TO MAKE IT GLUTEN-FREE
Use a GF flour mix without raising agent added.

PREP 15 minutes **COOK** 15 minutes **MAKES** about 18 crackers

It turns out that making your own crackers is ridiculously easy — it's a one-bowl wonder. Except that I normally have to make a double batch of these because one doesn't last long enough, largely due to the fact that they're so damn more-ish. We dip them into hummus straight out of the fridge, but they're also amazing with the Marinated Feta on page 198 and sliced tomato. Plus, your mates will be dazzled when they come round for drinks and all casually you suddenly serve up homemade crackers. *Kapow!*

Preheat the oven to 180°C regular bake.

Place a small dry pan over a medium heat, add the sesame seeds and cook for 5 minutes or so, shaking the pan to cook the seeds evenly, until they are golden brown. Don't go away and leave it, or you'll burn them!

Place all the ingredients in a mixing bowl and stir to combine evenly.

Tear off two pieces of baking paper about 40cm long. Shape the dough into a rough oblong and place between the sheets of paper. Roll out until it almost fills the baking paper — it should be nice and thin and even.

Carefully remove the top piece of baking paper. Score the dough with a sharp knife to mark out the size and shape of your desired crackers.

Lift the baking paper and dough onto a baking tray and drizzle with a little olive oil. Sprinkle with sea salt flakes and cracked pepper if you like. Bake for around 15 minutes, until golden brown — you may need to turn it around once during cooking.

Leave to cool, then snap into crackers along the lines you cut.

Store in an airtight container when cooled — they'll keep for a good week or so in a well-sealed container.

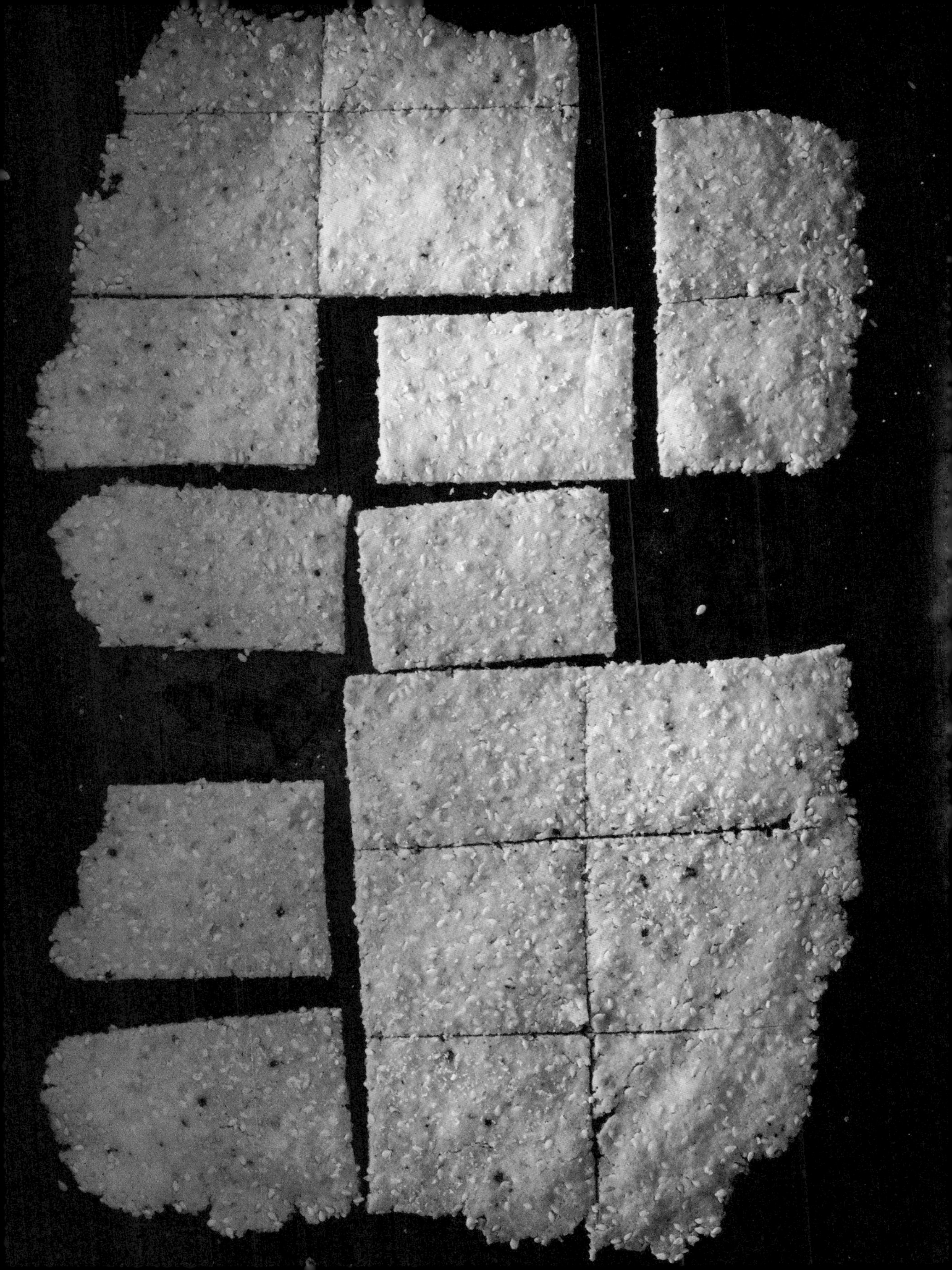

PLANT-BASED BUTTER

½ cup raw cashews
1 cup unflavoured coconut oil
½ cup canned chickpea liquid (aquafaba)
4 tsp grapeseed or sunflower oil
1 tsp lemon juice
½ tsp fine salt

PREP 30 minutes, plus 2+ hours to chill   **MAKES** 1 x 250g block

This plant-based butter is going to make life truly supergood once you start using it on everything. It's epic on toast (we put it under avocado on ours to be extra greedy), melted on hot cobs of sweetcorn, slathered on warm muffins, for lushing-up mashed potato and spreading on sammies. It's heavenly — creamy and slightly salty, and melts lusciously just like dairy butter. It's not suitable for cooking or baking, though — only as a buttery flourish on things. You simply must use an unflavoured coconut oil, though, or it will just taste like coconut and that gets old pretty quickly.

Place the cashews in a heatproof bowl and cover with boiling water. Leave to soak for 20 minutes, then drain.

Place all the ingredients in a high-speed blender or bullet blender, and whizz for about 10 seconds or until super-smooth.

Pour into a plastic container with a lid and refrigerate until firm (or use a loaf tin lined with baking paper).

Keeps in the fridge for a couple of weeks.

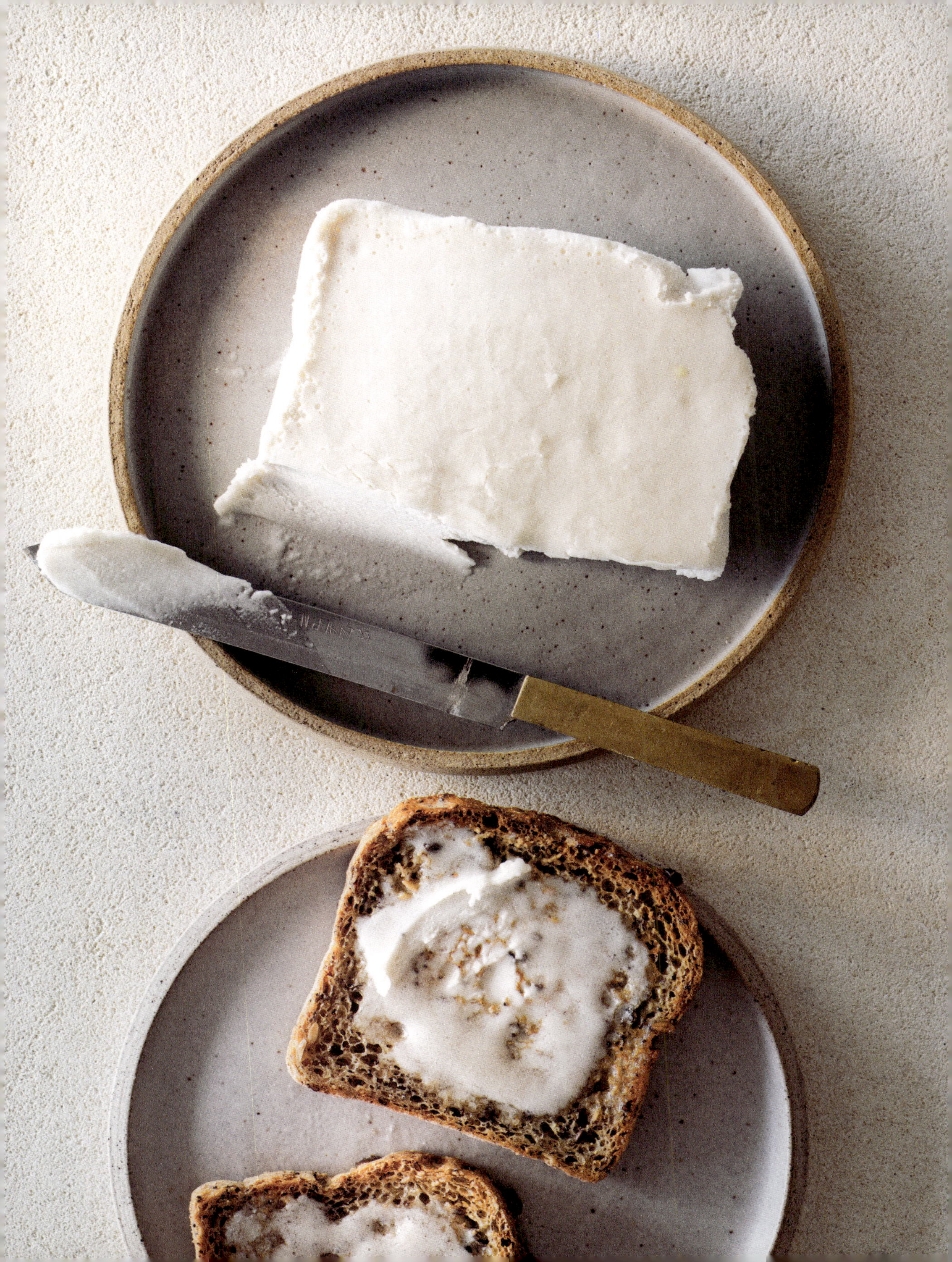

ELVISH TOAST BREAD

2½ cups quick or instant rolled oats
2 cups raw sunflower seeds
½ cup raw pumpkin seeds
1 cup whole linseeds (flax seeds)
⅓ cup sesame seeds
⅓ cup chia seeds
2½ cups water
1½ tsp fine salt

TO MAKE IT GLUTEN-FREE
Use GF flour or buckwheat flour instead of oats.

PREP 15 minutes   **COOK** 1 hour 15 minutes   **MAKES** 1 medium-sized loaf

This delicious, filling bread is designed to be sliced *thinly* and then toasted — that's when it gets crunchy and the seeds develop their nutty flavour. It only takes a few minutes to throw together, and it'll be your saviour for a quick meal — laden with either sweet or savoury toppings. For us, sometimes it's a big smear of almond or peanut butter with sliced banana and a drizzle of raw honey. Other times it's avocado, hummus, cherry tomatoes, olive oil and basil. It's also delicious under eggs or baked beans. Or serve it with soup for dinner. I called it Elvish bread because of the elves' bread in *The Lord of the Rings*. That's a special bread that keeps you full for ages — a bit like this one.

Preheat the oven to 150°C regular bake, and line a loaf tin with baking paper so that it covers the base and goes all the way up the sides.

Place all the ingredients in a large mixing bowl and stir well with a wooden spoon until well combined. Leave it to sit for 10 minutes for the water to be absorbed.

Scrape the mixture into the tin and squash it down as flat as you can with your hands, smoothing out the top and edges.

Cover with foil and bake for 1 hour 15 minutes, removing the foil with 15 minutes to go. When it is time to remove from the oven, pull the whole thing up out of the tin with the baking paper, and leave to cool completely. It will look and feel like a brick at this point — but have faith in your ol' mate Chelsea on this one.

When it's cooled down, slice with a very sharp, serrated knife. Toast it until golden and pile it with toppings. I just leave it in a block and slice off nice thin pieces as I go, or you could do the whole loaf and store it pre-sliced.

When cool, keep in a sealed container or paper bag in the fridge for up to a week. It freezes well for a couple of months, too.

TIP

+ If you can't find linseeds, you can use an extra ½ cup of pumpkin or sunflower seeds.
+ I find the loaf easiest to slice when I use ½ oats and ½ gluten-free/buckwheat flour.

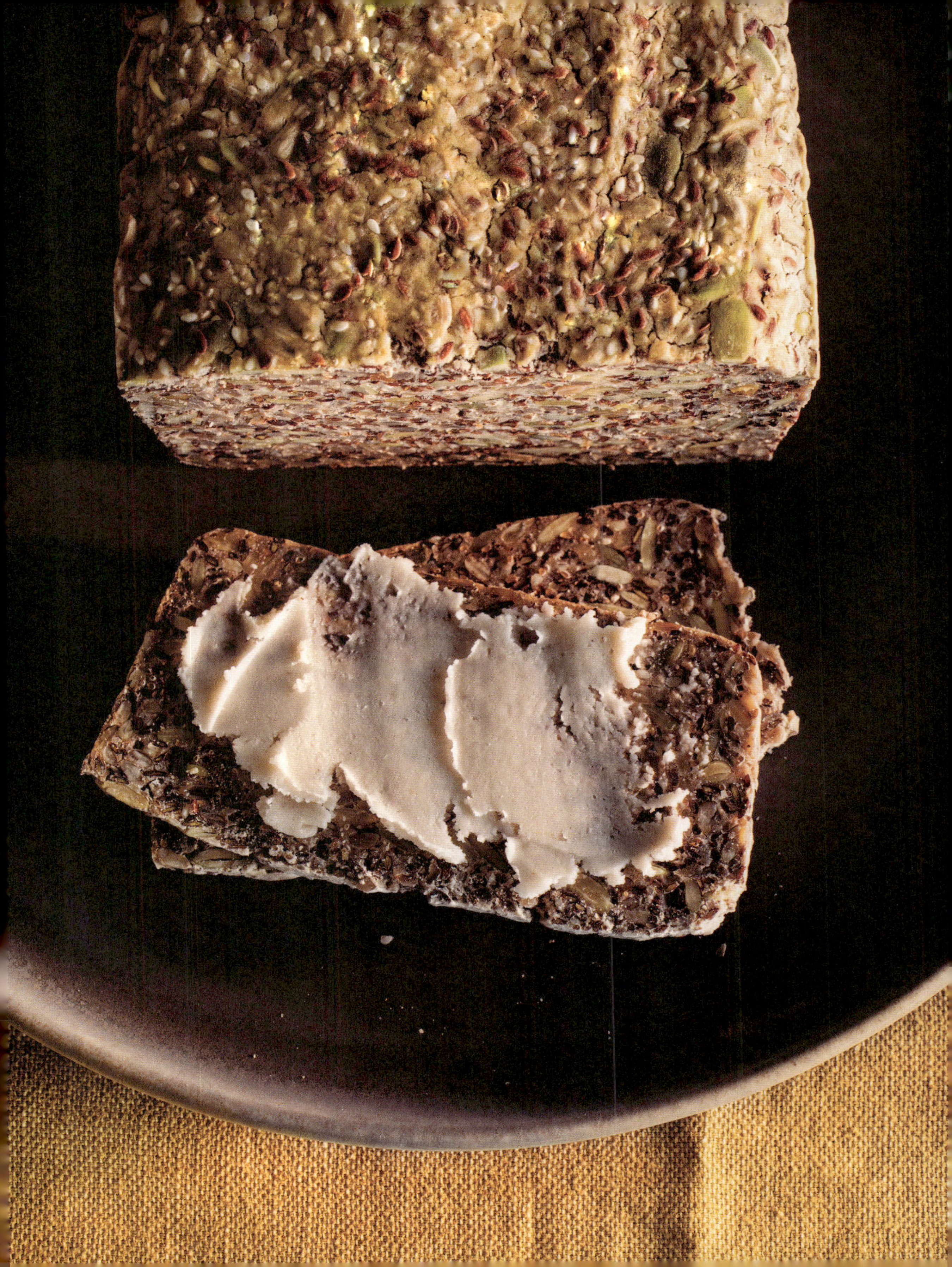

LOCKDOWN LOAF

3 cups plain flour (or use self-raising and omit the baking powder)

3 tsp baking powder

2 tsp sugar

1 tsp salt

375ml beer (lager is good — I use a 330ml bottle, then add a little water (roughly 3 tbsp, doesn't need to be exact) that I've swilled around in the empty beer bottle

toppings of choice, such as: finely chopped onion or red onion; grated dairy-free cheese; sweet chilli sauce; chipotle sauce; sprinkle of smoked paprika and/ or oregano; pesto; tapenade or olives; chopped sundried tomatoes; sunflower, pumpkin, sesame, poppy or cumin seeds

extra virgin olive oil, for drizzling

TO MAKE IT GLUTEN-FREE

Use a GF flour mix (if it's a self-raising one, omit the baking powder) and GF beer (see tips). Keep in mind that some GF flour works better than others, it's a case of trial and error for this one.

PREP 10 minutes **COOK** 45 minutes **MAKES** 1 small loaf

When New Zealand went into lockdown during the 2020 Covid-19 nightmare, I was chuffed to be able to help in my own small way. People wanted fresh bread, but they couldn't go out to the bakery and the yeast promptly disappeared from the supermarket shelves as people panic-bought supplies. Enter the now legendary Beer Bread, aptly renamed Lockdown Loaf! Boy, did it go viral. The easiest and arguably most delicious bread you could ever ask for. It's not light and crispy, it's dense; almost like a huge, delicious savoury scone you can slice. Keep in mind that if your loaf tin is large, it won't rise as impressively as it has in this photo.

Preheat the oven to 180°C regular bake and line a small loaf tin (mine was about 23cm x 13cm at the widest part) with baking paper.

Sift the flour, baking powder, sugar and salt into a large mixing bowl. Stir to combine.

Pour in the beer (and/or water) and stir again to combine into a sticky dough. Scrape into the prepared tin with a spatula and smooth out.

Finish with the toppings of your choice and a drizzle of olive oil.

Bake in the oven for about 45 minutes — it should have risen and puffed up and be all golden and delicious-looking. (When I make the gluten-free loaf, I find it needs more like an hour.)

This bread is best served warm, straight out of the oven, however once it's cooled down and starts firming up, it's amaaazing toasted (you'll probably need to put it down twice), or as a base for toasties.

Keep at room temperature in a bag or container. It's not gonna last long, though, I warn you now!

TIPS

- If making a gluten-free loaf, add 2 tbsp of either psyllium husk powder or ground chia seeds, along with ⅓ cup extra beer (or water). This helps give the loaf a springier, bread-like texture. After mixing the dough, let it rest for 10 minutes in the tin before it goes into the oven, to let the chia or husks swell up and do their thing. You can get psyllium husk powder and ground chia seeds at many supermarkets nowadays. If you have whole chia seeds at home, you can grind them to a powder in a mortar and pestle, coffee grinder or bullet.
- If you can't find a gluten-free beer, soda water works, but you'll miss that lovely flavour that makes beer bread so special.

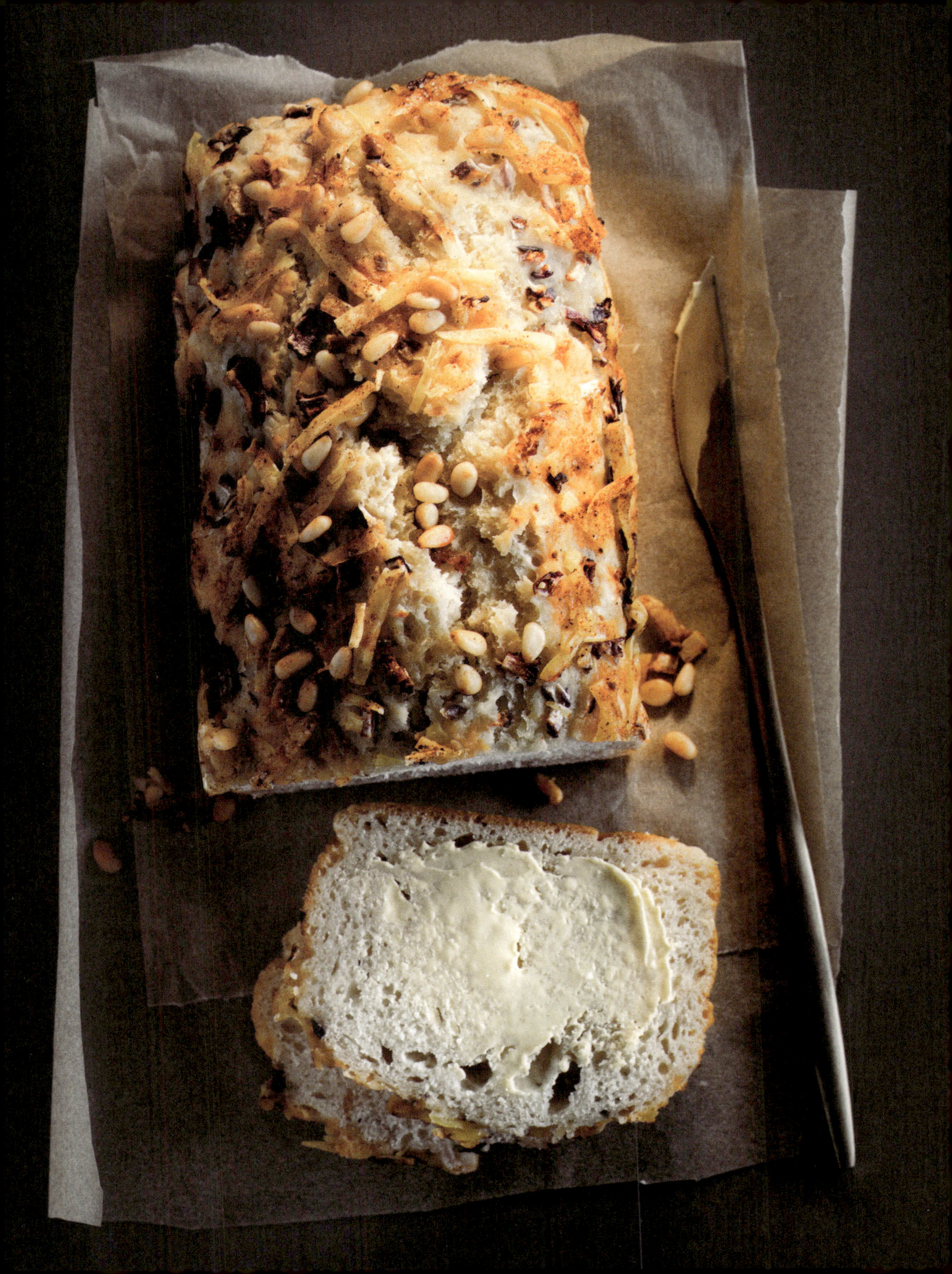

PLANT PARMESAN

½ cup raw walnuts
½ cup raw cashews
¼ cup nutritional yeast
2 tsp miso paste (optional)
1 clove garlic, crushed
1 tsp salt

TO MAKE IT GLUTEN-FREE
Use a GF miso paste.

PREP 5 minutes   **MAKES** just over 1 cup

This is a miraculous and über-tasty sprinkle that you'll want to keep on hand in the fridge at all times. Pile it on pasta, sandwiches, roasted veges, avocado toast, lasagne — anywhere you'd normally use Parmesan or where you feel like you want a nice salty burst of real savoury and umami flavour. Walnuts are a bit of a secret weapon in plant-based cooking — they make everything super scrumptious.

Place all the ingredients in a food processor and whizz until you have a fine crumb.

Store in a glass jar or airtight container in the fridge for a couple of weeks.

TIPS

+ You can leave the garlic out if you like and it will keep longer in the fridge, and still be tasty.
+ Don't worry if you don't have the miso, it's still awesome without it.

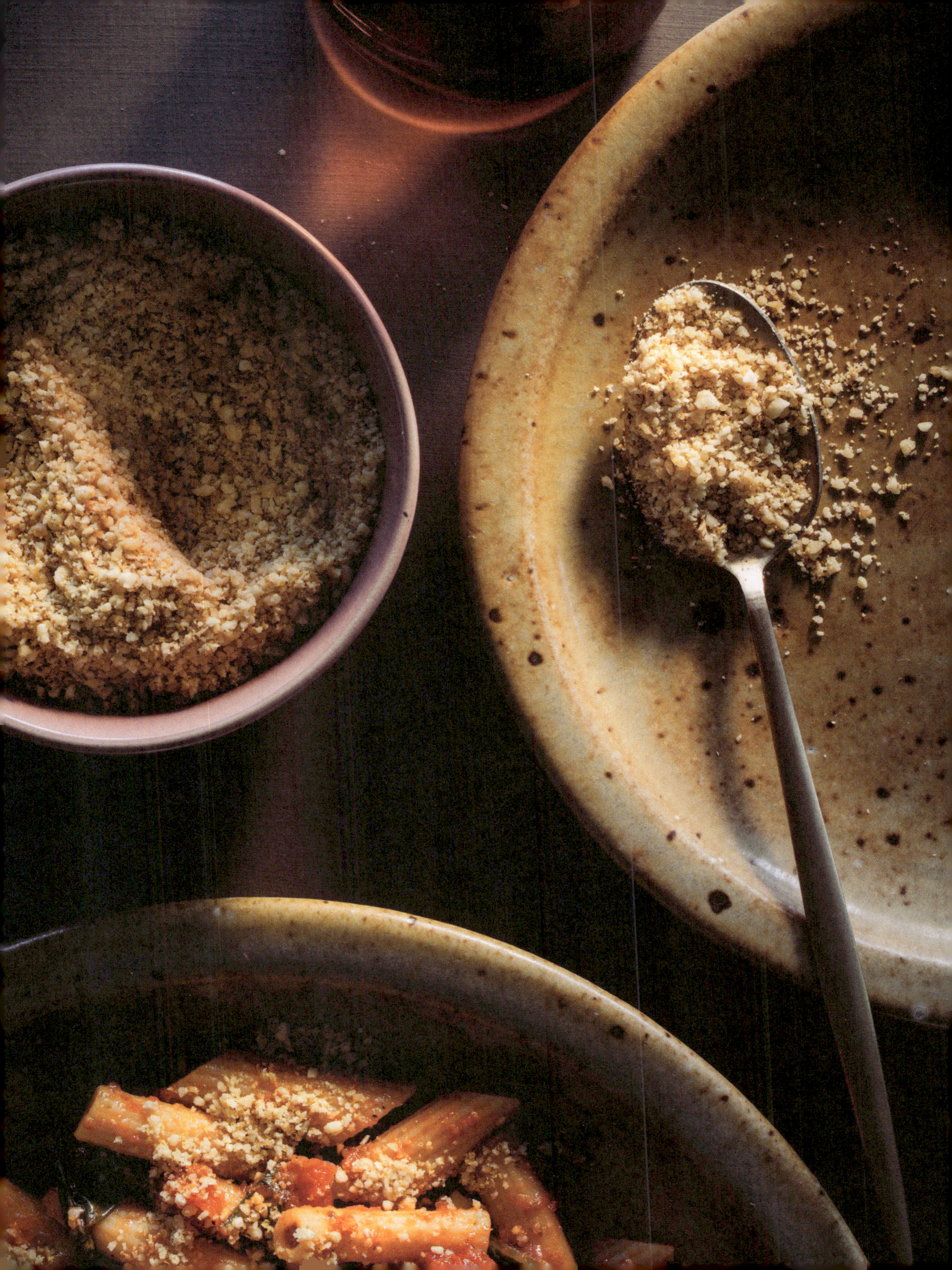

MARINATED FETA

1 cup raw cashews
½ cup melted coconut oil (it has to be unflavoured)
1½ tbsp hot water
1½ tbsp canned chickpea liquid (aquafaba)
1 tbsp nutritional yeast
1 clove garlic, peeled
1 tsp apple cider vinegar
1 tsp salt
¼ tsp finely ground black or white pepper

TO ASSEMBLE

2 x 350ml jars with lids (or one larger jar, or use a plastic container)
1 cup extra virgin olive oil
1 cup grapeseed or sunflower oil
2–4 small sprigs rosemary
20 whole peppercorns

IT'S GLUTEN-FREE

PREP 15 minutes, plus 1+ hour soaking time and overnight to set
MAKES 2 x 300ml jars

For ages we'd been buying jars of plant-based feta marinated in oil, and while it was unbelievably delish, it was also pretty spensy — we had to ration it out in slivers like it was war-time contraband. This homemade version is a lot kinder on the pocket, but delivers the same lightly salted, creamy, melt-in-the-mouth epicness. We have it on toast with avocado, tomato and basil — it's so good! It's also beautiful sprinkled on salads and smooshed on sandwiches. Because of the coconut oil it melts fairly quickly, so store it in the fridge, in the oil. And eat it as quickly as you can once it's out — which shouldn't be difficult!

Place the cashews in a heatproof bowl or jug and cover with just-boiled water. Leave to soak for at least an hour (or overnight), then drain.

Line a square loaf tin with plastic wrap or baking paper so that it covers the base and goes up the sides.

Transfer the cashews to a high-speed blender or bullet blender, add the remaining ingredients and blitz until silky smooth. This will probably only be 10 seconds or so in a really good bullet, or a minute or two in a blender — just keep testing as you go.

Scrape the mixture into the tin, cover and freeze to set (or you can refrigerate overnight, but freezing seems to help the cheese keep its shape better).

Prepare the jars by filling them three-quarters full with half each of the oils, and divide the rosemary and peppercorns between the two. You can also just use one larger jar.

Slice the cheese into cubes with a sharp knife and carefully drop them into the oil mixture until the jars are loosely filled. Refrigerate immediately, and keep refrigerated until you need it.

The cheese will melt fairly quickly in hot weather and on hot food, but that's part of its charm.

TIP

+ If your blender doesn't quite blitz properly because the mixture isn't catching the blades, you may need to double the mixture or add a little more liquid. Tilting and jiggling a bullet blender helps too.

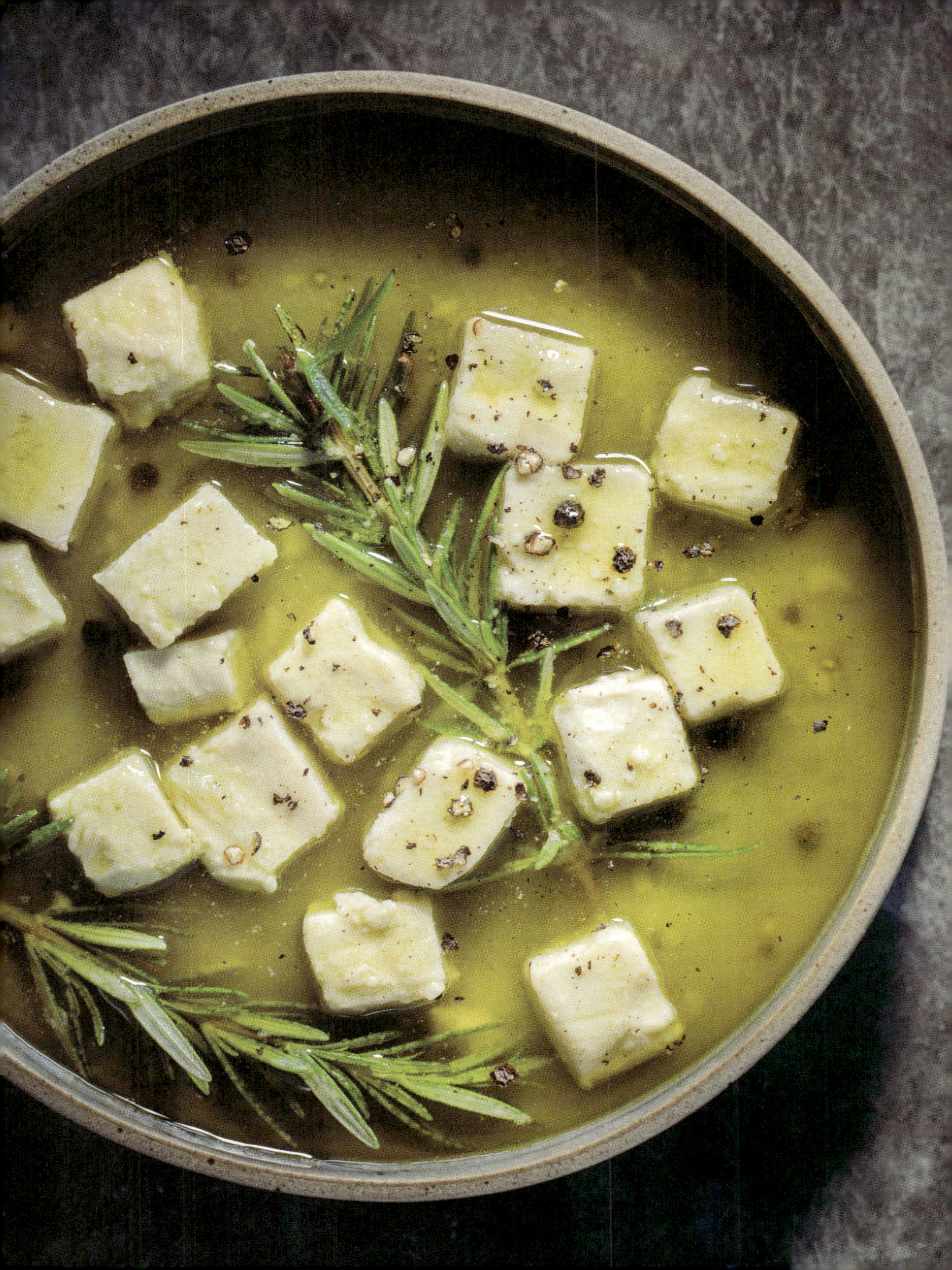

GLÖGG

½ cup soft brown sugar
½ cup water
1 x 750ml bottle red wine (I used cabernet sauvignon)
500ml port
1 cup brandy
few slices fresh ginger
10 whole cardamom pods
2 sticks cinnamon
8 whole cloves
2 tsp vanilla extract
zest of 1 orange

TO SERVE

1 cup raisins or sultanas
¾ cup toasted almonds

PREP 1 hour **SERVES** 8

What the heck is glögg, I hear you cry! Just think of it as Swedish mulled wine, a mid-winter treat for a special occasion. This saucy little number is pronounced something like 'glurg', which I feel is rather appropriate as you can 'glurgle' it down (although actually, it's better when sipped delicately). I thought it would be nice to include a mulled-wine recipe in this book and Douglas, who spent eight years living in Sweden, suggested this version that includes juicy raisins and toasted almonds. I made it for Christmas as an aperitif and it was a huge hit. It's like mulled wine on juicy, festive steroids!

Place the sugar and water in a small saucepan and simmer over a medium heat until the sugar has dissolved.

Pour this mixture into a larger saucepan and add the remaining ingredients. Reduce the heat right down — you want to get the mixture nice and hot, but not let it simmer at all. As soon as you do that, all the alcohol will evaporate and you'll have virgin glögg. Which won't taste quite as good.

Leave it on a low heat for 30–60 minutes, until the flavours from the aromatics have had time to release into the glögg. Before serving, strain out the ginger and other spices with a small sieve.

To serve, ladle hot glögg into small glasses (you don't need much). Add a few sultanas and almonds to the glass. By the time you've sipped your way delicately to the bottom, they will have soaked up flavour and juiciness from the liquid. Dig them out with a little spoon and enjoy!

TIPS

+ If you have some cheesecloth or muslin, you can put the spices on it and tie it up into a little bag. Then you can remove it at the end to save having to strain the glögg.
+ To toast raw almonds, bake at 180°C for 5 minutes or so until just turning golden.

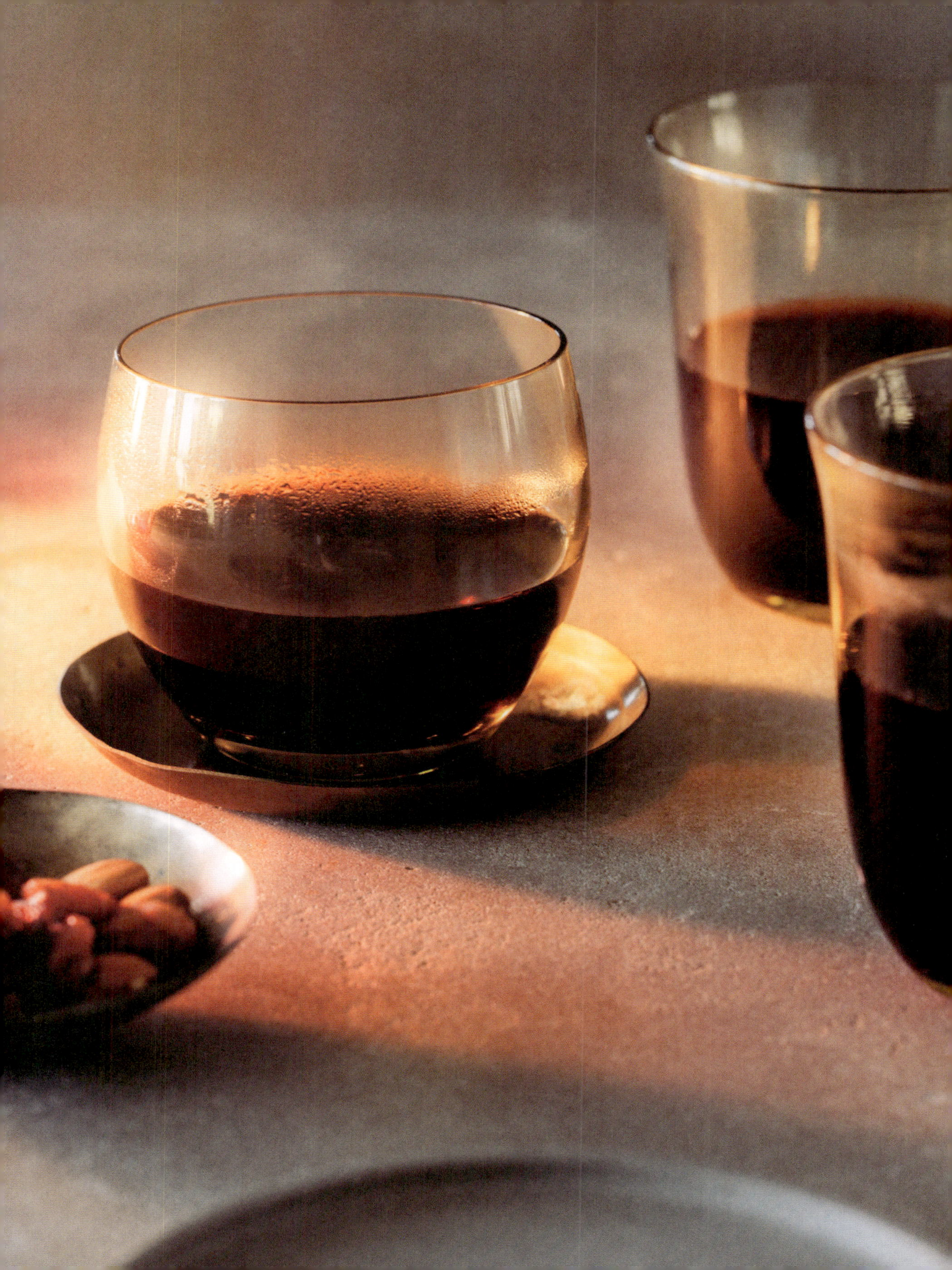

VERY HUNGRY CATERPILLAR

2 large apples

1 lemon

½ telegraph cucumber, peeled (or 2 short cucumbers)

3 large stalks celery

big handful spinach or silverbeet leaves (not baby spinach)

½ cup roughly chopped parsley or coriander (or a mixture; optional)

1cm slice ginger

PREP 15 minutes   **SERVES** 2–3

There are times when I realise that I haven't eaten many green veges in a while, or I'll be feeling tired after some late nights with Sky, or a bit jaded after travelling (or after a couple of glasses of red wine). I can feel my body craving something clean and revitalising, and this juice is what I turn to. You can almost feel the goodness leaching into your cells after you've finished it! All the energy in those fresh green leaves is transformed into such a pretty drink — a posh and snooty caterpillar would peer through his monocle and declare it a winner. Sky loves these juices, too!

Wash all the produce well. If your produce isn't organic and you're worried about sprays, soak it in water and apple cider vinegar as described on page 204, then peel the apples and scrub anything that might have been waxed.

Slice all the fruit and veges up into sizes that fit your juicer — the leaves can just be smooshed in. Juice as you normally would. I have a slow-press juicer that can get clogged easily, so I intersperse the apples between other things to help stop that happening.

Drink it right away when it's fresh.

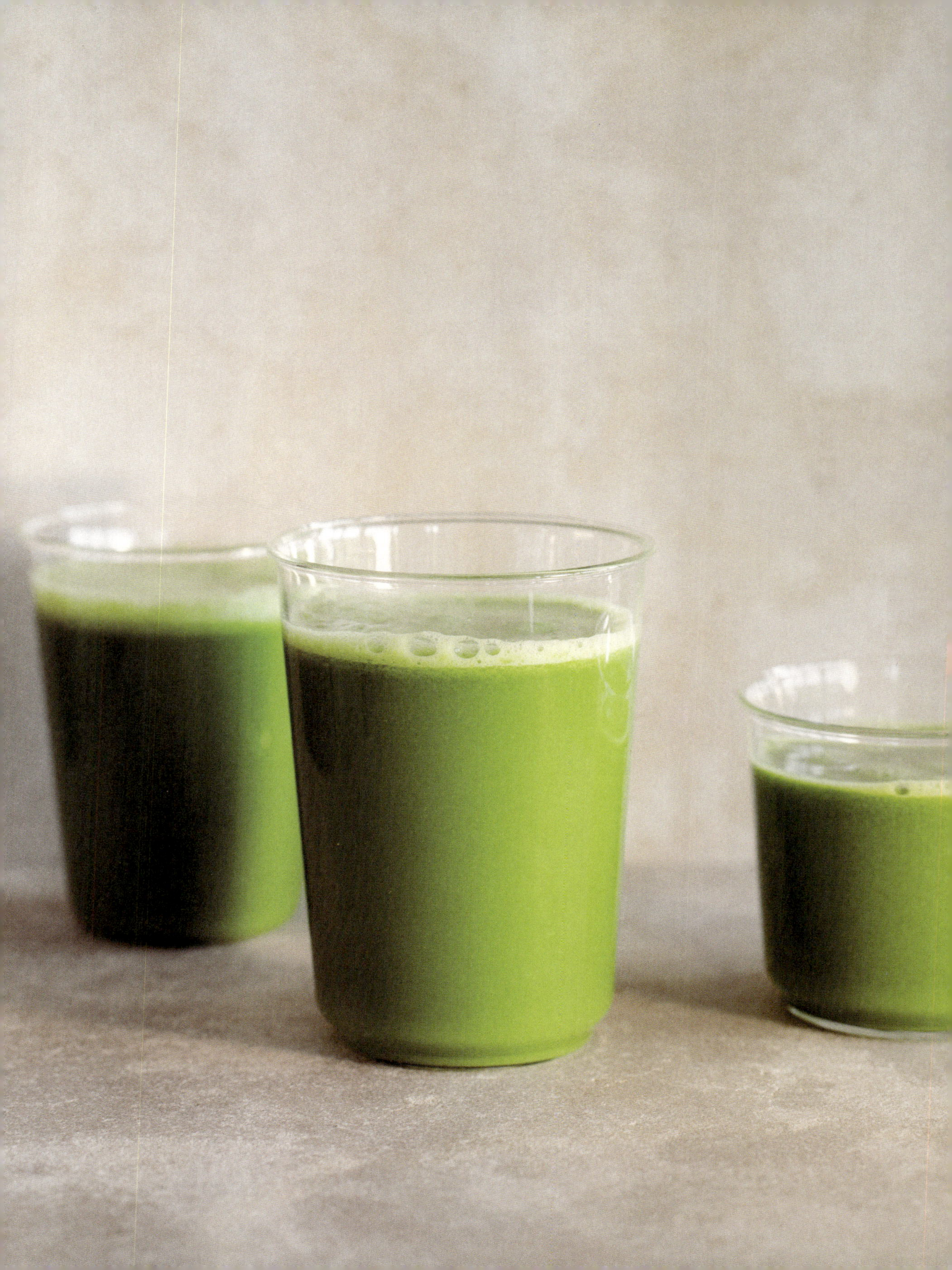

IN THE PINK JUICE

3 large apples
1 small lemon, unpeeled (or ½ a large one)
5 large carrots
1 small to medium beetroot

PREP 15 minutes   **SERVES** 3–4

A big serving of this glowing, vitamin-rich juice is great for boosting your immunity. It's loaded with goodness and I'll wager you'll feel damn fine afterwards. It's also delightfully delicious and surprisingly sweet. We try to make it every other day, alternating it with the Very Hungry Caterpillar juice on page 202. The recipe is easily doubled if you're wanting to make enough for the whole family or keep some in a Thermos or sealed container for later.

―

If your produce is organic, you don't need to peel any of it; just wash well and use.

If you're worried about sprays and pesticides (which are real and pretty nasty) you can soak your fruit in a bath of water and apple cider vinegar. In a large bowl or the sink, mix 4 parts water to 1 part vinegar and soak the fruit for 10 minutes.

Scrub any fruit that might be waxed (store-bought lemons and apples are often waxed). Rinse all the fruit before preparing.

Slice the fruit and veges into pieces that fit your juicer. For the lemon, you juice the whole thing — skin, pips and all. Trust me, it makes it taste incredible!

Juice everything as normal.

Best served immediately — I add ice if it's a hot day.

You can keep it in the fridge, well sealed, for up to a day, but the juice will slowly lose its nutrients the longer it's kept.

―

TIP

+ Just by owning a juicer and making homemade juice, you are already so awesome. But if you're wanting to get the best out of your juices, I can recommend a 'slow-press' or 'masticating' (that word, honestly!) juicer rather than a fast centrifugal one. The slow juicers extract juice without any heat, so most of the vitamins and enzymes in the produce remain, whereas apparently the friction from the fast juicers can create heat which compromises the quality of the juice. It takes longer the slow way, but it's sort of meditative standing there watching the magic happen.

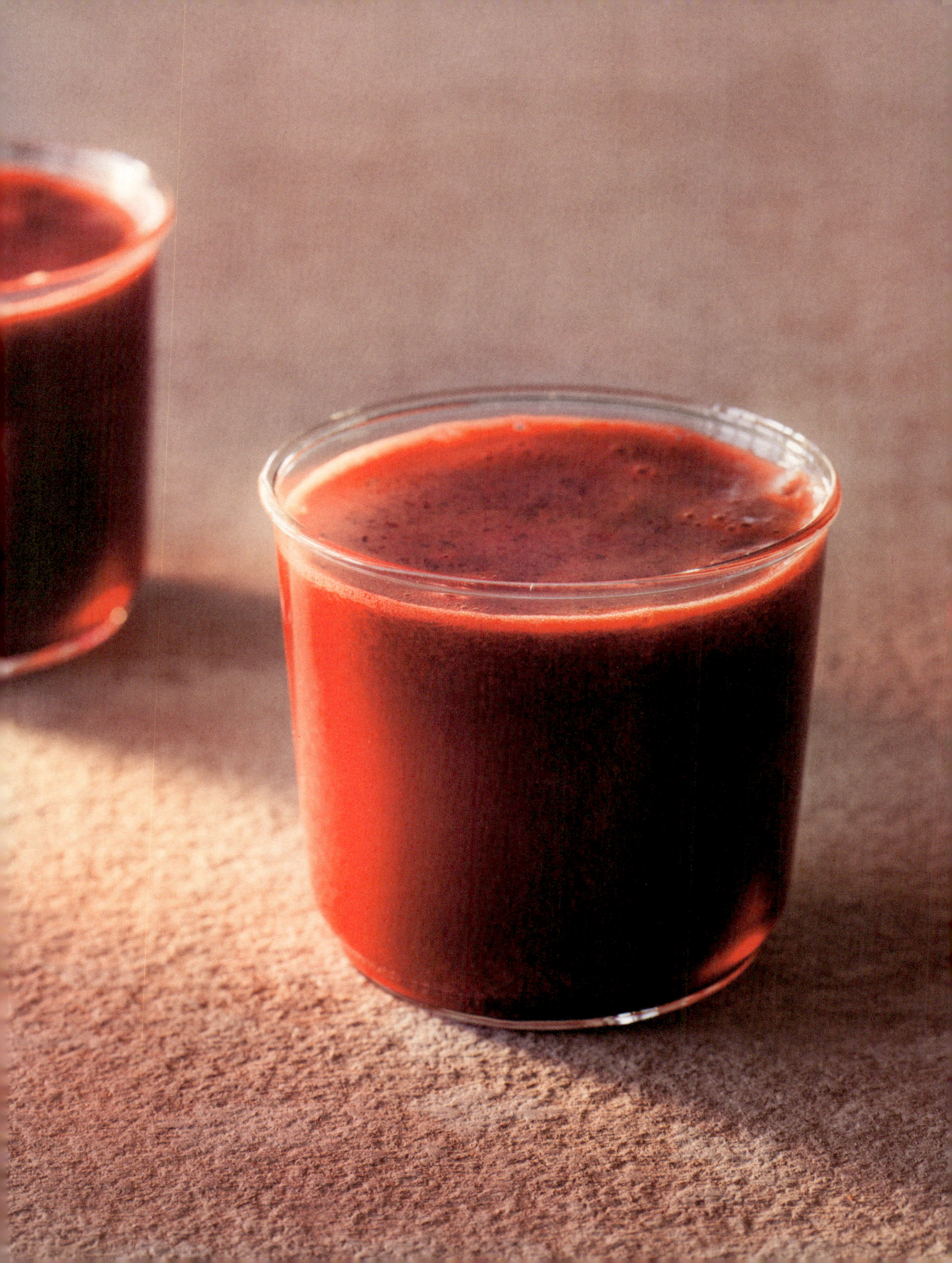

SUPER SMOOTHIE

3 ripe bananas, peeled and broken into chunks

2 cups plant-based milk (I use one with added calcium)

3 tbsp almond butter (or peanut butter)

2 tbsp good-quality cacao powder

2 tbsp hemp seed powder

2 tsp honey (optional)

5 cubes ice

toasted whole buckwheat groats, for serving (optional)

desiccated coconut (optional)

PREP 10 minutes   **SERVES** 2

This smoothie is full of protein and omega fats from the hemp powder, energy from the banana (the holy grail of fruit!), good fats from the almond butter, and calcium from the plant-based milk — and more, I could keep going . . . I use it as a pre-breakfast snack, or as something to keep me going between meals, but other people I've made it for say it keeps them full for ages and it feels like they've had a meal. It just depends on the person. If you're making it for one, you can keep the rest in a Thermos or sealed jar in the fridge for later. If your bananas are nice and ripe, you may not need the honey.

Put all the ingredients (apart from the buckwheat) in a high-speed or bullet blender and whizz until silky smooth. Pour into glasses and serve with toasted buckwheat and desiccated coconut for crunch, if you want to be fancy.

TIPS

+ Cacao is an uncooked, minimally processed version of cocoa, and therefore has much more nutritional value. It's one of the best plant-based sources of iron known to us. It's also rich in antioxidants and a natural mood enhancer.
+ You should be able to find hemp seed powder in the health-food aisle in the supermarket. It's considered a 'superfood', though I'm dubious about that word — let's just say that it's packed with protein, fibre, omega fats, vitamins and minerals and has a pleasant nutty flavour. Google it for more info. Hemp is a thing.
+ For an even richer, more filling smoothie, add ½ ripe avocado or 2 tbsp coconut oil.

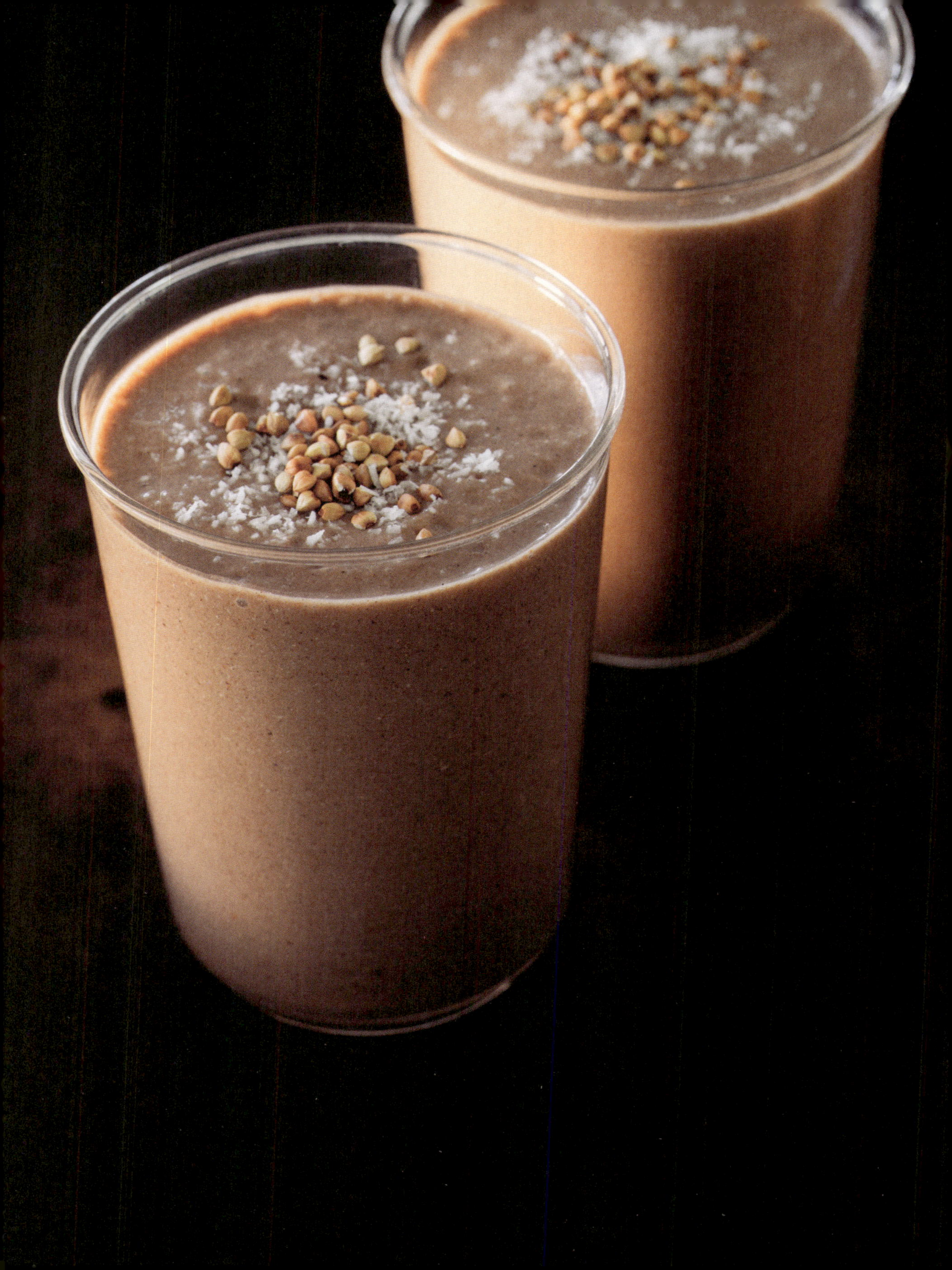

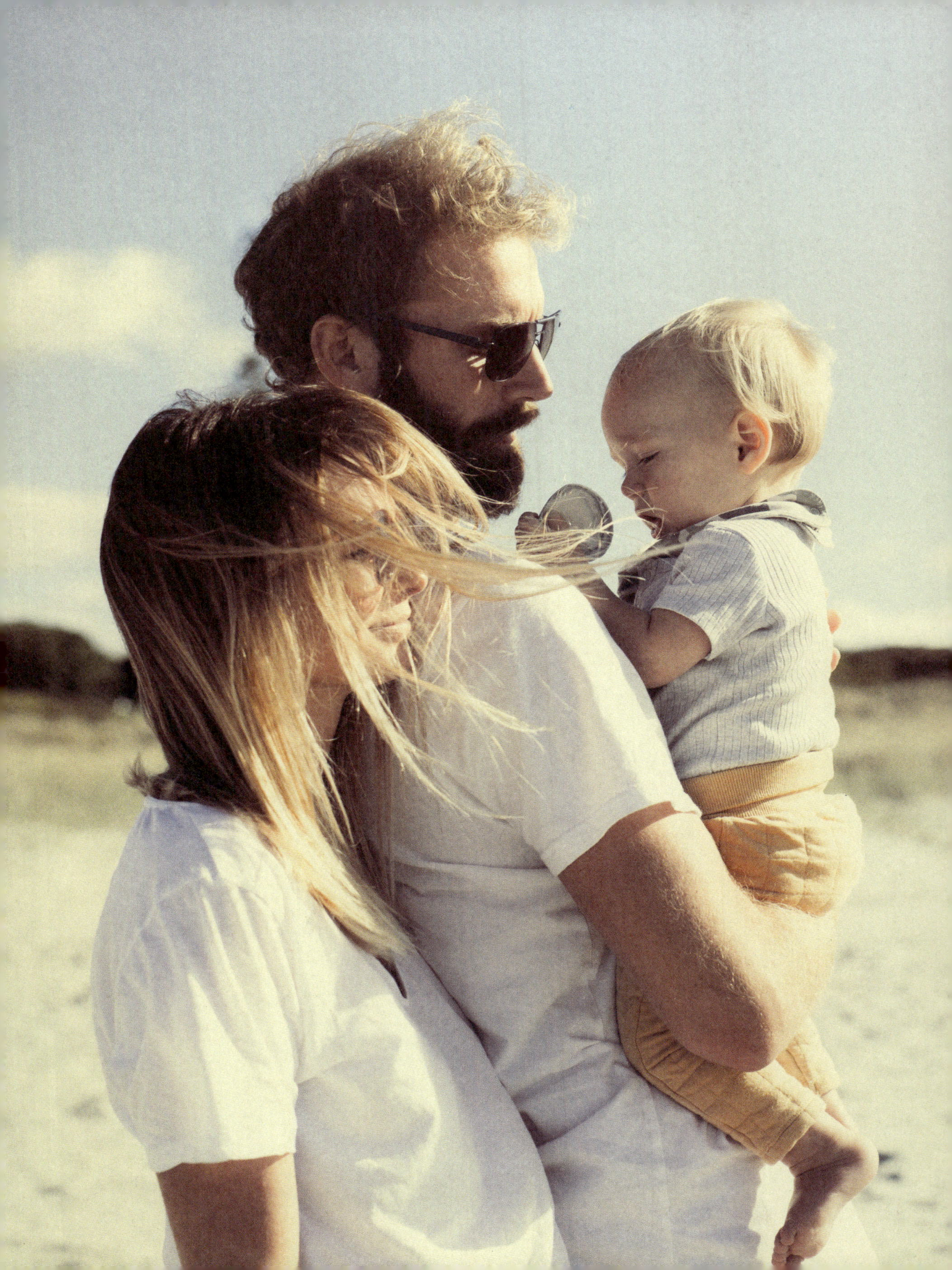

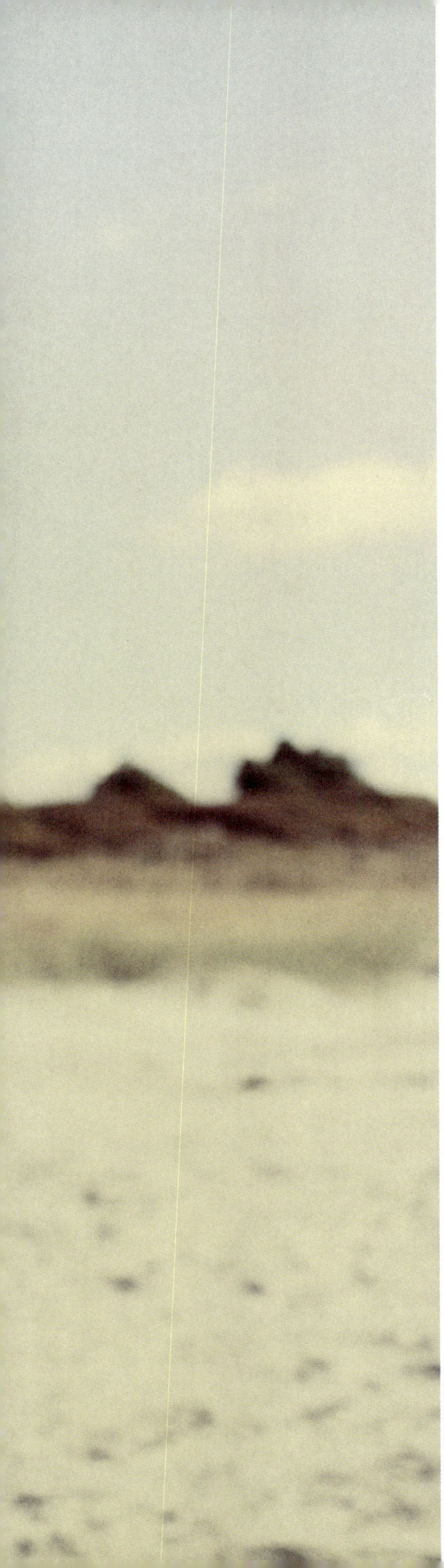
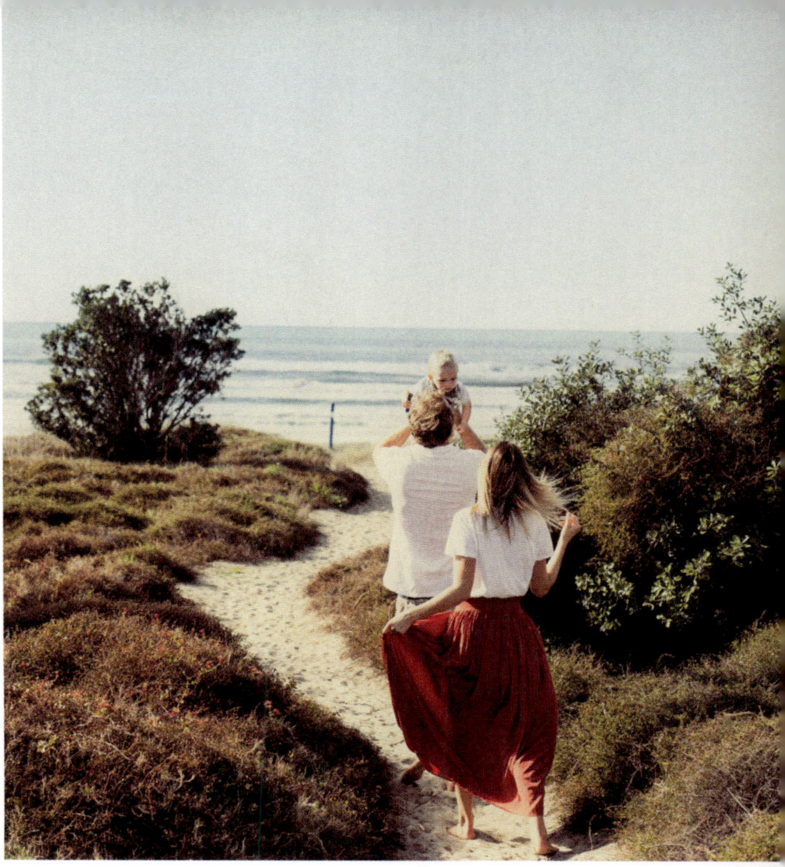
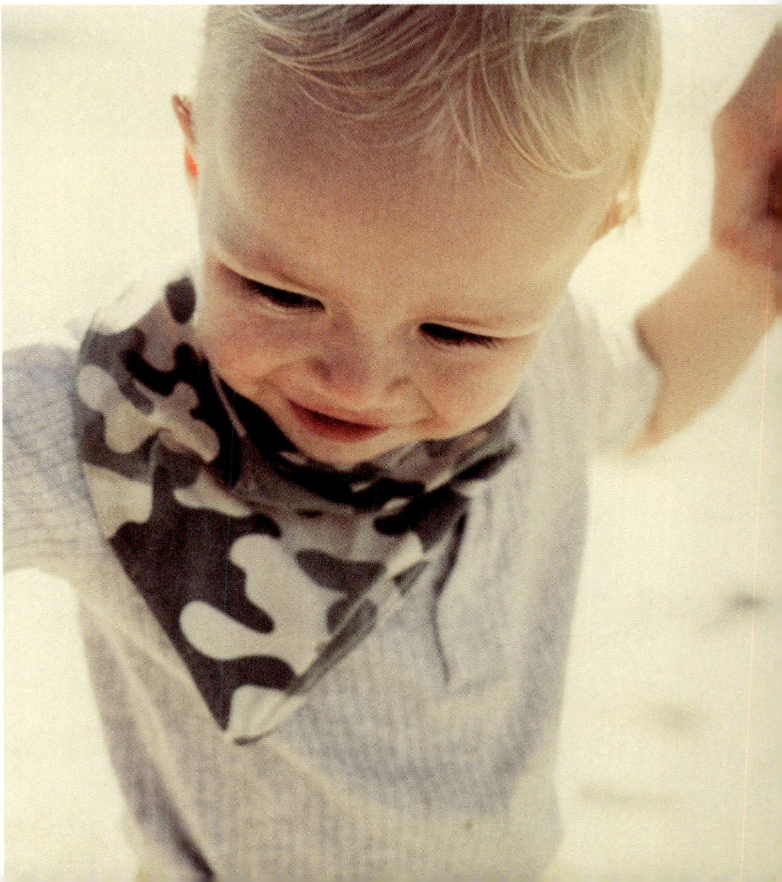

FLASH BROWNS

5–6 medium-sized Agria potatoes, peeled
¾ tsp salt
¾ tsp finely ground white or black pepper
grapeseed or sunflower oil, for frying

TO SERVE
plant-based aïoli (see page 182)
tomato sauce

IT'S GLUTEN-FREE

PREP 20 minutes, plus 2+ hours to chill   **COOK** 10 minutes   **MAKES** 4–5

Flash as! Hash browns are a popular choice for breakfast (or second breakfast) in our household. We used to buy them frozen . . . I am a little abashed to admit it but hey, they tasted good. But these are better! It was time to create a homemade hash brown recipe that was epic but wasn't just mushing raw grated potato into clumps. (I've never been overly happy with that method — the end product always feels a bit gooey.) These flash browns are kind of a cross between a roast potato and a potato fritter, which can't be bad, eh? Thanks to my friend Tony for the recipe inspo!

Bring a saucepan of salted cold water to a gentle boil, then add the whole peeled potatoes and set a timer for 20 minutes. They should be about three-quarters cooked by then.

Drain the potatoes and refrigerate for 2 hours until completely cold.

Grate the potatoes and add to the bowl with the salt and pepper. Scrunch to combine.

Shape the mixture into about 4–5 hash browns (more if you want them smaller). Really squash them tight. You can wet your hands a little to help with the final shaping. Set aside or refrigerate until needed — you can keep them overnight in the fridge in a covered container, as long as you haven't had the whole potatoes in the fridge overnight already.

Heat ½ cm of oil in a frying pan over a medium-high heat. Wait until the oil is nice and hot — the tip of a wooden spoon handle will bubble fizzily when dipped in. (If you have a thermometer, you want it around 180–190°C.) If the oil isn't hot enough the hash browns will go soggy and soak up too much oil.

When the oil is hot, add a few hash browns at a time and cook for about 5 minutes on each side — or until they are deep golden brown and crispy on both sides.

Drain on a wire rack sitting over paper towels and cool for a minute or two before eating. Sprinkle with a little extra salt if you like.

Serve with aïoli and tomato sauce. These are also nice with Scrambled Tofu (see page 212), or make it a big breakfast with some baked beans, roasted tomatoes and sliced avocado!

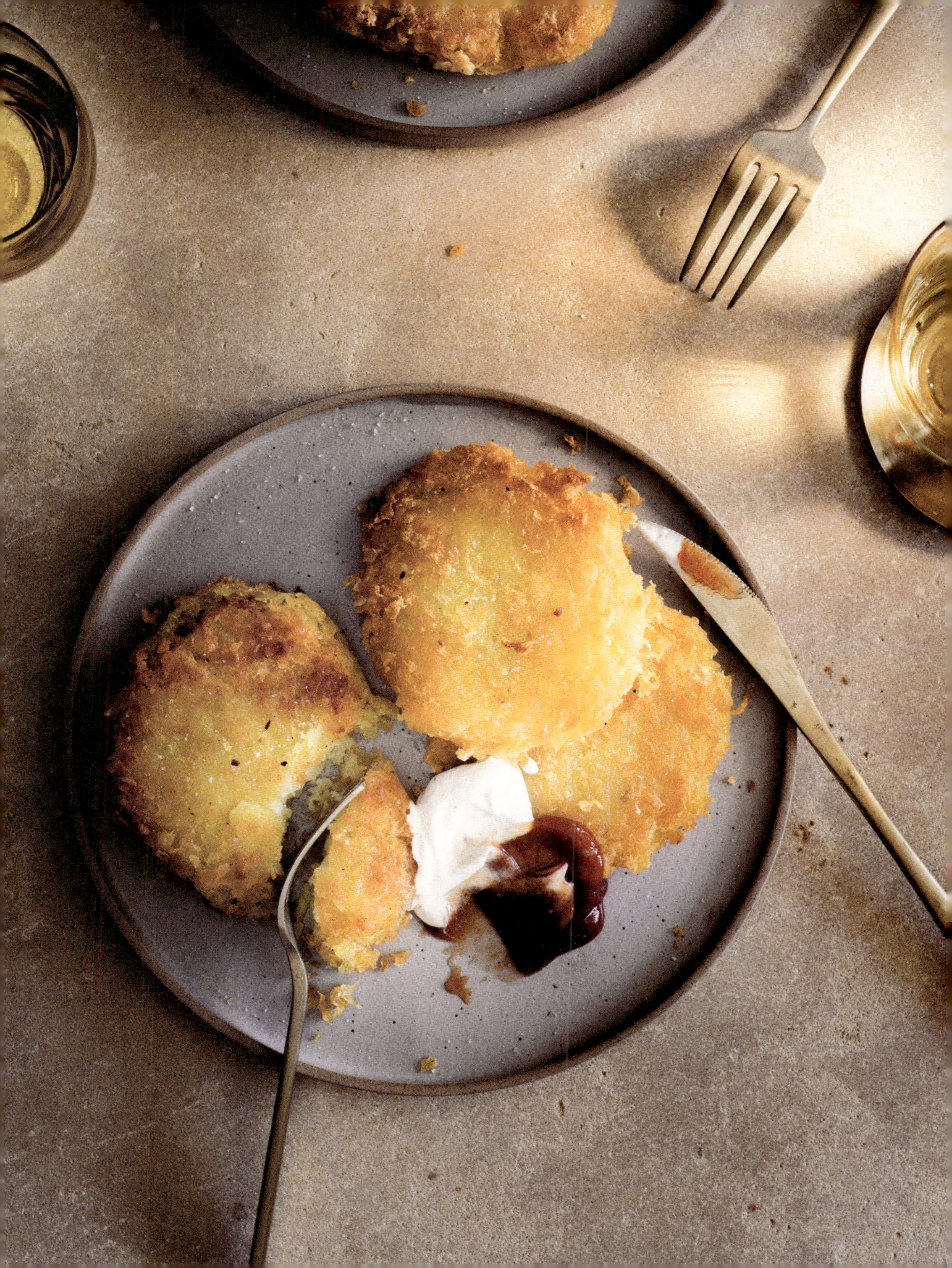

SCRAMBLED TOFU

- 1 x 300g block tofu (organic is best; I use Tonzu)
- 2 tbsp grapeseed oil or unflavoured coconut oil (or use dairy-free spread)
- ½ cup very finely chopped onion
- ½ tsp ground turmeric
- ⅓ cup plant-based milk
- 2 tsp cashew butter (optional)
- ¾ tsp salt
- ½ tsp finely ground black pepper
- ¼ cup chopped fresh parsley and chives, plus extra to garnish
- squeeze of lemon juice
- pinch chilli flakes (optional)

TO SERVE
- freshly toasted bread
- sliced avocado or tomato (optional)

PREP 10 minutes   **COOK** 10 minutes   **SERVES** 2–3

For me, the best part about scrambee eggs (that's what I call them, thanks to Jim Carrey in *The Cable Guy*) is the salt, parsley, pepper and butter! And as I really love tofu, this swap-over dish is a no-brainer for me. Tofu is a really great vehicle for flavour (think of it as a blank canvas), and when crumbled like this it has a texture incredibly similar to cooked egg (and with a little turmeric for colour, it really looks the part). If you're cooking for a crowd, double the recipe. The cashew butter makes it super creamy; I always try to have some on hand in my pantry.

Crumble the tofu up — not too finely, leave some chunkier bits in there. Set aside on a plate.

Heat the oil in a frying pan over a medium-low heat. Add the onion and cook, stirring, for about 7 minutes until softened. Add the turmeric and cook for another minute.

Add the tofu, milk, cashew butter (if using), salt and pepper, and cook for another few minutes until the liquid has almost evaporated. Taste and season with more salt and pepper if you think it needs it. Add the herbs and lemon juice and stir through.

Serve immediately on hot toast (a garnish of sliced avocado and/or tomato is nice) with the extra herbs scattered on top. If you have to leave your scrambled tofu sitting for a while, freshen it up with a little more milk before you serve it so that it isn't dry.

TIP

+ I like drizzling a little Tabasco sauce on top to take the flavours up a level.

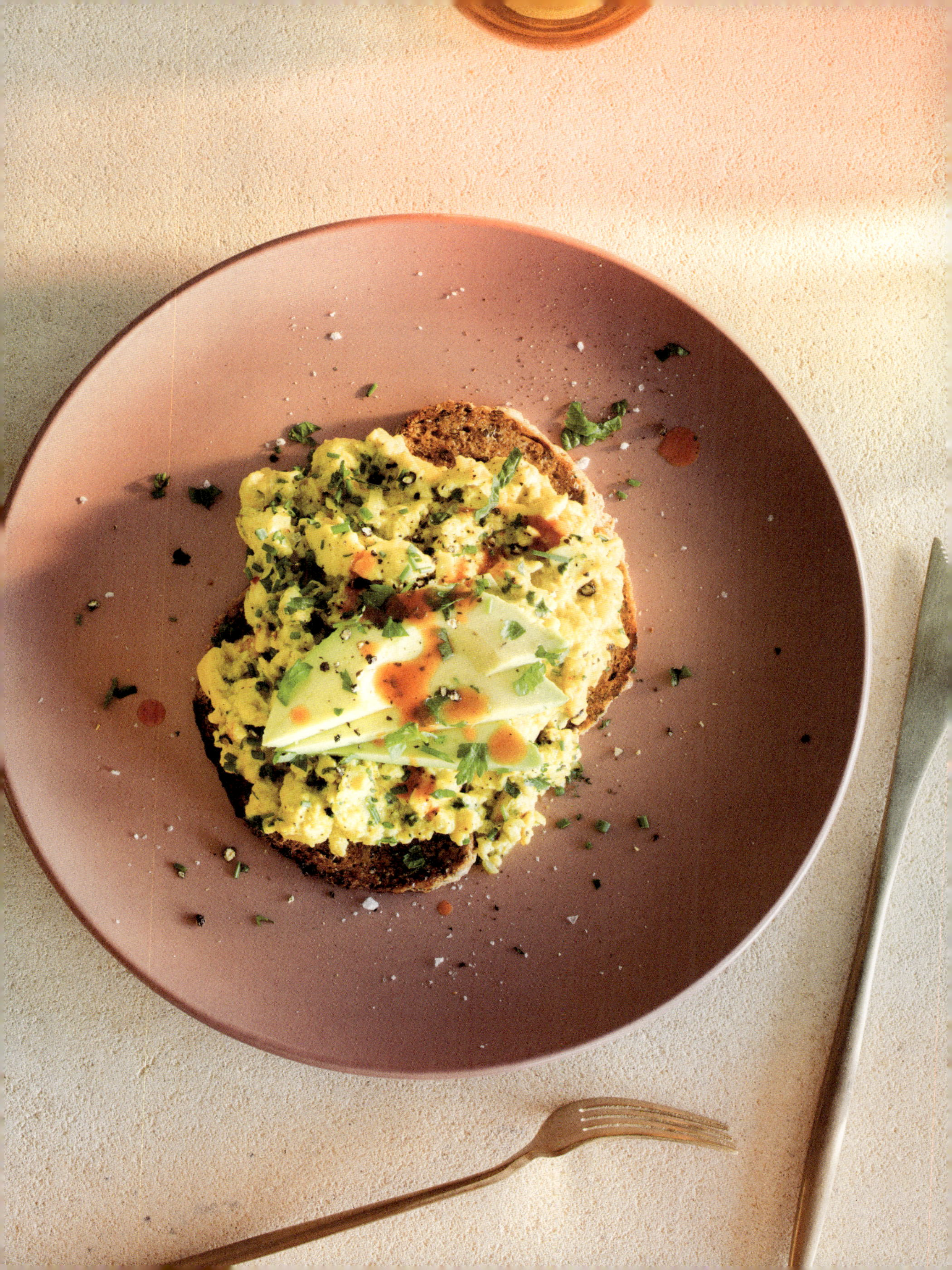

COCONUT PORRIDGE

2 cups rolled oats (I use organic and not wholegrain)
4 cups rice, oat or soy milk
¼ tsp salt
½ cup coconut cream
1 tsp vanilla extract

TO SERVE
almond or peanut butter
sliced banana
soft brown sugar or maple syrup

PREP 5 minutes   **COOK** 7 minutes   **SERVES** 4

This porridge is so creamy and decadent! I know, some people make porridge using water as well as milk, and I lie awake at night worrying about the amount of watery gruel being served up each morning. I just had to include this recipe since we literally ate it *every single day* during the winter when Sky was a newborn. Not only was it incredible fuel for breastfeeding at the time, but it's actually really delicious for everyone, all the time. The toppings make it more of a meal; I never used to find that porridge filled me up for very long until I started making this version.

Place the oats, milk and salt in a medium-sized saucepan, stir to combine and place over a medium-low heat. Cook for about 5 minutes, stirring frequently, or just until the porridge has thickened up.

Add the coconut cream and vanilla and cook for another couple of minutes, or until the consistency is to your liking.

Serve the hot porridge in bowls topped with a dollop of almond or peanut butter, some banana and nice lashings of maple syrup or brown sugar (or both, which is what we do).

TIPS

+ If blueberries are in season, throw a handful on top before serving. Same goes for raspberries.
+ In this photo, I added some sliced almonds for crunch. Some toasted shredded coconut would be amazing too.

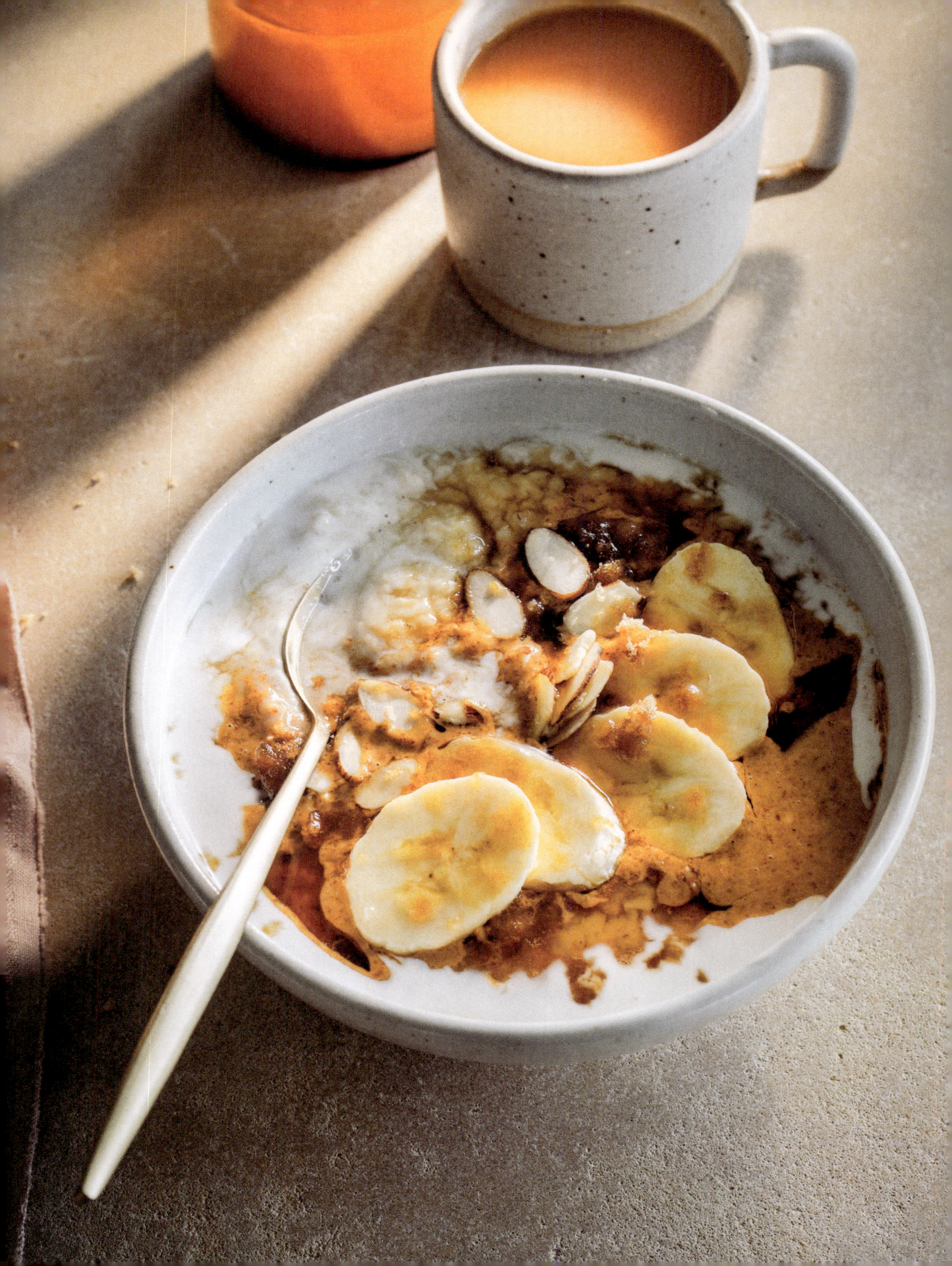

GLUTEN-FREE MUESLI

DRY INGREDIENTS
2½ cups sliced almonds
2 cups sunflower seeds
2 cups buckwheat groats
2 cups desiccated coconut
2 cups shredded coconut or coconut chips
2½ cups walnuts, roughly chopped
1½ cups pumpkin seeds
1 cup sesame seeds

DRIED FRUIT
2½ cups dried apricots, chopped
2½ cups dates, chopped (or use other dried fruit such as sultanas)

WET INGREDIENTS
⅓ cup almond butter
⅓ cup honey (or use maple syrup)
¼ cup maple syrup
1 tsp vanilla extract (optional)
½ tsp salt

IT'S GLUTEN-FREE

TIPS
+ This makes an amazing gift in a nice jar; whoever gets it will be so grateful. And the recipe makes enough for two batches so you can keep half!
+ If you can find sulphur-free apricots, they are amazing. Brown rather than orange, but way better for you.
+ You can add some pre-puffed grains of your choice if you like at the very end.

PREP 30 minutes   **MAKES** enough to last a while

Our summer breakfast go-to. Making your own muesli takes a little time, but with this recipe you'll never look back (the smell of it cooking alone is worth it). It features a deliciously unique blend of goodies (not just a whole load of oats), and it's unquestionably filling and nourishing as well as super-tasty (the almond butter and honey make it very special indeed). You can of course tweak the recipe to your liking — maybe add a couple of handfuls of oats if you like them, and mix it up with the types of nuts or dried fruit you use. You should be able to get buckwheat groats at the supermarket — just ask.

Preheat the oven to 180°C regular bake and get your biggest oven tray ready (or a huge metal roasting dish if you have one). You may have to cook this in two batches.

If your roasting dish has sides, you can use this to both toast the dry ingredients and mix the final muesli. Or, use a huge mixing bowl to combine things at the end.

Add the dry ingredients to the roasting dish/bowl and mix well to combine. Transfer to the oven tray if necessary and bake until you see the top and edges going slightly golden (5–10 minutes). Give it a stir, and however long it took to cook the first time, keep baking in those intervals, stirring after each time, until the whole lot is a little toasty — about 3 times usually does it. The coconut chips will brown first, so make you sure keep stirring it so it doesn't burn.

If necessary, tip it back into the mixing bowl. Add the dried fruit and mix to combine.

Heat the wet ingredients in a small saucepan until melted, then pour over the muesli and stir together to coat evenly.

Leave the muesli to cool completely, then transfer to airtight containers or jars. A jar of it looks very beautiful on the kitchen bench, and the rest is best stored in the fridge so that the oil in the nuts doesn't go rancid in warm weather.

Serve with nut milk, stewed or fresh fruit, Chia Pudding (see page 218) and yoghurt or coconut yoghurt. Stewed or canned black Doris plums are my favourite!

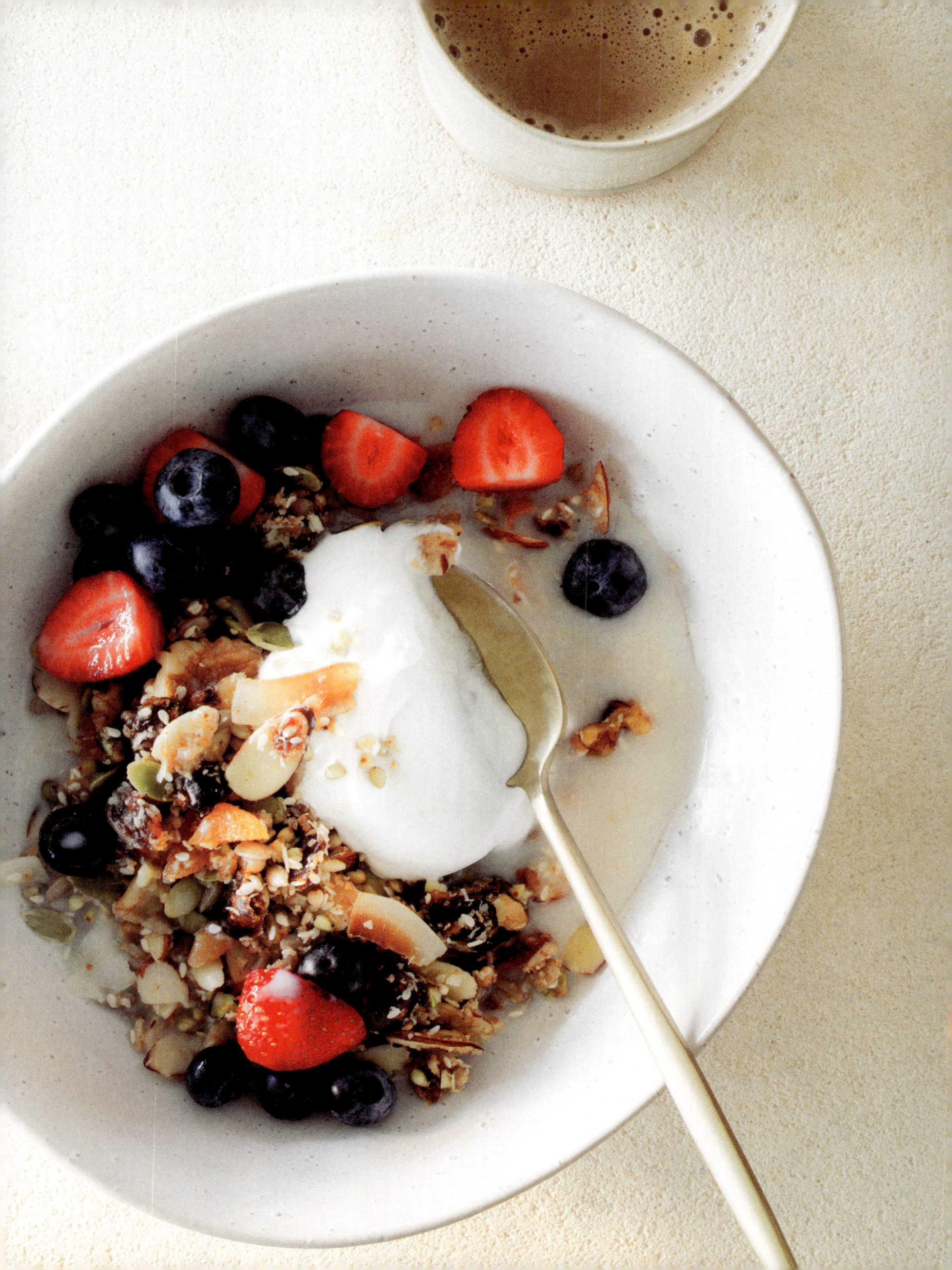

CHIA PUDDING

3 tbsp white or black chia seeds
1 x 400ml can coconut milk
2 tbsp maple syrup
½ tsp vanilla extract
small pinch salt

PREP 5 minutes, plus 30 minutes to set   **MAKES** about 2 cups

Chia pudding is no longer a newfangled thing; these days you'll find it in the cabinets of many cafés across the country, usually served in a wee glass with some muesli and fruit. After sampling a few and deciding that chia pudding was totally my bag, I began making my own a year or two ago and never looked back. I do a big ol' batch and keep it in the fridge to use it as you might use coconut yoghurt — on muesli, with a bowl of fruit salad, in a smoothie, or as a snack by itself (it's very delicious). Sky loves it, too. Chia seeds boast many health benefits (they're a kind of superfood and a good source of omega-3s), and in terms of cost you'll be laughing all the way to the bank.

Put all the ingredients in a jug and whisk or stir with a fork to combine. Let it sit for 5 minutes, then whisk again. Cover and put in the fridge for 30 minutes. Stir again before eating.

Serve as part of breakfast with fruit or on muesli, or as a virtuous dessert with fresh or tinned fruit (black Doris plums are *delish*).

TIPS

+ If you're not sure which coconut milk to buy, I recommend one that has around 16–17% fat content. Don't be scared — the oil in coconuts isn't a 'bad' fat; in fact, it's thought that consumption of coconut-derived foods may help protect the body from infections and viruses. Everything in moderation, as they say.
+ You could use any plant-based milk in place of coconut milk; the creamier the better, though (think cashew or soy).

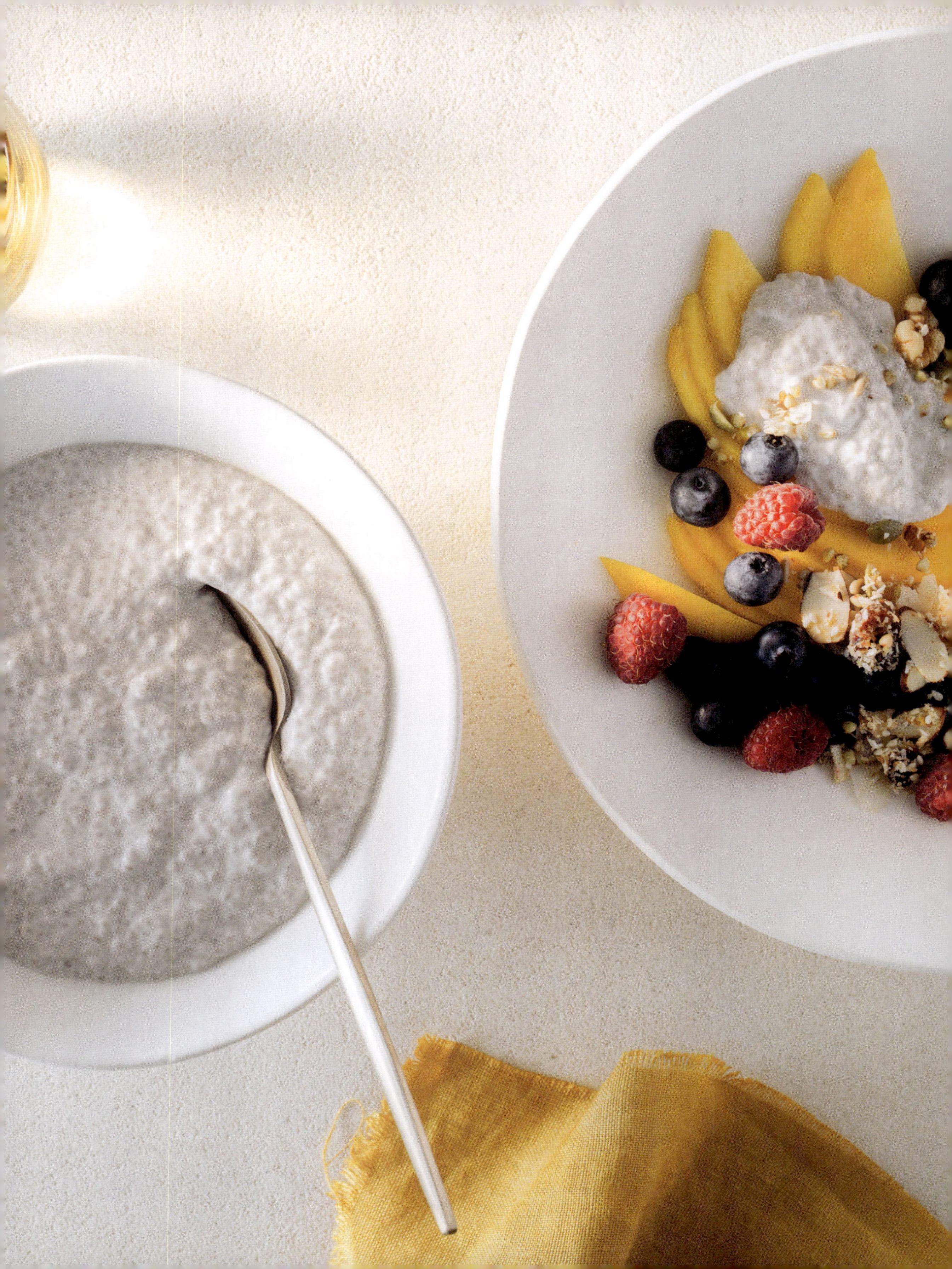

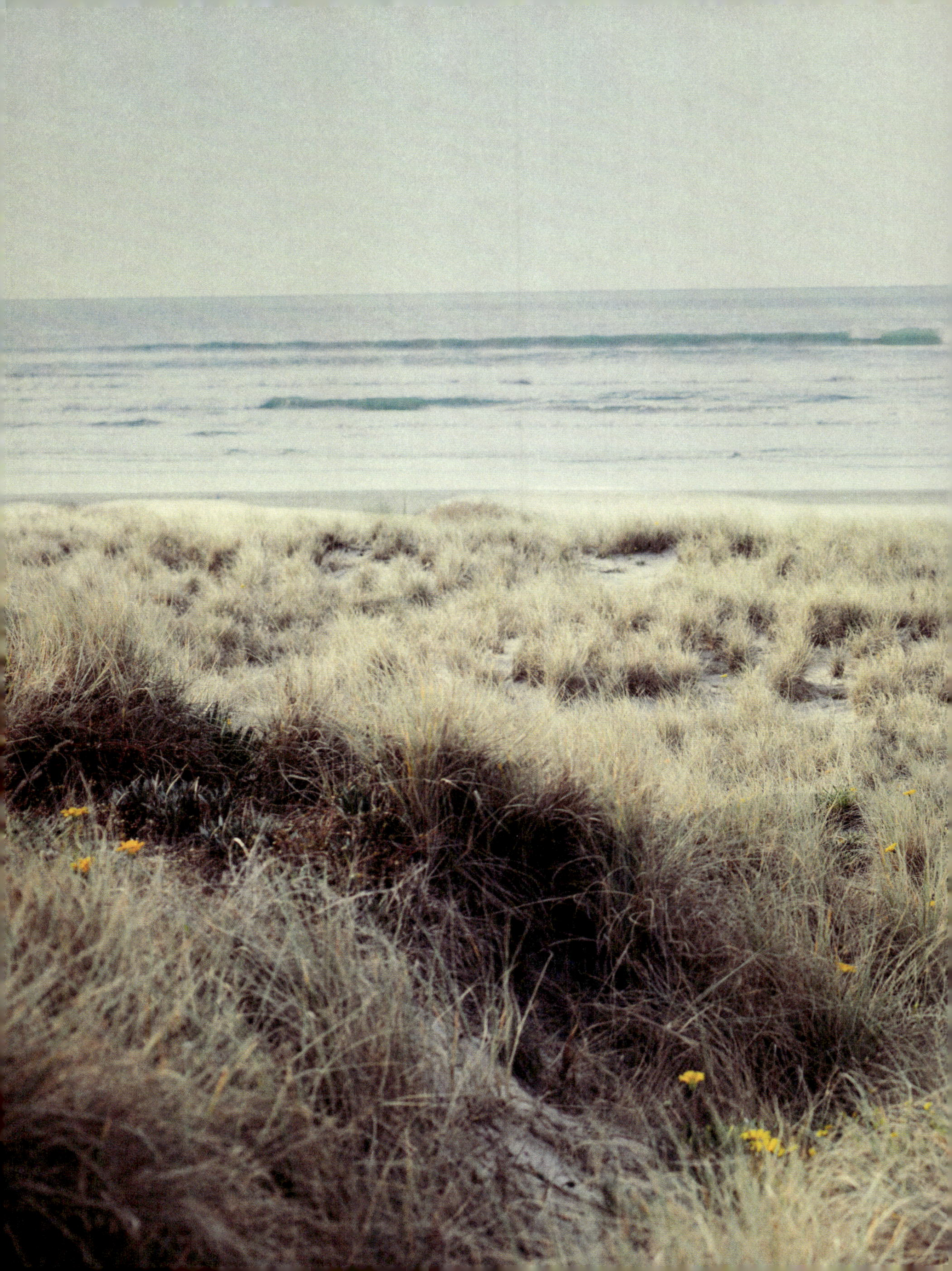

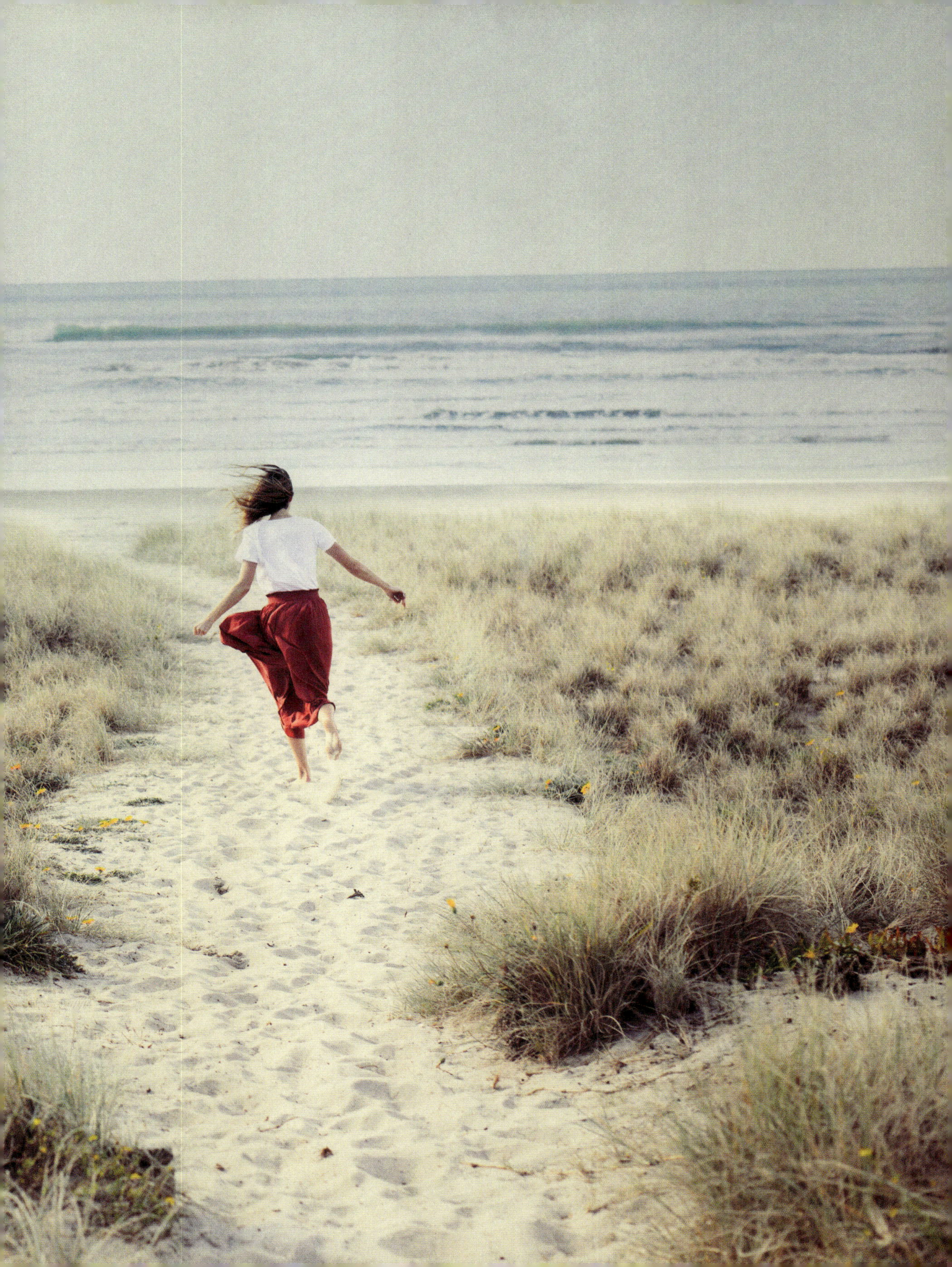

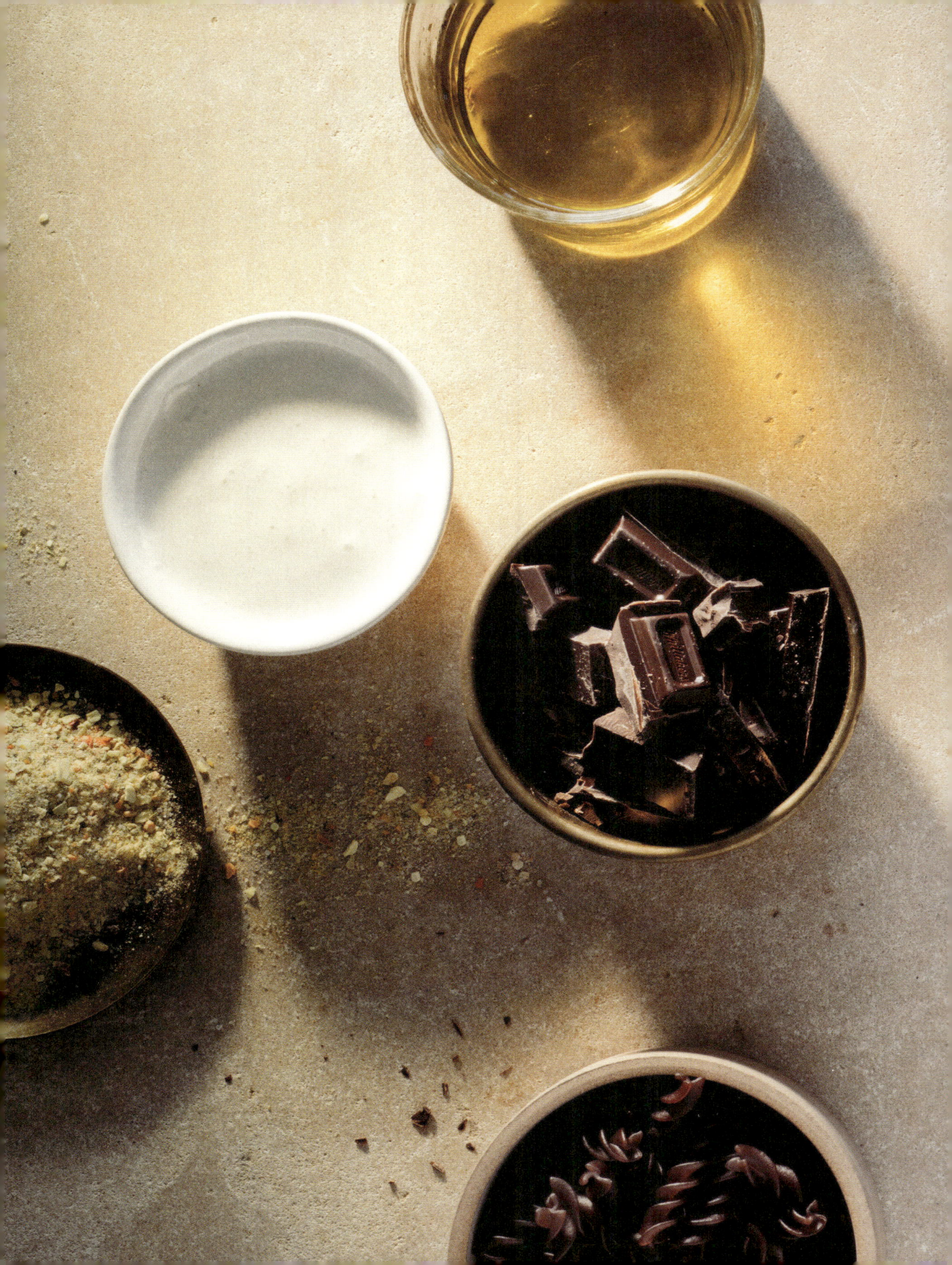

SAY HELLO TO YOUR NEW FRIENDS

I've always believed that you don't need a heap of fancy and unusual things in your pantry to make good food. My five previous cookbooks attest to that — all of those recipes call for everyday ingredients easily found at the supermarket. And that's how you guys like it (you tell me all the time!), so I intend to keep it that way. However, as plant-based cooking is a whole different ball game in many ways, it's only natural that I'll need to introduce a few new bits and pieces so that the recipes are up to my usual standard (in other words, each one must be a taste sensation — another thing I'm uncompromising about). There's nothing to be scared of here; it's all exciting and fun, and you'll probably still be able to find most things at your local. If not, online shopping is a thing — use it!

OILS

As always, in this book I use extra virgin olive oil (only extra virgin — never 'light' and never just 'olive oil') when it makes sense in a recipe. That means when I want the olive-y flavour and I'm only using it up to a medium-high heat. When I need an oil that's flavourless (like for aïoli, baking or Asian-style dishes) or for high-heat frying, I use grapeseed oil; apparently it's the least refined of the clean-tasting oils and the best for you. If you can't find that, I'd use sunflower oil. Avocado oil is super-healthy and is perfect for high-heat cooking and frying too, if you don't mind the strong flavour. For cold dressings I use extra virgin olive oil, or something else cold-pressed and unrefined like hemp, avocado or macadamia oil.

PEPPER

Whenever I mention pepper in my recipes, I'm referring to those really old-school black and white pepper powders you get in a drum. In my humble opinion I think we all need these in our pantry — at least for my recipes anyway. Don't skip them, or just haphazardly grind in some cracked black pepper; it won't have the same effect. Black and white peppers taste different to each other and add their own unique nuances to a dish; they can really take flavour to the next level, especially with plant-based dishes. Beware, though, they always make me sneeze.

When it comes to *serving* food, that's when I bust out the pepper grinder on the table.

SALT

Nowadays I usually use finely ground pink Himalayan salt for cooking and testing my recipes (that's what I've been measuring out in this book). For serving and garnishing, crunchy sea salt flakes are a nice touch. Celtic sea salt is also very good for you, if you can find it.

Heavily refined and bleached iodised table salt is my least-recommended salt (and the level of iodine present is so miniscule that you'd need to dump half the drum on your scrambled tofu to get any benefit whatsoever). Instead, I like to use a little kelp powder (see page 231) in my meals to solve the iodine problem.

COCONUT OIL

There's a great range of coconut oil available at most supermarkets nowadays, which is just brilliant. The two types I use are cold-pressed virgin oil, which has a lovely coconut flavour, and then a flavourless oil — usually labelled as having a 'neutral flavour'. You definitely want both varieties. The flavourless stuff still has a really lovely buttery texture, and is perfect for savoury recipes (like my plant-based butter) where you don't want to taste coconut.

COCONUT CREAM AND COCONUT MILK

Not all coconut creams are created equal, something that became glaringly obvious to me while writing this book (where coconut cream is used in different ways depending on the recipe).

Sometimes a recipe calls for a coconut cream that separates into solid and liquid parts when refrigerated (so you can use the solid part). Some people say you need to look for one without stabilisers and emulsifiers added, but I've found this hasn't been the case — the best one I've tried (Solo's Choice) contains both. Pacific Crown also works okay and Fia Fia isn't bad — they all need to be refrigerated overnight, though.

For curries, I usually want a coconut cream that's thick, creamy and luscious, so the Kara one that comes in a tetrapack (cardboard box) is perfect. Or just use something with a high fat content (I don't think I've ever bought a 'light' coconut cream in my life).

But really, aside from the recipes where you need to separate the solid and liquid, you can just use whatever you have on hand so long as it isn't fat-reduced. (Honestly, why would you?)

Oh, and coconut milk? Technically it's supposed to be a thinner, lighter version of coconut cream, but some are very similar to coconut cream while others are watery and sad. Try them out and see which ones you prefer.

PLANT-BASED MILKS

Okay, so I'm literally obsessed with these! I'm so used to drinking plant-based milk now that I don't know how I ever did without it (and I used to be one of those people who would just skull a massive glass of cow's milk because I loved it). It only takes about a week for your taste-buds to get used to plant-based milk.

When I was first cutting down on dairy, I used to make my own nut milk. It tasted epic, but we go through *waaay* too much of it now to bother with that (especially with a baby — yeesh). I've tried all the plant-based varieties and at the moment I love creamy soy milk (especially for coffees!), hemp seed milk, coconut milk, oat milk, almond milk and cashew milk. I always choose organic and non-GMO where I can.

The great thing about these milks is that you can get them fortified with plant-based calcium, which is super-easy for our bodies to soak up and use (unlike the calcium in dairy . . . but that's another story). When I was making my own almond milk I wasn't getting enough calcium, and when I started drinking calcium-fortified plant-based milks I could really feel the difference; it was awesome when I was pregnant, too. Also, these milks come in tetrapacks so you can keep a whole lot in the pantry at room temperature and never run out!

PASTA

I love a good-quality durum wheat pasta as much as the next person, but in terms of nutritional value it's not ideal to eat it all the time (I think we all know that deep in our hearts). Recently I discovered that you can buy pasta made from pulses and other grains: red lentils, chickpeas, mung beans, black beans, quinoa. The verdict is that pasta made from red lentils is amazing — you can't tell it's not regular pasta, and apparently it has twice the protein and four times the fibre of regular pasta as well as being gluten-free. You can get it in spirals (supermarket), and penne and rigatoni (my favourites, but you might need a specialty food store or health food shop for these). I've also found epic lasagne sheets made from green lentils. (Standard gluten-free pasta made from corn and rice is okay, but I find it a bit chalky and it's more or less devoid of nutrients.)

FLOURS

There are just so many varieties of flour out there nowadays — I could write a thesis on all of them and your head would implode with confusion, like mine already has. It seems that you can dry out and grind up just about anything these days and *bam*, you've got a funky new flour. Maybe in future I'll play with the different types a little more, but to keep things simple in this book I've stuck to just a few.

If you're okay with gluten, then plain white flour is perfect; however, I suggest you look for the unbleached organic flour that's popping up in many supermarkets these days. That's what I buy; it's much better for you and still works perfectly in everything. I've also used white spelt flour with success. Spelt is a type of wheat, but it's high in protein, fibre and B-vitamins.

For gluten-free, I've used a standard gluten-free flour mix that you can get at the supermarket; there are usually a couple of brands to choose from. It's a specially designed blend of flours, usually made up of rice, maize and tapioca, but the blend can vary widely and there's no set rule.

A couple of my recipes mention buckwheat flour, which is usually available at the supermarket these days. It's gluten-free, good for you and has quite a strong earthy, nutty flavour, which means I wouldn't recommend using it plain for baking.

CHOCOLATE

I use dairy-free chocolate a whole lot in this book because it's an easy way to make epic sweets. Believe it or not, quite a bit of everyday, good-quality eating chocolate containing 50% cocoa solids or more is dairy-free (i.e. vegan). You just need to check the ingredients list — so long as there's only *cocoa butter and/or cocoa solids*, you're fine. When you see the word *milk* as in *milk solids* or *cream*, then it's dairy-based and not the one for you.

TOFU

Up until a couple of years ago I don't think I'd ever cooked with tofu. I probably even turned my nose up at it, since it wasn't a lamb chop or a packet of mince. Ignoramus! Now I absolutely adore tofu, and I always have a few blocks in the fridge to use as a source of protein for meals. I love its versatility: I can bulk up a curry or stir-fry in a matter of seconds, whizz it up into a soft cheese, grate and fry it to add texture to a soup or pad Thai, add slices to a burger — even scramble it on toast! It has a mild flavour that takes on whatever vibe you have going on with the meal, and it's quick and easy to prep. Sometimes I just season cubes of it with salt and two types of pepper and fry it up to dunk in some sweet and sour sauce.

Tofu is made from soybeans that are ground with water, heated, made firm with minerals and pressed into a block. I suppose it's like a sort of soft, neutral cheese made out of soybeans. On the supermarket shelf it comes in silken, soft, firm and extra-firm varieties — I use firm unless stated otherwise in the recipe; often that's the only type you can get at the supermarket anyway. I try to always buy plain organic tofu (and always NZ-made).

And don't believe everything you hear about soy being full of hormones that will give blokes man-boobs — that's been debunked by recent research. Soy even apparently helps to *regulate* hormones. Anyway, tofu has been a staple in China for over 2000 years and if moobs from tofu were a thing I think we'd have clear proof by now.

JACKFRUIT

A large, bristly and somewhat ungainly looking fruit, its flesh has a knack for masquerading as shredded meat in some plant-based recipes. Grown in regions of Asia, it's one of the biggest fruit that grows on trees. When ripe, it apparently has a mango/pineapple-ish flavour vibe, though I've yet to try a ripe one. The jackfruit we have access to in New Zealand is the canned, young and green (unripe) kind. It has a pretty neutral flavour, but that just makes it an awesome base for savoury dishes where you want the look and feel of something meaty. I've used it in this book for Mexican-inspired dishes where there'd usually be pulled pork or brisket or something. It's relatively cheap and simple to prepare, and really looks the part — even the texture is pretty close. Bear in mind, though, that there's not a whole lot of protein there so it's not all that filling by itself. Plenty of added goodies like beans, brown rice, corn tortillas and avocado will help with that.

AQUAFABA

You'd better believe it — that murky water that chickpeas are cooked and canned in is *totally* a thing, and it has a name. Aquafaba has quickly become a vitally important ingredient that's helping to shape the way we prepare exciting and delicious plant-based food. Why? Because in many ways, aquafaba — seemingly magically — behaves just like egg white. To cut a long story short (google it if you want all the geeky deets), as the chickpeas cook, the cooking water takes on a unique combination of their properties. Protein is a big one: it's how, in truly spectacular fashion, one humble can's worth of aquafaba can fluff into a huge, fluffy cloud *exactly* like egg white (I think even better, to be honest). It even bakes like egg white! I had to try it myself to believe it. (Interestingly, it is said that organic canned chickpeas fluff up better — I always buy the organic ones, anyway.)

But aquafaba is so much more than just meringue. I've used it to make cheesecakes lighter, chocolate mousse fluffier, in my plant-based butter as an emulsifier, to give structure in cakes, as an 'egg wash' for golden pastry, as a thickener, as a binder . . . the list goes on. And then of course you can use the actual chickpeas to create nourishing, delicious food. Who'd have guessed that this reluctant superhero was waiting quietly on your pantry shelf to save the world all this time? (Aquafaba was only very recently discovered, in 2014 — by a French musician, naturally.) Well, I for one am excited about it and I know there's a whole lot more for me to discover and subsequently share with you all.

Note: aquafaba actually refers to the water that *all* pulses (the dried seeds of legumes) are cooked in, not just chickpeas — think beans, peas and lentils too. I always use chickpea aquafaba, though, as it seems to work the best. Also, you can cook your own chickpeas and use that water if you prefer, though it may need to be reduced a little. Oh, and don't worry — you can't taste any chickpeas when you use aquafaba in a recipe.

NUTRITIONAL YEAST (AKA SAVOURY YEAST FLAKES)

Aside from the unfortunate name (you suppressed a snigger — don't pretend you didn't), this new addition to my arsenal is probably the most important. With its cheesy, savoury, nutty flavour, it's easily the holy grail of cheese-free cooking (try my Mac & Cheese and you'll see). It also boasts some impressive health benefits: it's a good source of B-vitamins and often comes fortified with vitamin B_{12}. Affectionately known as 'nooch' or 'hippie dust', nutritional yeast is nothing new in the plant-based world. It's similar to the yeast used in baking but has been heated so that it's inactive. You can get it at some good supermarkets now and all health stores (often in the bulk bins). Needless to say, I always have some hippie dust on hand. It's the bomb and very versatile.

MARMITE AND VEGEMITE

Ah yes, these beloved little jars of gummy, dark, intensely flavoured spread, unique to New Zealand and Australia (oh yeah, and England if you must be pedantic). So awesome on toast, crumpets and muffin splits, but also — and most importantly — a little-known secret weapon in plant-based cooking! Both do contain gluten, but you may be able to get gluten-free varieties if you have a hunt. You can add 1 or 2 teaspoons to saucy, savoury dishes (like my Vege Bolognese or Ramen) to add a rich, salty, 'meaty' umami flavour — kind of like where people would normally use miso paste. Don't go crazy though, or you'll have a weird yeasty-flavoured meal.

SOY SAUCE AND TAMARI

Tamari might be new to some of you. While it seems very similar to soy sauce, there are a few differences. Both are by-products of fermented soybeans, but soy sauce is made using wheat, whereas tamari usually contains little or no wheat, making it a no-brainer for gluten-free folk (check the label, though). Tamari is Japanese; it's usually darker and richer than some Chinese soy sauces, but less salty and not as 'harsh'. This makes it a great dipping sauce by itself (or you can add a little sweet chilli sauce).

    I use these magic helpers in all kinds of dishes to add a full, savoury, umami flavour — another little hack for plant-based cooking. Experiment with it yourself to get a feel for how much you need to use.

STOCK POWDER

I use stock powder in many of my recipes as I find that spooning in powder is easier than having to dissolve cubes, although I still use both. In the past I haven't been a huge fan of stock powders because ones I tried left me rather unimpressed — too salty, nasty fake flavours, and some have a radioactive hue. Nowadays, though, you can get some really good vegetable stock powders which can be added to pretty much any savoury dish to give it a real boost.

Look for a stock that's plant-based, not too salty and without too many weird ingredients — the more dehydrated veges, the better. Sometimes you'll even find plant-based stock (usually cubes) labelled as 'chicken-style' or 'beef-style', which I love using as well. It just helps to achieve that lovely depth of flavour that meat would normally provide. Stock powder is also really handy when you're cooking bland things like rice, quinoa or pasta: add a couple of teaspoons to the water to make it extra yum.

I still use the liquid stock that comes in cartons when I need it for something with a bit of sauce, or a soup; even then, extra stock powder can still be added to ramp up the flavour.

KELP POWDER

I haven't really used kelp powder in the recipes in this book because it's not readily available at the supermarket and I didn't want you to freak out if you couldn't get it. It is, however, available in health shops and online, and it deserves a mention here because it's quite a miraculous product.

Kelp powder, made from a dried seaweed, is very useful in two ways. First, it adds an umami flavour to dishes in the absence of meat (in the same way that Marmite/Vegemite, nutritional yeast and mushrooms do). You don't need a lot — too much and things can start to feel a little seaweedy, but just enough adds a nice depth of flavour. Second, kelp is full of natural iodine, which is so important for a myriad of functions in your body (not just thyroid). It's highly likely that many of us are deficient in iodine because it's not present in our New Zealand soil and so is lacking in many of our foods. Kelp is also a good source of potassium, magnesium, calcium and iron. (Interestingly, as soon as I consciously started supplementing with iodine, my monthly cycle clicked into place after years of being worryingly inconsistent. Then I got pregnant. Coincidence? I don't know.)

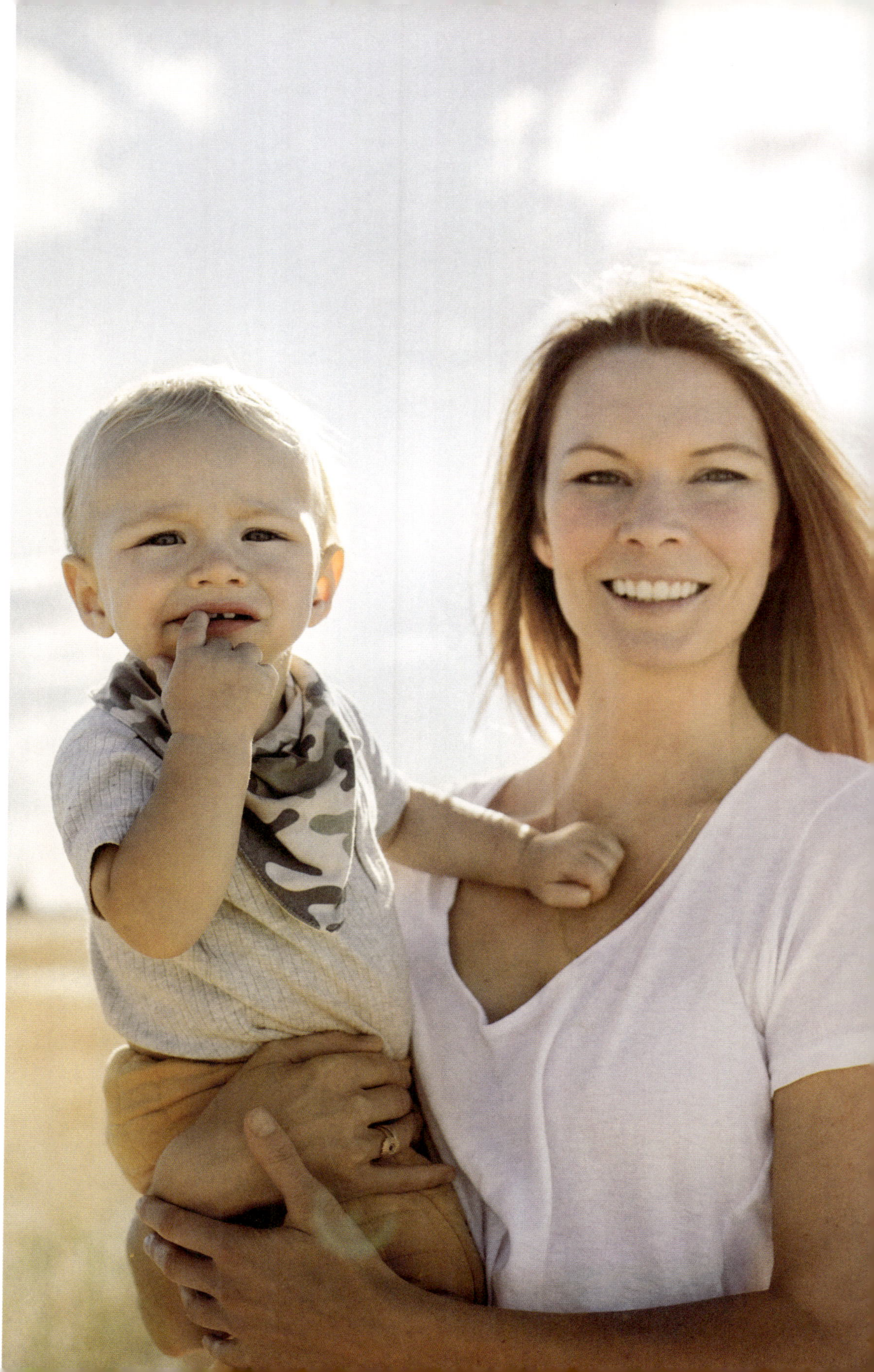

GRATITUDE

I started this book when Sky was just six months old, and assumed that because I'd been through the process five times before, I'd be a bit of a gun and be able to juggle a baby and a book pretty easily. I assumed wrong. No point acting like a hero here, it was a herculean effort and it nearly killed me. Learning how to be a new mum, as well as giving deep, focused energy to create these recipes and bring the book together took absolutely *everything* I had. I wouldn't have been able to produce *Supergood* without acres of support and some very hardworking people.

Thank you Douglas — you are a magical father, a fine palate, a mirror and a sounding board, a challenger, a man with a vision, an epic giver of hugs, beside me on every step of the journey.

Thank you Tam and Vic for 'seeing me', and telling the story of my food and my family with honesty and integrity. And for weaving the thread in your sensitive and inspired way to bring the rich tapestry of the book to life.

Thank you Helen for your beautiful, intelligent design, carried out with cheerful finesse.

Mum, Pauline and Heather, thank you for looking after our wee Skyrocket with such love and care.

Thanks to my team at Penguin Random House, especially Claire, Stu, Cat and Becky.

To the bookstores and booksellers, as always, I'm ever so grateful for your support.

Thanks Belinda for your hard graft behind the scenes.

Thanks to my beloved fans for being a part of my journey, for trusting me as a companion in your kitchen.

Thank you to Mem, you are an anchor and a light for me, always.

INDEX

A

aïoli
  Chelsea's Famous 10-second Aïoli 182
almonds, sliced
  Gluten-free Muesli 216
apples
  Branberry Muffins 164
  In the Pink Juice 204
  Very Hungry Caterpillar 202
apricots, dried
  Gluten-free Muesli 216
aquafaba (chickpea liquid)
  Chocolate Ice Cream 178
  Chocolate Mousse 170
  Plant-based Butter 190
  Sweet Little Meringues 144–6
Asian-style No-meatballs 68
avocados
  Hefty Green Salad 96
  Maumau's Strawberry Salad 106
  Warm Broccoli, Kumara & Avocado Salad 104

B

bananas
  Chocolate Banoffee Pie 136
  Strawberry Gelato 176
  Super Smoothie 206
banoffee pie
  Chocolate Banoffee Pie 136
Barrier Curry 56
BBQ Burgers with Crispy Onion Rings 76
beans, black
  Golden Tortilla Bake 46
  Macho Nachos 16
  Oozy Quesadillas 22
beans, cannellini
  Summer Vegetable Medley 92
beans, edamame
  Hefty Green Salad 96
beans, kidney
  Golden Tortilla Bake 46
  Oozy Quesadillas 22
beans, pinto
  Golden Tortilla Bake 46
  Oozy Quesadillas 22
beer
  Lockdown Loaf 194
beetroot
  In the Pink Juice 204
biscuits *see* cookies
blueberries
  Branberry Muffins 164
Bolognese
  Vege Bolognese 34
Branberry Muffins 164
bread
  Elvish Toast Bread 192
  Lockdown Loaf 194
Breakfasts, Bits & Pieces
  Chelsea's Famous 10-second Aïoli 182
  Chelsea's Hummus 186
  Chia Pudding 218
  Coconut Porridge 214
  Crispy Salted Sesame Crackers 188
  Elvish Toast Bread 192
  Flash Browns 210
  Fresh Herby Pesto 184
  Glögg 200
  Gluten-free Muesli 216
  In the Pink Juice 204
  Lockdown Loaf 194
  Marinated Feta 198
  Plant Parmesan 196
  Plant-based Butter 190
  Scrambled Tofu 212
  Super Smoothie 206
  Very Hungry Caterpillar 202
broccoli
  Warm Broccoli, Kumara & Avocado Salad 104
brownie
  Fudge Cake Brownie 158
burgers
  BBQ Burgers with Crispy Onion Rings 76
  Crispy Tofu Burgers 74
butter
  Plant-based Butter 190
butternut
  Lush Thai Green Curry 52
Butterscotch 142

C

cabbage
  Noodly Peanut Slaw 102
cakes
  Carrot Cake 130
  Chocolate Cupcakes & Whipped Ganache Icing 162
  Spiced Pear Velvet Cake 134
  Vanilla Celebration Cake 124–6
caramel
  Chocolate Banoffee Pie 136
  Gooey Caramel Slice 154
carrots
  Carrot Cake 130
  In the Pink Juice 204
  Moroccan Roasted Carrot & Quinoa Salad 100
  Noodly Peanut Slaw 102
  Not Dogs 78
cashews
  Creamy Alfredo 28
  Creamy Cashew Cheese 18
  Creamy Mushroom Soup 88
  French Tomato Tart 44

Lovely Lettuce Cups 110
Margherita Pizza 18–20
Marinated Feta 198
Pesto & Spinach Pasta 30
Plant Parmesan 196
cauliflower
  Crispy Sweet & Sour Cauliflower 116
Cheat's Chocolate 172
cheese, dairy-free
  Golden Tortilla Bake 46
  Mac & Cheese 24
  Oozy Quesadillas 22
cheesecakes
  Chocolate Cheesecake 138
  Jellytip Cheesecake 140
  Oreo Cheesecake 128
  Snickalicious Cheesecake 132
Chelsea's Famous 10-second Aïoli 182
Chelsea's Hummus 186
Chia Pudding 218
chickpeas *see also* aquafaba (chickpea liquid)
  Chelsea's Hummus 186
  Mayo Salad Sammies 118
  Pumpkin & Chickpea Curry 54
  That Moroccan Dish 70
chocolate
  Cheat's Chocolate 172
  Chocolate Banoffee Pie 136
  Chocolate Cheesecake 138
  Chocolate Cupcakes & Whipped Ganache Icing 162
  Chocolate Ice Cream 178
  Chocolate Mousse 170
  Freedom Chocolate Chip Cookies 150
  Fudge Cake Brownie 158
  Gooey Caramel Slice 154
  Jellytip Cheesecake 140
  Little Peanut Truffles 174
Coconut & Lemongrass Broth 84
Coconut Porridge 214
cookies
  Freedom Chocolate Chip Cookies 150

courgettes
  Fuss-free Tomato Pasta 26
  Summer Vegetable Medley 92
  Veg-out Lasagne 40
crackers
  Crispy Salted Sesame Crackers 188
Creamy Alfredo 28
Creamy Dahl & Crunchy Roast Potatoes 14
Creamy Mushroom Soup 88
Crispy Salted Sesame Crackers 188
Crispy Sweet & Sour Cauliflower 116
Crispy Tofu Burgers 74
cucumber
  Hefty Green Salad 96
  Maumau's Strawberry Salad 106
  Very Hungry Caterpillar 202
cupcakes
  Chocolate Cupcakes & Whipped Ganache Icing 162
curries
  Barrier Curry 56
  Creamy Dahl & Crunchy Roast Potatoes 14
  Lush Thai Green Curry 52
  Pumpkin & Chickpea Curry 54

D

dahl
  Creamy Dahl & Crunchy Roast Potatoes 14
dates
  Gluten-free Muesli 216
desserts
  Chocolate Banoffee Pie 136
  Chocolate Cheesecake 138
  Chocolate Ice Cream 178
  Chocolate Mousse 170
  Jellytip Cheesecake 140
  Little Peanut Truffles 174
  Oreo Cheesecake 128
  Snickalicious Cheesecake 132
  Strawberry Gelato 176
  Sweet Little Meringues 144–6
dinners *see* Meals, Big & Small

dip *see also* sauces
  Chelsea's Hummus 186
doughnuts
  Mini Sugared Doughnuts 168
dressings
  balsamic vinaigrette 106
  creamy peanut dressing 102
  tahini salad dressing 96
drinks
  Glögg 200
  In the Pink Juice 204
  Super Smoothie 206
  Very Hungry Caterpillar 202

E

Eatloaf 64
eggplant
  Asian-style No-meatballs 68
  Lush Thai Green Curry 52
  Veg-out Lasagne 40
Elvish Toast Bread 192

F

Festive Stuffed Mushrooms 114
feta
  Marinated Feta 198
Fireside Cottage Pie 62
Flash Browns 210
Freedom Chocolate Chip Cookies 150
French Onion Soup 82
French Tomato Tart 44
Fresh Herby Pesto 184
fudge
  Peanutty Russian Fudge 156
Fudge Cake Brownie 158
Fuss-free Tomato Pasta 26

G

gelato
  Strawberry Gelato 176
Ginger Slice 152
Glögg 200
Gluten-free Muesli 216
Golden Tortilla Bake 46

Gooey Caramel Slice 154
Grilled Sweetcorn 112

H

hash browns
   Flash Browns 210
Hedonistic Hotcakes 166
Hefty Green Salad 96
hot dogs
   Not Dogs 78
hotcakes
   Hedonistic Hotcakes 166
hummus
   Chelsea's Hummus 186

I

ice cream
   Chocolate Ice Cream 178
   Strawberry Gelato 176
icings
   ginger icing 152
   lemon icing 130
   vanilla icing 124–6
   whipped ganache icing 162
In the Pink Juice 204

J

jackfruit
   BBQ Burgers with Crispy Onion Rings 76
   Golden Tortilla Bake 46
   Soft Taco Fiesta 66
Jellytip Cheesecake 140
juices
   In the Pink Juice 204
   Very Hungry Caterpillar 202

K

kumara
   Eatloaf 64
   Sunday Roast Pie 60
   Warm Broccoli, Kumara & Avocado Salad 104

L

lasagne
   The Beast Mode Lasagne 36–8
   Veg-out Lasagne 40
lentils
   Barrier Curry 56
   Creamy Dahl & Crunchy Roast Potatoes 14
   Eatloaf 64
   Fireside Cottage Pie 62
   Golden Tortilla Bake 46
   Macho Nachos 16
   Snausage Rolls 120
   That Moroccan Dish 70
   The Beast Mode Lasagne 36–8
   Vege Bolognese 34
lettuce
   Lovely Lettuce Cups 110
   Maumau's Strawberry Salad 106
Little Peanut Truffles 174
Lockdown Loaf 194
Lovely Lettuce Cups 110
lunches *see* Meals, Big & Small
Lush Thai Green Curry 52

M

Mac & Cheese 24
Macho Nachos 16
Margherita Pizza 18–20
Marinated Feta 198
Maumau's Strawberry Salad 106
Mayo Salad Sammies 118
Meals, Big & Small
   Asian-style No-meatballs 68
   Barrier Curry 56
   BBQ Burgers with Crispy Onion Rings 76
   Coconut & Lemongrass Broth 84
   Creamy Alfredo 28
   Creamy Dahl & Crunchy Roast Potatoes 14
   Creamy Mushroom Soup 88
   Crispy Sweet & Sour Cauliflower 116
   Crispy Tofu Burgers 74
   Festive Stuffed Mushrooms 114
   Fireside Cottage Pie 62
   French Onion Soup 82
   French Tomato Tart 44
   Fuss-free Tomato Pasta 26
   Golden Tortilla Bake 46
   Grilled Sweetcorn 112
   Hefty Green Salad 96
   Lovely Lettuce Cups 110
   Lush Thai Green Curry 52
   Mac & Cheese 24
   Macho Nachos 16
   Margherita Pizza 18–20
   Maumau's Strawberry Salad 106
   Mayo Salad Sammies 118
   Moroccan Roasted Carrot & Quinoa Salad 100
   Noodly Peanut Slaw 102
   Not Dogs 78
   Oozy Quesadillas 22
   Pad Thai 50
   Pesto & Spinach Pasta 30
   Potato Salad 98
   Pumpkin & Chickpea Curry 54
   Ramen 90
   Rice Paper Rolls with Peanut Satay Sauce 48
   Samosa Stuffed Potatoes 72
   Snausage Rolls 120
   Soft Taco Fiesta 66
   Summer Vegetable Medley 92
   Sunday Roast Pie 60
   That Moroccan Dish 70
   The Beast Mode Lasagne 36–8
   Über-tasty Japanese Noodles & Crunchy Tofu 86
   Veg-out Lasagne 40
   Vege Bolognese 34
   Warm Broccoli, Kumara & Avocado Salad 104
meatballs
   Asian-style No-meatballs 68
meringues
   Sweet Little Meringues 144–6
Mini Sugared Doughnuts 168
Moroccan Roasted Carrot & Quinoa Salad 100
mousse
   Chocolate Mousse 170

muesli
  Gluten-free Muesli 216
muffins
  Branberry Muffins 164
mushrooms
  Creamy Mushroom Soup 88
  Eatloaf 64
  Festive Stuffed Mushrooms 114
  Fireside Cottage Pie 62
  Ramen 90
  The Beast Mode Lasagne 36–8
  Über-tasty Japanese Noodles & Crunchy Tofu 86
  Veg-out Lasagne 40
  Vege Bolognese 34

N

nachos
  Macho Nachos 16
noodles
  Coconut & Lemongrass Broth 84
  Noodly Peanut Slaw 102
  Pad Thai 50
  Ramen 90
  Über-tasty Japanese Noodles & Crunchy Tofu 86
Not Dogs 78

O

onions
  BBQ Burgers with Crispy Onion Rings 76
  French Onion Soup 82
Oozy Quesadillas 22
Oreo Cheesecake 128

P

Pad Thai 50
Parmesan
  Plant Parmesan 196
pasta
  Creamy Alfredo 28
  Fuss-free Tomato Pasta 26
  Mac & Cheese 24
  Pesto & Spinach Pasta 30
  The Beast Mode Lasagne 36–8

Veg-out Lasagne 40
Vege Bolognese 34
peanut butter
  Rice Paper Rolls with Peanut Satay Sauce 48
peanuts
  Little Peanut Truffles 174
  Noodly Peanut Slaw 102
  Peanutty Russian Fudge 156
pears
  Hefty Green Salad 96
  Spiced Pear Velvet Cake 134
pesto
  Fresh Herby Pesto 184
  Pesto & Spinach Pasta 30
pies
  Chocolate Banoffee Pie 136
  Fireside Cottage Pie 62
  Sunday Roast Pie 60
pizza
  Margherita Pizza 18–20
Plant Parmesan 196
Plant-based Butter 190
porridge
  Coconut Porridge 214
potatoes
  Barrier Curry 56
  Creamy Dahl & Crunchy Roast Potatoes 14
  Fireside Cottage Pie 62
  Flash Browns 210
  Potato Salad 98
  Samosa Stuffed Potatoes 72
  Sunday Roast Pie 60
pumpkin
  Lush Thai Green Curry 52
  Pumpkin & Chickpea Curry 54
  Sunday Roast Pie 60

Q

quesadillas
  Oozy Quesadillas 22
quinoa
  Moroccan Roasted Carrot & Quinoa Salad 100

R

Ramen 90
raspberries
  Jellytip Cheesecake 140
rice, brown
  Asian-style No-meatballs 68
  Festive Stuffed Mushrooms 114
Rice Paper Rolls with Peanut Satay Sauce 48
Russian fudge
  Peanutty Russian Fudge 156

S

salads
  Hefty Green Salad 96
  Maumau's Strawberry Salad 106
  Moroccan Roasted Carrot & Quinoa Salad 100
  Noodly Peanut Slaw 102
  Potato Salad 98
  slaw 66, 74
  Warm Broccoli, Kumara & Avocado Salad 104
salsa 110
Samosa Stuffed Potatoes 72
sandwiches
  Mayo Salad Sammies 118
sauces see also dip, dressings
  Asian-style sauce 68
  Butterscotch 142
  creamy white sauce 36, 40
  Fresh Herby Pesto 184
  pad Thai sauce 50
  peanut satay dipping sauce 48
  rich tomato sauce 40
  smoky sauce 112
  sweet & sour sauce 116
  sweet chilli burger sauce 74
  tomato sauce 18
  white sauce 60
Scrambled Tofu 212
slices
  Fudge Cake Brownie 158
  Ginger Slice 152
  Gooey Caramel Slice 154
  Peanutty Russian Fudge 156

smoothie
　Super Smoothie 206
Snausage Rolls 120
Snickalicious Cheesecake 132
Soft Taco Fiesta 66
soups & broths
　Coconut & Lemongrass Broth 84
　Creamy Mushroom Soup 88
　French Onion Soup 82
Spiced Pear Velvet Cake 134
spinach
　Pesto & Spinach Pasta 30
sprouts, alfalfa
　Hefty Green Salad 96
　Maumau's Strawberry Salad 106
sprouts, mung bean
　Hefty Green Salad 96
　Noodly Peanut Slaw 102
　Pad Thai 50
strawberries
　Maumau's Strawberry Salad 106
　Strawberry Gelato 176
Summer Vegetable Medley 92
Sunday Roast Pie 60
sunflower seeds
　Eatloaf 64
Super Smoothie 206
Sweet Little Meringues 144–6
sweetcorn
　Grilled Sweetcorn 112
　Summer Vegetable Medley 92
Sweets
　Branberry Muffins 164
　Butterscotch 142
　Carrot Cake 130
　Cheat's Chocolate 172
　Chocolate Banoffee Pie 136
　Chocolate Cheesecake 138
　Chocolate Cupcakes & Whipped
　　Ganache Icing 162
　Chocolate Ice Cream 178
　Chocolate Mousse 170
　Freedom Chocolate Chip Cookies
　　150
　Fudge Cake Brownie 158
　Ginger Slice 152
　Gooey Caramel Slice 154
　Hedonistic Hotcakes 166
　Jellytip Cheesecake 140
　Little Peanut Truffles 174
　Mini Sugared Doughnuts 168
　Oreo Cheesecake 128
　Peanutty Russian Fudge 156
　Snickalicious Cheesecake 132
　Spiced Pear Velvet Cake 134
　Strawberry Gelato 176
　Sweet Little Meringues 144–6
　Vanilla Celebration Cake 124–6

T

tacos
　Soft Taco Fiesta 66
tart
　French Tomato Tart 44
That Moroccan Dish 70
The Beast Mode Lasagne 36–8
tofu
　Asian-style No-meatballs 68
　Coconut & Lemongrass Broth 84
　Crispy Tofu Burgers 74
　Lush Thai Green Curry 52
　Pad Thai 50
　Rice Paper Rolls with Peanut Satay
　　Sauce 48
　Scrambled Tofu 212
　Über-tasty Japanese Noodles &
　　Crunchy Tofu 86
tomatoes
　French Tomato Tart 44
　Fuss-free Tomato Pasta 26
　Margherita Pizza 18–20
tortillas
　Golden Tortilla Bake 46
　Oozy Quesadillas 22
　Soft Taco Fiesta 66
truffles
　Little Peanut Truffles 174

U

Über-tasty Japanese Noodles &
　Crunchy Tofu 86

V

Vanilla Celebration Cake 124–6
Veg-out Lasagne 40
Vege Bolognese 34
Very Hungry Caterpillar 202

W

walnuts
　Eatloaf 64
　Gluten-free Muesli 216
　Lovely Lettuce Cups 110
　Pesto & Spinach Pasta 30
　Plant Parmesan 196
Warm Broccoli, Kumara & Avocado
　Salad 104
wine, mulled
　Glögg 200

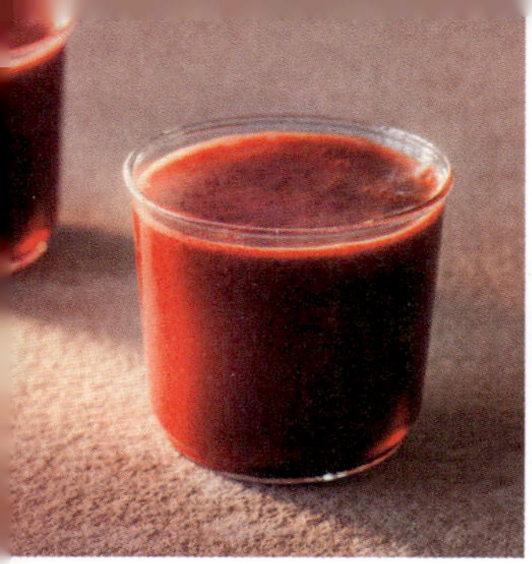
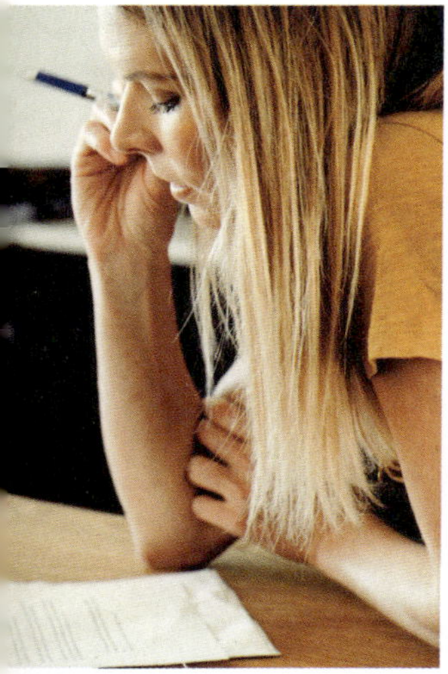
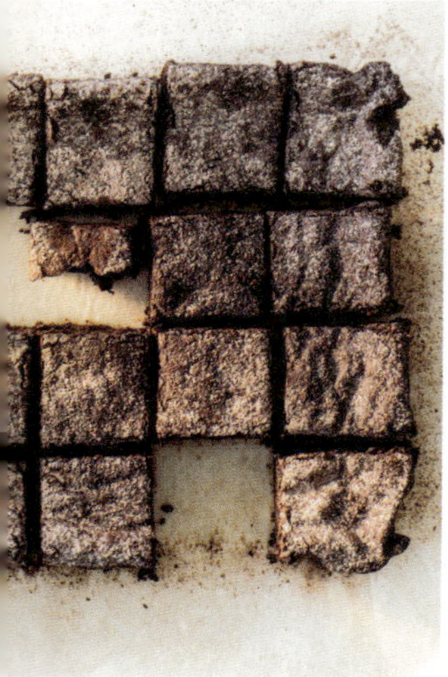
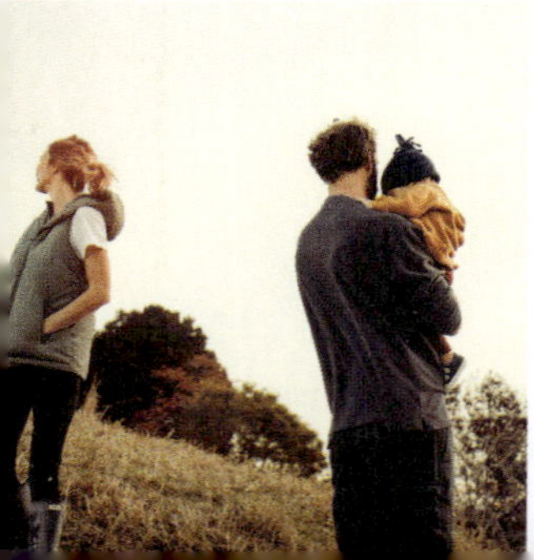
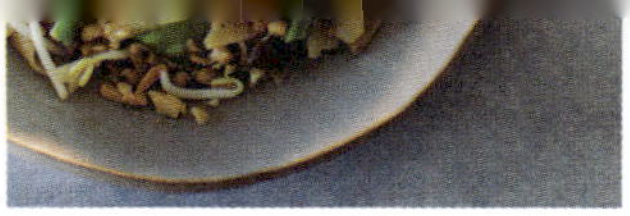
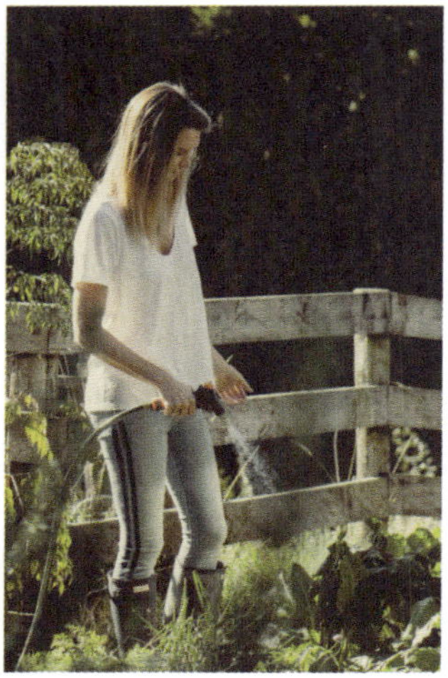
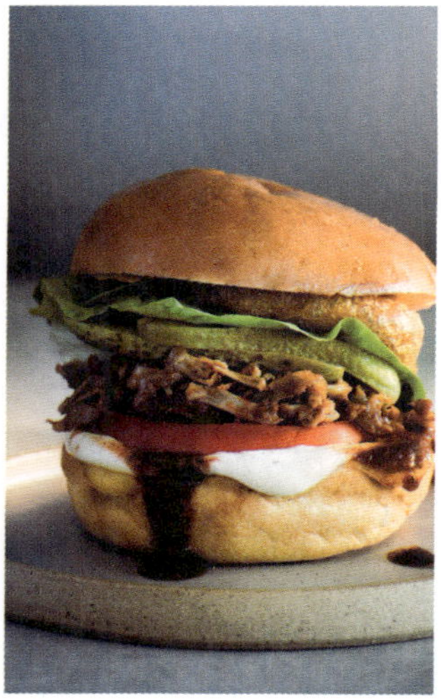
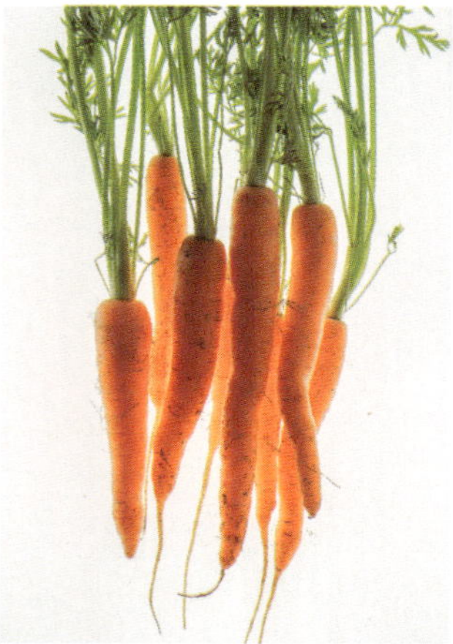

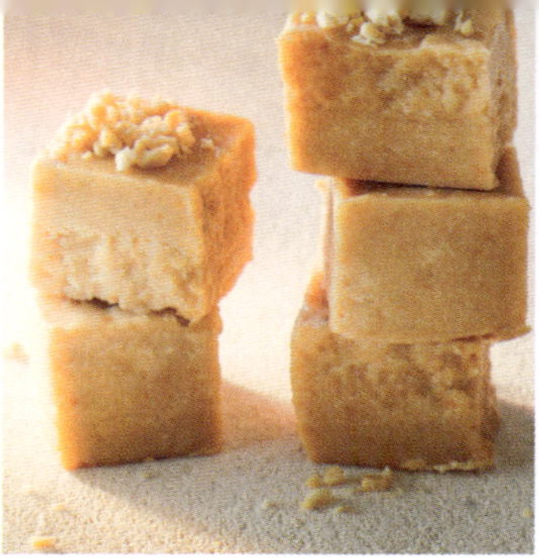
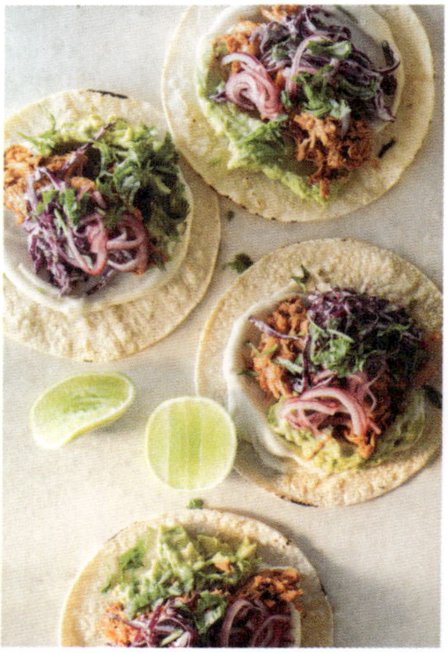
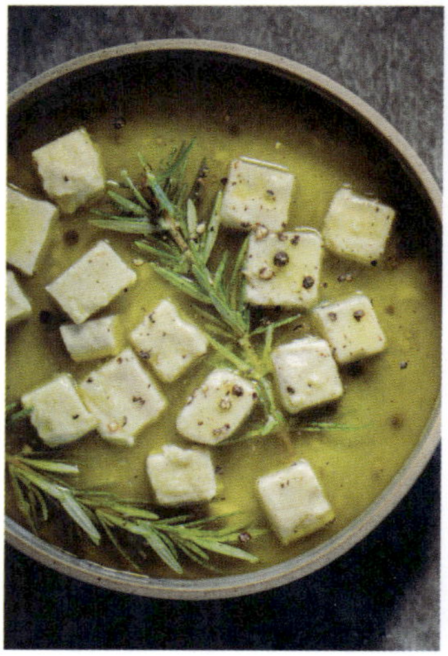
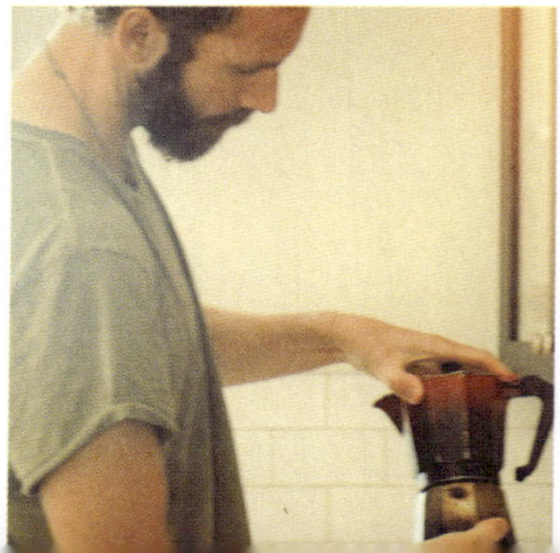
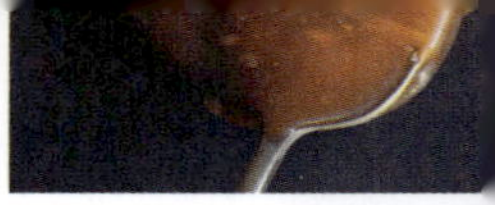
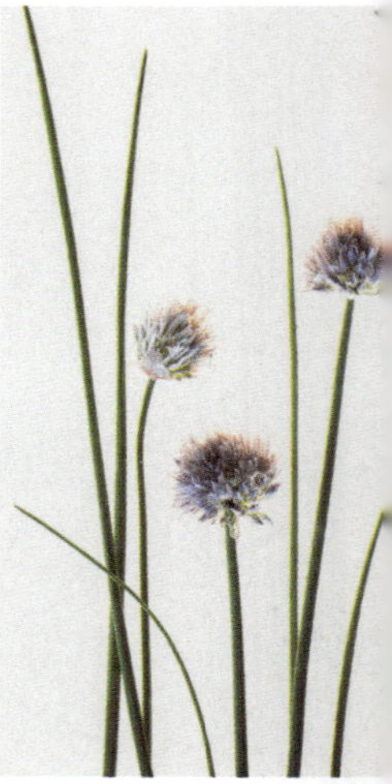
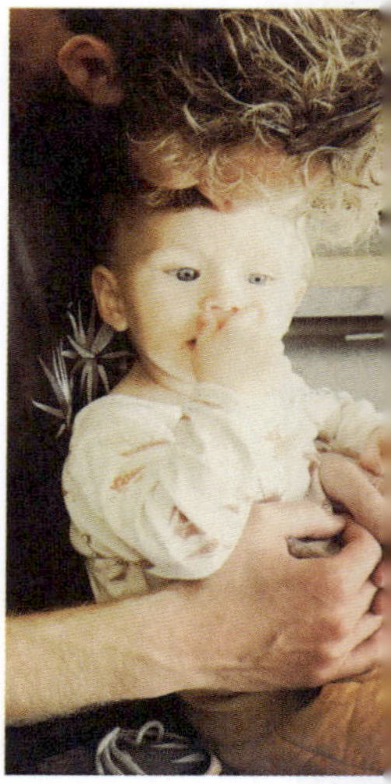
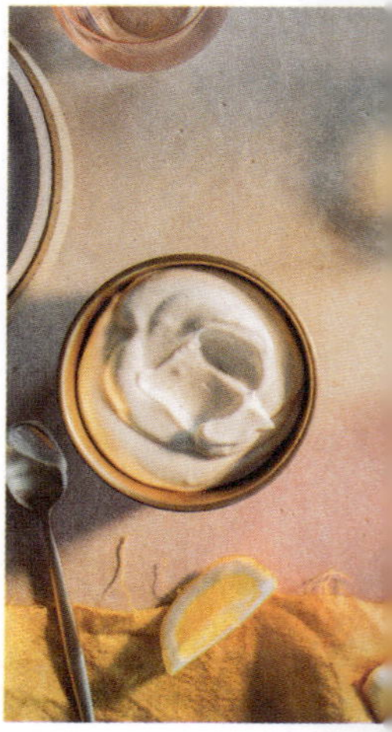